The Russian Memoir

The Russian Memoir

HISTORY AND LITERATURE

Edited and with an introduction
by Beth Holmgren

NORTHWESTERN UNIVERSITY PRESS / EVANSTON, ILLINOIS

Northwestern University Press
www.nupress.northwestern.edu

First paperback printing 2007

Printed in the United States of America

10 9 8 7 6 5 4 3 2 1

ISBN-13: 978-0-8101-2428-8
ISBN-10: 0-8101-2428-9

Library of Congress Cataloging-in-Publication Data

The Russian memoir : history and literature / edited and with an introduction by
    Beth Holmgren.
        p. cm. — (Studies in Russian literature and theory)
    Includes bibliographic references and index.
    ISBN 0-8101-1929-3 (cloth : alk. paper)
    1. Russian prose literature—History and criticism. 2. Autobiography.
    3. Biography as a literary form. 4. Self in literature. I. Holmgren, Beth, 1955–
    II. Series.
    PG3091.9.A93 R97 2003
    891.709′492—dc21

                                                                    2002154753

♾ The paper used in this publication meets the minimum requirements of the American National Standard for Information Sciences—Permanence of Paper for Printed Library Materials, ANSI Z39.48-1992.

Contents

Acknowledgments

I thank all the parties enlisted in realizing this volume: its assiduous and patient contributors; its meticulous anonymous readers for Northwestern University Press; Caryl Emerson as the Studies in Russian Literature and Theory series editor; Susan Harris as NUP editor extraordinaire; Mark Sidell as on-site technical support; and, of course, former graduate students in the UNC-Chapel Hill Department of Slavic Languages and Literatures, who can blame me for its belated appearance. An earlier version of Galya Diment's "English as Sanctuary: Nabokov's and Brodsky's Autobiographical Writings" appeared in *Slavic and East European Journal* 3 (fall 1988): 353–72; we reprint a revised and updated version of her essay with this journal's permission.

Beth Holmgren

Introduction

A good question prompted this volume. As my graduate students were perusing a list of required primary texts for their comprehensive examinations in Russian literature, they asked, quite sensibly, about the inclusion of certain memoirs. At the time I mumbled something about the arbitrary nature of canonization and resorted to a vague justification I later found repeated in various literary histories: that some memoirs qualify as superb works of verbal art and reward the specialist's close analysis and cultural contextualization.[1] These works of verbal art, I continued more brightly, yield a factual bonus—the eyewitness encounters and "backstage" news of the worlds they purport to record. After all, one can't know the engendering sociopolitical context of Russian realism without studying Aleksandr Herzen's *My Past and Thoughts*. One can't fathom the dread conditions of Stalinist culture without experiencing the memoirs of Evgeniia Ginzburg and Nadezhda Mandelstam.

While my students, at least to my face, appeared satisfied with my answer, I was not. Nor did I discover a more satisfactory justification among those other habitual assigners of memoirs—historians. Memoirs intermittently surface as documents rather than literary works in history course syllabi and reading lists. Historians recommend memoirs as primary sources which, despite their bias and stylization, proffer more compelling, coherent reading than other sorts of documents. In some cases, memoirs may be all that remain, the "unofficial" narratives that eluded political censure or academic regimentation. Herzen's *My Past and Thoughts*, dispatched from exile by an astute politician, at last made a full breast of the nineteenth-century revolutionary's history. The Stalinist camps were first and foremost exposed by their survivor-memoirists.

It seems, therefore, that for all its indispensability to the making and understanding of Russian culture and history, the memoir, with its generic slippage between art and document, subjective expression and dedicated record, often falls through the cracks separating the relatively recently developed academic fields of literary studies and historiography. We assign memoirs in our courses haphazardly, enjoy them enormously, yet rarely bother with their structural and stylistic analysis. We're intent either on general historical coverage or concentrating on a more traditional canon of fictional "greats." Yet we are developing the tools to teach otherwise: recent scholarship has begun to explore Russian modes of self-representation and self-expression, to interrogate Russians' specific, presumably non-Western conceptions and constructions of the self.[2] This inquiry, belatedly echoing renewed interest in Western autobiography, is in good part fired by the quest to recover silenced or censored subjects. I would argue that feminist scholars catalyzed the new focus on various Russian forms of autobiographical writing, testing and extending Barbara Heldt's hypothesis about Russian women's signal achievements in autobiography and lyric poetry, and producing such fine anthologies of primary sources and critical writings as *Russia Through Women's Eyes: Autobiographies from Tsarist Russia* and *Models of Self: Russian Women's Autobiographical Texts*.[3] This new scholarship naturally absorbs the memoir in its declared investigation of currently more fashionable concepts of autobiography and the self—in significant contrast, as one anthology notes, to "Russian and Soviet scholars' preference for the terms *memoir literature* or *documentary literature*" (*Russia Through Women's Eyes*, 6).

Our volume specifically heeds this preference and proposes a "genre"-specific focus—for it asserts that the memoir or *vospominaniia* (recollections, reminiscences), with their dual (if not always balanced) agendas of individualized expression and reliable reportage, has maintained an abiding national genre "contract" between Russian writers and readers. Promising to inscribe the memoirist's self among (often famous) others, with reference to and commentary about the real world, the memoir has powerfully attracted and obligated Russians who were eager to articulate their engagement with their singular, developing society, yet also muted by political censorship in other forms of writing. For centuries Russians have embraced the memoir as a form of autobiography with (depending on one's point of view) a conscience or an agenda, a legacy that encourages and troubles writers even in the post-Soviet present.

The Russian Memoir proffers readers both closer and extensive looks at this durable and elastic narrative form. The introduction opens by exploring the thorny questions of the memoir's definition and disciplinary appropriation. Its successive sections, titled "The Memoir and the World" and "The Memoir and the Word," lay out the framework for the essays to follow, respectively accenting, on the one hand, the memoir's various extraliterary functions (as interpretive history, social modeling, political expression or exposé) and, on the other, its overlap with Russian literature as textual masterpiece or authenticating source. In effect, these sections conduct brief sociopolitical and literary historical surveys of the genre in the modern period.

Although subjects of the essays in *The Russian Memoir* range chronologically from the late eighteenth century to the present day, these texts are not grouped and ordered to assay a comprehensive history of the Russian memoir. Each specific essay, however, more thoroughly contextualizes its subject text(s), for the memoir is shaped conceptually and formally by contemporary notions of history and the individual's role in making and relaying it. Above all, the essays in *The Russian Memoir*, written by literary scholars expert in their chosen subjects, analyze and appreciate the memoir as text, whatever the memoirist's literary skill and relationship to classic Russian culture. Highlighted memoirists vary widely in talent, reputation, and aspiration, including the "private person" Princess Natal'ia Dolgorukaia, sophisticated high culture writers (Nikolai Zabolotsky, Vladimir Nabokov, Joseph Brodsky), cultural critics and facilitators (Lidiia Ginzburg, Avdot'ia Panaeva), political dissidents (Elena Bonner, Evgeniia Ginzburg), and popular artists (El'dar Riazanov). It is my hope that this volume furnishes a useful set of answers to my students' and my question—that readers of *The Russian Memoir* will come away better equipped to evaluate the form and function of the many memoirs they encounter in their study of Russian history and literature.

WHAT A MEMOIR MAY BE

Over the last two centuries, codifiers of Russian literature have assayed valiant, inevitably inadequate definitions of the memoir, intoning certain recurring features of the genre even as they admit its wild variations.[4] In the memoir, they tentatively agree, the author narrates real events and contacts he or she has experienced or witnessed, usually foregrounding a subjective perspective and evaluation. The veracity of the memoir's related "facts" and the style of the memoirist's perception and expression differ greatly from text to text—in the main because the genre accepts all comers. Memoir writing has allured and empowered the polished professional, the public celebrity, the politically disenfranchised, and the barely educated. The memoir's accessibility renders it a treasure trove for historians and quicksand for prescriptive literary critics.

It is remarkable, therefore, that Russian literature scholars have not avoided the hazard, although their efforts have tended to shelter in collective generic schema. Since the early twentieth century, when the Russian Formalists displaced political judgment and subjective impressionism with notions of literary evolution and close analyses of all kinds of verbal texts, Russian critics have not only flagged the memoir and other "documentary" genres on the literary map, but also have insisted, quite prudently, on presenting that map in full:

There is an unbroken chain connecting artistic prose to the history, the memoir, the biography, and ultimately the "human document" of everyday life. The nature of this correlation is complex and has varied from one epoch to another. Depending on the historical preconditions, literature has either withdrawn into special, pointedly aesthetic forms, or it has moved closer to nonliterary discourse. The intermediate, documentary genres, without losing their specificity, without turning into either novel or tale, have accordingly sometimes acquired the status of verbal art. (Ginzburg 1991, 4)

The critic quoted here is Lidiia Ginzburg, an accomplished memoirist and important bridge figure between Formalism and Soviet Structuralism who emerged as one of the most incisive analysts and authors of the genre. According to Ginzburg, documentary genres stand distinct from imaginative literature in their "orientation toward authenticity" and "the peculiar cognitive and emotional possibilities deriving therefrom" (Ginzburg 1991, 6, 7). That orientation does not guarantee that the text "tells the truth," but it invokes a different dual relationship between author and reader in which the reader can presume independent knowledge of the events and experiences the writer represents (Ginzburg 1991, 8). Signal here is the text's projected connection with the true and the real. Yet Ginzburg resists equating documentary literature with primary documents, for she characterizes its organization—its "plot," narration, generalizations, and symbols—as aesthetic: "Memoirs, autobiographies and confessions are almost always literature presupposing readers in the future or in the present; they are a kind of plotted structuring of an image of reality and an image of a human being" (Ginzburg 1991, 9).[5] We should remark Ginzburg's cautious "cluster" definition; in her criticism the memoir merits overlapping categorization (memoirs, autobiographies, confessions) or singular analysis (for example, her studies of Saint Simon's *Memoires* and Herzen's *My Past and Thoughts*).[6]

Another renowned heir to the Formalists, Mikhail Bakhtin, projects an implicit antique view of the memoir's place among the genres, cataloging the features and gauging the impact of those classical genres that most approximate it—Greek and Roman autobiographical and biographical forms. Honoring these as distinctive genres, Bakhtin nonetheless ultimately implies their grander service in narrative history: with their articulation of "a new type of biographical time" and their increasing accent on private life and interiority, these forms "had a profound influence not only on the development of European biography, but also on the development of the European novel as a whole" (Bakhtin 1981, 130). For Bakhtin, an erudite, passionate scholar of narrative prose and the novel, the ultimate value of autobiography and biography (and the memoir between) lies in the material they proffer for fictional refurbishing.[7]

While Bakhtin and Ginzburg, so juxtaposed, point to the memoir's ever shifting incarnations between "human document" and fictional text, more recent critics of Russian literature have opted to sweep the genre into the larger denomination of autobiographical writing. Over the last several decades concepts of autobiography have subsumed an astonishingly varied typology of texts in terms of narrative voice, thematic coverage, structure, and address. In fact, as a host of scholars confess, autobiography poses perhaps the greatest challenge of literary definition and categorization.[8] The 1990 anthology intriguingly titled *Autobiographical Statements in Russian Literature* surveys texts that very differently realize "the autobiographical mode," ranging in type from such recognized memoirs as Nadezhda Mandelstam's *Hope Against Hope* and Vladimir Nabokov's *Speak, Memory* to the autobiographically inflected fictions of Iurii Trifonov and Eduard Limonov. A 1996 issue of the journal *a/b Autobiography*, devoted to Russian examples, declares at the very outset that none of its texts "can be placed in the category of 'pure' autobiographies," although that purity is never defined (Balina 1996, 3).

To a certain extent, such Western-based scholarship follows the lead of Western literary criticism, for the concept of autobiography has readily accommodated opposing critical points of view and remains ever fashionable. G. Thomas Couser traces the 180-degree spectrum of autobiographical criticism from the "literalist" insistence on the genre's facticity and truthful revelation of the author (Georges Gusdorf, John Sturrock) to the deconstructionist sleight of argument that "autobiography doesn't reveal reliable self-knowledge, but shows the real impossibility of closure and totalization" (Couser 1995, 39). Autobiography depends on the tension between textuality and referentiality that inheres in all documentary genres, but this capacious term seems especially to foreground the autobiographical subject and his or her play of subjective imagination.

Each of these different sitings of the memoir—within autobiography, narrative prose, and even documentary genres—spotlights its aesthetic properties and affinities. Yet other scholars have argued, with equally compelling evidence, that the memoir more readily intersects with the nonfictional forms of history and biography. The memoir may be filtered through the most idiosyncratic subject and as eccentrically narrated, elaborately plotted, and symbol packed as any work of fiction, but the memoirist is nevertheless bound to worldly reference. This contiguity does not deny the memoir's complexity as text, although it may encourage that text's uncritical reading as mere information. Indeed, a memoir's experiments with plot and style need not disqualify it as historiography. As Hayden White persuasively theorizes and Simon Schama flamboyantly demonstrates, the writing of history entails plotting, "troping," and in some happy instances, stylistic flair.[9]

In acts of painstaking historiographical imperialism, A. G. Tartakovskii's recent studies of Russian memoirs claim the genre expressly as a manifestation of "historical consciousness" and historiography (Tartakovskii

1997, 8). When Andrew Wachtel analyzes how "Russian writers never allowed themselves to be marginalized from the scene of historical writing," he identifies the impressive tip of the iceberg (Wachtel 1994, 17); Tartakovskii's textual evidence discloses a phenomenally widespread competition for personal recovery of a collective past, among writers and nonwriters. Individual memoirs, at first privately circulated and eventually published en masse, enjoyed dual prestige as primary and secondary sources for much of the nineteenth century. Only in the 1860s and 1870s, with the professionalization of the writing and teaching of history, did memoirs diminish in authority to mere documents and raw material (Tartakovskii 1997, 338; Tartakovskii 1991, 101–4). Yet, the memoir's claim to authoritative discourse was renewed in the twentieth century when the Stalinist authorities systematically destroyed evidence and blatantly distorted historical accounts. A 1998 Russian academic handbook on working with source materials states this inverse relationship as a matter of fact: "Memoirs are especially valuable because our history is so poorly documented " (*Istochnikovedenie* 1998, 636).[10]

In negotiating between self-expression and observation of others, the memoir also overlaps significantly with biography, a potently concentrated form of historical nonfiction. Whereas Bakhtin treasures the contributions of the biography to the novel, G. Vinokur's roughly contemporaneous definition of biography underscores the genre's absolutely validating intersection with history and its similar capacity for encompassing the complex unity of private life through its "mixture of observations, facts, and conjectures along with all other possible factors"—a mixture likewise concocted by the memoirist (Vinokur 1997, 27). In his thoroughgoing study of biography, Ira Bruce Nadel dwells on its malleable form, another notable congruence between biography and memoir (Nadel 1984, 3–18). The biographer in the text may opt for third-person omniscience or first-person presence, may play the detached analyst or the involved interlocutor—in short, may approximate the first-person performance of the memoirist. "A narrative which has as its primary task the enactment of character and place through language," the biography may utilize standard devices that figure frequently in the memoir—the "illuminating incident," the "substantiating quote," "selective description," concise evaluation, and, of course, "the suppression of uncomfortable or too revealing facts in an effort to maintain nobility of character" (Nadel 1984, 8, 17).[11]

In intriguing contrast to the autobiography, the biography also has elicited periodic attacks in the West, in large part, I submit, because scholars deem its art old-fashioned and its political influence conservative. Over the last few decades the biography has been faulted for its supposed mythologization of the individual and the great, its "reinforcement of the authority of origins, the precedence of creator over creation, of fact over fiction, and of the ideology of bourgeois individualism" (Wallen 1995, 51). Yet, for much of Russia's modern era, the mythologizing capacity inherent in both biography and the memoir proved exceptionally subversive and therefore appealing to the highly educated, politically discontented Russian intelligentsia who sought coded portrayals of real-life oppositional heroes and heroines (Nadel 1984, 178).[12] The biography, recast as the memoir of one's famous "contemporaries," not only commemorated actual role models for the intelligentsia's inspiration, but also held up a flattering mirror to their collective image outlawed elsewhere by tsarist and Soviet governments.

The biography and the memoir share one other ambiguous distinction— their endurance as highly *popular* forms of nonfiction (Nadel 1984, 1).[13] The "naive" messages the critics decry in biography—that great persons exist to be celebrated and scrutinized, that every life harbors delectable secrets and scandals—continue to compel both biographers and readers. Biography, both respectable and voyeuristic, has accrued enormous entertainment value, convincing editors to experiment with collective and serial publications. A few of the more "educational" examples range from the nineteenth-century Russian *Lives of Remarkable People*, which marketed "works on religious figures, state leaders and national heroes, scholars and scientists, philosophers, philanthropists and educators, explorers, inventors, writers, artists, musicians, and actors" to Oxford University Press's most recent (1999) edition of *American National Biography* (Brooks 1985, 344).[14] With its equal opportunity access and personalized purview, the memoir easily duplicates the popular biography's conventional uplift, sensational exposé, and mass appeal.

The memoir thus presents a remarkably fluid and affective genre, coincident with and sometimes indiscernible from fiction, autobiography, biography, history, and gossip; and capacious enough to combine fictional enhancements with nonfictional authority, confession with observation, personal license with verifiable facts, subversive rumors with celebrity worship. Yet—to intone a recurring feature—the memoir necessarily presumes to record its subject's different public performances on "real" stages: among family and intimates; in various social and political milieus; in the "real" space and time of history. For the term of reading, the narrator-subject assumes enormous authority as the reader's descriptive and evaluative guide to these depicted worlds. Unbound by scholarly strictures and privileged with firsthand knowledge, the memoirist wields interpretive power more overtly, freely, and intimately than either historian or biographer.

THE MEMOIR AND THE WORLD

This powerful, protean genre imprinted, vented, and at times helped to shape modern Russian society and politics. Its first appearance in eighteenth-century Russian literature reflected and reinforced fundamental changes that Peter I (1682–1725) had forcibly implemented in state-subject relations and empire building. The Muscovite world Peter sought to transform had privileged the collective identity and role of the extended family and the carefully codified literature of historical chronicles and religious texts. Self-expression surfaced more and more frequently in texts registering the religious and political turbulence of the seventeenth century, as the famous *Life of Archpriest Avvakum* examples, but the conservative religious values of Muscovy guaranteed that "the impersonal character of medieval historical narratives" dominated in print (Tartakovskii 1991, 7).

In ordering Muscovy's secularization and technological and cultural modernization along Western lines, Peter I fomented a cultural and psychological revolution. He exhorted his new elite to shift their allegiance from the family to the new imperial state; to acquire a Western-style education and to sample Western cultures beyond Muscovy; and to serve the state as trained professionals with the expectation that individual achievements (and not family connections) would earn them status and rewards. Derek Offord concludes that the Petrine reforms enabled Russians to conceive of and honor individual identity, paving the way "for the unleashing of personal potentialities and for speculation on the nature and status of the individual human" (Offord 1998, 14). The Petrine reforms, moreover, enabled this newly individualized elite's exposure to a new canon of Western literary genres, initiating a formative cultural intercourse that would affect Russian memoir production for decades to come. The many Western memoirs, confessions, and autobiographies read by the elite surely influenced the post-Petrine notion of selfhood.

Yet the Petrine cultivation of individual identity did not usher in the bourgeois individualism we are accustomed to standardize as Western. In a sense, Peter I liberated the self for immediate duty elsewhere; the value of the individual obtained only in his or her devoted state service. The first beneficiaries of Peter's revolution were too busy (and perhaps too traumatized) to do much more than serve, and the first, relatively few, accounts of individual lives produced by this service elite largely recapitulated specific assignments and achievements (Tartakovskii 1997, 9–10). By the reign of Peter's great successor, Catherine II (1762–96), the fruits of Peter's reforms, the ever increasing influence of Western literature, and the privileges conceded a less "serving" nobility facilitated a significant increase in memoirs that centered on self-reflection and individualized perception. Nevertheless, the conflicted selfhood Peter had promoted, harnessing self-development to external service and deriving individual distinction from government recognition, long remained a constant in Russian social thought and cultural works. Even those opposed to the state found alien the notion of a nonsacrificing, self-oriented individualism.

The memoir, then, was ideally designed for expressing this notion of the self, and throughout modern Russian history it demonstrated that dutiful, contextualized self's real-world influence, relying as much on its mode of transmission as its mode of address. The men and women who first ventured individualized memoirs in the 1760s and 1770s—memoirs organized by their specific point of view and way of remembering—nonetheless did not write for the public (Tartakovskii 1997, 11). There as yet existed no socially condoned practice of publishing memoirs. A Russian penned his or her memoirs not for self-display, but for private and familial benefit (Tartakovskii 1991, 96).

Yet delayed publication did not always prevent a memoir from reaching and influencing a select public. The tiny dimensions of the Russian elite and the intimate connections linking families and friends meant that a private or secret manuscript might be sampled by the major writers and thinkers of the day. By the early nineteenth century, A. N. Golitsyn and Aleksandr Turgenev had earned guarded renown as collectors of such "unpublished Russian history" as Catherine II's secret memoirs and politically dangerous accounts of Catherine's demise and her son Paul's accession to the throne (Tartakovskii 1997, 124, 131, 135). Turgenev, in turn, regularly supplied manuscripts to such influential men as Prince Petr Viazemskii and Aleksandr Pushkin. In this "self-censoring" sociopolitical climate, the rather naive public ambition of Aleksandr Radishchev's provocative memoir-travelogue, *A Journey from Petersburg to Moscow* (1790), published anonymously by the author, stands as a dangerous anomaly. Radishchev's arrest and exile stemmed directly from his exploitation of the memoir as published real-world guide: he had barbed his supposedly real journey with digressions against serfdom, censorship, and other anti-Enlightenment evils "found" in the Russian landscape.

With the turn into the nineteenth century and Russia's heroic world performance in the Napoleonic wars, memoir production proliferated as Russians hastened to record the lives of their very own national greats.[15] By the onset of Nicholas I's rule (1825–55), the combined quests to distinguish Russia's national history and to realize Russia's imperial destiny engaged most of the writing and reading elite and fueled a boom of published and commissioned memoirs. The enormous popularity of Nikolai Karamzin's *History of the Russian State* (1818–26) signaled this trend, with Karamzin's manifest "author-chronicler" breaching the boundary between memoir and history, while M. P. Pogodin's founding of the thick journal *The Muscovite* furnished a ready forum for memoir publication (Tartakovskii 1991, 14; 1997, 19–20, 107–8).[16] By the 1830s memoirists regularly published their efforts out of a sense of historical and national obligation and with the assurance of eager public consumption, if not state approval. Their work was condoned and courted by the most eminent figure then active in Russian culture, Aleksandr Pushkin:

> One of Russia's most jealous defenders of "memoir literature," and its collector, critic, and propagandist, [Pushkin] was preoccupied by the fact that the memory of remarkable people would quickly disappear owing to a paucity of historical memoirs. It was in the 1830s that Pushkin especially exhorted all those who had something to tell to write down their recollections. (Tartakovskii 1997, 175)

At the same time, as Pushkin the voracious manuscript reader well knew, there already existed memoirs that simply could not be committed to print on account of their politically suspect authorship or vantage point. Indeed, the exhortations of Pushkin and his associates to would-be memoirists comprised a relatively mild form of political subversion, for the Pushkin circle championed a distinctive gentry heritage and leadership in preserving the national past. Gentry memoirs could smuggle a kind of literary magna carta past government censors into the public eye. Bolder challenges to government authority remained in manuscript; this was the fate of the Decembrists' memoirs, composed after this gentry group's December 1825 coup d'état failed and its more fortunate members, exiled in Siberia, recorded their politically illicit stories (Tartakovskii 1997, 43).

The memoir's democratizing potential also came to be exploited to an extent that the highborn Pushkin circle might have found hard to condone, at least among Russians. Since the seventeenth century, France had outstripped the European world in memoir production, a trend commenced by its independent and powerful nobility and blown open to the masses with the social upheaval of the French Revolution (Ginzburg 1991, 6). After the overthrow of king and aristocracy, French citizens of all classes, and more astonishingly, both genders, felt beholden and empowered to tell their versions of unfolding history, and this practice persisted throughout the nineteenth century.[17]

By the 1830s and 1840s Russians were emulating this now established French tradition, as memoirs issued forth from a great variety of social types—merchants, clerks, lowly officers, nonnoble intelligentsia (Tartakovskii 1997, 42, 162). This era, for example, marks the startling debut of Nadezhda Durova's *Notes of a Cavalry Maiden* (1836), a publication expressly sponsored by Pushkin and clearly indicative of the memoir's growing accessibility.[18] A woman who successfully masqueraded as a tsarist officer in the Napoleonic Wars, Durova (1783–1866) was audacious in print as well, trespassing with her *Notes* onto the hallowed terrain of great military men's campaign reminiscences. Public consumption of such transgression suggests a Russian society that could countenance a provocatively different memoirist as long as the transgressor also professed her loyalty to the tsar.

Thus, the charged connection between memoir writing and political opposition, first assayed by the French, resonated with special force under Russian and later Soviet political conditions. In tsarist Russia an elite educated and professionalized by a modernizing, all-powerful state conceived a wide range of critical perspectives on its sponsor, but possessed no legal right to a collective oppositional voice. The memoir's propensities to document and interpret "reality," to spawn role models, and to proselytize its readers rendered it a fearsome potential weapon against a univocal authority. Alert to the danger, the state censor scrutinized the memoir's subject for religious and political unorthodoxy and limited the memoir's depiction of "real stages" to those that were perfectly timeless (the pastoral) or endorsed official state history.

The state thus did permit the publication of some of the most remarkable memoirs and, interestingly enough, pseudomemoirs in Russian culture, Sergei Aksakov's *Reminiscences* (1856) and his more famous semi-fictionalized *Family Chronicle* (1856).[19] In these texts Aksakov evoked his patriarchal provincial gentry family with great aesthetic skill and little sentimentality. His works seemed to deliver the fullest response to Pushkin's call for the gentry memoir, although their complex psychological portraiture and revelations on master-serf relations prevented their "unqualified endorsement" of gentry life (Durkin 1983, 243). Yet their "worldly" interpretation, schematized by Aksakov's reliance on character type and unifying motivations, posed no critique of a flawed present, voicing instead nostalgia for "a bright distant past, one that perhaps never existed and cannot be regained, but one in which the secure emotional circle of the family seemed a sure bulwark" (Durkin 1983, 45).

In sharp political contrast but with no less literary verve, the extraordinary memoir of Aleksandr Herzen, *My Past and Thoughts* (1855–67), was constructed quite deliberately to exert a competing authority. Already in Western European exile, Herzen wrote "free of the prohibitions of censorship" and equipped his memoir to engage, persuade, and impart freely expressed and freely lived experience to his politically frustrated readers at home (Ginzburg 1991, 196). His work focuses directly on the present and recent past without a plot's "partition between authorial consciousness and objective reality"; his narration builds on this impression of objectivity by analyzing rather than aestheticizing his experience. Perhaps most powerful is Herzen's self-portrayal "as the representative of a generation, of a particular historical stratum" (Ginzburg 1991, 209).[20] In a sense, Herzen fortifies this consummately subversive text with an alternative variation on the serving, representative Russian self.

Other subversive memoirs, safeguarded in manuscript or ventured after the relaxation of tsarist censorship in the early 1900s, replayed Herzen's smart strategy, albeit with much less rhetorical and analytical skill. This was especially the case for Russian radicals and revolutionists, who justified their highly critical representation of the authorities and the slow-to-revolt masses with the stance and voice of collective authority. The radical memoirists also frequently censored a complex self and a particular life story to foreground their cause. Because it aimed to engage the public—as public self-presentation and personalized persuasion—the Russian memoir very often offset transgression with sanction, one kind of unorthodoxy with another kind of orthodoxy. The revolutionaries, no less than other memoirists, disciplined their outrageous subjects to ensure their moral appeal.

It is intriguing to pose the parallel between Durova's politically loyal, yet socially stunning *Notes of a Cavalry Maiden* and the memoirs of Russian women revolutionaries, a group that gained steadily in number and public prominence from the 1870s through the early Soviet period. These radical women regimented their self-presentation—especially experiences that stigmatized them as different from their male colleagues (sexual experience, family obligations)—and wrote their memoirs as revolutionary history (Holmgren 1994). Barbara Alpern Engel and Clifford N. Rosenthal rightly observe that "personal and political liberation were intimately connected for these women," yet that connection flickers fitfully in their texts (Engel and Rosenthal 1975, xx).[21] For example, the memoir of Vera Figner (1852–1943), one of the most doctrinaire revolutionaries, marches inexorably from tales of a pampered girlhood to a dispassionate chronicle of revolutionary activities, only to be set adrift as she meditates about her long years in the Schlusselberg Fortress, revealing "the deepest layer of her personality, her character, one may even say her soul" (Stites 1991, x). A similar tension disfigures the *Autobiography of a Sexually Emancipated Communist Woman* (1926), the boldly titled memoir of Figner's more prominent heir, the Bolshevik feminist and high-ranking Soviet bureaucrat Aleksandra Kollontai. More than any other female radical, Kollontai struggled to join political with individual freedom in her life *and* writings, yet she dutifully (fearfully?) purged her memoir of what her Party deemed inappropriately personal.

Less overtly political memoir writing also flourished in late-nineteenth- and early-twentieth-century Russia. Despite its harsh autocratic government, Russian society in these decades was professionalizing and modernizing at an impressive pace evidenced by increasing literacy rates, expanding industries and markets, and the developments of mass transportation systems and a mass-circulation press. The growth of the press and the professions especially encouraged new candidates to undertake their memoirs, in good part because a burgeoning readership clamored for fresh topics and reflections of its own different images.

Indeed, the spread of Russian memoirs in the late tsarist period resembled the genre's cultivation in the capitalist West, delineating the emergence of an independent, diversifying civic society. Late nineteenth-century

Russia did not exactly reprise a mid-nineteenth-century France in which every bureaucrat felt entitled to tell his story, but more and more educated Russians sensed the print-worthy value of their specific lives as professionals and individuals. That is, their self-worth no longer derived solely from state service or political commitment, but also from professional achievements long celebrated and propagated in the West. Notions of professional identity and success had spawned such collective biographies as *The Lives of Indian Officers* (1867) and *The Lives of the Electricians* (1887) in Victorian England; in Russia they inspired lawyers, doctors, scientists, civil servants, and even qualified female professionals to take up the pen and write. Some of the first women doctors chronicled their arduous educational and professional journeys much as the female revolutionaries dedicated their memoirs to bear witness to the cause.[22]

Yet overall, Russian "professionals" differed strikingly from their Western peers in their cultural pretensions and, quite often, literary accomplishments. They did not write, as Western professionals did, to offer the striving public their example of "success." Rather, the public experience and self-confidence they gained through their work emboldened them to exercise the very considerable authority of the nineteenth-century Russian writer.[23] Anatolii Koni and Sergei Andreevskii (1847–1920?), whom D. S. Mirsky honors as "literary lawyers," composed essays and memoirs to cultivate their literary skills and to prove their profound understanding of human nature (Mirsky 1958, 358–59). When the mathematician Sofia Kovalevskaia penned her *Russian Childhood* (1890), she related no sensational wunderkind story, but mainly indulged in psychological analysis and lyrical evocation of her past. Doctors exploited memoirs as psychological outlet and social critique, lamenting in them their hard years in training and practice and highlighting "the difficult relationship between physicians and their superiors, both medical and nonmedical" (Frieden 1981, 208). Using their life's material, memoirists attempted to duplicate the keen insight and moral power they knew and admired from decades of Russian realist fiction.

In general, the reverence accorded the great Russian writer, at fever pitch by century's end, mightily influenced memoir production and reception. Readers hungered for personal disclosure and worldly guidance from the "greats." Writers, in turn, readily donned "greatness" and broadcast their worldly vision from the memoir's tailor-made soapbox. Such a reader-writer dynamic spanned all levels of literate fin de siècle society and inspired a wide variety of texts by serious and popular writers, by subjects who would be idols and subjects primed to pay idols homage. The refined loner Konstantin Leontiev (1831–91) relied on eccentric essays and brilliant recollections to impart his worldview, intimating the path later to be reworked by such writer-philosophers as Vasilii Rozanov and Nikolai Berdiaev. At the other end of the sociocultural spectrum, the memoirs of

Anastasiia Verbitskaia (1861–1928), the innovator of the Russian best-seller, propagandized her self-styled lofty purpose and summoned kindred spirits to buy her books and write in emulation. Even the "worshiping" memoirs ranged in type—from the deferential, lovingly detailed portraits of the artist by Kornei Chukovskii (1882–1969), a self-taught highbrow critic from the lower middle class, to the often disillusioned encounters with "great" Russians and the vaunted "folk" recounted by Maxim Gorky (Aleksei Peshkov, 1868–1936), one of the very few serious writers to have arisen from Russia's lower depths.

By the early twentieth century, then, the memoir had come to be used in Russia as a mode of wresting and bestowing power, of endorsing and subverting the sociopolitical status quo, and, almost invariably, of valuing the individual self insofar as it interpreted, served, and connected with the "real" context it depicted. To a significant degree, the memoir evolved in tandem and in a tug of war with the modern Russian state, enabled by the state's recognition of individual merit, nourished by state-cultivated contact with the West, reflective of the state's insistence on service, and competitive with the state's official vision and treatment of Russian reality. By writing memoirs, Russians dared to demarcate their own autonomous circles of presumably truthful perception and real-world influence, to pioneer the rights and capabilities of the individual in an autocratic, bureaucratic state.

The Soviet power that eventually triumphed over the tsarist empire aimed to improve the lot of Russia's poor masses and to ensure, at least on paper, the equality of all its citizens. But there inhered in its equitable outlook and redistribution of resources a vehement anti-individualism, for the ruling Bolshevik elite disdained individual rights and merits as bourgeois. In comparison with its tsarist predecessor, the Soviet state wielded stronger ideological motivation and more comprehensive institutional and material means to police individual expression, and it did so for the stated sake of various collectives—the Soviet people, the Communist Party, the good of the motherland. Some slippage occurred in the first decade of Soviet power, when the government had not yet corralled all writers into a single union and had not yet consolidated its censorship and management of the publishing industry. Thus, state-sponsored memoirs of the Bolshevik revolution and civil war coexisted with generally tolerated memoir-experiments in the 1920s. But once Joseph Stalin launched the comprehensive mobilization and regimentation of Soviet society in the early 1930s, both politically orthodox and aesthetically innovative memoirists faced an unprecedented set of strictures and dangers.

In effect, the Stalinist establishment enforced its "authoritative" interpretive discourse in the press and other media. Although the state's interpretation of past history, present conditions, and future goals was neither clear nor consistent, the state's power was such that writers either echoed or desperately tried to divine its point of view on any given subject. If the Stalinist secret police could arrest the author of a "seditious" poem left in manuscript, then only the most fearless or reckless memoirist would dare to articulate his or her specific reading of the world. Jane Gary Harris's opening essay in this section expertly traces how Lidiia Ginzburg, perhaps the most perceptive memoirist/analyst of the Russian and Soviet intelligentsia, at once elucidates and demonstrates the intelligentsia's complex psychological and clandestine textual response to this regimentation.

Those memoirs that could be published (see for example, Fedor Gladkov's *The Story of Childhood*) clung to politically approved formulas in choice of subject (preferably a stalwart young Communist) and reiterated Marxist-Leninist interpretations of (usually) a Russia on the eve of revolution. The extreme censorship and punishment of Stalin's regime (1929–53) posed yet another astonishing challenge to the memoir writer. The state not only censured alternative points of view, but also outlawed or tampered with all attempts to document a negative present, even when such documentation purported to be objective. Like other totalitarian societies, the Stalinist regime depended on a vast propaganda effort for its popular support; the government was adamant in equating the depicted with the real, and airbrushed that depiction accordingly. The Stalinist government could not tolerate the ambivalence and coded criticism the tsarist censor often overlooked in realist fiction and nonfiction: to name was to indict. The memoirist in the Stalin era was severely disciplined, therefore, as both distinctive subject and reporter/interpreter of real life. With its quasi-religious insistence on self-purification and unquestioning faith in the Party, the regime only permitted the self-representation of the true believer.[24] Although punishment for deviations lessened considerably after Stalin's death in 1953, its threat generally loomed until the late 1980s and the official declaration of glasnost, or "openness," in all public media.

A very few "nonbeliever" memoirists braved the dangers of Stalinist repression, among them Lidiia Chukovskaia in her transcribed meetings with the poet Anna Akhmatova (*The Akhmatova Journals*). But unofficial memoir production truly thrived and partially surfaced under the more liberal political conditions of the Thaw and de-Stalinization campaign in the late 1950s and early 1960s, when political leaders allowed and savvy editors actively solicited "true" documentation of the Stalinist experience. The call to de-Stalinize generated a host of memoirs, encompassing Il'ia Erenburg's published catalog of the repressed, *People, Years, Life* (1961–65), as well as such unpublishable memoir-exposés of Stalinist repression and the Stalinist labor camps as Nadezhda Mandelstam's *Hope Against Hope* and *Hope Abandoned* and Evgeniia Ginzburg's *Journey into the Whirlwind* and *Within the Whirlwind*. Sarah Pratt's essay on one such Thaw-era memoir,

Nikolai Zabolotsky's fascinating "Early Years," astutely marks this camp survivor's necessary compromises in chronological coverage and explicit allegiance and his glancing revelation of a taboo topic—his formative religious youth.

In contrast to their nineteenth-century predecessors, the post-Stalin memoirists could avail themselves of a more effective system of manuscript circulation. In tsarist times highly subversive manuscripts secretly made the rounds of the elite; post-Stalin liberalization facilitated a more sophisticated and widely practiced *samizdat,* or clandestine self-publishing. At the same time, the tensions of the Cold War contributed to *tamizdat,* or publishing abroad, a curious phenomenon underwritten by Western governments and Russian specialists in the West. In its "supplementary" offerings of the politically subversive and/or culturally valuable texts that the Soviet publishing establishment had disallowed, *tamizdat* produced a free Russian press for Soviet readers, as well as for all readers of Russian, and its frequent reprinting of *samizdat* texts put these into international circulation and durable form. Many unpublishable memoirs, including those of Evgeniia Ginzburg and Nadezhda Mandelstam, traveled this route west and out; eventually some Soviet dissidents themselves followed suit and promptly published their memoirs in exile.[25]

The new configuration of post-Stalin publishing in which a *samizdat-tamizdat* connection challenged the official press (*gosizdat*) abetted underground memoir production, enhancing these texts' authority and partially liberating their focus. Dissident memoirists' very experience of political repression entitled them to write, and such "writing for the drawer" could culminate in mass circulation and worldwide admiration. The sanctifying melodrama of *samizdat* and the Cold War urgency of *tamizdat* vouchsafed the memoirist a poignant global martyrdom. Some dissident writers, such as Irina Ratushinskaya in *Grey is the Color of Hope* and Andrei Sakharov in his monumental *Memoirs,* wielded their texts as prods to international activism. Others, such as Raisa Orlova, Liudmila Alekseeva, and Elena Bonner, retraced the now familiar patterns of the nineteenth-century revolutionists, generalizing a dissident role model from their signal political experience, yet sometimes at the cost of personal distinction and complexity. As Helena Goscilo deftly discerns in her analysis of Bonner's *Mothers and Daughters* (1990), this highly respected dissident disappoints, in contrast to her fiction-writing contemporaries, by politically straitening and psychologically repressing the fascinating relations her title promises to explore.

These twentieth-century heirs, embraced by the West as Cold War heroes, enjoyed a greater celebrity status and a better, more sophisticated press. They were also courted by a new breed of reader, the Soviet specialist. The Soviet moratorium on "objective" documentation and restrictions on archival access forced historians and social scientists to seek other infor-

national sources, and the memoir's implied eyewitness account and independent perceptions "eyemarked" it as more reliable material. As Aleksander Solzhenitsyn's *The Gulag Archipelago* (1976) demonstrated so importantly with his personal collection and presentation of camp testimonies, the post-Stalin era before glasnost became the heyday of the amateur, individualized Soviet historian, for historical "truth" could only be accessed via private, officially illicit connections and articulated by a personal voice uncompromised by official allegiance. An activist schooled in the memoir tradition of nineteenth-century Russian radicals perfectly fulfilled these requirements.

Although the advent of glasnost and the fall of the Soviet Union conduced to the uncensored rewriting of Soviet history, the memoir's value as historical source skyrocketed, rather than decreased, in the 1980s and 1990s. Memoir writing has boomed over the last fifteen years, initially as individual attempts to amplify or refute official Soviet historiography. But the memoir's unprecedented popularity in contemporary Russia also signifies a radical change in the genre's contents, for the conditions of the post-Soviet market have marginalized traditional Russian notions of the serving self and the instrumentalized life story. The buying Russian public's great appetite for memoirs, especially memoirs of media and political celebrities and their associates, confirms in bold the commercialization of Russian culture and the memoir's great durability as a commercial product. The memoir has positively thrived through the transition from socialism to capitalism because the life story always *sells,* the more so today when the Russian book market unabashedly centers on entertainment. It remains to be seen whether the political function and social prestige of the Russian memoir will wither away under market pressures. Alexander Prokhorov's intriguing essay on El'dar Riazanov's steady memoir output in the 1990s suggests that a certain social cachet remains, although its specific features reflect a not altogether clear reprioritization of the public's values and desires: Prokhorov points to Riazanov's recent embrace of the roles of both popular filmmaker and independent artist struggling with the new Russian market. Whatever its future approach and use, the memoir's mass appeal and circulation—for a capitalizing and/or nationalizing Russian society—seem assured.

THE MEMOIR AND THE WORD

Once it qualified as publishable and *published* writing, the Russian memoir acquired value as literature, earning its first literary codification in 1819 from the critic N. I. Grech.[26] By fortuitous coincidence the memoir at the same time yielded important building material to a developing Russian literature. The Sentimentalist movement, which so attracted the second generation of Westernized Russians in the late eighteenth century, had privileged human sensibility and explicitly subjective writing. In a few decades, the memoir's great capacities and specific focus—its narrative and stylistic experimentation, record of "real" experience, and emphasis on character study—would be championed and coveted by Pushkin, Viazemskii, and other literary men bent on cultivating a national Russian literature and, especially, Russian prose. Gitta Hammarberg's erudite essay on Princess Natal'ia Dolgorukaia's memoir in this section traces the multiple and diverse appropriations of one such "natural" record. Avid memoir consumers also admired and envied the new model of Walter Scott, whose popular novels transformed everyday history, the customary material of memoirs, into historical fiction.

Russian fiction's dependence on and interaction with the memoir intensified over the second third of the nineteenth century, as Russian writers and critics avidly pursued a poetics of realism built on psychologism and "a logical determinism, the search for causes and connections in the conception of the human being" (Ginzburg 1991, 82). By 1847, Vissarion Belinskii, a true critic-legislator of modern Russian literature, had declared that skillfully written memoirs "constitute something like the final frontier of the realm of the novel, themselves sealing it off."[27] Belinskii's less talented heir, the utilitarian critic Nikolai Chernyshevsky, characteristically savored the memoir as literature's "sustenance" (*pishcha*), specifically praising Aksakov's *Family Chronicle* for nourishing readers used to the spare diet of Russian fiction.[28] The memoir's analytical mode and free-ranging thematic scope thus "fed" a still embryonic prose that, according to Lidiia Ginzburg, would mature into the realist novel:

> The search in the first half of the 1850s for analytical incisiveness and scientific reliability in the comprehension of reality still had not discovered the form of the large-scale sociopsychological novel and it therefore frequently turned to the distinctive possibilities of the intermediate genres. (Ginzburg 1991, 197)

The memoir's sustenance eventually produced whopping fictional offspring. In the latter half of the nineteenth century Walter Scott's historical novels were overwhelmingly eclipsed by Lev Tolstoy's monument of historical fiction and fiction on history, *War and Peace*. Famed for its explicit reflections on the writing of history, this masterpiece also impresses and innovates in its convincing fictional transformation of the various memoirs Tolstoy consulted—I. T. Radozhitskii's accounts of the battles of the Napoleonic wars and S. M. Zhikharev's student observations of theatrical life in Moscow and St. Petersburg.[29] Russian realist novels won world renown in great part because they traversed the border between fiction and nonfiction, literary modeling and real life, with such impunity and skill.[30] Yet not all such "borrowings" resulted in salutary fiction; Hammarberg's survey of how Dolgorukaia's memoir was recycled in poetry and didactic prose painstakingly registers the numerous embellishments and distortions of this text's story and its narrator's persona.

The relationship between realist fiction and the memoir also proved reciprocal: while fiction "digested" and transformed the memoir, the memoir absorbed and flaunted literary features. Fiction's influence on the memoir became especially conventionalized in the wake of Aksakov's *Family Chronicle* and Tolstoy's trilogy, *Childhood* (1852), *Boyhood* (1854), and *Youth* (1857), for, as Andrew Wachtel demonstrates on scores of imitative gentry-authored texts, Tolstoy and Aksakov had forever identified the writing of a Russian gentry childhood as a weighty literary project (Wachtel 1990, 18–130). In our essay for this section, Jehanne Gheith and I identify a quite different fiction-memoir symbiosis in the oeuvre of Avdot'ia Panaeva (1819/20–93), a writer of nongentry provenance whose domestic purview and defiantly "humble" perspective shaped *first* her early autobiographical fiction and subsequently her oeuvre-culminating *Memoirs*.

By the first decade of the twentieth century, the realist approach had yielded its ethical and artistic monopoly on Russian literature, disdained for its aesthetic plainness by new modernist groups and attacked by writers and readers emerged from the lower classes for its privileging of the gentry experience. Such radical challenges did not render the memoir obsolete, but instead revitalized and varied its literary effects. In fact, the genre's link of individual impressions with world consciousness rendered it an all-purpose medium for protosocialists and esoteric poets alike. Gorky, for instance, most effectively channeled his romantic, revolutionary fervor through his autobiographical trilogy, *My Childhood, My Apprenticeship,* and *My Universities,* which deliberately counters Tolstoy's trilogy with its lower-class subject's brutalizing experience and folklore-influenced hero worship. The poet and essayist Zinaida Gippius (1869–1945), a self-declared Symbolist, successfully deployed her cultural memoirs not only to make her life observations art, but also to evince the absolute consonance *between* life and art that other Russian modernists avowed and contrived to enact.[31] The copious memoirs of the poet and novelist Andrei Belyi (1880–1934), produced over a decade later, nonetheless manifest much the same fin de siècle preference for personalized, idiosyncratic interpretation. The memoir could articulate the many desires and devices of a fin de siècle Russian society obsessed with individualism and more tolerant of diverse subjects: it authorized one's creative eccentricities or freshened one's sincere clichés.

The memoir enhanced its literary value after the 1917 Bolshevik Revolution, benefiting from a new critical regard for nonfiction, a fascination with "factography."[32] During the first decade of Soviet rule such writers as Boris Pil'niak and Konstantin Fedin experimented with intersplicing documents into their fiction; other authors trail blazed new forms of historical, biographical, and autobiographical art. Angela Brintlinger credits in part the interwar vogue for biographical novels (in the Soviet Union and interwar emigration) to Boris Eikhenbaum's and Iurii Tynianov's keen interest in the nonliterary text and Vladimir Weidle's attention to prose forms "loaded with factual or rational material."[33] For these astute critics, the memoir's worth lay in its nonrefinement, its potential abandonment of storytelling or novelistic conventions, its undigested display of the "facts." Other artists in this early Soviet period—perhaps most notably, Osip Mandelstam, Boris Pasternak, and Marina Tsvetaeva—resorted to the memoir to experiment with their own idiosyncratic linkage of art with history. Mandelstam in *The Noise of Time* (1922–23) and Pasternak in *Safe Conduct* (1931) similarly invoked the material base of recalled experiences, personages, and landscapes both to ground and to flourish their poetic vision. Writing in emigration during the early 1930s, Tsvetaeva utilized sketches of family members ("Mother and Music," "The House at Old Pimen' Street," "The Devil") and cultural figures ("My Pushkin," "Natal'ia Goncharova") as a means of tracing and asserting her peculiar poetic birthright. Swept up in the traumatic first decades of the Soviet state, these modernist writers conveyed (and to a certain extent contained) history as a vitalizing or terribly dramatizing influence on their art.

The Soviet government's increasing control over the arts soon stifled all types of experimentation, displacing diverse subjects with prescribed heroic models, and modernist innovative technique with conventional didactic prose. Gorky, reborn as a Soviet bureaucrat, contributed to this dull regimentation by resuscitating the series *Lives of Remarkable People*, published commercially in the nineteenth century, as a kind of state service. Once the doctrine of socialist realism, with its disjointed poetics of realist techniques conveying idealist visions, forcibly applied to the entire artistic establishment in the mid-1930s, the published memoir followed suit, regurgitating the approved plots, style, and character types of socialist realist fiction.[34] The Stalinist publishing establishment did not tolerate the political ambiguity of documentary literature or the aesthetic idiosyncrasies of a personalized narrator.

On the other hand, memoirs written secretly and later surfacing intermittently in the post-Stalin period often evinced a poetics intriguingly warped by censorship. These texts' modes of address and storytelling mark them as chamber works and, often, urgent communiqués—tales told by a narrator assured of his or her truthfulness to an audience whose ethical and artistic values he or she presumes to share. Dissident memoirists of the Stalinist and post-Stalin, preglasnost periods functioned within the confines of conspiracy, and their narratives incessantly reproduce the devices their closed circles relied upon to share information—the anecdote, with its salacious or subversive orientation and narrative punch, the frequently sentimentalized character sketch/encomium, and repeated gossip.[35] Even Lidiia Ginzburg's highly analytical notes on the era, titled *At the Writing Desk*, present a scholar's rambling private diary, a "human document" freely improvised for the drawer. Under the conditions of writing for *samizdat*, the memoir—unedited, unrevised, and often retold—converged with oral communication. As I have analyzed at length elsewhere, Nadezhda Mandelstam's two-volume memoirs transcribe her extraordinary sustained performance as a raconteur, a sharp-tongued gossip, and a highly gifted, as well as biased, observer of her times (Holmgren 1993, 127–38, 148–68).

Whereas Soviet dissident memoirists often reprised the teaching tone and investigative stance of famous nineteenth-century radicals and revolutionaries, they could no longer subscribe to nineteenth-century scenarios of tsarist oppression and socialist liberation, and so cast wide for generally humanist values and beliefs. Correspondingly, the literary forms they mustered often comprised a motley of high and popular genres, the stuff of "timeless truth" and immediate emotional effect. As Natasha Kolchevska richly elaborates in her essay for this section, the former Communist Evgeniia Ginzburg interweaves "multiple narrative modes" and invokes prerevolutionary Russian literature and classical tropes to endure her "journey" through the Stalinist prisons and camps, yet she also resorts to paradigms that recycle the popular features of melodrama (a black-and-white moral schema, tragic and transcendent sacrifice) and the adventure story (quick pacing, surprising plot turns, outsized physical tests and triumphs). In a sense, the post-Stalin increase in "amateur" memoirists who wrote in direct consequence of their repression inevitably inclined the dissident memoir toward the devices of socialist realism and mass-circulating popular fiction, as well as realist classics; new writers articulated their confounding life stories in the narrative forms they knew.

The keynote of poetry in Evgeniia Ginzburg's work sounds another important literary trend in above- and underground post-Stalin memoirs—the memoirist's self-conscious embrace of lyricism and aesthetic experiment. For Russians in the postwar period, the great poets of the early twentieth century—Anna Akhmatova, Aleksandr Blok, Osip Mandelstam, Boris Pasternak, Marina Tsvetaeva—had inherited the Russian realist authors' mantle of spiritual authority and prophetic insight; the memorized works of politically proscribed poets had fortified and inspired Ginzburg and countless others during the dark days of Stalinism. Predictably then, the post-Stalin Thaw, which commenced as a public call for emotional sincerity and fresh individual expression, fomented a poetry revival of massive and public proportions. It was no coincidence that an established poet, Ol'ga Berggolts (1910–75), helped realize the Thaw with her article "Discussion of Lyric Poetry" and published one of the first such poeticized memoirs, *Daylight Stars* (1959).

Nor did one have to qualify as a poet to attempt this sort of transformation, as is evident in the posthumously published memoir of the long-silent modernist writer Iurii Olesha, *No Day Without a Line* (1965), or in the late works of the well-known Soviet novelist Valentin Kataev (1897–1986), and the texts by younger artists of post-Stalin vintage intrigued by Kataev's example of "bad" writing. As Richard Borden observes in his monograph on Kataev's work and influence, this established author cultivated a "mauvist" approach that "deliberately obscure[d] the boundaries between the 'real' and the 'imagined,' creating a protean generic hybrid that fluctuates between memoir and pseudomemoir, autobiography and pseudoautobiography, lyrical diary and fiction" (Borden 1999, 48). Kataev's "excessive" textual play, which openly pitted solipsistic individualism against entrenched Soviet collectives and creative fancy against instrumentalized art, inspired and contributed to a steady stream of provocative "pseudomemoirs" and "fictional memoirs" by such writers as Vasilii Aksenov, Venedikt Erofeev, Eduard Limonov, and Sasha Sokolov (Borden 1999, 164).

Such deliberate aestheticization of the Russian memoir—marked by emphatically subjectivized narration, deliberately disordered plots, manipulation of time and space, incorporation of disparate "documents," and implicit resistance to political imperatives—represents the genre's boldest innovation over the last few decades, resuming and embellishing on the formal experimentation of prerevolutionary and pre-Stalinist literature. Certainly memoirs that inform or expose and presume to articulate a real world predominate in Russian publishing, be they produced in the Soviet Union, post-Soviet Russia, or the émigré diaspora. Decades of stringent censorship have necessitated such straightforward correctives. The market now favors sensational "inside" accounts and readers always readily empathize with and patronize individuals "simply" telling their life stories. But the extreme politicization of the Soviet era in Russian history has effected, in the cases of Kataev and other daring artists, what Russian readers *and* writers have never before permitted—a memoir that would eclipse or simply *disregard* reality. For Russian émigrés, who had in fact lost Russia, this was an inevitable development, and it was perhaps most brilliantly directed and verbalized in Vladimir Nabokov's *Speak, Memory* (1966), a luxuriously detailed memoir that admits some historical events and sketches a few famed contemporaries, yet primarily presumes to discern "the unseen design behind the apparent chaos of life," privileging the art of the memoirist's "radiant" recollection over the Russian memoir's dutiful functions as testimony and sociopolitical guide (Boyd 1991, 5; Diment 1999). This memoir's English-language articulation bolsters its self-sufficiency, for as Galya Diment perceptively argues in her essay, both Nabokov and another famous émigré, Joseph Brodsky, composed memoirs in English to exploit that medium's capacities for "authorial detachment" and creative freedom.

No memoirist remaining in Russia has matched the image-rich lyricism of Nabokov's autobiographical prose, but a similarly disdainful resistance to conventional memoir writing (what one author calls "the diary-memoir-autobiographical canvas") has crescendoed from politically muffled voices in the Thaw era into today's loud chorus of self-avowed "nonmemoirists" (Bitov 1999, 9). Andrei Sinyavsky (1926–97) boldly initiated this trend in *tamizdat*, insisting at once on his cohabitation with and authorial segregation from a pseudonymous alter ego named Abram Tertz. Tertz's authorship of Sinyavsky's most openly autobiographical texts—*Thoughts Unaware* (1966), *A Voice from the Chorus* (1976), and *Goodnight!* (1989)—not only proffered (at least initially) political camouflage, but also transgressed what Tertz deemed pedestrian boundaries between truth and art, between a scholarly, politically circumspect self and an extraordinarily imagined outlaw voice. Tertz's "novel" *Goodnight!* conjures up a fantastic memoir of Sinyavsky's experience to date—his family circle, school days, professional beginnings, labor camp sentence, and life in emigration.

The aesthetic audacity that once cost Sinyavsky his freedom and his country (he was sentenced to six years in a labor camp and forcibly exiled in 1973) now regularly informs Russian authors' published statements about their intents. In a 1999 roundtable on the memoir conducted by *Literary Issues* (*Voprosy literatury*), such writers as Andrei Bitov and Pavel Basinskii protested, with all due respect, any conventional classification of their works as memoir. Bitov ingenuously claims his inability to write autobiographically, asserting instead that style truly renders the self (Bitov 1999, 6–10). Basinskii, in a somewhat uncanny variation on the Sinyavsky-Tertz duality, disavows identification with the hero bearing his name and "almost" sharing his biography in *Prisoner of Moscow* (Basinskii 1999, 5–6). In her essay on late Soviet and post-Soviet memoirs, Marina Balina perceives this resistance as revulsion for a mandated political art (specifically, the straitjacketing socialist realist memoir) and smartly surveys creative responses ranging from Basinskii's and Anatolii Rybakov's knowing manipulations of the political memoir's plot and message to diverse accentuations of subjective experience in the works of Lev Ginzburg, Iurii Trifonov, Nina Gorlanova, and Sergei Gandlevskii.

Thus, in post-Soviet Russian culture, the memoir has positively blossomed as accessible formula and provocative form—variously manifest as a wildly popular commercial product, a corrective or confessional (and sometimes self-camouflaging) historical document, or an aesthetic point of departure for new experiments in prose. If we believe Gandlevskii, one such experimenter, Russian literature today has entered the era "of simple, direct narrative—memoirs, essays, and notes," when "the prose of life, once forbidden fruit, has become more desirable and poetic than poetry and invention" (Gandlevskii 1999, 15). Yet Gandlevskii himself, with a revealing post-Soviet sidestep, pointedly eschews the memoir's ethical obligation (and perhaps political residue) for aesthetic freedom and personal investment; his "novel," which he "does not consider a memoir in the exact sense of the word," consistently prefers legendary to documentary versions of real events. What the memoir affords Gandlevskii, and perhaps will still convey to other Russian writers in the twenty-first century, is an intensely affective mode of exchange, a familiar dutiful contract between writer and reader that now invites play with its assurances of reality, authority, responsibility, and intensity. The current kaleidoscope of memoir types, ascending from "authorized" gossip to sophisticated "nonmemoirs," promises to leaven a still tradition-bound Russian culture, subverting the longstanding Russian verities of the serving self and eyewitness truth and reveling in narratives that no longer serve, but exploit, Russian and Soviet history in pursuit of art, entertainment, and self-knowledge.

Notes

My profound thanks to these expert, generous readers: Marina Balina, Galya Diment, Helena Goscilo, Natasha Kolchevska, and the anonymous reviewers for Northwestern University Press. The mistakes are all mine.

1. D. S. Mirsky (1958), for example, lauds Apollon Grigor'ev's *My Literary and Moral Wanderings* as his "most significant prose work," arguing that "no one was more capable than [Grigor'ev] of reviving the smell and taste of a particular phase of time" (217). Victor Terras (1991) characterizes Aleksandr Herzen's *My Past and Thoughts* as a "masterpiece" that "combines the intimacy of an autobiography with the broad sweep of *Zeitgeschichte*" (323–24). Edward J. Brown (1982) observes that Nadezhda Mandelstam's *Memoirs* "are not only a literary and historical source of surpassing value, they are also a work of art" (47).

2. Excellent recent examples of this scholarship on constructions of the Russian self include the essays in *Self and Story in Russian History*, ed. Laura Engelstein and Stephanie Sandler (Ithaca and London: Cornell University Press, 2000), and in *Models of the Self: Russian Women's Autobiographical Texts*, ed. Marianne Liljestrom, Arja Rosenholm, and Irina Savkina (Helsinki: Kikimora Publications, 2000).

3. See Barbara Heldt's monograph, *Terrible Perfection: Women and Russian Literature*. Bloomington: Indiana University Press, 1987, 6–7, 9. For a sample of other pioneering examinations of Russian women's autobiography and memoir, see Jehanne Gheith's introduction to *The Memoirs of Princess Dashkova* (Durham and London: Duke University Press, 1995), 1–26. Beth Holmgren's *Women's Works in Stalin's Time: On Lidiia Chukovskaia and Nadezhda Mandelstam* (Bloomington: Indiana University Press, 1993); *Russia Through Women's Eyes: Autobiographies from Tsarist Russia*, ed. Toby W. Clyman and Judith Vowles (New Haven and London: Yale University Press, 1996); and *Models of the Self.*

4. Cf. the 1896 Brockhauz and Efron definition, quoted by M. Korallov in "Opyt nazhityi, opyt osoznannyi," *Voprosy literatury* 4 (1974): 61; and L. A. Levitskii 1967.

5. Ginzburg's cluster definition of memoirs, autobiographies, and confessions interestingly intersects with Gary Saul Morson's more foolproof definition of "literature" as texts wholly shaped by a "constructive principle" and "designed to be capable of meaning in manifold contexts" (Morson 1981, 41).

6. Ginzburg has offered her own sensible criticism of the quest for genre definition: "Generic nomenclature is not important in itself, after all, but only to the extent that it assists in clarifying, in making more precise for us the underlying principles of a particular creative apprehension of reality" (199).

7. According to Caryl Emerson's analyses of "types of selves" implied or delineated in the works of four major Russian cultural critics, Ginzburg's and Bakhtin's varying approaches to and evaluations of the memoir were predictable, given their "orientation toward the uttered or recorded word *as toward a primary reality*" (Emerson 2000, 23).

8. Of this host, see, in particular, William Spengemann, *The Forms of Autobiography: Episodes in the History of a Literary Genre* (1980), which claims that a confusingly wide array of texts qualify; and the smart, efficient critique of Elizabeth W. Bruss in *Autobiographical Acts: The Changing Situation of a Literary Genre* (1976).

9. Hayden White, *Metahistory: The Historical Imagination in Nineteenth-Century Europe*. See, among numerous examples, Simon Schama's *Citizens: A Chronicle of the French Revolution* (1990), and *Dead Certainties (Unwarranted Speculations)* (1992).

10. Although this handbook advises future historians against an uncritical reading of memoir sources and alerts them to the wide spectrum of memoir variations (from artistically refined reminiscences to memoirs evoked by questionnaire), it defines the genre as fundamentally documentary and an ever important source. I thank Marina Balina for bringing this interesting reference to my attention.

11. Brintlinger summarizes a "facts-to-fiction" spectrum of biographical forms delineated by other scholars, proceeding from "chronological outline" to "scholarly-historical" biography to literary biography to "narrative" biography to fictional biography (Brintlinger 2000, 12–13).

12. See also Ginzburg (1991, 7): "Events are given to [the memoirist], and he must reveal in them the latent energy of historical, philosophical, and psychological generalizations, thereby transforming them into the signs of those generalizations."

13. Iurii Lotman (1985) notes biography's durability even as he laments its frequent superficiality. In his January 23, 2000 review of the new edition of *American National Biography*, Richard Brookhiser remarks:

"The schools and universities may go astray, but people still know what they want, and book publishers, the Biography Channel and People magazine fill the gap. One thing—maybe the main thing—readers want from history, and what the A. N. B. commendably gives, is stories of lives: lives that both resemble our own (and that we can therefore understand), and that are more interesting than our own, whether the people who lived them were better, more talented or more dangerous."

14. The *Lives of Remarkable People* series was edited by the radical activist, F. F. Pavlenkov. See *American National Biography*, ed. John A. Garrarty and Mark C. Carnes (New York and London: Oxford University Press, 1999).

15. This is the central thesis of Tartakovskii's 1991 book. See Hammarberg's essay in this volume for somewhat surprising contemporary records of Russian *female* greats.

16. Nor did *The Muscovite* stand alone. Tartakovskii remarks that forty journals published more than fifteen hundred historical documents in the first third of the nineteenth century, an incredible number suggesting general reader interest (Tartakovskii 1997, 26).

17. A similar explosion in memoir writing accompanied the revolutions of 1848 to 1849 as individual observers felt compelled "to summarize what had taken place, to analyze the lessons of the revolution on the basis of prevolutionary and revolutionary experience" (Ginzburg 1991, 197).

18. For an excellent introduction to and translation of Durova's memoir, see *The Cavalry Maiden: Journals of a Female Russian Officer in the Napoleonic Wars*, trans. Mary Fleming Zirin (Bloomington: Indiana University Press, 1988).

19. See Durkin's 1983 monograph on Aksakov for details on these texts' publication after Nicholas I's death.

20. See also Margaret Morley Bullitt's dissertation, "The Voice of a Generation, the Generation of a Voice: Childhood in Herzen's *Byloe i dumy*" (Harvard, 1984).

21. The 1975 anthology, *Five Sisters Against the Tsar*, contains translated excerpts of five fascinating memoirs by female Russian revolutionaries.

22. See the translated excerpts from the memoirs of the women physicians Varvara Kashevarova-Rudneva and Ekaterina Slanskaia included in *Russia Through Women's Eyes: Autobiographies from Tsarist Russia*, pp. 158–216. See also the bibliography of Jeanette E. Tuve's *First Russian Women Physicians* (1984) for citations of the memoirs of Drs. Adelaide Lukanina, Nadezhda Suslova, and Anna Veretennikova.

23. Brooks notes that a third of F. F. Pavlenkov's subjects for *Lives of Remarkable People* were writers (1985, 344).

24. In his study of Alexander Afinogenov's intriguing "diary of 1937," Jochen Hellbeck argues that the Soviet playwright inscribed "a visible record of self-development" in accord with the Stalinist "revolutionary agenda of purification." It is important to note, however, that this text was neither designed for publication nor undertook the memoir's implicit task of reporting and interpreting the narrator's world.

25. See, for example, Lev Kopelev's *To Be Preserved Forever* and *Ease My Sorrows*, as well as the memoirs of his wife, Raisa Orlova.

26. Grech listed memoirs under the rubrics of "Russkaia slovesnost' i proza" in his *Rukovodstvo po russkoi slovesnosti* (Tartakovskii 1991, 50).

27. Quoted in Ginzburg 1991, 5.

28. Quoted in Tartakovskii 1991, 184.

29. Zhikharev's notes appeared as "Dnevnik studenta" ("Diary of a Student") in M. P. Pogodin's journal, *The Muscovite* (Tartakovskii 1991, 149, 154).

30. In *Chernyshevsky and the Age of Realism: A Study in the Semiotics of Behavior,* Irina Paperno remarks on realist fiction's deliberate non-literary quality ("a model that essentially involves the imitation of a lack of modeling, conventionality, or literariness"), as well as its profound extra-literary impact (1988, 9, 11).

31. For various analyses of the practice of *zhiznetvorchestvo* or "life creation," see the essays in *Creating Life: The Aesthetic Utopia of Russian Modernism* (1994).

32. In a 1913 essay, Eikhenbaum (1987) remarks on a parallel phenomenon, what he characterizes as the novel's shift to biography and *byli.*

33. Quoted in Brintlinger 2000, 10.

34. See also Marina Balina's essay in this volume, in which she argues the formation of a socialist realist memoir modeled on the Bolsheviks' propagandistic obituaries.

35. Sinyavsky 1990 identifies the anecdote as "the leading folklore genre" of Soviet culture (223–25).

Works Cited

Alexeyeva, Ludmila. *The Thaw Generation: Coming of Age in the Post-Stalin Era.* Boston: Little, Brown, 1990.

Autobiographical Statements in Russian Literature. Edited by Jane Gary Harris. Princeton: Princeton University Press, 1990.

Bakhtin, Mikhail. "Forms of Time and Chronotope in the Novel." In *The Dialogic Imagination: Four Essays by Mikhail Bakhtin.* Edited by Michael

Holquist, translated by Caryl Emerson and Michael Holquist. Austin: University of Texas Press, 1981, 84–258.

Balina, Marina. "Introduction: Russian Autobiographies of the Twentieth Century: Fictions of the Self." *A/b Autobiography* 2, no. 2 (fall 1996): 3–7.

Basinskii, Pavel. "Memuary—zhanr slozhnyi i blagorodnyi." *Voprosy literatury,* January–February 1999, 5–6.

Bitov, Andrei. "V poiskakh utrachennogo 'ia.'" *Voprosy literatury,* January–February 1999, 6–10.

Bonner, Elena. *Mothers and Daughters.* Translated by Antonina W. Bouis. New York: Alfred A. Knopf, 1992.

Borden, Richard C. *The Art of Writing Badly: Valentin Kataev's Mauvism and the Rebirth of Russian Modernism.* Evanston, Ill.: Northwestern University Press, 1999.

Boyd, Brian. *Vladimir Nabokov: The American Years.* Princeton: Princeton University Press, 1991.

Brintlinger, Angela. *Writing a Useable Past: Russian Literary Culture, 1917–1937.* Evanston, Ill.: Northwestern University Press, 2000.

Brookhiser, Richard. Review of *American National Biography. New York Times Book Review,* January 23, 2000, 14.

Brooks, Jeffrey. *When Russia Learned to Read: Literacy and Popular Literature, 1861–1917.* Princeton: Princeton University Press, 1985.

Brown, Edward J. *Russian Literature Since the Revolution.* Cambridge and London: Harvard University Press, 1982.

Bruss, Elizabeth W. *Autobiographical Acts: The Changing Situation of a Literary Genre.* Baltimore and London: Johns Hopkins University Press, 1976.

Bullitt, Margaret Morley. "The Voice of a Generation, the Generation of a Voice: Childhood in Herzen's *Byloe i dumy.*" Dissertation. Harvard University, 1984.

Couser, G. Thomas. "Authority." *A/b Autobiography* 10, no. 1 (spring 1995): 34–49.

Creating Life: The Aesthetic Utopia of Russian Modernism. Edited by Irina Paperno and Joan Delaney Grossman. Stanford: Stanford University Press, 1994.

Diment, Galya. "Vladimir Nabokov and the Art of Autobiography." In *Nabokov and His Fiction: New Perspectives,* edited by Julian Connolly. Cambridge: Cambridge University Press, 1999, 36–53.

Durkin, Andrew R. *Sergei Aksakov and the Russian Pastoral.* New Brunswick, N.J.: Rutgers University Press, 1983.

Durova, Nadezhda. *The Cavalry Maiden: Journals of a Female Russian Officer in the Napoleonic Wars.* Translated by Mary Fleming Zirin. Bloomington: Indiana University Press, 1988.

Eikhenbaum, Boris. "Roman i biografiia." In *O literature*. Moscow: Sovetskii pisatel', 1987, 288–89.

Emerson, Caryl. "Bakhtin, Lotman, Vygotsky, and Lidia Ginzburg on Types of Selves: A Tribute." In *Self and Story in Russian History*, edited by Laura Engelstein and Stephanie Sandler. Ithaca and London: Cornell University Press, 2000, 20–45.

Engel, Barbara Alpern and Clifford N. Rosenthal. Introduction to *Five Sisters: Women Against the Tsar*. New York: Alfred A. Knopf, 1975.

Frieden, Nancy Mandelker. *Russian Physicians in an Era of Reform and Revolution*. Princeton: Princeton University Press, 1981.

Gandlevskii, Sergei. "Vernut' iavi ubeditel'nost'." *Voprosy literatury*, January–February 1999, 13–15.

Gheith, Jehanne M. Introduction to *The Memoirs of Princess Dashkova*. Translated and edited by Kyril Fitzlyon, with an afterword by A. Woronzoff-Dashkoff. Durham and London: Duke University Press, 1995, 1–26.

Ginzburg, Lydia. *On Psychological Prose*. Translated and edited by Judson Rosengrant, with a foreword by Edward J. Brown. Princeton, N.J.: Princeton University Press, 1991.

Heldt, Barbara. *Terrible Perfection: Women and Russian Literature*. Bloomington: Indiana University Press, 1987.

Holmgren, Beth. *Women's Works in Stalin's Time: On Lidiia Chukovskaia and Nadezhda Mandelstam*. Bloomington: Indiana University Press, 1993.

———. "For the Good of the Cause: Russian Women's Autobiography in the Twentieth Century." In *Women in Russian Literature*, edited by Diana Greene and Toby Clyman. Greenwood Press, 1994, 127–48.

Istochnikovedenie. Teoriia. Istoriia. Metod. Istochniki rossiiskoi istorii. Edited by I. N. Danilevskii, V. V. Kabanov, O. M. Medushevskaia, M. F. Rumiantseva. Moscow: Rossiiskii Gosudarstvennyi Gumanitarnyi Universitet, 1998.

Kollontai, Aleksandra. *The Autobiography of a Sexually Emancipated Communist Woman*. Edited and with an afterword by Iring Fetscher, translated by Salvator Attanasio. New York: Herder and Herder, 1971.

Kopelev, Lev. *To Be Preserved Forever*. Edited and translated by Anthony Austin. Philadelphia: Lippincott, 1977.

———. *Ease My Sorrows*. Translated by Antonina W. Bouis. New York: Random House, 1983.

Korallov, M. "Opyt nazhityi, opyt osoznannyi." *Voprosy literatury* 4 (1974): 46–62.

Levitskii, L. A. "Memuary." *Kratkaia literaturnaia entsiklopediia*. Vol. 4. Moscow: Sovetskaia entsiklopediia, 1967, 759–62.

Lotman, Iurii. "Biografiia i zhivoe litso." *Novyi mir*, no. 2 (1985): 228–36.

Mirsky, D. S. *A History of Russian Literature From Its Beginnings to 1900*. Edited by Francis J. Whitfield. New York: Vintage Books, 1958.

Models of the Self: Russian Women's Autobiographical Texts. Edited by Marianne Liljestrom, Arja Rosenholm, and Irina Savkina. Helsinki: Kikimora Publications, 2000.

Morson, Gary Saul. *The Boundaries of Genre: Dostoevsky's Diary of a Writer and the Tradition of Literary Utopia.* Austin: University of Texas Press, 1981.

Nadel, Ira Bruce. *Biography: Fiction, Fact and Form.* New York: St. Martin's Press, 1984.

Offord, Derek. "Lichnost': Notions of Individual Identity." In *Constructing Russian Culture in the Age of Revolution: 1881–1940.* Edited by Catriona Kelly and David Shepherd. Oxford and New York: Oxford University Press, 1998, 13–25.

Orlova, Raisa. *Memoirs.* Translated by Samuel Cioran. New York: Random House, 1983.

Paperno, Irina. *Chernyshevsky and the Age of Realism: A Study in the Semiotics of Behavior.* Stanford: Stanford University Press, 1988.

Russia Through Women's Eyes: Autobiographies from Tsarist Russia. Edited by Toby W. Clyman and Judith Vowles. New Haven and London: Yale University Press, 1996.

Schama, Simon. *Citizens: A Chronicle of the French Revolution.* New York: Random House, 1990.

———. *Dead Certainties (Unwarranted Speculations).* New York: Vintage Books, 1992.

Self and Story in Russian History. Edited by Laura Engelstein and Stephanie Sandler. Ithaca and London: Cornell University Press, 2000.

Sinyavsky, Andrei. *Soviet Civilization: A Cultural History.* Translated by Joanne Turnbull with the assistance of Nikolai Formozov. New York: Little, Brown and Co., 1990.

Spengemann, William. *The Forms of Autobiography: Episodes in the History of a Literary Genre.* New Haven: Yale University Press, 1980.

Stites, Richard. "Introduction: A Study in Rebellion." In Vera Figner's *Memoir of a Russian Revolutionist.* Dekalb, Illinois: Northern Illinois University Press, 1991.

Tartakovskii, A. G. *Russkaia memuaristika XVIII–pervoi poloviny XIX veka.* Moscow: Nauka, 1991.

———. *Russkaia memuaristika i istoricheskoe soznanie XIX veka.* Moscow: Arkheograficheskii Tsentr, 1997.

Terras, Victor. *A History of Russian Literature.* New Haven and London: Yale University Press, 1991.

Tuve, Jeanette E. *The First Russian Women Physicians.* Newtonville, Mass.: Oriental Research Partners, 1984.

Vinokur, G. *Biografiia i kul'tura.* Moscow: Russkie slovari, 1997.

Wachtel, Andrew. *The Battle for Childhood: Creation of a Russian Myth.* Stanford: Stanford University Press, 1990.

———. *An Obsession with History: Russian Writers Confront the Past.* Stanford: Stanford University Press, 1994.

Wallen, Jeffrey. "Between Text and Image: The Literary Portrait." *A/b. Autobiography* 10, no. 1 (spring 1995): 50–65.

White, Hayden. *Metahistory: The Historical Imagination in Nineteenth-Century Europe.* 3rd ed. Baltimore: Johns Hopkins University Press, 1980.

The Russian Memoir

PART I

The Memoir and the World

Jane Gary Harris

Lidiia Ginzburg: Images of the Intelligentsia

LIDIIA IAKOVLEVNA GINZBURG, recognized to-
day as one of the most prominent scholars, distinguished writers, and reliable witnesses of the Leningrad intelligentsia, is best known outside Russia
for her theoretical writings and scholarly studies of nineteenth- and twentieth-
century narrative prose and lyric poetry.[1] From the very beginning of her
career, however, Ginzburg chose to identify herself broadly as a "litterateur" or "literary professional": "Literary science cannot develop out of itself alone, external stimuli and association with other realms of thought are
required . . . For those of us who do not view ourselves primarily as literary
historians or literary theorists, but as having broader interests—who see
ourselves rather as *littérateurs,* as literary professionals—that lack of nour-
ishment is fatal."[2] Public recognition of this remarkable personality and her
literary accomplishments came only in the last decade of her life, in the
1980s, when she herself was in her eighties. Only then was Ginzburg able
to reveal herself as a creative writer, a master practitioner of the genres of
"life writing," for which she established new principles of analysis and
which she practiced as new forms of contemporary prose. In a 1988 interview, she explained her interest in life writing as part of the "evolving literary process": "In contemporary prose the sense of the author's presence is
developing space. . . . You take up a pen *for a conversation about life*—not
to write an autobiography, *but to express directly your own life experience,
your views on reality.* . . . This is one of the paths of future literary development . . . the path I prefer" (emphasis added).[3]

Indeed, Ginzburg's lifelong contemplation of the correlations between
reality or "lived experience" and literary creation provides the key to all her
writing, above all, to her own wide-ranging art of the *zapis'* (journal entry),
which included the vast range of genres of self-expression, from poignant
self-analyses, simple anecdotes, recorded conversations, to lengthy philosophical and memoiristic essays, among other things. Major literary influences
on her writing include Michel Montaigne, Jean-Jacques Rousseau, Lev Tolstoy, Petr Viazemskii, Osip Mandelstam, and Marcel Proust, uniquely complex practitioners of self-reflexive and self-critical analytical prose.

Lidiia Ginzburg was born into a middle-class assimilated Jewish family of the Odessa intelligentsia on March 5 (18), 1902, and died in her beloved adopted city of Leningrad on July 15, 1990. She summarizes her own biography against the background of Soviet intellectual and cultural life in a decade-by-decade assessment of the Russian intelligentsia in its twentieth-century incarnation in two linked cultural memoirs or memoiristic essays dating from 1979 to 1980: "Pokolenie na povorote" ("The Turning Point of a Generation," 1979) and "'I zaodno s pravo-poriadkom'" ("'At One with the Prevailing Order,'" 1980). These cultural memoirs of 1979 to 1980 are the subject of this chapter. Here Ginzburg fills out her skeletal biography by interrogating it in the context of the behavior of the postrevolutionary intelligentsia. She bases her analyses both on the experience of her own thinking as typical of her generation and on the social, historical, psychological, and aesthetic conditions that she perceived as exerting pressure on that thinking, among which are the literary and cultural formations inherited from the nineteenth-century Russian intelligentsia. Thus, this reading theorizes the memoirs of 1979 to 1980 as a unique effort to examine a life, not as conventional autobiography or memoir, but as a semiotic model of the social and psychological behavior of the intelligentsia during the various phases of Soviet Russian intellectual and cultural history from the 1920s to the Thaw. In the process Ginzburg provides a cultural and philosophical assessment of the behavior of the Soviet intelligentsia, her own life serving as a "variant" on that model. The writing of these memoirs is highly significant for Ginzburg's own self-cognition and self-representation, standing as a major effort on her part to connect with the younger, post-Stalinist generation, her addressee. Indeed, at the conclusion of the second memoir, she problematizes biography with reference to her own experience, questioning how much of life is consciously self-willed, and how much is conditioned by forces beyond one's control.

The memoirs of 1979 to 1980 were selected for analysis for several reasons. In addition to summing up Ginzburg's biography in her own words, they culminate earlier efforts at cultural memoirs of friends and colleagues begun in the 1960s as a means to repudiate the official version of reality condemning them to pariah status. Moreover, the form, content, and genre of these memoirs are unique in that they seek to combine and integrate Ginzburg's two favorite modes of expression—literary theory and the journal entry. Hence, they reflect her psychological, philosophical, and literary search for genres adequate to meet her ever broadening need for self-expression. To create these memoirs Ginzburg invokes experience grounded in her own documented history of her self—her lifelong journal. Theoretically, this textual performance echoes and develops Ginzburg's critiques of eighteenth- and nineteenth-century examples of life writing examined in her seminal theoretical works, *On Psychological Prose* and *The Literary*

Hero. Thus, the memoirs of 1979 to 1980, although not designated as such, appear to be among the first in a long line of memoirs which, according to Marina Balina (see her chapter in this volume), seek to promote "life writing" as a new genre. They serve as a practicum in Ginzburg's ongoing experiments in life writing, and are pivotal for her creative writing, in that they were preceded by preliminary "memoirs of contemporaries" and succeeded by her better known and lengthier quasi memoir and prose masterpiece, "Zapiski blokadnogo cheloveka" ("Notes from the Leningrad Blockade," published in two parts in 1984 and 1991, respectively). Instead of narrating the story of her life as an example of individual or personal behavior, Ginzburg inscribes herself into Soviet history. She does this by interrogating her "self," her own recorded microhistory, contextualized in the macrohistory of the behavior of her generation's intelligentsia. Hence, these memoirs represent the creative endeavor of a member of the older generation—an experienced literary theorist and critic as well as a practitioner of life writing—to connect with the younger, post-Stalinist generation by reframing her individual life experience, her identity, as a semiotic representation of the thinking of her generation of the Russian-Soviet intelligentsia.

This chapter will first summarize Lidiia Ginzburg's biography with special reference to the decade-by-decade semiotic schema of Soviet cultural history she devises in the memoirs of 1979 to 1980. Then, before examining the memoirs in some detail, I will consider how Ginzburg came to construct the memoirs by discussing their sources and the impetus behind their style and structure, including the pivotal role of these memoirs in the context of Ginzburg's later journal entries that explore and promote life writing as the "contemporary literary genre."

Ginzburg's semiotic biography begins in 1917 at age fifteen, when, according to the memoirs of 1979 to 1980, Ginzburg points out how she and her schoolmates were caught up in the revolution's intellectual and emotional fervor. She captures the power of those feelings: "there was acceptance, no looking back, no questions asked. That may be cause for surprise, but I am not surprised. We were all like that—at age 15. And something remains with us from our youth." Equally significant, she observes how her generation's welcoming of the revolution reflected contemporary intellectual currents: "Revolution attracted the entire Russian avant-garde. The Symbolists as early as 1905 . . . [As for the] post-Symbolists . . . Osip Mandelstam's essays of the 1920s are incomprehensible without noting what he said in *Noise of Time* about reading the Erfurt Program at school, or the influence of the Narodnik movement on his best friend's family . . . And Boris Pasternak in 'The Year 1905' . . . and even Anna Akhmatova . . ." ("Turning Point of a Generation").[4]

Two years after her gymnasium graduation in 1920, Ginzburg set off for Leningrad (then Petrograd), where she enrolled in the State Institute of

History of the Arts (Gosudarstvennyi Institut Istorii Iskusstv, better known as GIII). Her teachers included the most formidable minds of the literary intelligentsia—Eikhenbaum, Tynianov, Tomashevskii, Zhirmunskii, and Vinogradov, among others. The result, Ginzburg claims, was that the 1920s taught her circle, the "young formalists," that they were "part of history in the making." Indeed, here she defines her generation in terms of the epoch's literary and cultural alignments as part of the "innocent opposition" of the independent-minded formalists. "It seemed to us—and so it was for a short time—that we were the principal actors in a segment of culture which had just begun. On the other hand, in the 1930s and 1940s, we became the passive property of the Stalinist epoch and the war years, with all that followed." ("'At One with the Prevailing Order,'" 1980). After graduating in 1926, Ginzburg worked at GIII as a research fellow (*nauchnyi sotrudnik*) and taught seminars in nineteenth-century Russian poetry. It was during this time that she broadly defined herself as a "litterateur," and initiated her private journal modeled at first on that of the nineteenth-century poet and litterateur, Petr Viazemskii, the subject of her first scholarly publication, "Viazemskii-literator" ("Viazemskii—Man of Letters"). This was how her double life, as published literary scholar and unpublished writer and witness, began.

With the closing of GIII by the hostile authorities in 1930, Ginzburg found herself leading a truly marginalized existence, effectively banned from teaching in institutions of higher education. Forced to find new employment, she worked for a time at the Childrens' Publishing House [Detgiz], along with the Oberiu poets Nikolai Oleinikov and Nikolai Zabolotsky, producing a detective novel for adolescents, *The Pinkerton Agency*.[5] She dedicated that work to her then lover, Rina Zelenaia, but as she stated in her journal, "it was not the novel" she would have chosen to write.[6] Lesbianism, another source of her marginality, was the subject of a few journal essays; none, however, were published during her lifetime.[7] Ginzburg also found temporary positions teaching adult education classes in language and literature at workers' schools (*rabfak*). In contrast to journal entries from the 1920s recording intense intellectual involvement and the taking of principled stands on a broad range of issues, entries from the 1930s express a complex, often ambivalent vision of that period, including personal bouts of severe depression, confusion, and moral anxiety, contemplation of class "privilege," of remorse and "penance," and recognition of the impossibility of publishing her major article on Proust. For example, a journal entry dated 1930 expresses ambivalence toward her students, emphasizing feelings of class consciousness and her sense of moral duty toward righting the wrongs of the masses:

> Right now my students at rabfak and I somehow balance each other out. That they are studying and generally feel fulfilled as people correlates with some part of my life being empty; that they are reading Oblomov (why precisely Oblomov?) correlates with my not being able to publish my article on Proust.

I harbor no hard feelings; I feel only kindness and sympathy . . .
From a critical perspective, I sense in myself certain pure vestiges of the intelligentsia's self-abasement. Social self-abnegation is our penance for privilege. The penitent gentry expiated the sin of power; now the penitent intelligentsia is expiating the sin of education. No poverty, no experience, no mental freeze can ever eradicate such vestiges of class privilege.[8]

Paradoxically, according to the memoirs of 1979 to 1980, the 1940s appeared "simpler" and more comprehensible, and offered psychological relief because of "the wartime convergence of private values with those of the state." Nevertheless, Ginzburg's powers of endurance were severely tested as she remained in Leningrad throughout World War II, caring for her sick mother who died during the first winter of the blockade, and working as an editor at the state radio, "quietly correcting the broadcasts of other writers' war literature" (Journal, 1987). The winter of 1942 she took up residence at the radio station to which she attributes her survival. "Zapiski blokadnogo cheloveka" ("Notes from the Leningrad Blockade"), Ginzburg's highly acclaimed existential narrative concerning the experience and behavior of a human being living under conditions of war, derived in part from her journal recording of conversations overheard in bomb shelters, on bread lines, and at work.[9] "Notes from the Leningrad Blockade" could not be published until decades later: part 1, predominantly narrative, appeared in the Leningrad magazine, *Neva* (1984);[10] part 2, comprised mainly of "Conversations from the Leningrad Blockade," appeared only posthumously in *Pretvorenie opyta* (*Transformation of Experience*, 1991).[11]

The immediate postwar years (1946–53), Ginzburg wrote in her memoirs of 1979 to 1980, were the most traumatic for her personally because the moral and psychological "variant" invoked by the "creative intelligentsia" in the 1930s "no longer worked." During that era of vicious anti-intellectual and anti-Semitic attacks Ginzburg taught at Petrozavodsk University (1947–50); it was considered safer for Jewish intellectuals to be employed outside the major cities. Subsequently, she described in her journal the intelligentsia's incredulous naïveté before the horror of what had been taking place around them ("The Kochetov Complex," 1962)[12] and repudiated as repulsive her work of those years, including her doctoral dissertation on Alexander Herzen defended only in 1958. She had defended her candidate's dissertation on Mikhail Lermontov twenty years earlier.

Ginzburg's second encounter with state security also occurred at the close of 1952. Unsuccessfully recruited in a frightening endeavor to develop a case against her teacher and mentor, Boris Eikhenbaum, she was saved by Stalin's death. Her first encounter with state security had been in 1933 in a botched effort to develop a case against Viktor Zhirmunskii ("Two Encounters").[13]

During the Thaw years, as she described them in her journal, her first feelings of renewal and hope paradoxically combined with a new sensation of being part of the "older generation" ("O starosti i infantilizme" ["Old Age and Infantilism," 1954]).[14] In fact, the Thaw years not only permitted Ginzburg to flourish, no longer marginalized by the system, but the 1960s initiated her most fruitful years. Sporadic publication was superseded by a new book or revised edition every two or three years. The popularity of *O lirike* (*On the Lyric*, 1964) demanded a revised and enlarged format ten years later. *On Psychological Prose* (1971) was revised and reissued in 1977. *The Literary Hero* appeared in 1979. The memoirs of 1979 to 1980 (though unpublished at the time) initiated a series of publications in the 1980s and 1990s that provide a kind of summing up of Ginzburg's life experience and intellectual activity. In the 1980s several volumes of collected writings appeared, and for the first time they included prose narratives; literary, philosophical, and memoiristic essays; and other excerpts from her journals: *O starom i novom* (*On the Old and the New*, 1982), *Literatura v poiskakh real'nosti* (*Literature in Search of Reality*, 1987), and *Chelovek za pis'mennym stolom* (*At the Writing Desk*, 1989).[15] The latter included slightly revised versions of the memoirs of 1979 to 1980. The early 1990s witnessed the posthumous publication of more journal excerpts in *Novyi mir* and *Literaturnaia gazeta*;[16] and Ginzburg's last authorized volume, *Transformation of Experience* (1991), containing not only the remarkable second part of "Notes from the Leningrad Blockade," but two essays on Osip Mandelstam, whom she regarded as the seminal poet of the twentieth century. Finally, in the mid-1980s Ginzburg gained the public recognition she deserved. Official celebrations of her eightieth and eighty-fifth birthdays were succeeded in 1988 by the prestigious State Prize for Literature. Thus, at the very end of her life, as one of the few representatives of her generation to have lived long enough to voice her opinion freely, Ginzburg surprised herself, becoming a publicly powerful spokesperson in the press and on television, expressing moral satisfaction in the principle of "openness" (glasnost): "The principle itself—that I can say whatever I think—is an event of enormous moral consequence."[17]

Ginzburg's fascination with life writing can be traced back to her first publication, "Viazemskii—Man of Letters" (1926), a piece which emerged from the famous Eikhenbaum-Tynianov seminar for a select group of students at GIII in 1925.[18] Almost simultaneously, Ginzburg initiated what would become her lifetime focus, the private journal she would maintain from 1925 until a year before her death in 1990. While mastering the art of the journal, Ginzburg reevaluated the nature of materials not previously considered "aesthetic," and reassessed the aesthetic nature of materials not previously considered "literature." Appreciation of both the processes by which life is transformed into art and by which literary and cultural models affect codes of social behavior and society's self-consciousness influences all Ginzburg's writing, her theory being an outgrowth of her writing practice (her journal) as well as her research.

Historians have traditionally argued over the definition of the Russian intelligentsia, although two alternative cultural models seem to predominate. On the one hand, Isaiah Berlin emphasizes elitism, stating, "The concept of the intelligentsia must not be confused with the notion of intellectuals. Its members thought of themselves as united by something more than mere interest in ideas; they conceived themselves as being a dedicated order, almost a secular priesthood, devoted to the spreading of a specific attitude to life, something like a gospel."[19] Sheila Fitzpatrick counters that the intelligentsia "did not see itself as an elite, but rather as a classless group united by moral concern for the betterment of society, the capacity for 'critical thought' and, in particular, a critical, semi-oppositionist attitude toward the regime."[20]

Ginzburg, in her cultural memoirs of 1979 to 1980, theorizes that the thinking of the postrevolutionary intelligentsia was complicated by its nineteenth-century legacy, which she describes as the convergence of the above-mentioned two alternative cultural models, two contradictory value systems. The first, with its emphasis on high culture, linked the intelligentsia to current Western European literary and cultural trends: "the complex of modernism, individualism, and elitism." The second, with its emphasis on the Narodnik tradition of social justice, came to influence the generic definitions of the Russian intelligentsia: the complex of populism, humanism, and social justice. To examine the transformation of this cultural phenomenon in twentieth-century Soviet cultural life and to endeavor to explain its impact on her own sense of identity, Ginzburg grounded her thesis in two major sources: first, in the principles and concepts developed in her theoretical and critical writings but expressed most cogently in *On Psychological Prose,* and second, in her own life experience, that of an eyewitness, a member of the intelligentsia just coming of age with the revolution, documented on the pages of her private journal.[21]

In *On Psychological Prose* Ginzburg demonstrates how the continuous interaction of art and reality resulted in a cultural fabric without clear-cut boundaries between life and art, and how particular signifying elements— specific literary and cultural models—were accepted as "real" and thereby transformed into actual behavior. On the other hand, Ginzburg examines the dominant cultural formations of the pre-Stalinist and Stalinist years by referring to the microhistory of the Soviet period found in her own contemporary journal entries and modeled on her own experiences, those of an actual personality, her self, a member of the intelligentsia. Thus, she employs her own life experience as a semiotic model of the thinking and behavior of the intelligentsia of her generation.

Before examining these cultural memoirs more closely to delineate Ginzburg's extraordinary textual performance as analyst, eyewitness, and semiotic model of her generation's intellectual and cultural history, it is necessary to situate them with respect to the circumstances of their composition, the audience for whom they were intended, and her choice of genre. With the publication of *On the Lyric* in 1964, Ginzburg began to move gradually back into the public eye. Her marginalized "outsider" status as scholar, writer, and witness during the Stalinist decades gave way to near cultlike admiration inside Leningrad's intellectual community in the post-Stalinist Thaw years; as mentor and support for the younger generation of writers and scholars unrecognized by the official Soviet hierarchy, she strongly influenced the reformulation of post-Stalinist values. Her publications of the 1980s frequently reflect their genesis in her journal or in conversations with colleagues and friends. For example, privately, she had begun to read excerpts from her journals of the 1920s to a group of younger writers and scholars whom she had been mentoring intellectually and helping financially since the Thaw years, a group who had come to regard Ginzburg not only as a scholar, but as a mentor, friend, and trusted witness. They saw her as a living conduit of ideas, values, and knowledge, especially of the cultural life and work at GIII in the 1920s. The group encouraged Ginzburg to publish her journal entries and to write memoirs based on conversations arising from these private readings.

The impetus to write and compose Ginzburg's cultural memoirs of 1979 to 1980 then grew out of two related intellectual processes—the rereading and editing of selected journal entries for publication and the conversations about them with the younger generation. In 1982 *O starom i novom (On the Old and New)* appeared in print,[22] Ginzburg's first publication to include cultural memoirs and journal entries from the 1920s to the 1930s along with her scholarly writings. That same year selected journal entries appeared in the June issue of *Novyi mir,* while that same month, Ginzburg participated in the first of a series of Tynianov Conferences (Tynianovskie chteniia), organized on the initiative of Veniamin Kaverin and Marietta Chudakova, in response to the post-Stalinist impetus to reconnect current Russian literary theory and scholarship with its sources, namely, GIII, where Kaverin and Ginzburg had been students of Tynianov and Eikhenbaum, among others. Ginzburg's first public reading of journal entries took place at the first Tynianov Conference, in Rezekne, Latvia.[23]

Although written in 1979 and 1980, Ginzburg's cultural memoirs were not to appear in print until the end of the decade in the proceedings of the Tynianov Conferences, the *Tynianov Anthologies* of 1986 and 1988, respectively. Addressing "the youth of today," a somewhat self-conscious and wistful Ginzburg states: "It is impossible to explain all this to those who did not experience it because it is generally impossible to explain emotions."

Nevertheless, she tries. Thus, emotionally, these essays represent Ginzburg's profound personal effort to overcome what she considered a severe generation gap in trying to relate to her eager and critical post-Stalinist audience the culture of another age, the "cognition of spiritual life" of the Russian intelligentsia during the Stalinist era, through the prism of her own life experience based on the eyewitness accounts found in her own contemporary journal entries.

In choosing a genre to grapple with "the cognition of spiritual life" and the semiotics of social behavior, Ginzburg sought a thoroughly "contemporary form" that she subsequently designated "a conversation about life." She defined this new genre or mode of interpretation first in an interview in *Smena* in 1988 (see above), and second, in a 1989 journal entry that begins "A conversation with Andrey Levkin on the future of prose." Here she asserts, *"The direct conversation about life . . . is today the only genre that is contemporary"* (emphasis added). In the same entry, she cites as brilliant models of the "new prose" of life writing Viktor Shklovsky's *Zoo, or Letters Not about Love* and Mandelstam's *Conversation about Dante.* In claiming that the latter is far more about Mandelstam than Dante, she suggests that her own life writing may serve a similar purpose; in referring to Shklovsky's *Zoo,* she emphasizes the complexities of the political and social significance of communication. Both subtexts highlight the personal, cultural, and political significance of life writing for Ginzburg's own creative production.[24]

Ginzburg's cultural memoirs of 1979 to 1980 may be read as her "direct conversation about life." It is here that she combines the essentials of the two genres for which she ultimately gained her claim to fame, literary theory and criticism on the one hand, and her journal on the other. These memoirs, then, are memoiristic in that they incorporate as testimony journal entries recording her own thoughts and experiences from the 1920s through the post-Stalinist Thaw years. They are theoretical in that her unique approach juxtaposes the problematics of group consciousness and group value—"shared identity"—to individual identity and individual choice by subjecting them both to historical, political, and social analyses as well as to the impulses of cultural, aesthetic, and psychological formations. Equally important is Ginzburg's emphasis on the distinction between traditional "subjective" (autobiographical) prose and life writing, and what she perceived as the new "unmediated" prose, or the "direct conversation about life." The direct and unmediated aspects of the "new prose," both as Ginzburg theorized and practiced it, rejected the canonical genres of narrative prose as inadequate to her needs in the late twentieth century. Indeed, in *At the Writing Desk* (1989), she categorizes her journal entries as "esse" (*essais* in the French tradition of Montaigne and Pascal).[25] Employing unmediated prose allowed her to produce cultural memoirs or memoiristic essays that incorporate into her text a mosaic of references, theoretical models, and testimony from her private journal. Thus, in contrast to the traditional genres she analyzed in *On Psychological Prose*, autobiography (Rousseau) and memoir (Herzen), Ginzburg's more essayistic form of life writing refocuses the eyewitness account, redirecting it back to the written testimony of her journal but also forward, passing it through the prism of contemporary life, cultural theory, and literary practice. Ginzburg essentially reaffirms her mentor Tynianov's concept of "literary evolution," namely that writers continue to adapt to changing historical needs by inventing new forms and altering the tasks of older genres. Most significant for Ginzburg is not that "the artistic expression is subjective," but that it is "unmediated." Thus, in the same journal entry for 1989 mentioned above, she defines this mode as follows: "*as if* there were no boundary between the author and the objective world, or as if the boundary was fully transparent" (emphasis added). The main principle of the "new prose," what makes it contemporary, is that it problematizes the dichotomy of unmediated/mediated rather than subjectivity/objectivity, while the aesthetic illusion of the "direct conversation about life" is stressed in the phrase "as if."

By drawing a distinction between "subjective" (autobiographical) prose and "unmediated" prose, Ginzburg confronts her "self" as object rather than subject, as a kind of semiotic model of her generation, a generalized representative who is, and is not, herself. This enables her to signify or symbolize her own experience as representative of a shared identity, the way poets employ images to signify a thematic idea. Ginzburg's generalized form of self-assessment was first defined in a 1931 journal entry, where she described herself as "an especially convenient object of observation" and as a "bit of reality."[26] Even earlier, in a journal entry of 1926, she refers to herself as "we," emphasizing her participation in the collective membership of the "young formalist" circle, her sense of belonging to a shared identity, a collective consciousness.[27] Here, in the memoirs of 1979 to 1980, when citing her own life experience, Ginzburg frequently alternates between first-person singular and first-person plural, and between first- and third-person pronouns: "What can I say about my own case? Basically, that we should have no illusions, no one escaped unscathed."

In her scholarship, Ginzburg had long been fascinated not only by the genesis and formation of literary models of personality and social relationships, but by the reverse influence of such models on codes of social behavior and contemporary life. In her introduction to *On Psychological Prose*,[28] Ginzburg defines its problematics as "the relationship between the conception of personality characteristic of a given era and social milieu and the artistic representation of that conception." She defines her method for understanding the "cognition of spiritual life" as based on "material taken from memoiristic or documentary writing as well as from canonical artistic

14

literature" (3). In documenting how literary models are formed, Ginzburg also points out how "images of personality are constructed . . . in life, and [how] that is a natural, inevitable, and continuous process" (20). Hence, her pride in asserting that "it is indeed the literary investigation of man that has opened up a wide thoroughfare from schematic typification and mechanically articulated qualities to the most complex structures beyond the reach of one-dimensional formulations" (14). In a word, she credits literary theory with making it possible to articulate the semiotics of social behavior.

Indeed, Boris Gasparov, in his introduction to *The Semiotics of Russian Cultural History*, points out that *On Psychological Prose* was "an important stimulant to the development of the semiotics of behavior" and the "first explicit formulation" of Russian poststructuralism, what he terms the new discipline of "the semiotics of social behavior." Although not a participant in the Moscow-Tartu school, Ginzburg "documents the formation of literary models of personality types, situations, and social relations, showing the decisive importance of these models for contemporary behavior and self-consciousness."[29]

Ginzburg draws analogies between the processes of art and life as she focuses on the complex nature of the interrelationships between literary and social models and their impact on society's self-consciousness. She cites contemporary semiotic literature as crucial for having "proposed the idea of the model and modeling" for understanding the "'creatibility' of psychic structures by means of selection, correlation, and symbolic interpretation of psychic elements—by means, that is, of a method analogous to that used by art" (12). She also affirms the importance of the idea of the model, stating that "the psychological structures that a person constructs and apprehends in life and in literature may be regarded as kinds of imaginary figurative models" (12), and she views "personality as we are concerned with it in sociology and history and even in everyday life [as] a structure that derives from our observations of both internal processes (introspection) and external ones" (9).

Nevertheless, Ginzburg also expresses her ambivalence toward the potential misapplication of models, strongly cautioning against oversimplification: "One should neither forget the conventionality and approximateness that this term has in the humanities, nor expect of it the precision that it has in the exact sciences and in technology" (12). And she warns scholars to "be cautious with sociopsychological typology, lest it turn into a means of crudely simplifying spiritual life and its literary embodiments." Ultimately, she declares her faith in the uniqueness of the individual personality: such "formulas are not representations of the individual, but merely frameworks for his identification" (14).

Beginning in the mid-1960s, Ginzburg began to publish "memoirs of contemporaries," each of which focused on a particular problem of literary or cultural significance. These revolved around her subtle repudiation of established truths or official positions, and hence initiated the rehabilitation of the subject of the memoir and the recovery of his or her fundamental ideological or value system. In addition, these memoirs helped to give shape to her own life by establishing links between the different stages of her own past and thoughts. A good example is Ginzburg's memoir of Tynianov. In the course of recalling a vibrant teacher-student relationship, she also demonstrates how his life and work are of a piece, namely, how a "special aesthetic quality distinguished both his scholarship and his life." This interpretation repudiates the official thesis that Tynianov's scholarship negated ideas supported in his creative writing, and vice versa. Indeed, Ginzburg emphasizes that the function of the aesthetic is of prime significance in all aspects of her own writing, including her scholarship. In her memoir of Eikhenbaum, she focuses on the crucial problem of "behavior" both as a "subject of scholarship and in his daily life," while she simultaneously reflects on the impact of his scholarly and personal behavior on her life and work. She thereby rejects the idea that Eikhenbaum was an incorrigible formalist who lacked any understanding of the social sphere. Additionally, in her reminiscences of Anna Akhmatova, Ginzburg not only recalls her youthful pleasure and pride at being praised for her student paper on Viazemskii, but tries to pinpoint what precisely differentiated Akhmatova's lyric treatment of an experience from that of other poets. In the process, she explains Akhmatova's power by deflating the official image of her as a poet of minor themes.[30]

In this way Ginzburg's cultural memoirs of 1979 to 1980 may also be read as the culmination of her "memoirs of contemporaries." Yet here, in lieu of serving as individual teacher, friend, or mentor, Ginzburg endeavors to understand and memorialize a collective, the entire generation of her peers—her "shared identity." Invoking her prerogative to have a "direct conversation about life" in order to generalize and explain the significance of her endeavor, Ginzburg seeks to develop a kind of semiotic assessment of the behavior of the postrevolutionary intelligentsia over the course of the Stalinist decades instead of writing a more conventional subjective memoir of an individual.

In the first of her two cultural memoirs, "The Turning Point of a Generation" (1979), Ginzburg focuses initially on demonstrating how a key image, a cultural icon particularly cherished by the Russian intelligentsia, namely, Pushkin's image of Pugachev, underwent a cultural transmutation in response to the social, psychological, and historical forces associated with the revolution and, consequently, exerted a powerful influence on intelligentsia consciousness. As she had theorized earlier in *On Psychological Prose*, "personality shapes itself, both internally and externally, by means of images, many of which have passed through literature" (14). Here, Ginzburg demonstrates how the image of Pugachev, first in Pushkin's literary representation, and then again in Tsvetaeva's and Dobin's, empowered an entire generation.

Second, she examines the modes of thinking and typology of the pre- and postrevolutionary intelligentsia based on their differing orientations toward the two alternative cultural formations of the intelligentsia inherited from the nineteenth century: the "complex of modernism, individualism and elitism" on the one hand, and the complex of populism, humanism, and social justice on the other. She accomplishes this by invoking other poetic images or what she terms "poetic documents." Hence, in the latter half of this memoir, Ginzburg demonstrates how the contradictory orientations of these two alternatives are realized in Pasternak's "agonized oxymorons." In fact, she argues that it is precisely the poet's "lack of synthesis" which makes his poem, "Vysokaia bolezn'" ("A Lofty Malady"),[31] an "incomparable poetic document" of the thinking of the intelligentsia of the 1920s. This is because the conflicting poetic images in Pasternak's work represent a convergence of two distinctly different and indeed antithetical sets of values, and are therefore "not . . . falsehoods," but "interactions at different levels: correlations between the instinct for self-preservation and traditional intellectual habits, between historical analysis and fear."

Finally, in her sequel, "'At One with the Prevailing Order'" (1980), which takes its title from Pasternak's 1932 lyric "Stolet'e s lishnym—ne vchera" ("A Century Plus—Not Yesterday"), Ginzburg shows that the central cultural conflict of the 1920s—a sharpened but still permissable antithesis in social thinking and behavior—was replaced in the 1930s by increased social pressure which conditioned the psychological desire "to belong" to the new age.[32] Here Ginzburg develops her theory of "accommodation" to explain the dominant social behavior of the intelligentsia in the 1930s—the impetus behind types of "shared identity"—and its ever more lethal variants in subsequent Stalinist decades.

"The Turning Point of a Generation," then, focuses Ginzburg's "direct conversation about life" on her efforts as a member of the older generation of the Soviet intelligentsia to define her own place in the intelligentsia tradition, hence her need to distinguish between the pre- and postrevolutionary systems. Before the revolution, she asserts, there "reigned *a remarkable blend* of modernism, individualism, Tolstoyan vegetarianism . . . and Sofia Perovskaia . . . and although Pugachev was never my personal hero, it was somehow clear to me that this could also be right" (emphasis added). But after 1917, the "psychological map changed" because the demands for conformity increased, and the "remarkable blend" of values became "contradictory impulses, which, though *antithetical, were harnessed together*" (emphasis added). In a word, after 1917, the emphasis was no longer on the diversity or coexistence of differing value systems, but on difference and contradiction, and eventually, conformism or expulsion.

Second, before 1917, the intelligentsia's view of its relationship to revolution appeared clear-cut; truth was on the side of revolution; the intelligentsia's primary sin was its privileged status vis-à-vis its disadvantaged brothers.[33] After 1917, the clarity and firmness of these values came into question as people began to review "the revolution's first draft of the fate of the individual, a fate connected dialectically with revolution."

Third, the concept of "opposition," fundamental to the generic definition of the intelligentsia, underwent significant transformation. While many of Russia's cultural leaders did not want revolution, and even condemned it, Ginzburg noted, "opposition to the existing state of affairs was found among all strata . . . All thinking people were in opposition one way or another . . . a highly valued immutable given. But later on, people discussed how to 'merge' it [i.e., opposition] with other values, even with contradictory values."

In applying theoretical models in her cultural memoirs of 1979 to 1980 analogous to those described in *On Psychological Prose*, Ginzburg shows how the value system of the intelligentsia was filtered through literary and cultural models. She also theorizes how "poetic documents" portraying social types become models for group social behavior because they idealize "the good" and downplay or ignore "evil." Privilege and obligation, even taking up the sword, were clear-cut principles before the Revolution, and retained great allure in its aftermath. For example, Bazarov, the protagonist in Ivan Turgenev's famous 1860s novel *Fathers and Sons,* provided such a model in *On Psychological Prose.* Ginzburg pointed out how "not infrequently the social type was an indictment, or on the contrary, a model against which contemporaries might measure themselves. To a greater or lesser degree this happens whenever any social group becomes aware of the need for the advent of a 'new man.' What was Bazarov? Not a norm, not an ideal, and certainly not a set of positive characteristics . . . he became a standard for the 'new men.' Moreover, his negative traits . . . received positive valuation as the signs of a new social position" (22–23). Interrogating herself and her generation, Ginzburg raises the question of the semiotic significance of Pugachev and Sofia Perovskaia. Did they serve as analogues for the intelligentsia of the twentieth century? Could their negative traits have also received positive valuation as signs of a "new social position"? And if so, how did this occur?

In "The Turning Point of a Generation," Ginzburg demonstrates how the extraordinarily powerful image of Pugachev with its romantic appeal, its representation of the strength and firmness of opposition, and its total dedication to the cause of revolution, merged in itself elements from both types of the prerevolutionary intelligentsia: the behavioral characteristics of egocentric individualism and self-confidence blended with the characteristics of populism and social justice. In addition, Ginzburg proposes that the

18

image of Sofia Perovskaia, who in addition incorporated the ideal of "self-sacrifice," subsequently gained even greater moral force for her generation.

Ginzburg claims first of all that the poetic, indeed, mythic image (versus the historic image) of Pugachev reimagined in Tsvetaeva's 1937 essay, "Pushkin and Pugachev," is emblematic because "Tsetaeva's thinking reflected her membership in the intelligentsia." Thus, "Tsvetaeva asserted . . . that Pugachev was a magnanimous and intrepid peasant Czar. . . . This is Tsvetaeva speaking of the good Pugachev as depicted in Pushkin's *Captain's Daughter*, not the 'evil Pugachev' of Pushkin's *History*." In denoting the specifics of this image, Ginzburg also identifies what Tsvetaeva considered "good" and "evil": "Pugachev was perceived as good because he was a noble brigand." On the other hand, Ginzburg also points out Tsvetaeva's omissions: indeed, how she omitted "murder" in her enumeration of Pugachev's "evil" traits. What is more, "evil" is ascribed only to his failure to fulfill "the behavioral norms of the noble brigand." Thus, in Ginzburg's reading of Tsvetaeva, Pugachev betrayed his friends, "permitted his truest disciple to be hanged, and begged pardon in response to a bloody blow to his face," but Tsvetaeva attributes the cause merely to his "fear of his comrades," not to his evil nature or to evil per se. Moreover, Ginzburg argues that even when Pugachev's sins are spelled out, "what remains fails to raise the question of why we admired him so." Thus, she cites yet another supportive representation of Pugachev in Efim Dobin's popular adolescent novel where unsavory aspects of Pugachev's behavior are rationalized and accepted in the course of interpreting Grinev's dream: "there is only one means to salvation: to ask the peasant's blessing."

In further developing her "conversation about life," Ginzburg raises thorny rhetorical questions to assess the impact of these cultural images on her generation of the intelligentsia, concluding, "Again there is acceptance, no looking back, no questions asked. Why did not the simplest mechanisms work: Tsvetaeva's sympathy, Dobin's kindness or fear?" In response, she invokes her own emotional experience and her own thought processes as a semiotic model for the thinking of her generation: "That may be cause for surprise, but I am not surprised. We were all like that—at age 15. And we could have grown up thinking the same way if the epoch had not changed us." Thus, such cultural behavior is viewed as typical of her privileged social class. The intelligentsia's naïveté and privilege are cited to explain the psychology behind its adolescent enthusiasm, romantic vision, and youthful capacity for sacrifice: "We had been raised from childhood to be ashamed of our privileges, thus although we did not repudiate them ourselves, if history took them away, we did not lodge complaints against history when it put an end to that evil."

Ginzburg further historicizes and semiotizes the thinking of her generation of the intelligentsia by identifying other literary and cultural constants which shaped it. For example, the theme of privilege and obligation is traced back to its origins in Herzen's *From the Other Shore,* and forward to its literary echoes in Blok and Briusov, as well as up through to Mandelstam's 1931 lyric, "Za vysokuiu doblest' griadushchikh vekov" ("For the Thundering Valor of Future Centuries"). Additionally, Ginzburg cites ample literary evidence for the allure of "the idea of revolution for the entire Russian avant-garde," including the appeal of the "good Pugachev."

To quote Ginzburg's theoretical explanations in *On Psychological Prose:* "Real-life symbolism finds a place both in the thinking of historians and in the conceptions of historical events and figures present in the consciousness of society" (8) and "[Social man] passes . . . through a series of images that are oriented toward shared norms and ideals, images that not only have a social function but also possess aesthetic coloration" (11). In the same way, analogous twentieth-century images are aestheticized and cleansed or purified, and hence the enormity of their collective impact.

Throughout the memoirs of 1979 to 1980, Ginzburg's strategy is not only to seek explanations in literary and cultural models, nor to cite her own emotional experience and thought processes, but to interrogate herself and her audience. From her perspective at the end of the twentieth century she continuously questions her own and her generation's efforts to explain the appeal of revolution and their choices: "The formula was clear and simple: the people are suffering, we must take up the sword. Later, both those who took up the sword and those who did not perished because of it. Among them were the fifteen-year-olds of my generation. But how should we interpret this—*as historical accident or as the responsibility of the fifteen year olds* who mentally picked up the sword?" (emphasis added). With hindsight, of course, Ginzburg can raise vexed questions not raised at the time, such as "What about the sacrifices of the innocent?" However, in recognizing how "this too was somehow assimilated into our set of values," she also cautions her younger audience against applying the moral judgments of a later historical epoch to an earlier one.

In the latter half of "The Turning Point of a Generation," Ginzburg proposes that, after 1917, the prerevolutionary "blend" or synthesis of values could no longer function because the resolute ideals and firm judgments of Blok and Briusov no longer ruled the thinking of the intelligentsia and no longer yielded productive cultural formations. Instead, intellectual ambivalence—Pasternak's "agonized oxymorons"—replaced the prerevolutionary synthesis with a "convergence of all levels of self-consciousness." According to Ginzburg, Pasternak's images represented the dominant cultural signs of the 1920s, signifying the transition from the prerevolutionary typology of the intelligentsia with its firm views on revolution to the postrevolutionary typology with its unresolved ambiguities. "All kinds of notions pertaining to the intelligentsia and the revolution appear and yet there is no apparent effort to *synthesize* them . . . [As opposed to Blok's firm evaluative judgments] in Pasternak's work evaluative judgments are not present; or more accurately, *judgments are made on both sides*" (emphasis added). In retrospect, Pasternak's "poetic document" provides Ginzburg with a strikingly accurate cultural model for the 1920s, for it conveys both the intelligentsia's "creative ingenuity and its historical foolishness."

In the second cultural memoir, "'At One with the Prevailing Order'" (1980), Ginzburg proceeds to chart the course of the thinking and behavior of the postrevolutionary intelligentsia, attempting to make sense of the "changed psychological map." Here she documents the impact of history on the intelligentsia, defining the semiotics of each decade and the interaction with the general laws of psychosocial behavior discussed previously in *On Psychological Prose*. In this critical monograph, Ginzburg points out how individuals realize themselves in given historical periods although they cannot avoid the collective consciousness of the epoch. Important processes occur by which "a personality finds realization in the historically regulated forms of collective consciousness. That personality may create those forms, it may modify them, it may introduce something of its own into them, *but it cannot avoid them*" (17–18, emphasis added).

Ginzburg theorizes that just as stable historical periods differ from unsettled and transitional times, so personality types and characteristic social positions will be affected as well. She differentiates between "politically and ideologically dynamic periods when *only one definite social position is possible* for the different members of a single social group" (emphasis added) and "transitional times" when there may be "several characteristic social positions available to people of a single stratum." Ginzburg thus proposes that while essential individual choices are made, they are also conditioned historically: each "choice is determined by personal attributes, possibilities, capacities, and circumstances, and ultimately by luck. Yet for those who would take part in the ideological life of their time, a choice is essential" (18).

In "'At One with the Prevailing Order,'" as in *On Psychological Prose*, Ginzburg draws sharp distinctions between historical periods. The 1920s are semiotized as a "transitional" period when there could be "several characteristic social positions available to people of a single stratum," when there was both "a certain clarity of alignments," permitting a certain healthy opposition, and "genuine faith in having accomplished the advent of a better world." On the other hand, while Ginzburg views the 1930s as a "politically and ideologically dynamic period," its significance lies in being identified as a time when only "one definite social position was possible." Thus, in the 1930s it became clear that the "main objective was to find some point of accommodation." Ginzburg further differentiates between the "dynamic" years of the 1930s and the postwar Stalinist years, which for her and her former colleagues at GIII proved the most traumatic, because "my variant no longer worked, and hence people like myself were completely silenced."

In *On Psychological Prose* Ginzburg had endeavored to elucidate the phenomenon of historical inevitability in terms of history's capacity to "recast" personality traits. Recognizing the great variety and complexity of historical and psychological pressures on individual choice, she concluded that history had the last word. "The correlations are varied and complex. A person's basic features, his 'genotype' in Pavlov's terminology, may turn out to be particularly appropriate or particularly inappropriate for a given historical model. But history recasts both the appropriate and the inappropriate" (18).

While Ginzburg clearly accepted the idea that "social positions are reflected in epochal personality types," she still needed to ask the painful question: "how does the universally significant historical model correlate with the private personality of the individual?" Her retrospective analysis found in the memoirs of 1979 to 1980 semiotizes the 1920s as a time in which her generation found themselves in harmony with the goals of the new age and in support of its ideals, although at the time she had believed that her circle was actually "confronting the epoch." Nevertheless, she takes pride in the fact that her generation had understood that "for a short time" they were "actors in a segment of culture which had just begun." Thus, her comments in *On Psychological Prose* that the phenomenon of "real life symbolization" is "most clearly evident at historical turning points when 'new men' with new principles of behavior are born" (16) and her invocation of Herzen's concept of "Russian epochal personality types" (17) are fully applicable to her cultural memoirs as she equates her own life story with that of her generation: "My generation and my circle passed through the various stages of historical consciousness; we were always pressured by time."

Ginzburg then summarizes her own biography as part of the collective cultural biography of the postrevolutionary intelligentsia: "Childhood and early youth represented passive links to the momentous events of the world war and revolution. The 1920s were for me the Institute of History of the Arts. . . . For us personally experiencing an historical epoch in all its details made it possible to comprehend much that was incomprehensible to others who had never before had an active historical existence. . . . It seemed to us—and so it was for a short time—that we were the beginning, the first actors in a segment of culture which had just begun. But then, in the 1930s and 1940s, we became the passive property of the Stalinist epoch and the war years, with all that followed from that."

In retrospect, for Ginzburg's generation the 1930s dramatized the starkly changed conditions of Soviet life. In her memoirs, that was when the problematics of "belonging" became the key "cultural-historical current," indeed, "the only possible definite social position," and the theme of "shared identity" came to dominate the creative process. Consequently, in the cultural memoirs of 1979 to 1980, she sought to define those "historical conditions" and to determine how they interacted with the "universal laws governing human social behavior" and the laws governing the creative process that enabled the postrevolutionary intelligentsia not only to live, but to thrive.

Because hindsight already colored historians' endeavors to examine this period due to the cumulative knowledge of the horrors of the 1930s collected since the de-Stalinization process, and because that process focused almost exclusively on the macroprocesses of history, Ginzburg posited the need to examine the psychological microprocesses—the expression of the private experiences of individuals in diaries, letters, and other documents. She recognized, however, that these microprocesses must also be reviewed in conjunction with the laws of social and psychological behavior governing the lives shaped and grounded in the traditions of enthusiasm for the revolution. Here Ginzburg again bases her argument on principles established in *On Psychological Prose*, namely, that "images of human beings are constructed in life itself, and an everyday psychology accumulates in the traces of letters, diaries, confessions and other 'human documents' where the aesthetic principle is present to a greater or lesser degree of conscious realization." As she argues, *"letters or diaries fix the indeterminate process of life with its as yet unknown denouement"* (9, emphasis added). Hence, it is the documentation of her journal entries that allowed Ginzburg to begin to comprehend how the 1930s was a period of "excitement and enthusiasm" for her generation, a time when the "desire to participate and glorify" overshadowed everything else. Analogous to the cultural images of Pugachev and Sofia Perovskaia cited to document the intelligentsia's acceptance of revolution, Pasternak's "agonized oxymorons," and the "poetic documents" cited to define the contradictions of the 1920s, Ginzburg finds traces of an "everyday psychology" in her own life writing, in the entries in her private journal, to document the 1930s.

In addition, Ginzburg historicizes the 1930s by introducing pertinent facts regarding the co-optation of the intelligentsia and their emotional responses to the Stalinist terror. First of all, she alleges that the elite's well-being and high standard of living was made possible because "Stalin created an elite not only of bureaucrats, but of writers, academicians, professors and other intellectuals." Second, regarding the terror and forced collectivization, she tries to explain that although the "terrifying events in the background never allowed the consciousness to rest," psychologically people "shielded or distracted themselves." Third, and perhaps most significant, Ginzburg declares that "because the situation was so typical . . . we were aware that this could happen to anyone. As in wartime." Thus, Ginzburg's journal testifies to the intelligentsia's struggle to live normal lives under abnormal conditions: "It is absurd for us to imagine that the disasters of past epochs were the only thing that absorbed peoples' lives." Rather, she concludes, the reverse was true: "The 1930s were characterized by far more than labor and fear . . . we truly enjoyed ourselves," especially during summer vacations. Her journal bears witness to the psychological microprocesses of the epoch: "Our old journals surprise us now with their focus on our group activities, with their genuine absence of interest in anything else. That does not mean they lack historical meaning, for in their own way they suggest another possible picture of the age." Furthermore, according to Ginzburg, without considering the complex interaction between these historical facts, emotional facts, and the fundamental laws of human behavior, the spiritual life and social behavior characterizing this period cannot be grasped. Ginzburg thereby identifies three fundamental social mechanisms of the Stalinist 1930s—"accommodation, justification, and indifference"—which, she claimed, functioned so efficiently that "no one escaped unscathed."

In theorizing how these universal laws functioned in the 1930s, Ginzburg first endeavors to show that they "did not always function." In fact, they applied to certain historical moments, but not to others. For example, "the mechanism of accommodation with its dual function of distraction from suffering and attraction to pleasure" worked in conjunction with the "indifference people show toward whatever does not concern them." Citing her own personal experience as typical of her generation, she highlights more specifically what "our cultural behavior" included and excluded: "Our cultural behavior did not include" either the facts of collectivization or the Ukrainian famine; both were just "suppressed rumors." Nor did it include "the arrests as long as those arrests occurred in another sphere and did not yet represent immediate danger to our milieu."

Such individual or group behavior can only be attributed to the general laws of human behavior, that is, social action or social consciousness is activated only toward something for which a person "is answerable and which he can change. This is the key to participation in social movements . . ." Consequently, Ginzburg asks how these laws applied specifically to herself and her group's "cultural behavior." Reactions would be expected only to "what directly touches our emotions, our nerves," and the "facts of [our] own self-realization."

In analyzing what "directly touched the emotions" of her generation and what affected their "self-realization," Ginzburg explores the influence of history in shaping the creative process, and how the intelligentsia's inner struggle was reflected in both their life and their creative work. While "a gifted individual requires, even demands, the experience of creativity, " she points out that *creativity is the formalization of one's own understanding of life*" (emphasis added). Again raising the thorny question of the relationship between life and art, she inquires how the intelligentsia "formalized" its understanding of life in the new society of the 1930s.

This brings Ginzburg back once more to Pasternak. Specifically, his lines "Trudu so vsemi soobshcha / I zaodno s pravoporiadkom" ("I'm Working with Everyone Together / At One with the Prevailing Order") serve as the title for her second cultural memoir. Pasternak's lines generalize Ginzburg's thesis that the imagery of "belonging" provides the key to the psychological and social behavior of the intelligentsia of the Stalinist years. Indeed, she points out "talented individuals, talented both as artists and as human beings, sought with particular intensity to find or create within themselves *recognizable spheres of shared identity with everyone else*" (emphasis added).

In demonstrating how widespread the theme of "shared identity" was in the 1930s and how it was expressed both in life and in art, Ginzburg theorizes that the stylistic emphasis on "simplicity" emerged in the creative work of the majority of writers at this time as they strove, consciously and unconsciously, to make their work accessible to the mass reader. For Pasternak, the "search for equality" appears both in his everyday life and in his aesthetic expression—in his thematics as well as in his efforts to simplify his style. Even Mandelstam, Ginzburg claims, in his everyday life "genuinely rejoiced in his participation" in the new society, namely, in his editorial position at the newspaper *Moscow Komsomolets* helping younger writers. On the other hand, Mandelstam could never simplify his style. Rather, he chose to express feelings pertaining to his desire to belong to the age and its mass culture on a thematic level, but never abandoned ambivalence as an essential stylistic component of his work: "You should know—I'm a contemporary . . . / I'm a man of the Moskvoshvei epoch,— / Look how my jacket puffs up on me."

By documenting how the fundamental psychological need to seek some sphere of shared identification with the new culture, to find some means of belonging to the new age, was expressed as a universal law of human behavior, Ginzburg sets out to prove that the mechanism of accommodation affected everyone, although in different ways. Thus, without either condemning or condoning the behavior of her generation, Ginzburg endeavored to explain how social and historical forces operating in conjunction with the basic laws of human behavior shaped the moral as well as the aesthetic consciousness of the intelligentsia, and how her own efforts to reestablish the context of that behavior is crucial to its understanding. Indeed, in *On Psychological Prose*, she had not only discussed how "history recasts both the appropriate and the inappropriate," and how no one can avoid being part of the collective consciousness of a given historical epoch, but with reference to the Russian intelligentsia of the 1830s and 1840s, she had also shown how "the same person, if he was someone particularly responsive to history, could sometimes pass through all the [various stages of social history during his lifetime]" (28).

In alluding specifically to her own life story as a semiotic model of the social and psychological behavior of the intelligentsia of her generation, Ginzburg personalizes her experience of the behavioral mechanisms behind the creation of shared spheres of identity: "What can I say about my own case? Basically, that we should have no illusions, no one escaped unscathed. *My personal experience is interesting here insofar as it is a typical case, one of the varieties of the experience of the epoch.* Everyone who functioned in society was subject to the above-mentioned mechanisms—accommodation, justification, and indifference, only with certain people these mechanisms operated intermittently, and decency or honesty at times interfered. In my own case, the mechanism of justification was the most weakly developed; my inborn analytical sense interfered. On the other hand, the mechanism of indifference never ceased to operate" (emphasis added).

Furthermore, in rejecting the idea that writers like herself might prove the exception and escape their historical fate, Ginzburg confesses her initial belief that she had maintained her individuality and originality in her study of Herzen's *Past and Thoughts* and her discovery two decades later that the discourse of the late Stalinist period had insinuated its presence into her writing as well. Consequently, in identifying her own social type, she states, "I decided that *I belonged with those people who, within the limits of the possible, retained their own opinions.* However, those limits would sometimes expand, sometimes contract. In the immediate postwar period (1946–53), for example, they narrowed to such an extent that there was no leeway at all. *My variant no longer worked,* and hence people like myself were completely *silenced*" (emphasis added).

Thus, by taking a semiotic approach to her own biography in her cultural memoirs of 1979 to 1980, Ginzburg confronts historical conditioning directly: her final vexed question concerns self-determination and the fate of the individual in history—the relationship between conscious choice and behavior not consciously determined. She asks whether what seemed to be conscious choices in her own case had played a role in the formation of her biography. Citing Vinokur's *Biography and Culture* (1923), which she claims "defines biography as 'the life of a personality in history,'" she asks, "But does a biography emerge from the alternation of passive experience under inordinate historical pressures with quasi-illusory action? If so, it is certainly not a biography that has willed itself into existence." By considering her "self" and her experience as an object of investigation, as a model of an active participant in a semiotized construction of Soviet cultural history, Ginzburg applies the larger philosophical issue to the behavior of the intelligentsia in Soviet times.

Knowing that Ginzburg consistently sought out principles in literature and life to broaden her understanding of human behavior or human culture, we can locate these cultural memoirs in her overall oeuvre. Ginzburg's focus is on the ongoing processes, on the correlations as well as the distinctions between literature and life, on the "transformation" of life into art and the reverse effects of art on life. We also see that because Ginzburg viewed "boundaries" between life and art not as finite or absolute, but as fluid and changing entities in history as well as in an ongoing aesthetic continuum, in writing about literature she chose to devote a large portion of her research to studying the noncanonical genres of life writing and the processes of aesthetic genesis, transformation, and change. In keeping a journal, she chose to participate in the ongoing aesthetic and historical continuum on a regular, firsthand basis. And in her memoirs of 1979 to 1980, recollecting and examining her own self-image in the context of the behavior of the Russian intelligentsia in the Soviet cultural environment, she chose to adapt modes of expression from both her scholarship and her journal to analyses of human culture, identifying and interpreting literary and cultural images returned to life in the form of consciously accepted historical facts and codes of human behavior. Hence, Ginzburg's cultural memoirs of 1979 to 1980 reflect her efforts to capture in time her fascination with human behavior in both art and life and to focus her interpretation on the semiotics of self-creation and laws of human behavior, including the impact of literary and social models on codes of social behavior and social self-consciousness from the 1920s to the Thaw years.

Notes

1. See Sarah Pratt, "Lidiia Ginzburg and the Fluidity of Genre," in *Autobiographical Statements in Twentieth-Century Russian Literature*, ed. Jane Gary Harris (Princeton: Princeton University Press, 1990), 207–16; and Sarah Pratt, ed., "Lidiia Ginzburg's Contribution to Literary Criticism," *Canadian-American Slavic Studies*, Special Issue 19 (summer 1985): 2. See also Beth Holmgren, "For the Good of the Cause: Russian Women's Autobiography in the Twentieth-Century," in *Women Writers in Russian Literature*, ed. Toby Clyman and Diana Greene (Westport, Conn.: Greenwood Press, 1994), 138–40; Catriona Kelly, *A History of Russian Women's Writing, 1820–1992* (Oxford: Clarendon Press, 1994), 370–71; and Caryl Emerson, "Bakhtin, Lotman, Vygotsky and Lydia Ginzburg," in *Self and Story in Russian History*, ed. Laura Engelstein and Stephanie Sandler (Ithaca: Cornell University Press, 2000), 20–45. On the other hand, Ginzburg's personal life, wit, conversational skills, and nonscholarly writings have been addressed by Irina Paperno, "Beyond Literary Criticism" and Victor Erlich, "Two Conversations with Lidiia Ginzburg" in *Lidiia Ginzburg's Contribution.*

Boris Gasparov, Alexander Kushner et al., "Tvorcheskii portret L. Ia. Ginzburg," in *Literaturnoe obozrenie* 10 (1989): 78–86; Elena Nevzgliadova, "Na samom dele, mysl' kak gost' . . . O proze Lidiia Ginzburg," *Avrora* 4 (1989); Jane G. Harris, "The Crafting of a Self: Lidiia Ginzburg's Early Journal," in *Gender and Russian Literature: New Perspectives*, ed. Rosalind Marsh (Cambridge: Cambridge University Press, 1996), 263–82; and Harris, "'The Direct Conversation about Life': Lidiia Ginzburg's Journal as a Contemporary Literary Genre," in *Neoformalist Papers: Contributions to the Silver Age Jubilee Conference to Mark 25 Years of the Neo-Formalist Circle*, ed. Joe Andrew and Robert Reid, *Studies in Slavic Literatures and Poetics* (Amsterdam: Rodopi) 32 (1998): 45–64; Patricia Carden, "Wit and Understanding: The Voices of Lidiia Ginzburg," and my "Biographical Introduction," both in *In Memoriam: Lidiia Ginzburg*, ed. Jane G. Harris, *Canadian-American Slavic Studies*, Special Issue 28 (summer 1994): 2–3.

2. Journal entry 1927, in Lidiia Ginzburg, *Chelovek za pis'mennym stolom* (*At the Writer's Desk*) (Leningrad: Sovetskii pisatel', 1989), 35.

3. Interview, *Smena* 262 (November 13, 1988): 2.

4. "Eshche raz o starom i novom (Pokolenie na povorote)" (1979) ("Once Again on the Old and New [Turning Point of a Generation]") first appeared in print in *Tynianovskii sbornik: Vtorye Tynianovskie Chteniia* (Riga, 1986), 132–40. Translated as "Tsvetaeva et Pougachev," *Lettre Internationale* 22 (1989): 69. This is the first of Ginzburg's two cultural memoirs treated in this chapter. The second, its sequel, is "I zaodno s pravoporiadkom'" ("'At One With the Prevailing Order,'" 1980), which first appeared in print in *Tynianovskii sbornik: Tret'i Tynianovskie Chteniia* (Riga, 1988): 218–30. Both memoirs were reprinted with a few changes in *Chelovek*, 294–319.

5. Lidiia Ginzburg, *Agentstvo Pinkertona* (Leningrad: Detgiz, 1932).

6. Journal entry of 1932, *Chelovek*, 131.

7. See Harris, "The Crafting of a Self." No journal entries were published before the early 1990s. See Ginzburg's statements about sexuality and homosexuality in her early journal entry "1925 (On Reading Gide's Corydon)," in *Russian Women Writers*, ed. Christine Tomei (New York: Garland Publishers, 1999), 1166–68.

8. Journal entry of 1930, *Chelovek*, 102–3.

9. See Boris Gasparov, "On 'Notes from the Leningrad Blockade,'" in *In Memoriam: Lidiia Ginzburg*, ed. Jane G. Harris, *Canadian-American Slavic Studies*, Special Issue 28 (summer 1994): 216–21.

10. First published in *Neva* 1 (1984): 84–108; republished in *Chelovek*, 517–78.

11. Nikolay Kononov, ed., *Pretvorenie opyta* (Leningrad: Assotsiatsiia 'Novaia Literatura', 1991), 3–81.

12. First appeared in the magazine *Rodnik* 3 (March 1990): 26–27.

13. "Dve Vstrechi," *Russkaia mysl'* 3852 (November 2, 1990); also in *Pretvorenie opyta.*

14. See *Literatura v poiskakh real'nosti* (Leningrad: Sovetskii pisatel', 1987), 272–80.

15. These works were all published at the Leningrad branch of the Sovetskii Pisatel' (Soviet Writer) Publishing House where, beginning in 1964, Ginzburg's editor, Mina Dikman, encouraged her not only to continue publishing, but by the mid-1980s, to submit her journal entries and cultural memoirs along with her scholarly writings. I am much obliged to Mina Dikman's husband, Yuri Davidovich Levin, for sharing this information with me.

16. See Alexander Kushner, "Vvedenie" and Alexander Chudakov, "Kommentarii," "L. Ginzburg, Zapisi 20–30-x godov (Iz neopublikovannogo)," *Novyi Mir* 6 (1992); and Alexander Kushner, ed., "Iz dnevnikov Lidii Ginzburg," *Literaturnaia gazeta* 41, no. 5469 (October 13, 1993): 6.

17. *Literaturnaia Rossiia* 51 (December 23, 1988): 8–9.

18. L. Ginzburg, "Viazemskii-Literator," in *Russkaia proza,* ed. Boris Eikhenbaum and Iurii Tynianov (Leningrad: Academiia, 1926), 102–34; English translation by Ray Parrott, *Russian Prose* (Ann Arbor, Mich.: Ardis Publishers, 1985), 87–108. See Jane G. Harris, "Lidiia Ginzburg, the 'Young Formalists,' and *Russkaia proza,*" in *In Memoriam: Lidiia Ginzburg,* ed. Jane G. Harris, *Canadian-American Slavic Studies,* Special Issue 28 (summer 1994): 161–82.

19. Isaiah Berlin, "The Birth of the Russian Intelligentsia," *Russian Thinkers* (New York: Penguin Books, 1979), 117.

20. Sheila Fitzpatrick, *The Russian Revolution: 1917–1932* (Oxford: Oxford University Press, 1982), 17.

21. See also V. S. Bibler, "Lidiia Iakovlevna Ginzburg i sud'by russkoi intelligentsii," *ARKhE: Kul'turologicheskii ezhegodnik* 1 (1993): 422–27.

22. On reading *O starom i novom* as an "autobiographical text," see Pratt, "Lydia Ginzburg and the Fluidity of Genre" in *Autobiographical Statements in Twentieth Century Russian Literature,* ed. Jane Gary Harris (Princeton: Princeton University Press, 1990), 207–16.

23. For information about Ginzburg's life and circle, I am much indebted to personal conversations with Marietta and Alexander Chudakov, Irina Paperno, Alexander Kushner, Elena Nevzgliadova, among other close friends and colleagues, and to Elena Vaulina, Ginzburg's literary secretary from 1988 to 1990. See also Alexander Goldshtein's interview with Vaulina in *Okna* (Tel Aviv), March 11, 1993.

24. This was first published in *Rodnik* 3 (March 1990): 30, and then, with a few changes, in *Pretvorenie opyta* (1991): 171–72. At the time, Andrey Levkin was a Leningrad writer and an editor at *Rodnik*. For a more

detailed discussion of this journal entry and its significance, see Harris, "'The Direct Conversation about Life': Lidiia Ginzburg's Journal as a Contemporary Literary Genre," *Neoformalist Papers: Contributions to the Silver Age Jubilee Conference to Mark 25 Years of the Neo-Formalist Circle,* ed. Joe Andrew and Robert Reid, Studies in Slavic Literatures and Poetics (Amsterdam: Rodopi) 32 (1998): 45–64.

25. *Chelovek,* 4–350.

26. *Chelovek,* 116–18.

27. *Chelovek,* 22–23. For more details, see Harris, "The Crafting of a Self: Lidiia Ginzburg's Early Journal," in *Gender and Russian Literature: New Perspectives,* ed. Rosalind Marsh (Cambridge: Cambridge University Press, 1996): 263–82.

28. Lydia Ginzburg, introduction to *O psikhologicheskoi proze.*

29. See Boris Gasparov, introduction to *The Semiotics of Russian Cultural History,* ed. and trans. Alexander D. and Alice Stone Nakhimovsky (Ithaca: Cornell University Press, 1985), 16–19, in which Gasparov explicates the relationship between Ginzburg's and Lotman's scholarship. In placing Ginzburg's approach within the "ideological tradition of Russian literary criticism," Gasparov clearly differentiates it from the "ideas of Vissarion Belinskii . . ." He writes: "For Ginzburg, 'psychological prose' is not a secondary reflection or description of actual human consciousness, it is a highly organized artistic model with a powerful reverse influence on society's self-consciousness. The primacy of life in relation to literature is the primacy of raw, chaotic material. Defined and structured by a literary model, this material is given a new idealized existence in the minds of members of the society." In the same book, see also Yury Lotman, "The Decembrist in Daily Life (Everyday Behavior as a Historical-Psychological Category," 29: "Individuals do not select routine behavior but rather acquire it from their society, from the historical period in which they live or from their own psychological or physiological makeup; there is no alternative to it. Signifying behavior, on the contrary, is always the result of choice. It always involves individuals' free activity, their choice of language they will use in relations with society." For a current discussion of Ginzburg's place among contemporary literary theorists, see Emerson, "Bakhtin, Lotman, Vygotsky and Lydia Ginzburg."

30. The first of Ginzburg's cultural memoirs (on Bagritsky and Tynianov), based on revised journal entries, appeared in 1966. Ten years later, in 1977, more memoirs (on Akhmatova and Zabolotsky) began to appear. In 1978, Ginzburg gave her first interview. See "Vstrechi s Bagritskim," in *Den' poezii.Vospominaniia. Razmyshleniia. Vstrechi* (Moscow: Molodaia gvardiia, 1966), 86–100, and "Tynianov-Uchenyi," in *Vospominaniia o Iu. Tynianove. Portrety i vstrechi* (Moscow: Sovetskii pisatel', 1983), 147–72; "O Zabolotskom kontsa dvadtsatyx godov," in *Vospominaniia o Zabolotskom*

(Moscow: Sovetskii pisatel', 1977), 120–32; "Akhmatova (Neskol'ko stranits vospominanii)," in *Den' poezii* (1977), 216–17; and "Chtoby skazat' novoe i svoe, nado myslit' v izbrannom napravlenii . . ." (Interv'iu. Besedu vela A. Latynina), in *Voprosy literatury* 4 (1978): 182–97. The memoirs of Eikhenbaum included "Energiia tvorcheskogo uma" (K 100-letiiu so dnia rozhdeniia B. M. Eikhenbauma), *Literaturnaia gazeta* 44 (October 29, 1986), and "Problema povedeniia," in *Chelovek*, 353–58; "Nikolai Oleinikov," also in *Chelovek*, 379–400.

31. First published in *LEF* 1 (1924): 10–18, and then with a few changes in *Novyi mir* 11 (1928): 18–20.

32. Published in *Novyi mir* 5 (1932): 67.

33. Ginzburg stated of Blok: "His evaluative judgments are firmly in place: truth is always on the side of revolution, while the primary sin of the intelligentsia is their advantage over their underprivileged brothers."

Works Cited

Berlin, Isaiah. "The Birth of the Russian Intelligentsia." *Russian Thinkers*. New York: Penguin Books. 1979.

Bibler, V. S. "Lidiia Iakovlevna Ginzburg i sud'by russkoi intelligentsii." *ARKhE: Kul'turologicheskii ezhegodnik* 1 (1993): 422–27.

Carden, Patricia. "Wit and Understanding: The Voices of Lidiia Ginzburg." In *In Memoriam: Lidiia Ginzburg*, edited by Jane G. Harris. *Canadian-American Slavic Studies*, Special Issue 28 (summer 1994): 2–3.

Chudakov, Aleksandr. "Vvedenie i Kommentarii," "L. Ginzburg, Zapisi 20–30-x godov (Iz neopublikovannogo)." *Novyi Mir* 6 (1992).

Emerson, Caryl. "Bakhtin, Lotman, Vygotsky and Lydia Ginzburg." In *Self and Story in Russian History*, edited by Laura Engelstein and Stephanie Sandler. Ithaca: Cornell University Press, 2000, 20–45.

Erlich, Victor. "Two Conversations with Lidiia Ginzburg." In *Lidiia Ginzburg's Contribution to Literary Criticism. CASS*, Special Issue 19 (summer 1985): 2.

Fitzpatrick, Sheila. *The Russian Revolution: 1917–1932*. Oxford: Oxford University Press, 1982.

Gasparov, Boris, et al., "Tvorcheskii portret L. Ia. Ginzburg." In *Literaturnoe obozrenie* 10 (1989): 78–86.

———. "On 'Notes from the Leningrad Blockade.'" In *In Memoriam: Lidiia Ginzburg*, edited by Jane G. Harris. *Canadian-American Slavic Studies*, Special Issue 28 (summer 1994): 216–21.

———. Introduction to *The Semiotics of Russian Cultural History*, edited by Alexander D. and Alice Stone Nakhimovsky. Ithaca: Cornell University Press, 1985.

Ginzburg, Lidiia. "Viazemskii-Literator." In *Russkaia proza*, edited by Boris Eikhenbaum and Iurii Tynianov. Leningrad: Academia, 1926, 102–34. In English: In *Russian Prose*. Translated by Ray Parrott. Ann Arbor, Mich.: Ardis Publishers, 1985, 87–108.

————. *Agentstvo Pinkertona*. Leningrad: Detgiz, 1932.

————. *O lyrike (On the Lyric)*. Leningrad: Sovetskii pisatel', 1964.

————. "Vstrechi s Bagritskim." In *Den' poezii.Vospominaniia. Razmyshleniia. Vstrechi*. Moscow: Molodaia gvardiia. 1966, 86–100.

————. *O Psikhologicheskoi proze (On Psychological Prose)*. Leningrad: Sovetskii pisatel', 1971; revised, 1977. English translation by Judson Rosengrant. Princeton: Princeton University Press, 1991.

————. "O Zabolotskom kontsa dvadtsatyx godov." In *Vospominaniia o Zabolotskom*. Moscow: Sovetskii pisatel'. 1977, 120–32.

————. "Akhmatova (Neskol'ko stranits vospominanii)." *Den' poezii*. 1977, 216–17.

————. "Chtoby skazat' novoe i svoe, nado myslit' v izbrannom napravlenii . . ." (Interv'iu. Besedu vela A. Latynina). *Voprosy literatury* 4 (1978): 182–97.

————. *O literaturnom geroe (On the Literary Hero)*. Leningrad: Sovetskii pisatel', 1979.

————. *O starom i novom (On the Old and the New)*. Leningrad: Sovetskii pisatel', 1982.

————. "Chelovek za pis'mennym stolom: Po starym zapisnym knizhkam." *Novyi Mir* 6 (1982): 234–45.

————. "Tynianov-Uchenyi." In *Vospominaniia o Iu. Tynianove. Portrety i vstrechi*. Moscow: Sovetskii pisatel', 1983, 147–72.

————. "Zapiski blokadnogo cheloveka, I" ("Notes from the Leningrad Blockade"). *Neva* 1 (1984): 84–108; republished in *Chelovek,* 517–78. "Zapiski blokadnogo cheloveka, II." In *Pretvorenie opyta*. Edited by Nikolay Kononov. Leningrad: Assotsiatsiia 'Novaia Literatura', 1991, 3–81.

————. "Eshche raz o starom i novom (Pokolenie na povorote)" ("Once Again on the Old and New [Turning Point of a Generation]," 1979), first appeared in print in *Tynianovskii sbornik: Vtorye Tynianovskie Chteniia. Riga,* 1986, 132–40. Translated as "Tsvetaeva et Pougachev," *Lettre Internationale* 22 (1989): 69.

————. "Energiia tvorcheskogo uma" (K 100-letiiu so dnia rozhdeniia B. M. Eikhenbauma). *Literaturnaia gazeta*, no. 44 (October 29, 1986).

————. "Za pis'mennym stolom. Iz zapisei 1950–60-x godov." *Neva* 3 (1986): 112–39.

————. "I zaodno s pravoporiadkom'" ("'At One with the Prevailing Order,'" 1980), first appeared in print in *Tynianovskii sbornik: Tret'ie Tynianovskie Chteniia*. Riga, 1988, 218–30.

Lidiia Ginzburg

———. "O starosti i infantilism," 1954. In *Literatura v poiskakh real'nosti*. Leningrad: Sovietskii pisatel', 1987.

———. "Vybor budushchego. Iz zapisei 1920–1930-x godov." *Neva* 12 (1988): 131–57.

———. "Nikolay Oleinikov." *Iunost'* 1 (1988): 54–58.

———. Interview. *Smena* 262 (November 13, 1988): 2.

———. Interview. *Literaturnaia Rossiia* 51 (December 23, 1988): 8–9.

———. *Chelovek za pis'mennym stolom: Esse, iz vospominanii, chetyre povestvovaniia (At the Writer's Desk: Essays, from the Memoirs, Four Narratives)* Leningrad: Sovetskii pisatel', 1989.

———. "Problema povedeniia. Boris Mikhailovich Eikhenbaum." In *Chelovek za pis'mennym stolom*. Leningrad: Sovetskii pisatel'. 1989, 353–58

———. "Zapisi raznyx let" (including "The Kochetov Complex" and "A Conversation with Andrey Levkin on the Future of Prose"). *Rodnik* 3 (March 1990): 26–30. Reprinted in *Pretvorenie opyta*. 1991, 171–72.

———. "Dve vstrechi" ("Two Encounters"). *Russkaia mysl'* 3852 (November 2, 1990), reprinted in *Pretvorenie opyta*.

———. *Pretvorenie opyta (Transformation of Experience)*. Edited by Nikolay Kononov. Leningrad: Assotsiatsiia 'Novaia Literatura', 1991.

———. "Selected Works: From The Journals." Translated by Jane G. Harris. In vol. 2, *Russian Women Writers*, edited by Christine Tomei. New York: Garland Publishers, 1999, 1166–78.

Goldshtein, Alexander. Interview with Elena Vaulina in *Okna* (Tel Aviv) (March 11, 1993).

Gordin, Iakov. "Mashtabnost' issledovaniia." *Voprosy literatury* 1 (1981): 273–81.

Harris, Jane G., ed. *Autobiographical Statements in Twentieth-Century Russian Literature*. Princeton: Princeton University Press, 1990.

———, ed. *In Memoriam: Lidiia Ginzburg. Canadian-American Slavic Studies*. Special Issue 28 (summer 1994): 2–3.

———. "Lidiia Ginzburg, the 'Young Formalists,' and Russkaia Proza." In *In Memoriam: Lidiia Ginzburg. Canadian-American Slavic Studies*. Special Issue 28 (summer 1994): 161–82.

———. "The Crafting of a Self: Lidiia Ginzburg's Early Journal." In *Gender and Russian Literature: New Perspectives*, edited by Rosalind Marsh. Cambridge: Cambridge University Press, 1996, 263–82.

———. "'The Direct Conversation about Life': Lidiia Ginzburg's Journal as a Contemporary Literary Genre." In *Neoformalist Papers: Contributions to the Silver Age Jubilee Conference to Mark 25 Years of the Neo-Formalist Circle*, edited by Joe Andrew and Robert Reid. *Studies in Slavic Literatures and Poetics*. Amsterdam: Rodopi. 32 (1998): 45–64.

————. "Lidiia Ginzburg." "Selected Works: From The Journals." In vol. 2, *Russian Women Writers*, edited by Christine Tomei. New York: Garland Publishers, 1999, 1157–78.

Holmgren, Beth. "For the Good of the Cause: Russian Women's Autobiography in the Twentieth Century." In *Women Writers in Russian Literature*. Edited by Toby Clyman and Diana Greene. Westport, Conn.: Greenwood Press, 1994, 127–48.

Kelly, Catriona. *A History of Russian Women's Writing, 1820–1992.* Oxford: Clarendon Press, 1994.

Kushner, Aleksandr. "Vvedenie." "L. Ginzburg, Zapisi 20–30-x godov (Iz neopublikovannogo)." *Novyi Mir* 6 (1992).

————, ed. "Iz dnevnikov Lidii Ginzburg." *Literaturnaia gazeta* 41, no. 5469 (October 13, 1993): 6.

Lotman, Iuri. "The Decembrist in Daily Life (Everyday Behavior as a Historical-Psychological Category)." In *The Semiotics of Russian Cultural History.* Ithaca: Cornell University Press, 1985.

Nakhimovsky, Alexander D., and Alice Stone, eds. and trans. *The Semiotics of Russian Cultural History.* Ithaca: Cornell University Press, 1985.

Nevzgliadova, Elena. "Na samom dele, mysl' kak gost' . . . O proze Lidii Ginzburg." *Avrora* 4 (1989).

Paperno, Irina. "Beyond Literary Criticism." In *Lidiia Ginzburg's Contribution to Literary Criticism. Canadian-American Slavic Studies*, Special Issue 19 (summer 1980): 2.

Pasternak, Boris. "Vysokaia bolezn'." *LEF* 1 (1924): 10–18; republished with a few changes in *Novyi mir* 11 (1928): 18–20.

————. "Stolet'e s lishnym—ne vchera." In *Novyi mir* 5 (1932): 67.

Pratt, Sarah, ed. *Lidiia Ginzburg's Contribution to Literary Criticism Canadian-American Slavic Studies*, Special Issue 19 (summer 1985): 2.

————. "Lidiia Ginzburg and the Fluidity of Genre." In *Autobiographical Statements in Twentieth-Century Russian Literature.* Edited by Jane Gary Harris. Princeton: Princeton University Press, 1990, 207–16.

Sarah Pratt

The Stuffed Shirt Unstuffed: Zabolotsky's "Early Years" and the Complexity of Soviet Culture

THE FIGURE OF Nikolai Zabolotsky generally comes down to us as a "Soviet poet."[1] This term carries several implications. It means that Zabolotsky lived primarily during the Soviet period. It means that we perceive him primarily as the author of works acceptable to the Soviet regime. In addition, because Zabolotsky began his career as a member of the avant-garde, served a term in prison camp during the Stalinist purges for corrupting Soviet youth with "nonsense" literature, and emerged a stylistically conservative poet, his designation as a "Soviet poet" prompts us to assume that at some point he gave up an original, true identity for the sake of political, literary, and possibly physical survival.

We are not necessarily mistaken, for Zabolotsky seems to represent himself repeatedly in these same terms. Given the fact that during the Soviet period virtually any utterance bore the stamp of political self-representation, we are justified in seeking details of Zabolotsky's self-portrait in writings ranging from an unabashed article of political apology from 1936 called *"Pravda* Articles Open Our Eyes" ("Stat'i *Pravdy* otkryvaiut nam glaza") to such innocuously simple but pointedly *non*-avant-garde poems as "The Ugly Little Girl" ("Nekrasivaia devochka"), "The Aged Actress" ("Staraia aktrisa"), and the pseudo–socialist realist poem "The Creators of Roads" ("Tvortsy dorog") from the 1940s and 1950s.[2]

Within this context, the sixteen-page, unabashedly autobiographical essay entitled "The Early Years" ("Rannie gody") from 1955 stands out as an anomaly.[3] The essay was not published until 1972, when it appeared in the two-volume annotated edition of Zabolotsky's selected works and then passed into the annals of Soviet literature essentially unnoticed. The fact that the narrative ends before the Russian revolution of 1917 might be seen as a form of protective self-censorship and a continuation of the pattern noted above. Perhaps as a former convict, Zabolotsky felt it wiser not to deal with the inevitable political complexities of life during and after the revolution. At the same time, however, it is equally plausible that the aging poet felt simply that it was time to identify and articulate the forces that formed him as a person and perceived that formation as occurring during the first fourteen years of his life, hence the explicitness of the title "The Early Years."

As the first even remotely comprehensive collection of Zabolotsky's works, the 1972 edition lists only one additional piece under the heading "Autobiographical Prose," a lyrical nature essay entitled "Pictures of the Far East" ("Kartiny dal'nego vostoka").[4] Although the essay is based on Zabolotsky's experience in camp and exile, these circumstances are not stated in the text or the accompanying notes. Moreover, the essay lacks the typical markers of autobiography or memoir, such as the presence of the first person in the text, an undercurrent of issues related to self-representation, a sense of chronological progression, or a presumption of historical relevance. This is clearly not autobiography in the standard sense. Other prose pieces by the poet, "Thought—Image—Music" ("Mysl'—obraz—muzyka") and "Why I Am Not a Pessimist" ("Pochemu ia ne pessimist") might be called "autobiographical" in the sense that they present a personal artistic credo, but "The Early Years" stands alone as the only chronologically organized first-person narrative of events in the poet's life.

Like the major part of the poet's prose, very little of Zabolotsky's poetry can be considered autobiographical in a direct sense. In "Farewell to Friends" ("Proshchanie s druz'iami") from 1952, for example, Zabolotsky offers a poignant reminiscence of his friends Daniil Kharms and Alexander Vvedenskii, who had been dead for many years. There are few markers to set the context, and Kharms and Vvedenskii remain unnamed. The poem can easily be read in terms of more generalized human experience, giving credence to Lidiia Ginzburg's paradoxical description of lyric poetry as "the most subjective genre," which, "more than any other, moves toward commonality, toward the depiction of spiritual life as a generalized phenomenon."[5] Or, to take another example, "Morning Song" ("Utrenniaia pesnia") from 1932 mentions the antics of the poet's young son Nikitushka and is clearly based on a family outing on a summer morning in the countryside. In similar fashion, the late poem "The Flight into Egypt" ("Begstvo v Egipet") reflects the poet's own experience of illness and delirium. Yet in each case, a reader with no knowledge of the poet's life could achieve a fully functional reading of the poems.

Still more common in Zabolotsky's works are what might be called his "autophilosophical" poems. Modeled on the term "autopsychological" invented by Lidiia Ginzburg to describe the psychologically self-reflexive thrust of Tolstoy's prose, the term "autophilosophical" refers to the self-reflexive philosophical quality of whole segments of Zabolotsky's oeuvre. In particular, it refers to the constant reexamination of the concepts of immortality and transfiguration that run through Zabolotsky's poetry and correspondence from the beginning to the end of his career, and that crop up as well in the writing of others about conversations with Zabolotsky.[6] It is significant that the only piece of autobiographical writing available to us, Zabolotsky's "Early Years," focuses in notable measure on the poet's experience as a young boy whose life was steeped in the traditions of Russian Orthodoxy, and that Russian Orthodox theology is particularly concerned with the achievement of immortality through the deification and transfiguration of the material world. The autophilosophical element begins here.

Before we get to the underlying concerns of "The Early Years," though, we need to return to the context of Zabolotsky's attempts at reconciliation with Soviet reality. His repeated assertions in letters and elsewhere that his worldview had been shaped by the thought of Friedrich Engels, the utterly proper tenor of his official autobiographical blurbs, and his continuing attempts to write officially acceptable poetry all suggest a poet traumatized by a term in camp, removed from any deep or original sense of poetic or personal self, and a person fully and fearfully engaged in creating the myth of Soviet culture.[7] He comes across as a man unwilling to think beyond the confines of a system that has engulfed the very essence of his being. It is hardly surprising, then, that Zabolotsky's intense involvement with the Russian avant-garde during the twenties flickers briefly across the screen of literary history and disappears. Time and time again, contradictory elements in the poet's oeuvre and personality fade almost instantaneously into the background in official Soviet assessments.

The politically enhanced image that remains after this treatment is the equivalent of the airbrushed portraits sprinkled through Soviet reference books and inserted into various editions of Zabolotsky's works. The photographs in the *Short Literary Encyclopedia* (*Kratkaia literaturnaia entsiklopediia*) and in the 1972 edition of Zabolotsky's poetry, for example, show the "Soviet poet" staring impassively into the camera, somehow managing to look uncomfortable and pompous at the same time, a stuffed shirt par excellence.[8]

And yet one must also consider other images. There is Zabolotsky's angst-ridden, protocubist self-portrait from 1925, drawn when the young poet was much taken with the work of Pavel Filonov. There is the caricature by Malakhovsky from the thirties in which the bespectacled poet, gazing heavenward, sits astride a puzzled-looking cow (who is endowed with both an udder and horns), and sings of the triumph of agriculture. And there is a photograph taken not long before the poet's death, in which the erstwhile stuffed shirt, now apparently wearing striped pajamas, leans out a window with a subdued yet impish expression on his face and shows off his balding head draped with wilted daisies; and yet another photo in which he wears the same striped top and the same mischievous expression while making a rude gesture with his right hand.[9]

In similar fashion, a close examination of Zabolotsky's writings yields a cumulative image far more complex than the politically and intellectually sanitized "Soviet poet" of the official biographical statements. As he portrays himself through both officially published poetry and works not for publication, including letters and occasional verse, Zabolotsky emerges as a person with more worries and more whimsy, and above all, a person of greater spiritual and intellectual depth than we are usually led to expect. Like the "Soviet poet" Zabolotsky, Soviet culture can be represented by a complex amalgam of images: the official and rigid ones that we so often took for reality, as well as the more creative, occasionally sillier, and inevitably deeper ones that fractured the rigid surface and yielded a fuller and more genuine portrait of reality. Likewise, it can be argued that Zabolotsky's identity functions as a cultural paradigm of the Soviet era, and that the underlying complexity of his personality represents the very forces that split the Soviet mold.

The broad outlines of Zabolotsky's experience make him an emblematic character for his era. His life mirrors the fortunes of many writers who, of necessity, sought an identity that encompassed the intoxication of the early years of the Soviet state, the grim experience of repression and camp, and, if they were lucky, the glimmering hope of the Thaw. In terms of age and social class, Zabolotsky represented the new, rather spottily educated, distinctly Soviet intelligentsia culled from rural and proletarian youth in the twenties—people like the writer Andrei Platonov who set out on their professional paths under Soviet rule.[10] For this group, the revolution per se was rarely an issue. They were less than twenty years old when it occurred. Many, including Zabolotsky and Platonov, worked for local offices of the newborn Soviet bureaucracy with varying degrees of ideological involvement.[11] They also shared certain tasks with an older generation of poets that included Pasternak, Mandelstam, and Akhmatova, among others. All of these figures, irrespective of age, faced the problem of how to be writers in an era when old definitions of being a writer no longer applied, new definitions came into existence by means of a tortuous and occasionally lethal process, and few actually knew what the current definition might be.

On a more abstract level, Zabolotsky's intellectual universe can be seen as a reflection of the ideological mélange from which Soviet culture was formed and into which it decomposed. The poet's forward-looking qualities partake of utopian currents from the work of the Futurists and the art of the avant-garde; positivist elements from the thought of Engels and the heterogeneous phenomena of Russian Marxism; and aspects of the utopian thought of Konstantin Tsiolkovsky and Nikolai Fedorov, as well as traces of what might be called "biological philosophy" from the work of Vladimir Vernadsky.[12] But for Zabolotsky, as for Soviet culture in general, ways of thinking and ways of looking at the world were still very often built upon a bedrock of Russian Orthodoxy, even if the bedrock was covered by layers of progressive ideology. Religion per se may have been overcome by the Soviet dogma of "militant atheism," but religious holidays were often recycled in a secular guise, Bolshevik holiday street processions bore a striking resemblance to the outdoor processions of the Orthodox church, and Bolshevik and Orthodox hagiography celebrated many of the same characteristics in the individuals portrayed as "saints."[13] In this context, one could simultaneously agree and disagree with the historian cited in the introduction to this volume, who believes that "memoirs are especially valuable because our history is so poorly documented."[14] In the case of "The Early Years," it is not the historical particulars that are so valuable, but rather the overall pattern that documents the hidden, but powerful dynamism of the continuity of culture.

As in many of Zabolotsky's poems, the moving force in "The Early Years" comes from intellectual and emotional tension, a tightly wound spring of linked but opposing ideas and feelings. On the one hand, the poet attempts to recapture the political unself-consciousness of his ten-year-old self as he portrays his prerevolutionary childhood. Similar to Aksakov's "bright distant past, one that perhaps never existed and cannot be regained, but one in which the secure emotional circle of the family seemed a sure bulwark," Zabolotsky's past is anchored not so much by the family, as by the wonder and solace of nature and Russian Orthodoxy.[15] At the same time, however, the aging author can in no way escape the grim postrevolutionary reality that holds his consciousness in a death grip, a grip so brutal that he kept several pairs of boots and a field coat in the vestibule of his Moscow apartment well into the 1950s just in case the KGB came by to cart him off to camp again.[16] It is Zabolotsky's attempt, and ultimately the reader's attempt, to achieve equilibrium between these two forces that makes the essay so compelling.

The political consciousness of the older Zabolotsky was inevitably informed by the generic Soviet myth to which he earnestly sought to contribute at various times in his life, yet wittingly or unwittingly undercut with considerable regularity.[17] A particular version of this myth tends to occur in coming-of-age stories, whether the stories are presented as fiction or non-fiction, autobiography or third-person narrative, and it would be reasonable to expect "The Early Years" to fit loosely into the established paradigm. Take, for example, the proto-Soviet coming-of-age story in Gorky's *Mother* (*Mat'*), the early Soviet coming-of-age story in the introductory essay in Andrei Platonov's *Blue Depths* (*Golubaia glubina*), or the Stalinist version in Ostrovsky's *How the Steel Was Tempered* (*Kak zakalialas' stal'*). In very rough form, the morphology of the Soviet coming-of-age myth for boys involves an impoverished childhood; an oppressed and oppressive father, often dead, physically absent, or consumed by drunkenness by the time the main narrative begins; a heroic, if politically naive, mother; tyrannical and deceitful parish priests, teachers, and government officials; and a teacher or mentor whose revolutionary consciousness transforms the protagonist's view of the world. The boy has a hard time in school or is expelled from school because his probing mind causes him to question dogma and his natural empathy causes him to question the inequities of the social structure. He comes to recognize the oppressive nature of the old regime and religion, begins to rebel, emerges from the constrained world of his family and immediate surroundings, and with the help of his mentor, comes to understand the larger revolutionary meaning in his own life.

This paradigm obviously has much in common with the master plot of the socialist realist novel explicated by Katerina Clark in *The Soviet Novel: History as Ritual*.[18] But instead of (or in addition to) arriving physically in the "microcosm," as Clark calls the small, fairly closed world of the novel, the hero of the coming-of-age story arrives mentally: he grows up enough to perceive the problems of the microcosm, and then proceeds through the trials that ultimately lead to political and personal triumph. The boy who comes of age often embodies Clark's "spontaneity-consciousness dialectic" as well, the dialectic representing a zigzagging path toward maturity in which the personal and political are fused. In the context of such a well-established pattern, deviations from the norm carry considerable weight. What the author chooses to omit or place in a less prominent role is just as important as what the author chooses to include.

Perhaps predictably, Zabolotsky's memoir both reinforces the Soviet myth and undercuts it. In the most general terms, "The Early Years" presents the tale of Zabolotsky's impoverished childhood in the countryside outside of Kazan in a family he describes as "somewhere halfway between the peasantry and the intelligentsia of the times."[19] Zabolotsky's mother is presented to us as a vague figure, possibly from a clerical family given her maiden name of D'iakonova (*d'iakon* meaning "deacon"). She is neither as oppressed nor as politically committed as Vlasova in Gorky's *Mother,* but her role as a morally alert woman beaten down by physical and spiritual hardship runs parallel to Vlasova's if one allows for a slightly higher educational and economic level.[20] As he describes his mother in "The Early Years," Zabolotsky demonstrates both his respect for the revolutionary movement and his lack of overwhelming enthusiasm for it. The possibility of a commitment to the revolution, of engagement with the world beyond the village and the surrounding countryside, serves Zabolotsky as a counterpoint to the senselessness of the narrow life to which his mother felt herself condemned:

> Buried by domestic cares, my mother aged before her time and languished out in the desolate countryside. Once joyful and fun loving, she eventually realized that she was trapped in an unsuccessful marriage and put all her pent-up energy into blind love for her children. She sensed that a genuine, vital

form of life was going on somewhere far away from her, and that she was doomed to die a slow spiritual death. She proudly told us that there were people in the world who wished poor people well and would fight for them, but who were harassed and persecuted for their efforts; and that her sister, Aunt Milia, had been in prison for illegal activities.[21]

Continuing his thought about the revolution and the potentially larger meaning of life, Zabolotsky shifts his focus to another relative who had served time in prison for revolutionary acts.

[O]ne of my father's nephews had also been in prison, a student known in our family by the nickname "Big Kolya," while I was known as "Little Kolya." Big Kolya used to visit us, always with the same old guitar, and he gathered a whole crowd of local young people around him. It was great the way he sang student songs we didn't know, and with his fun-loving demeanor he didn't resemble a political zealot who had suffered on behalf of the people at all.[22]

The young Zabolotsky clearly respects "Big Kolya" and "Aunt Milia" for their suffering and their revolutionary ardor. The main point of the passage, however, is not the revolution per se, but his mother's sense of being trapped by the narrowness of her circumstances and his own sense of the incongruity between Big Kolya's past suffering and present gaiety. It is this personal focus coupled with the productive friction between the perceptions of the boy living that life and the worldly wise author looking back on it that motivate the passage and drive it forward. The larger political meaning, although present, is muted.

In more general terms, Zabolotsky conveys a genuine concern for the appalling poverty and injustice of life in the Russian countryside in which he grew up, and he implicitly acknowledges the limited effectiveness of prerevolutionary religious and educational establishments in addressing human needs. It is easy to assume the author believes that such needs should be met more fully, and perhaps to assume a prorevolutionary undercurrent in the essay. Because the memoirs stop with the year 1914, however, the issue of the revolution need not be met head-on, and in any case, Zabolotsky does not herald the impending revolution with a fanfare of trumpets and drums.

Zabolotsky's father, an agronomist, stands out more clearly than his mother in "The Early Years." Indeed, he is a pronounced presence—not at all the dead or missing father of the standard Soviet coming-of-age story. The name "Aleksei Agafonovich Zabolotsky" marks the father as a figure close to the peasantry, "Agafon" being a name used almost solely among peasants by the late nineteenth century. Moreover, the name "Zabolotsky" proved so redolent of the backwater in its denotation of a clan living "beyond the swamp" (*za bolotom*) that the young poet changed the spelling apparently in a futile attempt to lessen its suggestion of an unregenerate country hick.[23] The aging author of the memoirs states with some pride that Aleksei Agafonovich was the first of the Zabolotskys to do "intellectual work." This means that Aleksei Agafonovich studied at the Kazan School of Agriculture and worked in the fields as an agronomist. He was "not so much a theoretician," writes the son, "as a confirmed pragmatist, [who] worked with the peasants for something like forty years."[24]

Aleksei Agafonovich seems to have been occasionally oppressed by economic conditions and was not always able to find work suitable for a graduate of the Kazan School of Agriculture, but he also did rather well much of the time. He apparently did a great deal to improve the cultivation of clover, rye, and flax in his region, and achieved some fame for successfully soliciting a contribution from the singer Fedor Chaliapin, also a product of the Urzhum district, when money was needed to support soup kitchens during a period of poor harvests.[25] One senses from the son's narrative that the elder Zabolotsky was, perhaps, oppressive but nonetheless respected within the family, and that if he drank, it was not to a degree that prevented him from earning a reasonable living much of the time. The introductory description of the father's demeanor is telling:

> My father bore many traits of the ancient patriarchal system (*starozavetnoi patriarkhal'nosti*), which in some strange manner coexisted with his reverence for scientific knowledge and his struggle against the agricultural indolence of the peasants. Tall, handsome, with nice dark hair, he wore his reddish beard in two wedges, dressed in an old style Russian coat and Russian boots, was moderately religious, respected learning, and preferred not to meddle in the larger matters of this world, devoting his life to the work that directly concerned him and to the needs of his large family.[26]

What is interesting here is the complexity of the father in relation to the political and ideological axes of the standard Soviet coming-of-age story. He is clearly peasantlike, which could be either good or bad depending on his circumstances and political outlook. He believes in science and struggles against agricultural indolence, which is good. He is moderately religious, which is bad to the degree that any religious belief is bad, but good in the sense that it is not a blind, all-consuming religiosity that precludes belief in science. Within his own family, he is perceived as neither an evil oppressor nor the victim of oppression by the authorities. He fits no particular paradigm, but comes across simply as a man "halfway between the peasantry and the intelligentsia of the times" doing his best within the confines of life's vicissitudes.

The most unusual aspect of "The Early Years"—and the point at which the erstwhile stuffed shirt becomes most obviously unstuffed—has to do with religion. The poet makes neither a statement of belief nor a statement of nonbelief, the latter being an absence that reeks of ideological heresy in the Stalinist context. Rather, in a highly extraordinary act, this "Soviet poet" writes about his religious upbringing at some length with a tone that comes across as "objective" and with a dynamism suggesting that religion played a significant role during these formative years. Even after the lessons of his term in camp, Zabolotsky neither forgot his religious training, nor did he edit it out of his memoirs for the sake of political expedience.

Here again, he diverges from the more standard Soviet coming-of-age story. Both Platonov and Ostrovsky portray religious education as irrelevant at best, evil at worst, and always oppressive. *How the Steel Was Tempered* opens as the hero is berated by a bad-tempered priest. The priest is presented to the reader not simply as "a priest," a term that might acknowledge some sense of a religious calling, but as "a corpulent man *in the garb of a priest,* with a heavy cross dangling from his neck," with "small, hard eyes" and a "baleful glare" (emphasis added). When Pavel questions the biblical story of the creation on the basis of something another teacher has told him, the "damned priest" (as Pavel later describes him) seizes him by the ears, bangs his head against the wall, and throws him out of class—inadvertently setting Pavel on the path to revolutionary heroism. Platonov's memoir makes a similar, though less dramatic case against religion. As portrayed by Ostrovsky and Platonov, the main good of parish school is that it could inculcate the first inklings of revolutionary consciousness.[27]

In "The Early Years," those responsible for the young Zabolotsky's religious training are hardly portrayed as inspiring models of saintly presence. Father Sergius in the parish school in the village of Sernur, where Zabolotsky spent most of his childhood, is remembered especially for his penchant for making unruly pupils kneel on dried peas in the corner, and Father Mikhail in the Realschule attended by Zabolotsky in Urzhum is described as "an incredible loser" who "didn't count for anything."[28] At the same time, however, both priests contributed to an environment that allowed the boy to hone the spiritual tools and foster the intuitions that would serve him again and again later on.

If, as Zabolotsky reports, his father "had many of the characteristics of the old patriarchal system" and was "moderately religious," the family most likely said daily prayers and attended church with some regularity.[29] Moreover, the boy undoubtedly studied religion (*Zakon Bozhii*) both in the parish school in Sernur and at the Realschule in Urzhum. He remembers not only passing the Realschule entrance examination in religion but, more than forty years later, he still remembers the short religious service with which every school day began: the auditorium with the huge gold-framed portrait of the tsar in his robes; the choir standing in front of the pupils on the left; the singing of the prayer "O Heavenly King" ("Tsariu nebesnyi") by "some baby first-year student" (*mladenets-novichok*); the priest, Father Mikhail, with his bad gums and quavering tenor voice reciting the daily chapter from the Gospels; and the closing singing of "God Save the Tsar." "After that," he reports, "we all ran off to our classrooms with a huge sense of relief."[30] In addition, Zabolotsky reminisces about obligatory attendance at both morning and evening services on Saturdays and Sundays, and serving as an altar boy in the cathedral. This latter assignment involved not only lighting and putting out candles, but also, much to the delight of the participants, taking gulps of communion wine on the sly and carrying notes between the boys from the Realschule and the girls from the local girls' gymnasium.[31]

Although the point of some of these passages is the author's amusement that religious experiences were undercut by pranks or subverted by the quavering tenor voice of the priest with bad gums, the fact that religious experiences are so clearly remembered, portrayed in such detail, and make up such a significant portion of the text should not be overlooked. Still more important is the fact that the two points of greatest emotional intensity in "The Early Years" are events associated with religious ceremonies. The first grows out of a description of a cold winter and the poverty of the local population during the poet's childhood in Sernur. Zabolotsky evokes the memory of his schoolmate Vania Mamaev, who came from a poor family and was given the honor of accompanying a wonder-working icon in the holy procession around the village.

> One winter, during a terrible cold spell, a wonder-working icon was brought to our village, and my friend, the Mari boy Vania Mamaev, walked with the monks from house to house from morning until night in his threadbare clothes, carrying a church lantern on a long pole. The poor fellow nearly froze to death, he was exhausted, and he received a lacquered picture of Nicholas the Wonder-worker as a reward. His luck made me absolutely green with envy (*Ia zavidoval ego schast'iu samoi chernoi zavist'iu*).[32]

The older Zabolotsky may be interjecting a touch of self-irony into this episode since, on the surface at any rate, it seems rather silly to envy someone who froze half to death and received only a lacquered picture in return. Yet the picture was of Saint Nicholas, quite possibly young Nikolai Zabolotsky's patron saint, and it is clear that the younger Zabolotsky regarded the incident with utter seriousness.

Perhaps the most profound expression of any boyhood experience comes in Zabolotsky's description of the vespers service. Here again, the older memoirist may impute a certain naïveté to the young boy's faith, but the passage is marked more by sweet nostalgia for that young self than by any potential for self-irony:

> [T]he quiet vespers service in the half-dark church glimmering with candles inclined one involuntarily to pensiveness and a feeling of sweet sorrow. The choir was excellent, and when the treble voices sang "Glory to God in the

highest" ("Slava v vyshnikh Bogu") or "O gentle light" ("Svete tikhii") my throat tightened and I, in my childlike way, believed in something lofty and merciful that soared high above us and would surely help me achieve true human happiness.[33]

Other future Soviet writers certainly attended similar Orthodox vespers services, and they may even have had the same reaction to the ceremony, but nowhere in any widely known Soviet coming-of-age story is there any such sense of religious hope and joy.

"The Early Years" runs only to the beginning of the First World War. There is, understandably, no written discussion of Zabolotsky's religious experience during the postrevolutionary period, but we do know that some aspects of the Orthodox tradition remained alive in his memory. In a letter to a boyhood friend written from Petrograd in 1921, for example, he mentions fond memories of Christmas at home:

> Today I remembered my early childhood. The Christmas tree, Christmas. The stove radiating heat. Steam seeping out through its doors. Some little boys come to the door with frost on their clothes. "Can we sing you some Christmas carols?"
>
> I lay on my bed and sang to myself, "Your Birth, O Christ Our God" ("Rozhdestvo Tvoe Khriste Bozhe Nash").
>
> A bunch of girls were standing outside my door and they started to laugh.[34]

Zabolotsky then closes the letter with the suggestion that his friend visit him "for Christmas" (na Rozhdestvo), even though Christmas had in theory been abolished several years earlier.

A roommate of the young poet reports another incident a few years later, when a spontaneous songfest among friends included not only the predictable "Evening Bells" ("Vechernii zvon") and "Down Along the Mother Volga" ("Vniz po matushke, po Volge"), but also the hymns "Praise the Name of the Lord" ("Khvalite imia Gospodne"), "The Bridegroom Cometh" ("Se zhenikh"), and "Thy Mansion" ("Chertog Tvoi"). While the roommate pointedly disclaims any religious inclinations on the part of the impromptu choristers, he nonetheless adds that the hymns were sung especially well.[35] In light of all this, it is not particularly surprising that a Bible was one of the books confiscated when the poet was arrested in 1938, or that even in the 1950s Zabolotsky turned to an aspect of the nativity theme in the poem mentioned earlier entitled "The Flight into Egypt" ("Begstvo v Egipet").[36] In keeping with most of Zabolotsky's work from this period, the poem portrays the experience of everyday life, but unlike the rest, it has an added layer of overtly religious meaning. The poet here imagines himself both as the Christ Child, whose family must flee into Egypt to save him, and as an aging man suffering through the "everyday life" experience of illness, nursed by someone he calls his "guardian angel" (angel khranitel').

Even though the poem overall is a "realistic" narration rather than a prayer, the opening words of the poem, "Angel, dnei moikh khranitel'" ("[An] angel, the guardian of my days"), suggest a truncated, modernized version of the opening of the Russian Orthodox prayer to one's guardian angel, "Angele Khristov, khraniteliu moi sviatyi, i pokroviteliu dushi i tela moego" ("Angel of Christ, my holy guardian and protector of my soul and body").[37] And finally, at the time of his death, Zabolotsky was working on a trilogy entitled "The Adoration of the Magi" ("Poklonenie volkhvov").[38] The sheet of paper left on his desk showed the beginning of a plan:

1. Shepherds, animals, angels.
2. ————————————————

The second point remained blank. Clearly, the significance of the religious training of Zabolotsky's early years—indeed, the pivotal experiences we see in "The Early Years"—had not been lost even during the stormy events of the intervening period. Neither his intense involvement with the rebellious avant-garde, nor the brutal experience of critical attacks, camp, and exile could dim this formative force. Although the extent of Zabolotsky's Orthodox belief remains open to question, the poet clearly retained a large measure of his childlike faith in *faith*, faith in "something lofty and merciful" that would help one achieve "true human happiness."

In the end, it is neither insignificant nor surprising that religious experience plays such a key role in "The Early Years." Nor is it insignificant or surprising that the last Russian tsar has now been put to rest with an Orthodox funeral attended by the most powerful political figures of the Russian state. Zabolotsky was indeed a "Soviet" poet, just as the Russian state was indeed a "Soviet" entity. An overlay of Marxism, "political correctness," and existence as a stuffed shirt, persevered in Zabolotsky's life—and the life of the Russian state—for a time, but it was just an overlay, a veneer. Zabolotsky's "Early Years" are a memoir of the childhood experiences of one person, but more than that, they are an argument for the continuity of culture in the development of both individual and collective identity.

Notes

1. See Andrei Turkov, "Nikolai Zabolotskii," in Nikolai Zabolotskii, *Stikhotvoreniia i poemy* (Moscow-Leningrad: Sovetskii pisatel', 1965), 5–58, and *Nikolai Zabolotskii* (Moscow: Khudozhestvennaia literatura, 1966); A. M. Makedonov, *Nikolai Zabolotskii. Zhizn', tvorchestvo, metamorfozy* (Leningrad: Sovetskii pisatel, 1968; expanded version, 1987); Darra Goldstein, *Nikolai Zabolotsky. Play for Mortal Stakes* (Cambridge: Cambridge University Press, 1993); Nikita Zabolotsky, *The Life of Zabolotsky*, ed. R. R.

Milner-Gulland (Cardiff: University of Wales Press, 1994) and *Zhizn'*
Zabolotskogo (Moscow: Soglasie, 1998); Nikolai Zabolotskii, *Ogon', mer-*
tsaiushchii v sosude, ed. Nikita Zabolotskii (Moscow: Pedagogika-Press, 1995).

2. "The Creators of Roads" is arguably the most subversive piece in
Zabolotsky's repertoire. It is based on the poet's experience in camp and
the "heroes" of Soviet labor he portrays are actually convict laborers. The
poem's apparent vision of Soviet reality was so appealing to the political-
literary establishment, however, that the second canto was made into the
libretto for a cantata entitled "The Builders of the Future" ("Stroiteli
griadushchego"). The subversion was not a conscious or purposeful act of
political dissent. Zabolotsky needed to produce a work that was politically
acceptable for the sake of his rehabilitation as a Soviet poet and, according
to all the available evidence, intended to do so. Nikolai Zabolotskii, *Izbran-*
nye proizvedeniia v dvukh tomakh, vol. 1 (Moscow: Khudozhestvennaia literatura, 1972), 387–88, hereafter cited as *Izbrannye.* For further discussion
of "The Creators of Roads," see Sarah Pratt, *Nikolai Zabolotsky: Enigma and*
Cultural Paradigm (Evanston, Ill.: Northwestern University Press, 2000).
See also Kevin Platt, "Nikolai Zabolotsky on the Pages of *Izvestiia:* Towards
a Biography of the Years 1934–1937," in *70 let OBERIU,* ed. Andrey Ustinov (Berkeley: Berkeley Slavic Specialties, 1998). For a detailed discussion
of Zabolotsky's arrest and experience in camp, see Goldstein, *Nikolai*
Zabolotsky, 86–98; Nikolai Zabolotsky, "The Story of My Imprisonment,"
trans. Robin Milner-Gulland, *The Times Literary Supplement* (October 9,
1981), 1179–81; Sil'va Gitovich, "Arest N. A. Zabolotskogo," *Pamiat'* (Paris,
1982), 336–53.

3. Ibid. 269–90.

4. Zabolotskii, *Izbrannye* 2: 227.

5. Lidiia Ginzburg, *O lirike* (Leningrad: Sovetskii pisatel', 1974), 8.

6. See, for example, Nikolai Chukovskii's description of evenings
spent with the poet: "He would get drunk slowly, becoming jollier and jollier. Then he would begin to frown and with growing urgency repeat that
we would not die, but simply be transformed," Nikolai Chukovskii, "Vstrechi s Zabolotskom," in *Vospominaniia o Zabolotskom,* ed. E. V. Zabolotskaia
and A. V. Makedonov (Moscow: Sovetskii pisatel', 1977; expanded edition
with N. N. Zabolotskii 1984), 218–33. All references are from the 1977 edition unless otherwise noted. Among Zabolotsky's autophilosophical poems
on immortality are the following: "Na lestnitskakh" (originally entitled "Bess-
mertie"); "Utreniaia pesnia;" "Pekarnia;" "Metamorfozy;" "Zaveshchanie;"
"Vchera, o smerti razmyshliaia;" "Lodeinikov;" and "Vecher na Oke."

7. See Nikita Zabolotskii, "K tvorcheskoi biografii Nikolaia Zabolotskogo," *Voprosy literatury* 11 (1979): 223.

8. *Kratkaia literaturnaia entsiklopediia,* vol. 2 (Moscow: Sovetskaia
entsiklopediia, 1964), 967; Zabolotskii, *Izbrannye,* frontispiece. See also

Nikita Zabolotskii, *Zhizn' N. A. Zabolotskogo*, photographs labeled Leningrad 1929, prefigured by Urzhum 1913 and Petrograd 1921, all in the section following page 80; and photographs labeled Leningrad 1932 and September 1953 in the section following page 400.

9. *Ogon' mertsaiushchii v sosude*. The self-portrait is reproduced immediately preceding page 321; the caricature is in the section following page 192; the picture with the daisies is in the section following page 320. In Nikita Zabolotsky, *Zhizn' N. A. Zabolotskogo*, the self-portrait is reproduced following page 80, and the caricature, picture with the daisies, and the rude gesture following page 400.

10. See Thomas Seifrid, *Andrei Platonov: Uncertainties of Spirit* (Cambridge: Cambridge University Press, 1992); Ayleen Teskey, *Platonov and Fyodorov: The Influence of Christian Philosophy on a Soviet Writer* (England [sic]: Avebury, 1982); M.Iu. [initials only], "Predislovie" in A. Platonov, *Golubaia glubina. Kniga stikhov* (Krasnodar: Burevestnik, 1922); S. G. Bocharov, "'Veshchestvo sushchestvovaniia.' Vyrazhenie v proze," in *Problema khudozhestvennoi formy sotsialisticheskogo realizma*, vol. 2, ed. N. K. Gei et al. (Moscow: Nauka, 1971), 310–50. I am indebted to Thomas Seifrid for providing me with a copy of the foreword to *Golubaia glubina* and for sharing his considerable knowledge of Platonov. On issues related to the new Soviet intelligentsia, see Sheila Fitzpatrick, *The Cultural Front: Power and Culture in Revolutionary Russia* (Ithaca: Cornell University Press, 1992) and *Cultural Revolution in Russia, 1928–1931* (Bloomington: Indiana University Press, 1978); Fitzpatrick, "The Problem of Class Identity in NEP Society," and Katerina Clark, "The 'Quiet Revolution' in Soviet Intellectual Life," in Fitzpatrick et al., *Russia in the Era of NEP: Explorations in Soviet Society and Culture* (Bloomington: Indiana University Press, 1991).

11. Zabolotsky's boyhood friend Mikhail Kas'ianov reports that in 1919 Zabolotsky worked in "some kind of Soviet office" and was even evacuated along with the office from Urzhum to the village of Kichma with the approach of Kolchak. M. Kas'ianov, "O iunosti poeta," in Zabolotskaia, *Vospominaniia o Zabolotskom* (1984), 33. In an article entitled "Detskie i iunosheskie gody poeta" in the same volume L. D'iakonov, a relative of Zabolotsky's wife, writes, "During the first years after the revolution, Zabolotskii became close to Viatsk area Komsomol members. In one of his letters . . . he writes about the Viatsk Komsomol poet Shchelkanov (Aleksandr Rabochii) as a good friend" (30). On Platonov, see Seifrid, *Andrei Platonov*, 4–6. In addition to the obvious differences between Platonov the prosaist and Zabolotsky the poet, one might note that Platonov, who grew up near the railroad yards of Voronezh and loved machines, was closer to the proletariat than Zabolotsky, the "half-peasant" and provincial *intelligent*. In addition, Platonov was more often than not practically and politically engaged, using his skills as a journalist and land reclamation engineer to further the

cause of the Soviet state. Zabolotsky may have seemed at times to be politically engaged, but the engagement, such as it was, was always tempered by his paramount concern for his identity as a poet.

12. See Goldstein, *Nikolai Zabolotsky,* especially chapters 2 and 3.

13. Richard Stites, *Revolutionary Dreams. Utopian Vision and Experimental Life in the Russian Revolution,* part 2, chapters 4, 5 (New York: Oxford University Press, 1989), especially 61, 109–14. Vladimir Tolstoy, Irina Bibikova, and Catherine Cooke, *Street Art of the Revolution: Festivals and Celebrations in Russia 1918–33* (New York: Vendome Press, 1993). Szymon Bojko, "Agit-Prop Art: The Streets Were Their Theater," in *The Avant-Garde in Russia 1910–1930: New Perspectives,* ed. Stephanie Barron and Maurice Tuchman, Catalogue, Los Angeles County Museum of Art (Cambridge, Mass.: M.I.T. Press, 1980), 72–77. Katerina Clark, *The Soviet Novel: History as Ritual* (Chicago: University of Chicago Press, 1981), 4–5, 47–67, 151–52, 181–82.

15. Cited from the introduction to this volume (xiv). I. N. Danilevskii, V. V. Kabanov, O. M. Medushevskaia, M. F. Rumiantseva, eds. *Istochnikovedenie. Teoriia. Istoriia. Metod. Istochniki rossiiskoi istorii* (Moscow: Rossiiskii Gosudarstvennyi Gumanitarnyi Universitet, 1998), 636.

14. Cited from the introduction to this volume (xix). Andrew R. Durkin, *Sergei Aksakov and the Russian Pastoral* (New Brunswick, N.J.: Rutgers University Press, 1983), 45

16. Nikita Zabolotskii, "Kratkie vospominaniia ob ottse i o nashei zhizni," in Zabolotskaia, *Vospominaniia o Zabolotskom,* 188. Goldstein reports that Zabolotsky would have been detained in 1948 had Nikolai Stepanov not managed to hide him. Goldstein, *Nikolai Zabolotsky,* 104.

17. See Pratt, *Nikolai Zabolotsky,* especially chapter 6, "Orthodoxies and Subversions in the Quest for Immortality."

18. Clark, *The Soviet Novel.*

19. Zabolotskii, *Izbrannye* 2: 208.

20. Ibid., 208, 222; Vasin, "Russkii poet mariiskogo kraia," 138.

21. Zabolotskii, *Izbrannye,* 2: 222.

22. Ibid.

23. The spelling change, which does not come across in transliteration, involves the substitution of the single Cyrillic letter "ts" for the separate "t" and "s" that divide the name more clearly into the separate morphemes *za* (beyond) + *boloto* (swamp) + *skii* (masculine ending). This change has no effect at all on the pronunciation of the name and, in the end, seems virtually pointless. Indeed, a certain A. Amsterdam makes precisely the pun the poet sought to avoid, as he attacks Zabolotsky's *Columns* in an article with the title, "Bolotnoe i Zabolotskii," which might be translated "That Which is Swampy and Zabolotsky" or "That Which is Swampy and Beyond-the-Swamp-skii" in *Rezets* 4 (1930).

24. Zabolotskii, *Izbrannye* 2: 208.

25. Vasin, "Russkii poet mariiskogo kraia," 137, 138.

26. Zabolotskii, *Izbrannye* 2: 208.

27. See the excerpt from Platonov's autobiography in the foreword to *Golubaia glubina*, p. vi; Seifrid, *Andrei Platonov*; and the opening pages in Nikolai Ostrovskii, *Sobranie sochinenii v trekh tomakh* (Moscow: Molodaia gvardiia, 1984) or Nikolai Ostrovsky, *How the Steel Was Tempered* (Moscow: Progress Publishers, 1973).

28. Zabolotskii, *Izbrannye* 2: 210, 216. On the generally low quality of the provincial clergy in the early twentieth century, see the introduction and chapter 10 in Gregory L. Freeze, *The Parish Clergy in Nineteenth Century Russia* (Princeton: Princeton University Press, 1983).

29. Zabolotskii, *Izbrannye* 2: 208.

30. Ibid., 210, 213.

31. Ibid., 220.

32. Ibid., 210.

33. Ibid., 220.

34. Zabolotsky, letter to Kas'ianov, November 11, 1921, ibid., 228.

35. N. Sboev, "Mansarda na Petrogradskoi (Zabolotskii v 1925–1926 godakh)" in Zabolotskaia, *Vospominaniia o Zabolotskom*, 43–44.

36. Zabolotsky, *The Life of Zabolotsky*, 138–39, 169.

37. Zabolotskii, *Izbrannye* 1: 287. *Bozhestvennaia liturgiia Sv. Ioanna Zlatoustago* (New York: Russian Theological Seminary of North America, 1960), 286–87.

38. Nikita Zabolotskii, "Kratkie vospominaniia ob ottse i o nashei zhizni," p. 205. Zabolotskii, *Izbrannye* 2: 295.

Works Cited

Bocharov, S. G. " 'Veshchestvo sushchestvovaniia.' Vyrazhenie v proze." In vol. 2, *Problema khudozhestvennoi formy sotsialisticheskogo realizma*, edited by N. K. Gei et al. Moscow: Nauka, 1971, 310–50.

Bojko, Szymon. "Agit-Prop Art: The Streets Were Their Theater." In *The Avant-Garde in Russia 1910–1930: New Perspectives*, edited by Stephanie Barron and Maurice Tuchman. Catalogue, Los Angeles County Museum of Art. Cambridge, Mass.: M.I.T. Press, 1980, 72–77.

Bozhestvennaia liturgiia Sv. Ioanna Zlatoustago. New York: Russian Theological Seminary of North America, 1960.

Chukovskii, Nikolai. "Vstrechi s Zabolotskom." In *Vospominaniia o Zabolotskom*, edited by E. V. Zabolotskaia and A. V. Makedonov. Moscow: Sovetskii pisatel', 1977, 218–33.

Clark, Katerina. *The Soviet Novel: History as Ritual.* Chicago: University of Chicago Press, 1981.

———. "The 'Quiet Revolution' in Soviet Intellectual Life." In Sheila Fitzpatrick et al., *Russia in the Era of NEP: Explorations in Soviet Society and Culture.* Bloomington: Indiana University Press, 1991.

Danilevskii, I. N., V. V. Kabanov, O. M. Medushevskaia, and M. F. Rumiantseva, eds. *Istochnikovedenie. Teoriia. Istoriia. Metod. Istochniki rossiiskoi istorii.* Moscow: Rossiiskii Gosudarstvennyi Gumanitarnyi Universitet, 1998.

D'iakonov, L. "Detskie i iunosheskie gody poeta." In *Vospominaniia o Zabolotskom,* edited by E. V. Zabolotskaia et al. Moscow: Sovetskii pisatel', 1984.

Durkin, Andrew R. *Sergei Aksakov and the Russian Pastoral.* New Brunswick, N.J.: Rutgers University Press, 1983.

Fitzpatrick, Sheila. *Cultural Revolution in Russia, 1928–1931.* Bloomington: Indiana University Press, 1978.

———. "The Problem of Class Identity in NEP Society," in Fitzpatrick et al., *Russia in the Era of NEP: Explorations in Soviet Society and Culture.* Bloomington: Indiana University Press, 1991.

———. *The Cultural Front: Power and Culture in Revolutionary Russia.* Ithaca: Cornell University Press, 1992.

Freeze, Gregory L. *The Parish Clergy in Nineteenth Century Russia.* Princeton: Princeton University Press, 1983.

Ginzburg, Lidiia. *O lirike.* Leningrad: Sovetskii pisatel', 1974.

Gitovich, Sil'va. "Arest N. A. Zabolotskogo." *Pamiat'.* Paris, 1982, 336–53.

Goldstein, Darra. *Nikolai Zabolotsky. Play for Mortal Stakes.* Cambridge: Cambridge University Press, 1993.

Kas'ianov, M. "O iunosti poeta." In *Vospominaniia o Zabolotskom,* edited by E. V. Zabolotskaia et al. Moscow: Sovetskii pisatel', 1984.

Kratkaia literaturnaia entsiklopediia. Moscow: Sovetskaia entsiklopediia, 1964.

M.Iu. [initials only]. "Predislovie." In A. Platonov, *Golubaia glubina. Kniga stikhov.* Krasnodar: Burevestnik, 1922.

Makedonov, A. M. *Nikolai Zabolotskii. Zhizn', tvorchestvo, metamorfozy.* Leningrad: Sovetskii pisatel', 1968; expanded version, 1987.

Ostrovskii, Nikolai. *Sobranie sochinenii v trekh tomakh.* Moscow: Molodaia gvardiia, 1984.

Ostrovsky, Nikolai. *How the Steel Was Tempered.* Moscow: Progress Publishers, 1973.

Platt, Kevin. "Nikolai Zabolotsky on the Pages of *Izvestiia:* Towards a Biography of the Years 1934–37." In *70 let OBERIU,* edited by Andrey Ustinov. Berkeley: Berkeley Slavic Specialties, 1998.

Pratt, Sarah. *Nikolai Zabolotsky: Enigma and Cultural Paradigm.* Evanston, Ill.: Northwestern University Press, 2000.

Sboev, N. "Mansarda na Petrogradskoi (Zabolotskii v 1925–26 godakh)." In *Vospominaniia o Zabolotskom,* edited by Zabolotskaia and Makedonov. Moscow: Sovetskii pisatel', 1977, 43–44.

Seifrid, Thomas. *Andrei Platonov: Uncertainties of Spirit.* Cambridge: Cambridge University Press, 1992.

Stites, Richard. *Revolutionary Dreams. Utopian Vision and Experimental Life in the Russian Revolution.* New York: Oxford University Press, 1989.

Teskey, Ayleen. *Platonov and Fyodorov: The Influence of Christian Philosophy on a Soviet Writer.* England [sic]: Avebury, 1982.

Tolstoy, Vladimir, Irina Bibikova, and Catherine Cooke. *Street Art of the Revolution: Festivals and Celebrations in Russia 1918–33.* New York: Vendome Press, 1993.

Turkov, Andrei. "Nikolai Zabolotskii" In Nikolai Zabolotskii, *Stikhotvoreniia i poemy.* Moscow-Leningrad: Sovetskii pisatel', 1965, 5–58.

———. *Nikolai Zabolotskii.* Moscow: Khudozhestvennaia literature, 1966.

Zabolotskaia, E. V., and A. V. Makedonov, eds. *Vospominaniia o Zabolotskom.* Moscow: Sovetskii pisatel', 1977; expanded edition with Nikita Zabolotskii, 1984.

Zabolotskii, Nikita. "Kratkie vospominaniia ob ottse i o nashei zhizni." In *Vospominaniia o Zabolotskom,* edited by Zabolotskaia and Makedonov. Moscow: Sovetskii pisatel', 1977.

———. "K tvorcheskoi biografii Nikolaia Zabolotskogo," *Voprosy literatury* 11 (1979), 223.

Zabolotskii, Nikolai. *Izbrannye proizvedeniia v dvukh tomakh.* Moscow: Khudozhestvennaia literature, 1972.

———. "The Story of My Imprisonment." Translated by Robin Milner-Gulland. *The Times Literary Supplement* (October 9, 1981): 1179–81.

———. *Ogon', mertsaiushchii v sosude,* edited by Nikita Zabolotskii. Moscow: Pedagogika Press, 1995.

Zabolotsky, Nikita. *The Life of Zabolotsky,* edited by R. R. Milner-Gulland. Cardiff: University of Wales Press, 1994

Helena Goscilo

The Italics Are Hers: Matrophobia and the Family Romance in Elena Bonner's *Mothers and Daughters*

> Matrophobia can be seen as a womanly splitting of the self, in the desire to become purged once and for all of our mothers' bondage, to become individuated and free. [. . .] Our personalities seem dangerously to blur and envelope with our mothers'; and, in a desperate attempt to know where mother ends and daughter begins, we perform radical surgery.
>
> —Adrienne Rich, *Of Woman Born*

> The thoughts of a daughter are a kind of memorial.
>
> —Enid Bagnold, *The Chalk Garden*

> The maternal function underlies the social order as well as the order of desire, but it is always restricted to the dimension of need.
>
> —Luce Irigaray, "Body Against Body: In Relation to the Mother"

BETWEEN MAMA AND MOMMIE DEAREST

Few cultures have extolled the sanctity of motherhood as doggedly and vociferously as Soviet Russia. Those hosannas, however, have been thoroughly gendered, with specifically *male* impassioned glorification of maternity ranging from Maxim Gorky's stirringly politicized quasi hagiography, *Mother* (*Mat'*, 1907), to numerous bathetic wartime poems, posters, and films troping nationhood as Mother Russia (Aleksandr Tvardovskii, Konstantin Simonov "The Motherland Summons You!"; *She Defends the Motherland*), secularized pictorial reprisals of the iconic Madonna cum Savior (Petrov-Vodkin), and, most recently, musical lyrics by the macho rock group Liube sentimentalizing mother/son bonds.[1] Although contemporary Russian women's prose, apart from Liudmila Petrushevskaia's chilling *Night Time* (*Vremia noch'*, 1992), rarely treads the virulent path of *Mommie Dearest* exposés, it has cast an appreciably more jaundiced and differentiated eye on maternity, problematizing it instead of basking in the cozy rosy glow of the near-beatification beamed by male authors. While the extratextual embrace by daughters such as Julia Latynina, Ekaterina Sadur, and Ekaterina Shcherbakova of their mothers' writerly legacy misleadingly suggests a seamless filial self-identification,[2] the fiction of such prosaists as Nina Katerli, Elena Makarova, Irina Polianskaia, Svetlana Vasilenko, and especially Galina Shcherbakova has unsparingly exposed the warts and wounds of multigenerational female interaction. In short, women's writing of the last few decades emphatically severs motherhood from sainthood.

To read Elena Bonner's childhood memoirs, *Mothers and Daughters* (*Dochki-Materi*, 1991), in the context of this fiction may strike card-carrying formalists as a fanciful trespass across genre boundaries.[3] Yet Paul de Man's tightly argued deconstructionist rejection of the autobiographical subject as a privileged form of referentiality dissuades me from analyzing autobiography as a bona fide discrete genre, since I share de Man's skeptically antitaxonomizing view that any text "with a readable title-page is, to some extent, autobiographical" (922). Or, in Sidonie Smith's reformulation, "Since all gesture and rhetoric is revealing of the subject, autobiography can be defined as any written or verbal communication" (Smith, 19). Whatever their claims to "truth," memoirs and autobiography, like fiction, present a life "shaped by the exigencies of narrative art" (Jay, 16). The premise that all narrative has the ultimate referent of temporality likewise leads Paul Ricoeur in *Time and Narrative* to subsume autobiography, according to the argument that the self, once "purged by the effects of narrative," is profoundly textual (Nalbantian, 39). Hence my de Man-and-Ricoeur-indebted treatment of Bonner's self-reflexive text as a supremely rhetorical category on the outskirts of historical documentation, with a foot tentatively planted in female fictions.

In titling her memoirs *Mothers and Daughters*,[4] Bonner (born 1923) inevitably fosters expectations of a gendered counterpart to Ivan Turgenev's *Fathers and Sons* (*Ottsy i deti*). Moreover, the pluralization in her title intimates the breadth of a sociological survey or the validation of a paradigmatic model of maternal-filial relations. Indeed, as in Turgenev's most famous novel, general tensions around values, allegiances, and modes of conduct figure centrally in Bonner's account, the conclusion of which implicitly generalizes her own case as a symptomatic, if not universal, configuration ("you can't protect yourself from feeling guilty toward the dead, if only because they are dead and you are alive. Mama felt guilty toward her mother because her fate ricocheted into her mother's life. I feel guilty toward my mother for my life and happiness. Mothers and daughters! Mothers and daughters" [332–33]).

Indefinitely postponing the boundlessly rich topos of generational guilt, which Soviet history unwittingly nurtured, here I merely note that the pluralism that marks the actual text belongs to a somewhat different order, for it reinstates a factor suppressed in the binarism of the title: namely, the primacy of the father in the triangulation that decisively shapes Bonner's subjectivity and structures the psychological dynamics of her narrative. The titular (female) dyad masks the narratively inscribed triad featuring the (male) father/husband as an object of unacknowledged contention across generations.

TEMPORALITY, ORIGINS, AND TOUCHSTONES

Bonner's memoirs adhere to a number of long-standing genre conventions: interweaving introspection and retrospection, they attempt to convey the flavor of a specific era and location (notably, Moscow and St. Petersburg during early Stalinism); purvey character sketches of sundry famous and obscure individuals; trace the encroachment of historical and sociopolitical forces upon family life; and focus on a series of memorable, presumably watershed incidents that, mutatis mutandis, influence identity formation.[5] They satisfy the reader's expectations of "an artistically pleasing amalgam of historical background and personal development" (Zweers 2). More intriguingly, through a series of flash-forwards to Bonner's stint in the army, her children, and her relationship with the internationally sanctified dissident Andrei Sakharov, they set the stage for the next volume of memoirs, about her adulthood.

That next volume, paradoxically, came first: *Alone Together*, almost exclusively devoted to the period of her exile with Sakharov in Gorky (1980–86), preceded *Mothers and Daughters* by five years. According to Bonner, *Alone Together* "was supposed to be about Andrei, but it turned out to be about [her]. However, every word was written for [sic] him" (Bonner 1986, foreword). This earlier set of memoirs illuminates Bonner's concept of the form as shaped by narrative devices characteristic of fiction: "Yes, I have most of the ingredients for a Christmas tale. Now all I need is the happy ending, but I can't make one up. [. . .] *Thanks to God, you are free/In Russia, in Boldino, in quarantine. —David Samoilov.* Yes, that must be it, the happy ending" (226).[6] For Bonner, memoirs patently serve as memorials or monuments: death catalyzes her impulse to write. Whereas in Peter Brooks's Freudian scenario narrative and its prolongation defer the inevitability of death,[7] for Bonner storytelling or telling *her* story sooner functions as an act of resurrection. As Marianne Hirsch comments, "Dead mothers do elicit a certain nostalgia" (48). Tellingly, the opening chapter of *Mothers and*

Daughters traces the text's origins to Bonner's dream about her mother, Ruth Bonner, forty days after the latter's death. The torrent of recollections about Bonner's parents and their families apparently unleashed by this dream became the embryo of *Mothers and Daughters* in the form of a letter resembling a family tree (11). Seven years after Sakharov's death Bonner would pay a similar tribute to him by publishing *Freestyle Notes about Andrei Sakharov's Genealogy* (*Vol'nye zametki k rodoslovnoi Andreia Sakharova,* 1996), replete with detailed genealogical charts and dates. "Internally, I wrote them [the memoirs] for him [Sakharov]," she confides (3), though "externally," the book, like *Mothers and Daughters,* addresses a broad general audience. Both volumes seek to establish continuity in the midst of personal and historical ruptures.

Missing from these painstaking retrievals cum postmortems, which smack of moral imperatives, is a coverage of Bonner's own life from the age of fourteen to fifty-seven: *Mothers and Daughters* ends with the year 1937 and the arrest of both parents. It offers but fleeting glimpses of those four-plus decades, in the italicized sections of the text—the italics designed to signal a later perspective on events and thereby to authenticate the fiction that everything else proceeds from a viewpoint contemporaneous with those events. Through the device of typographically distinguishing between this markedly retrospective ("mature") vantage point and the bulk of the memoirs, Bonner endeavors to emphasize the transparent immediacy of her recollected childhood—no mean feat in light of the sixty-odd years separating those experiences (in the late 1920s and 1930s) from her (re)construction of them in 1991.[8]

Indeed, *Mothers and Daughters* pulls strongly toward the "corrective" of the more recent temporality partly because of Andrei Sakharov's culturally overdetermined presence in it as a moral touchstone. And Bonner regularly leans on his authority as an icon of impeccable conscience and clear-sightedness to solidify, by association, her own credentials as a plausible reporting intelligence. Moreover, the interplay between the split temporal frames urges the reader to accept the young Bonner and her purported thoughts, responses, and actions as "accurately recalled" in part *because* the older and wiser Bonner's strategically "subsequent" reassessments point to the limitations of her childhood perspective, which the editorializing italics mutate from an orienting subjectivity to an analyzable object. Bonner's critical backward glance, in other words, preempts ours.

THE SURPLUS VALUE OF LIES AND CONFESSIONS

The issue of "accuracy" in self-presentation is inseparable from the reception of memoirs, for myriad forces—the pressure of desire on memory, psychological censoring mechanisms, rhetorical stratagems, and the bifocalism intrinsic to the task of inscribing immediacy from hindsight—conspire to undermine the memoirist's reliability as a truth teller. Whether deliberately or involuntarily, self-presentation risks degenerating into self-promotion or self-justification, as in the notoriously controversial case of Rousseau's *Confessions*. Moreover, as recent studies of autobiography and memoirs have increasingly contended, the self becomes (re)constituted through the process of recollection, ultimately inscribing a textual self—the only communicable self possible.

Awareness of readers' dependence on the memoirist's trustworthiness doubtlessly motivates the translator Antonina Bouis's ingenuous endorsement, in the introduction to the English version of *Dochki-materi*, of Bonner's "honesty": "Another of her [Bonner's] best-known characteristics was and is honesty. And she demands as much honesty of herself as she does of others" (x). As Sakharov's wife and widow, as an indefatigable, eloquent proponent of human rights, and as a courageous, educated, and savvy member of the Russian intelligentsia, Bonner deservedly enjoys a reputation for integrity and risk-laden outspokenness on volatile issues. *Mothers and Daughters*, however, aims to document not Bonner's political critique and resistance, but her childhood experiences within her parents' advantaged yet unmistakably troubled household; the focus is profoundly personal. Politics and family life may overlap, but cannot be equated, and political probity hardly vouchsafes sincerity in matters of filiation and domestic relations.

Bouis's assertion smacks of fanciful gloss not only in light of Bonner's overall treatment of dishonesty in the memoirs, but in its bald contradiction of Bonner's own acknowledgement: "I was a terrible liar (am I still?). . . . I would swear never to lie again, though I knew that I would, and, most importantly, I knew that lying didn't bother me and I didn't consider it a flaw. . . . I am astounded to encounter people like Andrei[,] who are completely free of it" (Bonner 1992, 49). Singling out her schoolmate Elka as the object of her teenage affection, Bonner notes, "I never knew whether she was lying or not" (221)—an uncertainty untouched by any dismay. In fact, Elka's debatable honesty enhances her aura of mystery, which Bonner finds so seductive. Elsewhere Bonner freely confesses to repeated instances of what might impress even the least exacting moralist as gratuitous fibs ("The summer passed as if it hadn't happened, because there was nothing to tell about it except for my lying" [109]), especially to her father, whose admiration she courts by whatever means prove effective. She falsely claims to have prepared a dish he enjoys ("Was I ashamed to lie about the jam? Not a bit, I don't think" [247]) and pretends familiarity with Shakespeare's *Romeo and Juliet* ("I had read *Othello* . . . [b]ut I hadn't read any other Shakespeare. But I nodded. Another lie!" [268]). When questioned by the housekeeper about her unexpected return to the family apartment, Bonner experiences relief that "[s]he didn't wait for a reply, and *I didn't have to start the day with a lie"* (307, emphasis added). Visiting her mother in the prison camp, she feels alienation, on top of which "there was the additional burden of *being forced to lie about Batanya"* (328–29, emphasis added). The wording in the last two comments, which perform startling rhetorical legerdemain, presupposes falsehood as an inherent and irresistible condition of life rather than one of several options available to a conscious agent confronting a moral choice. Although Bonner thematizes lies, she avoids contemplating the relationship of her own, seemingly innocuous, minor untruths (107)—as well as her habit of eavesdropping and spying (145, 147)—to the prevailing climate of duplicity and cowardice that made the horrors of Russia's 1930s possible.

On one hand, admitting to mendacity in a literary mode traditionally so preoccupied with veracity seems uncommonly guileless, for the logical reader might reasonably ask whether Bonner's propensity for lying compromises the integrity of her memoirs in their entirety. On the other hand, the price of admitting to what Bonner deems trifling fibs purchases the reader's credulity in her candor when more weighty issues are at stake, for little falsehoods presumably pale beside a disarming readiness to acknowledge them.[9] A passage in the memoirs attests to Bonner's recognition of the subtle complexities linking and separating the ontological status of truth, facts, and events, particularly in reminiscences: "If you ask me, 'Did this happen?' I will reply, 'No.' If you ask me, 'Is this true?' I will say, 'Of course'" (prologue).

Bonner's sophistication in formulating such distinctions relevant to retrospection is not matched, disappointingly, by a depth of introspection. Paul Jay rightly observes that "autobiographical writers . . . discovered the psychoanalytical process before Freud himself practised it. The psychoanalytical function of the process of self-reflexive composition" made explicit in Augustine's *Confessions* (23) and so richly exploited, for example, in Mikhail Zoshchenko's *Before Sunrise* (*Pered voskhodom solntsa*), optimally culminates in increased self-understanding. A disconcerting aspect of *Mothers and Daughters* in this regard is Bonner's reluctance to submit herself and others to that enabling examination. Reticence and exteriorization substitute for psychological inquiry even when the occasion begs for the sort of probing that illuminates motivations, inner conflicts, and self-delusion or personal myths. Although willing to concede selective unpalatable truths, Bonner gingerly steers around questions of sexuality and seems preposterously unaware of her own repressions. Psychological scrutiny is precisely what *Mothers and Daughters* lacks. Consequently, Bonner emerges as a surprisingly unself-conscious narrator of her own and others' biographies. What explains Bonner's reluctance, for instance, to hazard an interpretation of her mother's painfully eloquent body language before her arrest: "She raised both hands, pulling me closer with one, pushing me away with the other" (303)? Bonner's disabling blindness to the psychological division so vividly materialized in her mother's physical gestures extend, regrettably, to the sphere of her own repressions: to a post-Freudian reader, what patently constitutes the unsaid of Bonner's text (cathected at such overloaded yet narratively bypassed moments) is a life-narrative firmly anchored in Oedipal attachment and family romance.

MATROPHOBIA AND OEDIPAL (AF)FILIATIONS

If desire complicated by a clash between hero and villain propels the plot of most narratives, that dynamic in *Mothers and Daughters* plays itself out as the incompletely articulated antagonism between Bonner and her mother, Ruth. On the sociohistorical plane, this ostensibly private, familial tension metonymizes Bonner's rejection of Stalinism. As Natasha Kolchevska in her excellent commentary on the text observes, Ruth Bonner remains an enigma in the memoirs that she, in a sense, inspired—a shadowy, fractionally drawn figure whose inner world Bonner never explores, instead projecting onto her mother the negative features of Soviet orthodoxy, from which Bonner considers herself immaculately exempt and against which she and Sakharov would agitate during the dross-and-moss of stagnation.[10]

Bonner's matrophobia manifests itself in a distancing from her mother not only as a failed progenitor, but also—and relatedly—as the dread personification of Soviet womanhood, the product of an ideology the adult Bonner finds morally and politically repugnant. To what extent, however, could Bonner as child perceive connections between her mother's personal role denial and her political conformism? Bonner's reflex of dissociative self-identification, whereby her tastes, behavior, and desires define themselves antithetically to her mother's, conjures up neat adult reconstellations of messy, disparate elements from childhood scenes so as to weld her animus to principled convictions. Through that paradigmatic stratagem, which Marianne Hirsch detects in *Electra* and innumerable kindred texts, the daughter "presents herself as everything her mother is not" (31)—in Bonner's case, subversive, passionate, willful, and attracted to "bourgeois" luxuries (the "bad girl" countermodel). Bonner never entertains the notion that psychologically based factors disavowed or repressed by her, rather than dissenting convictions, or the state's nationwide appropriation of adult women's time and energies (accounting for Ruth's chronic absences), rather than chilly neglect, might explain, if incompletely, Ruth's treatment of her and her own wounded resentment against her mother.

A party worker, the exact nature of whose official activities Bonner never clarifies, Ruth Bonner in her daughter's disjointed portrait appears cold, puritanical, punitive, and withholding: "Antibourgeois and maximalist, . . . [she] never allowed herself to use a tender word to Egorka [Bonner's brother] or me" (90). She incarnates the unquestioning, myopic loyalty to the policies and mandates of the Soviet regime, along with its ethic of dutiful self-denial, disdain for creature comforts, and rigid self-control that Bonner associates, tellingly, with stone ("[*litso*] *okamenelo, pobelelo*," [140, 154]) and that by the 1990s, when Bonner published her memoirs, would be utterly discredited.

Ruth encompasses the traits exemplified by the postrevolutionary New Woman, fictionally codified in Dasha, the heroine of Fedor Gladkov's *Cement* (1922–24, 1934, 1941):[11] impassive and unwavering compliance with state imperatives; a blind belief in the system despite copious horrifying evidence of its ruthless inhumanity; and indifference to domestic, including maternal, "duties": "Mama was never home. And what if she were? What could she do, when she couldn't even make cream of wheat without lumps? And what about the laundry? And the shopping? Or keeping track of the money? Or washing us?" (Bonner 1992, 105). "Mama never took part at all in running the household. Nura [the housekeeper] was given expense money and she made the decisions on how to spend it. Mama gave the others nannies money once a week (I think), and grew very angry when they tried to account for their expenses to her" (126). Accordingly, Bonner relegates Ruth to the outer periphery of "home," while foregrounding her Grandmother Batyana; Nura, the gastronomical wonder nicknamed the Nun (242); and finally (though, in covert, mediated form), herself.

Bonner casts her mother's presence as perennial absence, and in her telling Ruth's utter ineptness in household matters is surpassed only by her violation of all conventional maternal desiderata. Unloving, eternally critical of her daughter, Ruth denigrates and humiliates her,[12] dwelling on Bonner's supposed physical weakness, stupidity, and ugliness ("'You're ugly' were words Mama said to me repeatedly before she was arrested" [46]).[13] By eroding Bonner's self-confidence, Ruth prompts her to forge an oppositional identity and to find affirmation elsewhere. Ruth's "villainy" enables Bonner's "heroinism."

Alternating neglect and callous insensitivity from her mother, in fact, lead Bonner to adopt a series of contrastive, "unruthian" surrogates: friends such as Elka, Lena Krebs, Lida, and Olya, the capable housekeeper Nura ("The house wouldn't be a home without Nura" [105]), and, above all, her grandmother, Tatyana (Batyana), who completely supplants Ruth: "Batyana, not Mama, was the center of my life, the peak, the most important person, and I could not imagine life without her" (27). In fact, Bonner "documents" her own entry into the world, which takes place at her paternal grandparents' house in Turkmenia, by reproducing the telegram announcing the event to Batyana (90). Not Ruth, who actually bears the child, but Batyana presides as the dominant persona and thereafter becomes the most powerful female presence in Bonner's life—a usurpation that Bonner, citing from a lyric by Vladimir Kornilov, universalizes into a national historical phenomenon: "'and it seemed that in our years there were no mothers. There were only grandmothers. . . .' Grandmothers there were!" (17).

Ruth has no place in an overly rationalized familial constellation that appoints Batanya the peerless female ancestor/house mother and makes Bonner's father, the Armenian Bolshevik Gevork Alikhanov (a key executive in the Comintern), the magnet for Bonner's egotistical heterosexual love. As the object of Bonner's worship, Alikhanov not only personifies virtues of the intelligentsia, but, until Andrei Sakharov's appearance, constitutes the masculine (i.e., social and "universal") ideal in Bonner's hierarchized world. Throughout the memoirs Bonner dwells on their mutual, wordless understanding ("Papa understood everything. I hadn't said a word" [174]), the special bond that invariably prompts him to "side" with his daughter against his wife whenever conflicts over values arise. In her imagination, Bonner displaces her mother as Alikhanov's "soulmate."

Nowhere is that displacement more dramatically evident than in Bonner's breathtakingly clueless revelation of her Oedipal obsession with her father. Visits by Dolores Ibarruri arouse her irritated jealousy: "I didn't like her in our house. She paid no attention to anyone but Papa" (236). Alone with her father in their Moscow home during one summer, Bonner enjoys feeling "like the lady of the house" and proceeds to bolster her suitability for that role through showcasing her culinary skills—one of the chief areas of Ruth's haplessness. In the adult-coded italicized segment of this episode, Bonner states, *"That month, that hot urban August, was a gift from the gods because I spent it with Papa"* (249). Unfettered by the company of others, in the evenings they go out "on sprees," with Bonner wearing a yellow dress, a flower in her hair, and the exciting glow of being called Carmen by her father (248). They dine at the Aragvi or other, equally fashionable, restaurants: "Papa had never had so much time for me before. This was the only way to talk, just the two of us" (248). The discourse sooner evokes typical romantic rendezvous à deux than father/daughter eating habits. And, perhaps most remarkably, Bonner's memoirs leave few doubts that during her teen years her subsequently intellectualized Oedipal desire interfused with her classic enactment of the family romance.

THE FAMILY ROMANCE: SURROGATES
AND DISPLACEMENTS

Freud's blueprint of personality formation posits the family romance as "an imaginary interrogation of origins [. . .] which embeds the engenderment of narrative" within the experience of the discursively structured family (Hirsch, 9). As a defensive fantasy common to all pubertal children disillusioned with formerly idolized parents, in Freudian terms the process rep-

resents a normal stage in maturation. It entails projecting one's own estrangement onto the mother or father, who as a consequence becomes not
the genuine, biological parent, but an inferior substitute for the real and
vastly more impressive progenitor.[14] Whether Bonner's alienation from her
mother, which indisputably feeds on her wounded deprivation of motherly
love, also stems from disappointed idolatry remains debatable. But her radical, persistent notion of Ruth as a lesser maternal surrogate affords an exemplary instantiation of Freud's scenario: "The image of the stepmother
often transformed itself into Mama, and shedding copious tears I imagined
that she was my stepmother and watched her closely for signs that it was
true" (Bonner, 46). Recalling a particularly corrosive moment of total estrangement, she writes, "I was certain that she was the 'mean stepmother,'
and she would kill me or give me to an orphanage" (Bonner, 62). Bonner's
narrative of generational relations vividly illustrates how "mothers . . . become the targets of [the] process of disidentification and the primary negative models for the daughter" (Hirsch 11), thereby facilitating the latter's
maturation into womanhood. Bonner's female singularity, her perceived
subjectivity, rests squarely on this matrophobic disidentification: "'I'm not
a gypsy,' I always responded, because I thought that this somehow separated me from Mama, that it might somehow make it clear that I was not
Mama's child and that she was my stepmother" (106).

Whereas Bonner's mother reportedly lacks the characteristic features
equated with the totalizing nurture of the imaginary, Bonner's father affirms
her links with the symbolic order via her intellectual abilities, a love of reading ("we read poetry to each other" [248]), and a precocious ability to master space in the outside world (a point of pride for Bonner [59]). Like her
passion for tools and repair work, learned from a surrogate grandfather
(Deda, 68–69), these are the "masculine" traits mirroring the paternal persona, persistently and dissociatively contrasted to Ruth in phrases inscribing difference: "I could easily imagine my mother as my stepmother, but
I never thought of Papa as an evil stepfather" (47). Yet the single greatest
irony of Bonner's memoirs is that not Ruth but Alikhanov was, quite literally, the parental surrogate: "I was only two when my first nanny, Tonya, told
me that Papa, my Alikhanov [sic], wasn't my papa at all. I remembered that
forever. . . . Certainly Alikhanov was no stepfather" (47). Indeed, the fact
that Alikhanov *was* Bonner's stepfather endlessly complicates her protracted
Oedipal fixation on him, which one might expect to have weakened with her
marriage in 1950 to Ivan Semenov, presumably an appropriate male figure
for a transference: "Papa . . . [was] not all that successful, powerful, and
strong, beloved by others. . . . *I put all this together and into words only
later, after Papa was gone*" (249). Yet Semenov, with whom Bonner had two
children, belongs to the "never-never land" of the temporal segment excluded from her memoirs, which nonetheless recognize Sakharov, and him

alone, in the role of spouse and beloved. Relying exclusively on Bonner's memoirs, one might conclude that the most significant—indeed, the only *genuine*—heterosexual loves of her life were her stepfather and Sakharov, prominent men who occupied highly influential sociopolitical positions in Russia during their respective eras.

Although *Mothers and Daughters* resuscitates the first fourteen years of Bonner's biography, Sakharov, whom she met approximately three decades later, in 1970, is a vital presence in the text. As elsewhere in Bonner's works, he functions as a yardstick, an ideal beyond criticism whose persona provides the position from which most judgments, whether explicitly or by implication, proceed.[15] If Bonner came to a belated realization of her stepfather's sundry human weaknesses, those flaws surely contrasted with the soul-searching moral rectitude that Sakharov during perestroika incarnated not only for Bonner but for the entire nation.

Bonner's eventual and qualified "rehabilitation" of her mother is riddled with ambiguities and retains the disidentifying perspective so crucial to the (non)maternal portrait Bonner constructs. Ruth finally succumbs to demonstrative (and demonstrable) nurturing sentiments only as a grandmother and great-grandmother—that is, when she is "beyond womanhood" and disempowered in old age—after her camp sentence and loss of husband, job, and party connections. By then she has metamorphosed, in Bonner's words, "into a 'crazy' grandmother and great-grandmother, for whom her grandchildren and great-grandchildren . . . [are] the chief 'light in the window'" (90). At this stage, Ruth sooner resembles Bonner's child, in a role reversal that permits Bonner to display *her* contrasting capacity to nourish and love. Softened through age and myriad vulnerabilities, Ruth nonetheless retains her perceived persona of overly self-contained and distant critic. Though she relies on Bonner's medical skills, she continues to fault them: "Mama was always making sarcastic comments about me as a doctor, but at the same time she was absolutely convinced that I could always help her and always spare her suffering" (7). The memoirs allow Ruth's own voice to emerge only when she has shrunk to the position of a frail, helpless dependent. The contents of her last notebook (for August–September 1987) reveal both Ruth's acuity and the depth of her psychological suffering, a suffering Bonner recognizes yet cannot integrate into a more searching, ego-muted view of her mother:

> They're [Bonner and Sakharov] basically happy, very busy and closely welded to each other. They don't need anyone else around; they're happy together. The only thing that worries them is being separated. . . .
>
> My daughter feels that seeing people . . . is bad for me. What a stupid doctor she is. How could I possibly learn anything from anyone that would be more horrible than my own life. . . . I feel that I am in solitary confinement. (332)

Ultimately, the "true mothers" of the memoirs are Batyana and Bonner herself. The text, in effect, eliminates Ruth as mother, assigning her the diminished functions of unconvincing imposter (the stepmother of family romance), dupe of the Soviet system, and powerless old lady who repudiates her own past and in so doing partially vindicates Bonner's childhood self. Although at memoirs' end Bonner largely resists what Sidonie Smith has aptly called "the summative tendency of memory" within autobiography (Smith 142), under the temporally alinear surface of *Mothers and Daughters* one perceives the teleological drive to establish the rightness of Bonner's relationship to life's circumstances.

In her astute, wide-ranging analysis of twentieth-century Russian women's autobiography, Beth Holmgren convincingly argues that the best-known representative texts within the "genre"—by Lidiia Chukovskaia, Lidiia Ginzburg, Evgeniia Ginzburg, Mariia Ioffe—"for the good of the cause" genuflect before authoritative male mentors and intelligentsia values, while simultaneously imposing conformist models on women who enact culturally enriching difference (e.g., peasants and gypsies, lesbians, bona fide criminals). Above all, with the exception of Nadezhda Mandelstam's two milestone volumes,[16] memoirs by women copiously illustrate their cult of domesticity/family, their rigid notions of gendered propriety, and their automatic, credulous insistence on a positive interpretation of the most hideous Soviet realities. A recent collection of women's Gulag memoirs, *Till My Tale Is Told* (*Dodnes' tiagoteet*, 1999), which recounts instances of inconceivably inhumane torture inflicted upon arbitrarily imprisoned Soviet citizens, teems with examples of blinkered faith in the "motherland's" fundamental decency and benign responsiveness to its people's irrational loyalty. Countless women incarcerated for no crime other than being themselves penned impassioned letters to Stalin, convinced that he knew nothing of the Gulags and would liberate them immediately upon learning of their unjust "fate." By her own account Zaraya Vesyolaya, who spent years in exile and transferred from one prison to another, in conversation "leaped to the defense of the Soviet state" and upon hearing of an unimaginably brutal punishment of prisoners "could not believe it: 'In our camps? That can't be true!'" (Vilensky, 307, 333). The frequently encountered, ineradicable conviction that "our" (Soviet) camps, unlike their less "enlightened" Nazi equivalents, adhered to some indefinable humanitarian principles pervades women's camp memoirs. It reflects the more comprehensive incapacity of intelligentsia women, who demonstrate formidable stoicism and survival skills under appalling circumstances, to voice the unsaid.

Insofar as they openly and iteratively acknowledge mother/daughter tensions Bonner's memoirs promise deviation from a cardinal tenet of Russia's standard memoiristic etiquette. Yet numerous aporetic passages in

Mothers and Daughters ally Bonner with an all too familiar repressive decorum; they betray the degree to which intelligentsia women (Bonner among them) have practiced their own form of "varnishing reality" (*lakirovka*), to evade a radical self-confrontation that can make for painful reading, but also to consolidate the ethos of the group to which they belong, if only as second-class citizens.[17]

Notes

1. For the role of mothers in posters and other visual materials, see Waters. For an investigation of maternity as trope and allegory in Soviet and post-Soviet culture, see Goscilo, *Dehexing Sex*, especially 32–44. For a discussion of the persistence of motherhood as psychological phenomenon in Russia, especially in folkloric genres, see Barker.

2. For a survey of this phenomenon, see Goscilo, "Perestroika and Postsoviet Prose."

3. A comparison of Bonner's memoirs with Christa Wolf's *Kinderheitmuster* (*A Model Childhood*), so penetratingly analyzed by Marianne Hirsch (154–61), would offer valuable insights into female child autobiography.

4. The English rendition of the original Russian title, literally *Daughters— Mothers*, not only reverses the order of generations, but supplies the conjunction signaling continuity and union that the more ambiguous dash avoids.

5. Felicity Nussbaum commonsensically observes that "the 'self' is an ideological construct that is recruited into place within specific historical formations rather than always present as an eternal truth. It is less an essence than an ensemble of social and political relations" (xii).

6. The quote from Samoilov's verses refers to Pushkin's enforced stay, owing to an epidemic, in Boldino, located near Gorky.

7. See especially Brooks 60–61.

8. Thus through the simple expedient of a typographical change Bonner tries to solve the dilemma that so vexed Augustine in his *Confessions*: "the inability of language to bridge the distance between what he takes to be a past self and a present self" (Jay 1984, 30). For a cogent assessment of the problems faced by an author of childhood memoirs, see Zweers's study of Ivan Bunin's *Life of Arsen'ev*, 6–18.

9. On the rhetorical and psychological benefits of confession, see Goscilo, "Gilded Guilt."

10. Its more comprehensive focus aside, Kolchevska's sensitive reading of *Dochki-materi*, early versions of which antedate this article, intersects at many junctures with my own and forms a chapter in her forthcoming study of women's memoirs.

11. On the ethos driving that novel, see Clark 78.

12. A particularly painful episode involves her mother's reaction when Bonner returns home late after spending most of the night in conversation with her "boyfriend" Seva (Bagritsky). Without explanation Ruth orders her uncomprehending daughter, "'Show me your panties'" (280), provoking both pity and hatred in Bonner, who nonetheless obeys the offensive command.

13. In terms of the memoirs, then, Bonner's delighted discovery of her attractiveness represents the triumph of self-affirming, independent "personality" over belittling experience, or more precisely, daughters' capacity to overcome mothers' objectifying projections: "When Lion Feuchtwanger's book *The Ugly Duckling* was published in Russia, I was twelve years old. Mama started calling me that. I found the novel on her shelf, read it, and was outraged, and even said a lot of harsh and nasty things to her about it. But then in the summer of 1936 I looked in the mirror and decided that I was very pretty, so pretty that it took my breath away with an incredible feeling of joy and happiness and some other feeling I didn't know, filling my entire being. I can recall that moment to this day, and I've never experienced another one like it" (47). This symbolic moment of self-discovery in a mirror marks both an internal and external separation from her mother. It occurs, in Bonner's story of self, at approximately the time of her father's, then her mother's, arrest and Bonner's resultant transition from a privileged child of party functionaries to a "strange orphan" (the term coined by Il'ia Erenburg for offspring of people who fell victim to Stalin's purges, associated above all with the year 1937).

14. For an insightful examination of the family romance in the European novel, see M. B. Goscilo, especially chapter 1, which contains the theoretical framework in highly readable form.

15. For instance, Bonner expresses amazement that he can be "completely free" of lying (49), experiences joy when, after reading her memoirs, he informs her, "You write better than I do" (319), finds him "radiat[ing] a feeling of concentration and peace" (135), and never seems to question or challenge his assessments of any situation or individual. By comparison with the utterly honest Sakharov, Bonner's father lied, or was caught doing so, "only twice" (151).

16. Especially the second volume of Mandelstam's unaccommodated memoirs (*Hope Abandoned* [*Vtoraia kniga*]) triggered an avalanche of resentful criticism among the intelligentsia, many of whom stopped speaking with the author, primarily because she had violated the "good girl" conventions of the intelligentsia by expressing herself forthrightly, naming names, and voicing profound doubts that implicitly "cast aspersions on" (*ona brosaet ten' na nas*) them as an entire category. According to Liudmila Petrushevskaia (personal conversation with author in 1990), she underwent the same ostracism after the publication of her hard-hitting story "Our Crowd" ("Svoi krug").

17. Anyone seeking a counterexample within memoirs and autobiography could not find a more vivid illustration of its subversive potential than Mariia Arbatova's recent volume, *They Call Me [a] Woman* (*Menia zovut zhenshchina*, 1999), which ignores the major enduring taboos of the intelligentsia, notably sexual explicitness, the interrogation of male superiority, self-promotion, and skepticism about the unassailability of the intelligentsia. For an intelligent examination of Arbatova's text as a feminist statement, see Sutcliffe.

Works Cited

Barker, Adele M. *The Mother Syndrome in the Russian Folk Imagination.* Columbus: Slavica Publishers, 1986.

Bonner, Elena. *Alone Together.* New York: Alfred A. Knopf, 1986.

———. *Dochki-materi.* Moscow: "Progress"/"Litera," 1994.

———. *Mothers and Daughters.* New York: Alfred A. Knopf, 1992.

———. *Vol'nye zametki k rodoslovnoi Andreia Sakharova.* Moscow: Izd. "Prava cheloveka," 1996.

Brooks, Peter. *Reading for the Plot: Design and Intention in Narrative.* New York: Alfred A. Knopf, 1984.

Chevigny, Bell Gale. "Daughter Writing: Toward a Theory of Women's Biography." *Feminist Studies* 9, no. 1 (1983): 51–69.

Chodorow, Nancy, and Susan Contratto. "The Fantasy of the Perfect Mother." In *Rethinking the Family,* ed. Barrie Thorne and Marilyn Yalom. New York: Longman, 1982.

Clark, Katerina. *The Soviet Novel: History as Ritual.* Chicago and London: University of Chicago Press, 1985.

Contratto, Susan W. "Maternal Sexuality and Asexual Motherhood." *Signs* 5, no. 4 (summer 1980): 766–82.

De Man, Paul. "Autobiography as De-Facement." *Modern Language Notes* 94 (December 1979): 918–38.

Engel, Barbara Alpern. *Mothers and Daughters: Women of the Intelligentsia in Nineteenth-Century Russia.* Cambridge: Cambridge University Press, 1983.

Freud, Sigmund. "Family Romances." In vol. 2, *Collected Papers,* edited by James Strachey. London: Hogarth Press, 1953.

Goscilo, Helena. *Dehexing Sex: Russian Womanhood During and After Glasnost.* Ann Arbor: University of Michigan Press, 1996.

———. "Gilded Guilt: Confession in Russian Romantic Prose." *Russian Literature,* Special Issue: Russian Romanticism I, 14, no. 2 (August 1983): 54–66.

———. "Perestroika and Postsoviet Prose: From Dazzle to Dispersal." In *History of Russian Women's Writing,* edited by A. Barker and J. Gheith. Cambridge: Cambridge University Press, 2002.

Goscilo, Margaret Bozenna. *The Bastard Hero in the Novel.* New York and London: Garland Publishers, 1990.

Hirsch, Marianne. *The Mother/Daughter Plot: Narrative, Psychoanalysis, Feminism.* Bloomington: Indiana University Press, 1989.

Holmgren, Beth. "For the Good of the Cause: Russian Women's Autobiography in the Twentieth Century." In *Women Writers in Russian Literature,* edited by Toby W. Clyman and Diana Greene. Westport, Conn.: Greenwood Press, 1994.

Irigaray, Luce. "Body Against Body: In Relation to the Mother" (1980). In *Sexes and Genealogies,* translated by Gillian C. Gill. New York: Columbia University Press, 1992.

Jay, Paul. *Being in the Text: Self-Representation from Wordsworth to Roland Barthes.* Ithaca: Cornell University Press, 1984.

Kolchevska, Natasha. "Women's Childhood Memoirs and the Recovery of Memory." Talk delivered at the American Association for the Advancement of Slavic Studies conference in November 1994.

Kristeva, Julia. *Tales of Love.* Translated by Léon S. Roudiez. New York: Columbia University Press, 1986.

Nalbantian, Suzanne. *Aesthetic Autobiography: From Life to Art in Marcel Proust, James Joyce, Virginia Woolf and Anais Nin.* New York: St. Martin's Press, 1994.

Nussbaum, Felicity A. *The Autobiographical Subject: Gender and Ideology in Eighteenth-Century England.* Baltimore and London: Johns Hopkins University Press, 1989.

Rich, Adrienne. "Motherhood in Bondage" (1976). In *On Lies, Secrets, and Silence: Selected Prose 1966–1978.* New York and London: W. W. Norton, 1979.

———. "Motherhood: The Contemporary Emergency and the Quantum Leap" (1978). In *On Lies, Secrets, and Silence: Selected Prose 1966–1978.* New York and London: W. W. Norton, 1979.

———. *Of Woman Born: Motherhood as Experience and Institution.* New York and London: W. W. Norton, 1986.

Sagan, Eli. *Freud, Women, and Morality: The Psychology of Good and Evil.* New York: Basic Books, 1988.

Smith, Sidonie. *A Poetics of Women's Autobiography: Marginality and the Fictions of Self-Representation.* Bloomington: Indiana University Press, 1987.

Spengemann, William C. *The Forms of Autobiography: Episodes in the History of a Literary Genre.* New Haven and London: Yale University Press, 1980.

Stanton, Domna. "Difference on Trial: A Critique of The Maternal Meta-
phor in Cixous, Irigaray and Kristeva." In *The Poetics of Gender*, edited
by Nancy K. Miller. New York: Columbia University Press, 1986.

Suleiman, Susan Rubin. "Writing and Motherhood." In *The (M)Other Tongue:
Essays in Feminist Psychoanalytic Interpretation*, edited by Shirley Nel-
son Garner, Claire Kahane, Madelon Sprengnether. Ithaca: Cornell University Press, 1985.

Sutcliffe, Benjamin. "Establishing the Feminist Autobiographical Self in
Mariia Arbatova's *They Call Me a Woman*." Forthcoming.

Vilensky, Simeon, ed. *Till My Tale Is Told: Women's Memoirs of the Gulag*.
Bloomington: Indiana University Press, 1999.

Waters, Elizabeth. "The Female Form in Soviet Political Iconography,
1917–32." In *Russia's Women: Accommodation, Resistance, Transformation*, edited by Barbara Evans Clements, Barbara Alpern Engel, Christine D. Worobec. Berkeley: University of California Press, 1991.

Young-Bruehl, Elisabeth. *Freud on Women: A Reader*. New York and London: W. W. Norton, 1990.

Zweers, Alexander F. *The Narratology of the Autobiography: An Analysis
of the Literary Devices Employed in Ivan Bunin's "The Life of Arsen'ev."*
New York: Peter Lang, 1997.

Alexander Prokhorov

Accommodating Consumers' Desires: El'dar Riazanov's Memoirs in Soviet and Post-Soviet Russia

ENTERTAINING MEMORIES

In post-Soviet Russia, memoirs have become best-selling entertainment. Geia Publishers issues a series of spy memoirs, *Declassified Lives*, among whose best-known authors is the sinister spy master Pavel Sudoplatov.[1] In 1998 AST Feniks publisher launched a series of male celebrity biographies titled Man-Myth, featuring such diverse male icons as Russian poet Aleksandr Pushkin (Luk'ianov) and Elvis Presley (Whitmer), Russian actor and bard Vladimir Vysotskii (Zubrilina), and Casanova (Flem). On its web page, the Russian publishing house Vagrius presents memoirs as its top-selling genre. Vagrius now issues the memoirs series *Literary Memoirs* and *My Twentieth Century;* the latter includes the reminiscences of famous actors, musicians, writers, diplomats, and politicians. The memoirs of the famous Russian film director El'dar Riazanov (born 1927) have been published four times in this series.

For many readers, the memoirs of popular cultural and political figures evoke pleasant reminiscences of their youth. Older readers often perceive memoirs as recollections of a more secure and stable life. Many recently published memoirs of Russian celebrities—hockey player Viacheslav Fetisov, film director El'dar Riazanov, actress Lidiia Smirnova, actor Innokentii Smoktunovskii—sell readers their star status. Such stars are typically first consumed visually, on TV and movie screens, and then verbally through their memoirs. As objects of consumption, these celebrities combine the extraordinary with the ordinary. On the one hand, Fetisov, a star of the NHL and the Russian hockey league, is the unattainable object of desire and an all-Russian champion. On the other hand, Fetisov is a Russian everyman, "just like us," with whom the viewer and reader can identify.[2]

Christine Gledhill notes that stars have emblematic as well as cultural value, "as condensers of moral, social, and ideological values" (215). A star—through her or his celebrity status—transcends the social contradictions that the consumers of culture experience in their own lives. The celebrity status of El'dar Riazanov inspires the former Soviet intelligentsia, in particular, because in his persona and memoirs he attempts to reconcile important cultural tensions: first, between popular culture (as a filmmaker) and high art (as a poet) and second, between the myth of the artist (independent, creative, and nonconformist) and the mass-produced, industrial nature of modern culture (the artist's labor subordinated to the entrepreneurial talent of the producer).

El'dar Riazanov has made more than twenty feature films, most of them comedies or melodramas, and until recently he enjoyed the status of one of the most popular film directors in the former Soviet Union. Until the 1990s most of his films were blockbusters, and several have been recognized as symbols of entire historical periods in Russian culture—*Carnival Night* (1956) of Khrushchev's Thaw,[3] and *Irony of Fate* (1975) of Brezhnev's Stagnation.[4] Riazanov is also a popular talk show personality; he hosted *Kinopanorama* from 1979 till the late 1980s[5] and produced numerous popular TV programs.[6] After Yeltsin ordered troops to shoot at the Russian parliament building (White House) in October 1993 and public opinion turned against him, the president's press service asked Riazanov to conduct an interview with Yeltsin in order to raise the latter's popularity. Riazanov complied, and also interviewed Yeltsin before the national referendum. By including this episode in his book Riazanov emphasizes that his popularity goes beyond the world of the arts and can even influence an entire nation's opinion of its leader and his policies.

Since 1977 Riazanov has published eight editions of his memoirs, four of them after the collapse of the Soviet Union. Since the mid-1980s Riazanov has produced such "television memoirs" as *Four Evenings with Vladimir Vysotskii*,[7] *Six Evenings with Iurii Nikulin*,[8] and *Russian Muses*.[9] In his writing and television memoirs Riazanov bridges various cultural divides in an unsuccessful attempt to construct a unified, harmonious self and to vouchsafe the vicarious pleasures of his narrative persona to his post-Soviet readers, and, above all, to the intelligentsia.

As this volume's introduction details, the recent Russian fashion for memoirs has its origins in a well-established tradition of memoir writing that goes back to the preromantic age. One of the important factors that recently expanded the market for memoir literature is "the tidal wave of nostalgia sweeping through postsoviet society" (Goscilo, 9). Helena Goscilo notes that Russia's honeymoon with the West ended around 1995 and Russians turned to their common Soviet and Russian past. The fast food chain

Russkoe Bistro was established to challenge McDonald's Happy Meals. Russian Radio became the most popular radio station, with 664,000 daily listeners in almost forty cities. New Russia-minded programs and channels emerged on Russian television. The Moscow area channel was renamed Muscovy, a medieval pre-Petrine name for Russia, and one of the most successful programs on the channel was *Russia House,* a witty title for a program with a strong Orthodox flavor discussing issues of Russian identity (Goscilo 9–10).

The 1990s boom in memoirs, both published and broadcast, catered to the new fashion for nostalgia. In this period, three major Russian TV channels—ORT, RTR, and NTV—offered numerous memoir programs, including *Lives of Remarkable People* (on ORT). The title of the program derives from the nineteenth-century memoir series revived by Maxim Gorky in the Soviet era. ORT also offered the program *Women's Stories,* a talk show focusing on celebrity women and their lives and careers. On ORT, the Russian actor Leonid Filatov hosted a biographical program, *Lives to Remember,* about forgotten film and theater actors and actresses. The RTR channel aired several memoir programs: *My Twentieth Century, Silver Ball,* and *Man and Woman.* NTV also broadcast several weekly and monthly memoir programs: the best known were *A Witness of the Century* and *Children of the Famous.*[10]

The popularity of memoirs in post-Soviet Russia may be partly explained by the exhaustion of paradigms for writing official historical accounts. In her article in this volume Marina Balina contends that in order to narrate the public life of an individual, Soviet culture developed "a stern and all-controlling etiquette" for memoir writing. Soviet memoirs usually described the life of a martyr for the revolutionary cause, provided individual confirmation of official history, and fulfilled the function of didactic propaganda. Most important, Soviet memoirs paralyzed the temporality of remembrance and favored the temporality of anticipation: reading about the life of a martyr was important because such an exemplary life brought closer the apocalyptic coming of the bright future.

The educated estates of the Soviet empire, especially the intelligentsia, took advantage of the genre. The Soviet intelligentsia, or in Vera Dunham's wording, the Soviet middle class, emerged as the state service estate.[11] This estate's legitimacy and cultural validity were based, above all, on its public professional life. Memoirs spotlighting the public performances of the protagonist/main narrator became a primary mode of the Soviet/Russian elite's self-portraiture.[12] Post-Soviet memoirs function differently not only from official Soviet memoirs of the 1920s and 1930s, but also from the official and unofficial memoirs of the late Soviet era. Post-Stalinist memoirs still served as martyrdom stories either for the newly redefined official cause, or for the "right" cause, which anti-Soviet memoirists defined as the opposite to the party line. On the one hand, the Thaw-era memoirs of Il'ia Erenburg, published in the 1960s by state publishing houses, resurrected the cultural authority of Isaak Babel, Boris Pil'niak, Marina Tsvetaeva, and many others—the cultural producers who had lost the fight for political and cultural power during the Stalin era. On the other hand, works by Lidiia Chukovskaia, Lidiia Ginzburg, and Nadezhda Mandelstam provided alternative martyrdom narratives of Soviet cultural history, circulated widely in both *samizdat* and *tamizdat* during most of the Soviet era, and became appropriated by Soviet culture during late perestroika.

Post-Soviet memoirs, in contrast, do not pursue any didactic or propagandistic goals; political veracity is hardly their prime purpose. Rather, they offer an anecdotal account of a famous life that may be consumed as entertainment or, for more traditional readers, truth. Such memoirs favor the success stories of (Western or Russo-Soviet) show business celebrities and public figures. An important new feature of the Soviet celebrity persona is the continuity of her or his success story. Indispensable martyrdom (dissidence, emigration, tsarist prison, or Soviet camp experience) is no longer a standard feature of a memoir persona. The protagonist may have encountered problems during the Soviet period, but these only foreground an ability to function successfully within the system. That is probably why the print run of the memoirs of Stalin's associate Lazar Kaganovich exceeded by three times the print run of Riazanov's memoir (Melik-Karamov): it was at least three times as difficult to survive and succeed under Stalin than after the Great Leader's death. This instinct for success and the implied happy ending transcend political formations and provide both continuity and the unity of the post-Soviet memoiristic self.

As Beth Holmgren points out in the introduction, the first wave of Russian professional memoirs in the late tsarist period differed from Western success stories in their attempt to generate a surplus value by exercising "the very considerable authority of the nineteenth-century writer." In contrast, post-Soviet professional memoirs do not covet literary authority, in part because literature ceased to be the most authoritative cultural medium after the dissolution of the Soviet Union. Memoirists concentrate on promoting themselves as successful figures, rather then on demonstrating their literary accomplishments. Even Riazanov, who writes about his poetic achievements, puts this part of his life in the larger framework of popular culture production. In the final analysis, the new Russian mass reader mirrors the Western reader counterpart, who definitely prefers stories of power and success.

Riazanov's memoirs provide especially interesting material for analysis because the author manifests an enviable self-centeredness and obsession with self-promotion already in the first edition of his memoirs. In tune with the spirit of the Brezhnev era, Riazanov transforms the story about his public life (his service to Soviet cinema muse) into a promotional self-presentation of the best comedy director in the Soviet Union. In this respect the earlier editions of Riazanov's text are less oriented toward the Soviet memoir canon than the perestroika-era editions, which include numerous pages about the film director's confrontations with censors and evoke moralistic similarities to dissident memoirs. Although post-Soviet editions of the film-maker's memoirs preserve the narratives about his dissent, they primarily favor the success story of Riazanov and his blockbusters.

Riazanov narrated different success stories depending on the values and limits of what was permissible at different periods of Russo-Soviet history. The first edition (1977), published under the title *The Sad Face of Comedy* (*Grustnoe litso komedii*), focused primarily on Riazanov's experiences as a director of comedy films. The subsequent three editions (1983, 1986, 1991) appeared under the title *A Non-Summing Up* (*Nepodvedennye itogi*) and focused on Riazanov less as a comedy director and more as a multifaceted artist: director, poet, TV host, professor, playwright, and screenwriter. The two post-Soviet editions (1995, 1997) bore the same titles but were released as part of the series *My Twentieth Century.* They contextualized the life of the popular film director not only in the history of Russian culture, but also in the history of world film. In 1997 and 2000 Riazanov published two final editions of his memoirs. In a savvy marketing move he changed its title (*Summing Up* [*Podvedennye itogi*]) and sold another twenty to thirty thousand copies of the book.[13]

One of the reasons for Riazanov's numerous rewritings of his memoirs lies in what Paul Jay refers to as the "dissimilarity between identity and discourse" (29). Within the text this dissimilarity often projects a conflict between the identity of the protagonist/narrator/author and the conventionalizing features that a given culture tries to impose on that identity. In the Russian context Riazanov's self-representation is potentially flawed because of his association with popular film. Russian culture still favors what Andreas Huyssen refers to as the Great Divide ("the discourse which insists on the categorical distinction between high art and mass culture" [viii]),[14] and the producer of mass culture texts has to pay homage to high art in order to achieve full recognition as a cultural authority. Constructing his memoiristic self, Riazanov constantly emphasizes that he does not strictly belong to the popular side of the "Great Divide": he also writes serious poetry, for example. The second problematic aspect of Riazanov's self is his success within the Soviet film industry under heavy party and state censorship. How may one reconcile such success with his memoirs' narrative of a nonconformist artist preserving his artistic integrity within an oppressive cultural environment? In short, the self of Riazanov's memoirs embraces both poles of the high versus low opposition (poetry and popular film) and also claims to retain authenticity and freedom of artistic expression "in an age of its technical reproducibility" and micromanaged Soviet "film factories."

TRANSCENDING THE "GREAT DIVIDE"

Riazanov became famous because of his work in two popular film genres: comedy and melodrama. Every Russian knows his films and millions consider Riazanov their favorite director. Russian film scholarship of the Soviet era, in contrast, traditionally concentrated on *auteur* cinema and did not devote much attention to Riazanov's work.[15] De-Sovietization, however, disrupted this privileging of high art cinema over popular film. Whereas during the Soviet era official culture and the intelligentsia enforced the cult of high art, post-Soviet culture is more tolerant of its own popular forms and pays attention to its producers. The numerous editions of Riazanov's memoirs reflect this change in the status of popular culture, especially evident in the way Riazanov discusses his two main teachers: Grigorii Kozintsev and Ivan Pyr'ev.

The Soviet and post-Soviet editions of Riazanov's memoirs offer different evaluations of the roles played by Kozintsev and Pyr'ev in Riazanov's life. In the first, Soviet-era edition of *A Non-Summing Up* Riazanov talks more about Kozintsev, whose creative workshop he attended at VGIK,[16] than Pyr'ev, whom he relegates to the background of the narrative. Kozintsev was and still remains a cult figure for the intelligentsia—one of the founders of FEKS in the 1920s,[17] the author of famous film adaptations of Shakespeare's *Hamlet* (1964) and *King Lear* (1969) and Cervantes's *Don Quixote* (1957). Pyr'ev, on the other hand, was cast as a "cultural villain," the director of Stalinist musicals, which both the party leadership after Stalin and the intelligentsia denounced for depicting happy peasants in the age of repressions and man-made famines. After Khrushchev officially denounced "the depiction of kolkhoz life with tables collapsing under the weight of turkeys and geese" (Khrushchev 71), the so-called liberal Thaw intelligentsia joined the chorus of denunciation and Pyr'ev—following the canonical script of Soviet cultural politics—acknowledged his mistakes. In short, with the change of cultural politics after Stalin's death the Stalinist musical became a scapegoat for the crimes of the system.

In the Stagnation era, and even during perestroika, critics could not afford to examine the complexity of Pyr'ev's role in film art, production, and cultural politics of the time. As a film director Pyr'ev worked mostly in the popular genres of the musical and the melodrama, those despised by the post-Stalinist intelligentsia, yet extremely popular with mass audiences and still shown on Russian TV. The intelligentsia, however, cherished the division of film culture into high and popular, the former representing the intelligentsia's realm and the latter the gutter, which was controlled by official

discourse and patronized by lower-class consumers. In 1983, when Riazanov first published his book under the title *A Non-Summing Up,* Pyr'ev was
still the intelligentsia's *bête noire.* Had Riazanov favored Pyr'ev over Kozintsev as his mentor, at least part of the intelligentsia would have interpreted that priority as a betrayal of the intelligentsia's high moral values and
an avowal of Soviet orthodoxy.

Pyr'ev's cultural rehabilitation began only during perestroika, and continued in the post-Soviet era. The demise of the Soviet Union and the dissolution of the intelligentsia as a state-financed professional class also meant
the end of the intelligentsia's high-culture dictatorship. It subsequently led
to Russian cultural critics' reevaluation of the legacy of popular culture producers like Pyr'ev.[18] In addition to being one of the most talented Russian
filmmakers, Pyr'ev was instrumental in loosening censorship during the
Thaw, increasing the number of films made by Mosfilm, and bringing young
directors to the studio. Riazanov was his major discovery and creation.

In the 1995 edition of his memoirs Riazanov rearranged the hierarchy
of his teachers: Pyr'ev and Kozintsev switched places and roles. Riazanov
placed Pyr'ev's portrait right after Eisenstein's and called him "my mentor,"
while characterizing Kozintsev as a talented director and professor who introduced young Riazanov to the basics of directing: "Kozintsev opened the
profession . . . Pyr'ev introduced me to filmmaking and many other things,
he determined my life's path" (Riazanov 1995, 495). According to Riazanov,
Kozintsev taught mostly through negative comments: Riazanov was almost
expelled from VGIK and never heard a kind word from the great pedagogue during his studies. In contrast, the 1995, 1997, and 2000 editions of
the memoirs feature Pyr'ev as the guide who taught Riazanov the secrets of
film art and production, and, in many respects, shaped his directorial style.

The later editions of Riazanov's memoirs contributed to the rehabilitation of Pyr'ev. The famous pupil writes how Pyr'ev, as the head of Mosfilm, overcame the Stalin-era dearth of films known as *malokartin'e:*[19] "Ivan
Aleksandrovich . . . devoted all his talent and infinite energy to the creation
of the new cinema. He hired new film directors, many of whom were the
pride of our art for many years" (1995, 50). Pyr'ev encouraged filmmakers
to work in popular forms, especially comedy, which, as Riazanov notes, was
a genre feared by directors and treated suspiciously by the authorities:
"Pyr'ev tried to make everyone he invited to Mosfilm do film comedy . . .
Everyone, however, avoided comedy like the plague" (1995, 50).

Riazanov articulates his artistic identity regarding the opposition of
high art versus popular culture not only through a discussion of his two major teachers, but also through the links he establishes between his own film
art and the art of the cultural producers whom he credits with influencing
his work. On the one hand, it is his VGIK professor, Sergei Eisenstein, the
patriarch of Russian film, whom he fetes equally in all the versions of his

memoirs and whose art Riazanov (like most film specialists) considers the summit of Russian avant-garde film. On the other hand, in the 1995 edition Riazanov adds to Eisenstein's name the name of Iakov Protazanov, who worked his entire life in popular narrative film, especially comedy and melodrama (495). From the Soviet to post-Soviet editions of his memoirs Riazanov reverses the hierarchy of his mentors and predecessors: those working in popular genres, such as Pyr'ev or Protazanov, acquire more legitimacy. Riazanov's own identity as an artist, however, is never completely secure because his major success was in the realm of popular cinema and not in the cinema considered high or avant-garde art.

As if reflecting the insecurities of his cinematic persona, Riazanov's memoirs emphasize that his creative self is not limited to film: in addition to directing, he writes plays, prose, and poetry. Riazanov perceives the two extremes of his artistic personality in directing popular film on the one hand, and writing serious poetry, on the other. Film allows Riazanov to have contact with a mass audience. Cinema for him is both an industry (1995, 495) and a communal (kollektivnoe) art, where the personal finds only partial self-expression: "one can expect this [to express one's personal world] from film art only with obvious reservations" (492). Poetry, on the other hand, gives Riazanov the opportunity to express his inner self: "Why did I start writing poetry and prose? Evidently, I felt a certain lack of confessionality in film art. I needed to express my deep inner self" (492). Riazanov's book, in this respect, aspires to join the tradition of Russian writers' memoirs that make poetic genesis the center of their writing.[20]

In addition, poetry, as the privileged discourse in Russian culture, provides Riazanov with an opportunity to move from the cultural periphery to the center. Poetry also confirms Riazanov's creative maturity: Riazanov notes in the memoirs that he wrote only talentless imitations in his youth and stopped writing poetry altogether until his late forties and early fifties, when original poetic inspiration finally visited him.

To strengthen the reader's perception of him as a producer of high culture, Riazanov emphasizes that his poetry was published in thick journals, for example, in Znamia (1983). During the Thaw and even Stagnation such a publication would have ensured the intelligentsia's acceptance of his poetry as serious art. Riazanov's poetry, however, appeared on the pages of thick journals when poetry was slowly going out of fashion. First, during perestroika, the unpublished prose of dissident and prohibited writers displaced contemporary poetry. Second, with the end of the Soviet Union the thick journals lost their position as literature's most prestigious venue. Thus, just as Riazanov became intimate with the master discourse of Russian literature, poetry's authority itself was put into question by the new values of the time.

Riazanov only obliquely refers to the neglect of high culture—with poetry at its apex—as an unfortunate consequence of desovietization, but he never questions the status of poetry and high culture itself within Russian life. In a society where literature, and especially poetry, still fulfills for some the role of a quasi religion, Riazanov apparently feels insufficiently recognized as a cultural producer, his considerable fame resting chiefly on his film comedies. The popular filmmaker continued to include chapters about his poetry even in the later, post-Soviet editions of his memoirs, implying that Riazanov the poet is closer than Riazanov the film director to the sacred core of Russian culture.

According to the memoirs, even Riazanov's introduction into film art occurred in the shadow of his desire for literature: his spiritual link to Eisenstein was forged not so much through celluloid as through their shared love of the written word. Eisenstein collected antique books and passed his interest in literature and book collecting on to Riazanov: "Thanks to Sergei Mikhailovich I've got into collecting books . . . Sergei Mikhailovich dragged me to second-hand bookstores, introduced me to book connoisseurs, opened for me the unique world of old books and ancient publications" (Riazanov 1983, 23). In the memoirs, poetry validates Riazanov's artistic self, placing him at the verbal center of Russian culture, as opposed to its "visual periphery." The filmmaker's memoirs create a portrait of an artist who was able to embrace the best of both: popularity with the masses and sophistication in high art. As an example of his successful transcendence of the "Great Divide" the filmmaker refers to his popular films, peppered with the high poetry of Pasternak, Tsvetaeva, Akhmadulina, and his own modest contributions. In the 1970s Riazanov's poetry also started appearing in his films in the form of song lyrics. He initially disguised his authorship, however, and presented his creations as the poems of William Blake, Rudyard Kipling, David Samoilov, and Iunna Morits. Surprisingly, the highbrow Soviet intelligentsia never noticed the trick until Riazanov confessed to the artistic misdemeanor. In his memoirs, Riazanov-the-celebrity thus seems to resolve one of the intelligentsia's cursed dilemmas: the gulf between high and popular modes of Russian culture.

A PORTRAIT OF THE ARTIST IN THE AGE OF MECHANICAL REPRODUCTION

If the alternation of chapters dealing with poetry and popular film demonstrates Riazanov's ability at least to move between high culture and mass entertainment, then the chapters describing Riazanov's struggle with both Soviet cultural administrators and post-Soviet producers present the filmmaker as an artist who preserved his artistic integrity against all odds under the constraints of modern cultural production—both in its command and market incarnations. The tone of those passages about Riazanov fighting for his artistic integrity evokes Soviet-era dissident memoirs, which promote the author as the martyr for the noble cause.

Riazanov devotes many pages to his conflicts with state censors during the Soviet era. He carefully explains what he planned to say or show in his films and what he was made to show by various cultural administrators. For example, he writes at length about the films he never made because Goskino (State Committee on Cinematography) prohibited or stopped his work at the preparatory stage. In the early 1980s, according to Riazanov, he tried to make film adaptations of Mikhail Bulgakov's *Master and Margarita*, Evgenii Shvarts's *Dragon*, and Nikolai Erdman's *The Suicide* (1995, 495). Goskino buried all these projects for political reasons. A chapter titled "Twenty-Four Hours to Reconsider" gives Riazanov's account of his work in the late 1960s on the film adaptation of *Cyrano de Bergerac* by Edmond Rostand. Yevgeny Yevtushenko, a popular and controversial poet of Khrushchev's Thaw, played the lead. Vladimir Baskakov, the deputy minister of Goskino from 1962 to 1974, ordered Riazanov either to replace Yevtushenko with any other actor or to stop shooting the film; Riazanov refused and work on the film was terminated. Recollected incidents of this sort serve as intelligentsia credentials, a proof that Riazanov sacrificed both material reward and possible artistic recognition for the higher cause of political opposition.

The chapter "Put in a Word" narrates Riazanov's troubles with his 1980 film *Put in a Word for the Poor Cavalry Man.* Riazanov recollects in detail how both Goskino and Gosteleradio (State Committee on Radio and Television) participated in rewriting the screenplay (written originally by Grigorii Gorin and Riazanov) and censored the production of the film itself. Riazanov's narrative self confirms his integrity by distinguishing between what, in his opinion, is genuinely *his* and the changes made by the state agencies that financed and supervised film production during the Soviet era.

In the post-Soviet editions of the memoirs just as many pages target market-era producers, who, according to Riazanov, often treat him without regard for his artistic authority and do not allow him to shoot films according to his experienced preferences. Riazanov's comments are symptomatic of many Soviet intellectuals' reactions to the changes in filmmaking and power distribution in the industry. Market considerations have replaced the primacy of the director in filmmaking with a shared authority between the director and the producer. For Western producers working with Riazanov and not familiar with Soviet-era hierarchies, even a director who is famous in Russia is just an employee. In Riazanov's memoirs those producers who limit his free self-expression usually appear as Westerners. Later editions preserve Riazanov's chapter about filming a Soviet-Italian coproduction, *The Extraordinary Adventures of Italians in Russia* (1974): during his work in Italy, according to the author, he was constantly harassed by stingy local producers who would not find him a decent hotel, neglected him, and interfered with his shooting schedule.

As in the Soviet era, some of Riazanov's most cherished plans could not be realized even in the 1990s because of misunderstandings on key issues between the artist and the producer, who was no longer a Soviet bureaucrat but a representative of the free market. Riazanov's negotiations with British producer Eric Abraham about a film adaptation of *The Life and Extraordinary Adventures of Private Ivan Chonkin* (Vladimir Voinovich 1975–79) serve as the major example. In the chapter "Farewell, Chonkin" Riazanov recounts how he was not able to make an adaptation of Voinovich's novel because Abraham's Portobello Pictures, which owned the rights to the adaptation, disagreed with Riazanov on how the film should be shot, who would play the leads, and how the film would be distributed. Riazanov feels that Abraham treated both him and Russian film administrators as second-class citizens. Unable to find common ground, Portobello finally hired a Czech director, Jiří Menzel, and made the film without Riazanov.[21]

Responding in 1995 to a question about whether he had abandoned all intentions of making films, Riazanov said, "There are plans but I need a very rich producer . . . I do not want to run around begging for money and then stop in the middle of production" (1995, 503). Riazanov's artistic personality matured at a period when the dominance of the director in the filmmaking process and full state financing of film projects were sine qua non conditions. At the end of his career he had to adjust to a new model of filmmaking that allotted the producer a more prominent role. His memoirs tell the story of how he has remained true to his artistic self while adjusting to new conditions.[22]

Being an artist, according to Riazanov, means not only resisting a hostile cultural environment, but also preserving the ability to generate original works of art. The author obsessively returns to his main fear—that of repeating himself (1995, 490), which he equates with artistic death.[23] Narratives about preserving his artistic integrity alternate in Riazanov's memoirs with narratives about the maturation of his unique status as a film director and poet. The chapters dealing with Riazanov's maturation in both capacities emphasize the transition from a disciple's imitations to the acquisition of his own point of view, his own voice. The author recollects that Kozintsev was dissatisfied with Riazanov's student projects when they lacked originality. Riazanov also remembers that Konstantin Simonov criticized his first book of poems for imitating the poetry of Pushkin, Lermontov, Nadson, and Esenin: "He advised me to be original and told me to stop imitating other poets . . . Poetry should be unique and express the individuality of the author" (1995, 255).

The foils to Riazanov as a unique artist are pseudo artists, who either repeat someone's words or claim authorship of texts they never wrote. The chapter "Who Is the Author?!" treats the author-impostor of the play "Long Long Ago" on which Riazanov's film *Hussar's Ballad* (1962) is based. General consensus attributed the play to Aleksandr Gladkov (1940), so when Riazanov started working on his film, he invited Gladkov to rework his play into a script. The financial director of the film, Shevkunenko, however, told Riazanov that they would have to pay Gladkov half of the royalty because Gladkov was not the real author of the play and they would need to hire a ghost writer to work on the screenplay. According to Shevkunenko, Gladkov only began writing poetry after his 1940 release from prison (sentenced for stealing books from the Lenin Library), when he published "Long Long Ago"—a play in verse. When the play was staged in Sverdlovsk in 1942 and Gladkov was asked to rework a couple of lines, he simply disappeared until the director abandoned all hope of finding him and asked somebody else to rework the text. Riazanov writes that he had exactly the same experience with Gladkov and eventually had to write part of the play himself. He concludes: "If even I . . . managed to translate prose into poetry within a week, then the author of the play could have done it within three days" (1995, 135). In Riazanov's memoirs Gladkov not only merely imitates somebody else's style, but also imitates the persona of a poet: "you can pretend so well that you are the author of someone's else work that you will start to believe in your authorship yourself" (1995, 139–40).

In contrast to such impostors, Riazanov, as the protagonist of his memoirs, often writes a text and modestly conceals his authorship, as in the case of rewriting Gladkov's play. With such a gesture Riazanov links his own behavior with the anonymous author who, Riazanov suggests, probably never left prison and passed his manuscript on to Gladkov. Thus, the author-impostor as a secondary character of Riazanov's memoirs foregrounds the protagonist: a unique and original artist.

ESTABLISHING ARTISTIC IDENTITY
THROUGH SINCERE NARRATION

Riazanov links the free self-expression of an artist with presenting himself as a sincere narrator of his life and times. The ability to tell an honest history of the self and the mores of the era (1995, 489) validates his unique artistic voice. The stance of sincerity, however, is articulated differently in chapters about the Soviet and the post-Soviet periods of Riazanov's life.

The section devoted to the Soviet period combines a detailed account of Riazanov's creative life with less known or previously proscribed details about the cultural life of the era. In this respect Riazanov's memoirs become more informative with every new edition because he adds new chapters about cultural figures who could not be mentioned in earlier editions. Vladimir Vysotskii, for example, appears only in later editions because of his

controversial, semiofficial status. Some sharp comments by Sergei Eisenstein about still-living cultural authorities were also beyond the limits of the
permissible in the earlier editions.[24] High-placed apparatchiks, such as Filipp Ermash or Sergei Lapin, likewise could not be mentioned because arguments between filmmakers and apparatchiks were not a legitimate subject
for memoirs of the Soviet period.[25]

In the second part of the memoirs, which covers the late Soviet and
post-Soviet periods, Riazanov changes the devices that shape the sincere
narrative about his self and his time. His main concern is no longer state
censorship but the unstable status of cultural producers in the transitional
economy of post-Soviet Russia. The insecurities of a former Soviet intellectual
elite manifest themselves in a switch to a narrative collage that lacks a stable
hierarchy of narrative voices and is filled with "authenticating evidence": a
mixture of diary entries, reminiscences, letters, and most notably, business
contracts with film producers. For example, Riazanov includes in the memoir
a draft of what, from his point of view, is an unfair contract between Mosfilm
Studios and Portobello Pictures for the film adaptation of Voinovich's *Chonkin*
novel (1995, 457–58). Riazanov's recollections become fragmented, non-
chronological, and stylistically omnivorous. The memoir loses its unitary
narrative perspective and eschews finalizing evaluations of events. Marlene
Kadar defines this pastichelike narration about self as "life writing," which
she says, "includes the conventional genres of autobiography, journals, memoirs, letters, and other texts that neither objectify nor subjectify the nature
of a particular cultural truth" (10). In her article in this volume Marina Balina
argues that life writing has recently emerged in Russian memoirs as a new
narrative mode characterized by: (1) a fragmented structure; (2) an ambivalent evaluation of events; and (3) a polyphony of voices narrating these events.
Riazanov as the main narrator implies that he can recount a single-voiced
truth about the preglasnost part of his life, but the Gorbachev and post-Soviet
eras seem to require multivoiced and fragmented discourse in order to convey his persona's sincerity. Through this *heteroglossia* later editions of Riazanov's memoirs reflect such new post-Soviet trends in self-representation.

In the second part of *A Non-Summing Up* such a polyphony manifests
itself, above all, in the diversity of lexical registers engaged by the memoirist. The language in the second part is spiced with colloquial expressions
and emotionally charged poetic interpolations. For example, Riazanov uses
colloquialisms and even slang when describing how Abraham, the head of
Portobello, mistreated Mosfilm and the film director personally:

> My vosprinimali eto tak: vy tam v svoem leprozorii mozhete delat', chto
> khotite. Vprochem, esli my zakhotim, to vse, chto vy tam naludite, budet pri-
> nadlezhat' tol'ko nam . . . na russkoi kartine mozhno zarabotat', ne vlozhiv ni
> edinogo tsenta. I mina khoroshaia—vrode kak blagodetel', i igra neplokhaia.
> (1995, 458)

We understood it this way: you guys in your leper colony can do whatever you want. Meanwhile, if we want, we will repossess everything that you crank out over there . . . A Russian film can make us [Portobello] money without our investing a cent. We'll look charitable toward Russians and play a fine business game.

Naludit' is a word from Moscow youth slang of the 1980s,[26] while *khoroshaia mina* and *plokhaia igra* are colloquial expressions. Emotionally charged vocabulary and the colloquial syntax—the *Vy tam* structure, for example—of marketplace bargaining emphasize Riazanov's anxiety about the current state of the film industry and his status as a filmmaker. The lowering of style also suggests Riazanov's relative "helplessness" as an "average" Russian confronting the new market-driven Russia. By equating via language his celebrity persona with the Russian everyman, Riazanov creates intimacy between his constructed self and his implied reader.

Riazanov enhances the sincerity of his memoirs by interpolating stanzas "from the heart" about his experience of living in contemporary Russia:

> Zhit' by mne v takoi strane,
> Chtoby ei gordit'sia.
> Tol'ko mne v bol'shom govne
> Dovelos' rodit'sia.
>
> I wish I lived in a country
> Of which I would be proud.
> I, however, was born
> In deep shit.
> (1995, 505)

The range of vocabulary unthinkable for Soviet-era memoirs—the rhyme links the words "country" and "shit"—gives no new factual information about the cultural politics of the time, but certainly provides an insight into the dire straits of an artist and his frustration with the current situation in Russia's culture industry.

Finally, probably the most striking device used to inscribe the sincerity of Riazanov's account is the narrator's silence. The narrator's voice stumbles at humiliating or emotionally traumatic episodes in his life. Riazanov notes that some emotional moments of his life can be registered, but not expressed. Two major instances of such verbal numbness occur in the last part of the book: the death of his wife and the financial circumstances of his film *Prophecy*. In both cases failure to write signals a total loss of context. His family, about whom he never talks in his memoirs apart from the moment of his final separation with his wife, turns into an emotional void. At the same time, the new rules of the game, which have replaced the old ways of conducting business in film industry, create a void in Riazanov's career of a successful filmmaker. After reporting his wife's death, Riazanov interrupts the entries in the diary part of the memoirs with three lines of ellipses (1995, 486). About his Russian-French coproduction, *Prophecy*, which was financed by a French company, Riazanov refuses to write out of profound disgust at his treatment. He employs Hamlet's most telling device—"The rest is silence."

> It disgusts me to recall how we looked for a French partner—it was complicated, unsuccessful, at times humiliating. I'll not go into it . . . From Jean-Louis Levi, who in conversation evaluated our work highly and enthusiastically praised our film, I never even got a single note. Either he doesn't know anything about good manners or sees us as third-class citizens. Maybe both. (1995, 482–84)

Whereas in the first case the graphic silence of ellipses expresses the emotional surge of personal grief, in the second the refusal to write about the financing of his film indicates Riazanov's discomfort with the changed production circumstances in the film industry and with the unviable status of the artist. The silenced narrative reflects the instability of Riazanov's post-Soviet self-identity. The self-image of an artist who can cope with the cultural tensions of the era literally vanishes from the text.

This instability, however, brings Riazanov closer to his implied post-Soviet readers with all their anxieties and apprehensions. At the same time the author presents to the consumers/readers a celebrity persona, who entertains them through nostalgic encounters with the characters and actors from the most popular comedies and melodramas of the Soviet era. Most important, the protagonist of Riazanov's work copes with issues that the Russian intelligentsia could not resolve in the course of the twentieth century. Riazanov the artist bridges the gap between high art and popular culture by embracing in his creative work the best of both worlds: his comedies are popular with the masses, but he is also appreciated as a connoisseur and writer of poetry.

Riazanov's memoirs, however, produce an ambiguous pleasure. If the narrative—rewritten six times—attempts to create an artist's identity that resolves and transcends cultural tensions and aporias, then the discourse of the memoirs, especially the concluding chapters, betrays the self as far from harmonious or secure. Riazanov's failure, however, rescues the work from reiterating the traditional paradigms of Russo-Soviet memoirs. Riazanov serves neither the official cause nor the noble antiofficial cause, as did numerous Russian dissident-martyrs from Archpriest Avvakum to Andrei Sakharov. Riazanov as memoirist is more humble and reader-friendly: he entertains his reader and, as the five-figure print runs show, his success in *lettres* matches his success in film art.

Notes

1. Pavel Sudoplatov (1907–96) was a Soviet spymaster who directed Trotskii's assassination and controlled Department S of the NKVD, the organization responsible for gathering intelligence on atomic bomb research in the West. Robert Conquest called the English translation of his memoirs "the most sensational, the most devastating, and in many ways the most informative autobiography to emerge out of the Stalinist milieu" (Sudoplatov 1994, cover).

2. For a detailed discussion of the star as fetish see Richard Dyer, *Heavenly Bodies: Film Stars and Society,* and John Ellis, *Visible Fictions.*

3. Mikhail Kozakov in his film *Pokrovskie Gates* (Mosfilm 1982) uses the 1950s posters advertising *Carnival Night* and visual quotes from the film to evoke the spirit of Khrushchev's Thaw.

4 . The New Year issue of *Ogonek* 1 (1996) included a front-page portrait of Riazanov and the headline "A Fairy Tale for All Times: For Twenty Years *Irony of Fate* Has Brought Happiness to Millions of Russians." The issue celebrated the twentieth anniversary of Riazanov's comedy and its phenomenal success with viewers. The film, indeed, has acquired a status similar to that of *It's a Wonderful Life* in American culture: since the late 1970s it has been a Russian tradition to watch *Irony of Fate* on New Year's Eve (Minaev, 66–67).

5. A Soviet equivalent of Siskel and Ebert–like programs, *Kinopanorama* was a TV talk show covering the news of the Soviet and world film industries.

6. The series was broadcast on Russia's NTV in 1994. Riazanov notes that NTV is the most "intelligent" (the epithet, *intelligentnyi,* derives from "intelligentsia") channel in Russia, but many Russians, unfortunately, do not watch NTV's programs (Riazanov 1995, 486).

7. Vladimir Vysotskii (1938–80) was a popular film and theater actor and bard (a performer of his own guitar poetry). To this day he remains a cult figure in Russia.

8. Iurii Nikulin (1921–97) was a popular actor, clown, and director of the Moscow Circus on Tsvetnoi Boulevard. Vagrius recently published his memoirs, *Pochti ser'ezno (Almost Seriously).*

9. *Russian Muses* was a TV program about Russian women, primarily wives of French poets and artists.

10. I am grateful to Natal'ia Prokhorova and Tat'iana Sopina for information on TV shows.

11. Vera Dunham discusses the middle class as a state-financed professional and bureaucratic elite that emerged in the Soviet Union after the end of World War II. The common name for this social group is the Soviet intelligentsia.

12. In my analysis I use Mikhail Bakhtin's definition of memoir as a genre. In his "Form of Time and Chronotope in the Novel" Bakhtin analyzes ancient memoirs as a type of autobiographical writing that emphasizes the life of a public persona against the background of his time: "Such autobiographies are documents testifying to a family-clan consciousness of self. But on such family-clan soil, autobiographical self-consciousness does not become private or intimately personal. It retains a deeply public character" (137). Although Bakhtin discusses ancient biography and autobiography—specifically the memoirs of the Roman patrician family that "fused directly with the state" (137)—his discussion is useful for analyzing the memoirs of a Soviet intellectual who represented a professional estate financed by and fused with the state.

13. The first syllable in the title *Nepodvedennye itogi* appears with an "X" superimposed over the prefix "Ne."

14. Huyssen notes that the belief in the "Great Divide" is still part of the academy today. Postmodernism, however, challenges the "theories and practices of the Great Divide" (1986, viii).

15. Though slighted, Riazanov was not completely neglected by Russian film studies. In the 1970s Neia Zorkaia edited a volume on his art and in 1989 Evgenii Gromov published a book about the director.

16. VGIK is a Russian acronym for the All-Union State Institute of Film Art—the major Russian film school.

17. FEKS (Factory of the Eccentric Actor) is an avant-garde group of film and theater actors and directors. Kozintsev, Leonid Trauberg, and Sergei Iutkevich founded the group in 1922.

18. Maia Turovskaia's 1988 article about Pyr'ev was a key text in his rehabilitation. It prompted acknowledgment that his cinematic art and Stalinist politics had a complex and mediated relationship: specifically, the article rejected the formerly unchallenged, simplistic point of view of Pyr'ev's musicals as a disguise for Stalin's Gulag. Critics also acknowledged his role in post-Stalinist film. In the 1950s Pyr'ev became the head of Mosfilm and from 1957 until 1965 he chaired the Organizing Committee of the Union of Soviet Cinematographers, which had been established "to defend the interests of Soviet filmmaking against the incursions of the party state bureaucracy, unlike the Writers' Union" (Taylor, 144). In 1994 the series *One Hundred Years of Film Art*, with Riazanov on the editorial board, published a collection of articles about Pyr'ev, acknowledging his major contribution to Russian film art.

19. *Malokartin'e* is a term that refers to the drop in Soviet film production during the late 1940s and early 1950s.

20. Jane Harris notes that Russian critics emphasize the lyrical stance in much of Russian literary memoirs. It is usually "lyrical prose that focuses on the relationship between lyric poetry and contemporary nonfictional memoirs" (15).

21. The film *Život a neobyčejná dobrodružství vojáka Ivana Čonkina*, directed by Jirí Menzel (1994), is a joint production by the Czech Republic, France, Italy, Russia, and the United Kingdom.

22. Anna Lawton notes that beginning in late Stagnation the films of the famous comedy director grew "progressively disenchanted and his vein took a turn toward tragedy, which peaked in *Dear Elena Sergeevna* (1988)" (196). Despite financial trouble and less uplifting genre forms, Riazanov still remains one of the most prolific Russian filmmakers.

23. Riazanov's early comedies represent the sublime manifestation of the filmmaker's fear of repetition. He constantly tries his talent in new genre forms: *Carnival Night* is a backstage musical; *A Man from Nowhere*— a grotesque comedy; *Hussar's Ballad*—a fairy-tale musical; *Give Me a Complaint Book* and *A Girl without an Address*—melodramas; *Beware of a Car*—an ironic parody of a Soviet detective film. Time and again Riazanov tries to bridge the gap between the formulaic nature of popular culture genres and the cult of defamiliarization characteristic of high art.

24. Riazanov as narrator never says anything negative about actors, writers, or film directors. He, however, allows other characters in his memoirs to joke about their colleagues. For instance, he recalls Sergei Eisenstein's cutting remarks about his famous colleagues: "Eisenstein had a very sharp tongue . . . For example, he called Grigorii Roshal' 'a volcano erupting with cotton balls.' About Sergei Iutkevich he noted, 'a man with a refined bad taste.' He was brief about Sergei Gerasimov: 'Red Nazi'" (1995, 28).

25. Filipp Ermash was the head of Goskino and Sergei Lapin was the head of Gosteleradio during the Brezhnev era.

26. The *Dictionary of Moscow Argot* defines *naludit'* as "to do something fast, intensely, in one shot" (Elistratov, 156).

Works Cited

Bakhtin, Mikhail. "Form of Time and Chronotope in the Novel." *The Dialogic Imagination. Four Essays by M. M. Bakhtin.* Austin: University of Texas Press, 1981, 84–259.

Dunham, Vera. *In Stalin's Time: Middleclass Values in Soviet Fiction.* Cambridge: Cambridge University Press, 1976.

Dyer, Richard. *Heavenly Bodies: Film Stars and Society.* Basingstoke: Macmillan, 1986.

Ellis, John. *Visible Fictions: Cinema, Television, Video.* London: Routledge and Kegan Paul, 1982.

Elistratov, Vladimir. *Slovar' moskovskogo argo (materialy 1980–1994).* Moscow: Russkie slovari, 1994.

Fetisov, Viacheslav. *Overtaim.* Moscow: Vagrius, 1998.

Flem, Lidiia. *Kazanova, ili voploshchennoe schast'e*. Rostov na Donu: Feniks, 1998.

Gledhill, Christine, ed. *Stardom: The Industry of Desire*. London: Routledge, 1991.

Goscilo, Helena. Introduction to *Russian Culture of the 1990s: A Special Issue of Studies in Twentieth Century Literature* 24, no. 1 (winter 2000): 7–15.

Gromov, Evgenii. *Komedii i ne tol'ko komedii: rezhisser Riazanov*. Moscow: Kinotsentr, 1989.

Harris, Jane Gary. *Autobiographical Statements in Twentieth-Century Russian Literature*. Princeton: Princeton University Press, 1990.

Huyssen, Andreas. *After the Great Divide*. Bloomington: Indiana University Press, 1986.

Jay, Paul. *Being in the Text: Self-Representation from Wordsworth to Roland Barthes*. Ithaca: Cornell University Press, 1984.

Kadar, Marlene. "Coming to Terms: Life Writing—From Genre to Critical Practice." In *Essays on Life Writing: From Genre to Critical Practice*, edited by Marlene Kadar. Toronto: University of Toronto Press, 1992, 3–12.

Kaganovich, Lazar'. *Pamiatnye zapiski rabochego, kommunista-bol'shevika, profsoiuznogo, partiinogo i sovetsko-gosudarstvennogo rabotnika*. Moscow: Vagrius, 1996.

Khrushchev, Nikita. *The "Secret" Speech: Delivered to the Closed Session of the Twentieth Congress of the Communist Party*. Nottingham: Spokesman Books for the Bertrand Russell Peace Foundation, 1976.

Lawton, Anna. *Kinoglasnost: Soviet Cinema in Our Time*. Cambridge: Cambridge University Press, 1992.

Luk'ianov, Aleksandr. *Aleksandr Pushkin v liubvi: intimnaia psikhobiografiia poeta*. Moscow: AST Feniks, 1999.

Mar'iamov, Grigorii, ed. *Ivan Pyr'ev v zhizni i na ekrane: stranitsy vospominanii*. Moscow: Kinotsentr, 1994.

Melik-Karamov, Vitalii. "Chto s nami sdelalos', brat'ia?" *Ogonek* 28 (2001).

Minaev, Boris. "Kazhdyi raz pod Novyi god my otpravliaemsia v baniu." *Ogonek* 1 (1996): 66–67.

Nikulin, Iurii. *Pochti ser'ezno*. Moscow: Vagrius, 1998.

Riazanov, El'dar. *Nepodvedennye itogi*. Moscow: Vagrius, 2000.

———. *Nepodvedennye itogi*. Moscow: Vagrius, 1997.

———. *Nepodvedennye itogi*. Moscow: Vagrius, 1997.

———. *Nepodvedennye itogi*. Moscow: Vagrius, 1995.

———. *Nepodvedennye itogi*. Leningrad: Soiuzteatr, 1991.

———. *Nepodvedennye itogi*. Moscow: Iskusstvo, 1986.

———. *Nepodvedennye itogi*. Moscow: Iskusstvo, 1983.

———. *Grustnoe litso komedii*. Moscow: Molodaia gvardiia, 1977.

Smirnova, Lidiia. *Moia liubov'*. Moscow: Vagrius, 1997.

Smoktunovskii, Innokentii. *Byt'!* Moscow: Algoritm, 1999.

Sudoplatov, Pavel. *Razvedka i Kreml': zapiski nezhelatel'nogo svidetelia.* Moscow: Geia, 1996.

Sudoplatov, Pavel, Anatolii Sudoplatov, Leona Schecter, and Jerrold Schecter. *Special Tasks: The Memoirs of an Unwanted Witness—A Soviet Spymaster.* Boston: Little Brown and Company, 1994.

Taylor, Richard. "Singing on the Steppes for Stalin: Ivan Pyr'ev and the Kolkhoz Musical in Soviet Cinema." *Slavic Review* (spring 1999): 143–60.

Turovskaia, Maiia. "I. A. Pyr'ev i ego muzykal'nye komedii." *Kinovedcheskie zapiski* 1 (1988): 111–46.

Whitmer, Peter O. *Elvis Presli: psikhobiografiia pevtsa.* Rostov na Donu: Feniks, 1999.

Zorkaia, Neia. *El'dar Riazanov: Sbornik.* Moscow: Iskusstvo, 1974.

Zubrilina, S. *Vladimir Vysotskii: stranitsy biografii.* Rostov na Donu: Feniks, 1998.

PART II

The Memoir and the Word

Gitta Hammarberg

The Canonization of Dolgorukaia

AT AGE FIFTY-THREE Natal'ia Borisovna Dolgoru-
kaia (1714–71) was persuaded by her son to write her memoirs. Born a
Sheremeteva, she was part of the most privileged Moscow aristocracy and
after a happy childhood she was betrothed to Ivan Dolgorukii, favorite of
Peter II, in 1729. She married Ivan even though the large Dolgorukii family
was rapidly falling from favor. They were finally exiled after Peter's sudden
death and Anna's accession to the throne in 1730. She spent ten difficult
years in Berezov, beyond the Ural mountains in Siberia, where she bore two
children and remained for almost two years after her husband was removed
in great secrecy for eventual execution. Dolgorukaia was released from exile
and arrived with her sons in Moscow in 1740. There she suffered more humiliation in her dependence on her older brother and further hardship as
she strived to educate her sons properly and to restore the good name and
fortunes of the Dolgorukii family. After her older son had embarked on a
military career and married she left for Kiev with her younger son, who had
developed severe psychological problems. There she entered the Frolovskii
convent and took the strict vows of the schema and the name Nektariia.
Her younger son died two years before she herself died in 1771.[1]

Dolgorukaia wrote her memoirs in the convent to dispel her "gloom"
and "disturbing thoughts" after her older son and his family had urged her
to write "a journal about what had happened to me that was worth recalling,
how I had passed my life" (33).[2] The memoirs were produced as a private
document and center on Dolgorukaia herself.[3] She writes under certain
constraints: age and maturity color her retrospective view, the intended audience knows a great deal about the topic, and her status as a nun requires
pious references (appeals to God's judgment or mercy, references to Biblical precedents),[4] and prohibits such topics as the details of her engagement
ceremony (39). Although Dolgorukaia, like most memoirists, tends to select
situations that do her credit, at times she gives credit to past customs for her
own favorable image (37, 43) and at times she admits personal foolishness
(59). Her conversational style and her freely shared reactions to events point
to an intimate circle of readers.[5] She is writing "just as if I were talking to

93

you" (37) and her account is frequently interrupted by emotional exclamations and direct addresses to her readers.[6] She may, however, also be envisioning a wider audience in references to "those who want to know" or need to be consoled (41).[7]

Although Dolgorukaia vows to "tell the absolute truth" (43), she frequently stresses the vagaries of memory (63, 67, 71) and she worries that her weak health may impede her description (33, 71). She justifiably takes pride in her accomplishments, but tries to downplay them according to the dictates of feminine modesty and her monastic station. She vows not to expose the vices of others, yet she does not always refrain from doing so, which makes her self-image refreshingly human. Empress Anna, for instance, is so negatively described (most terrible to look at, repugnant face, taller than most men, extraordinarily fat, 46) that Dolgorukaia's descendants saw fit to omit the passage in the early published versions, together with nasty counterfactual references to Biron's lowly birth (51).[8] Her evaluation of her own life as a series of calamities is revealed in intermittent vows "to write of my own misfortunes" (51).[9] Her misfortunes start with the sudden reversal of the Dolgorukii family's favored status at court at the very time she was planning her marriage into that family, and continue with the family's travails en route to Berezov. Her misfortunes sound all the more striking against the introductory description of her pampered childhood and happy betrothal. The memoirs end with the Dolgorukii family's arrival in Berezov when her personal misfortunes had merely begun.

Dolgorukaia's text has been recognized as an important historical account of the relatively neglected period in Russian history between its two eighteenth-century "greats," Peter I and Catherine II. It has been hailed as a linguistically rare written document using the spoken language of an educated Russian eighteenth-century woman—the kind of language that was advocated as the model for the Russian literary language. Dolgorukaia is the first private person in Russia to write a published autobiography and belongs to a relatively small number of women memoirists born in the eighteenth century. Catherine II wrote and edited her memoirs throughout her life, but they were not made public until 1859 when Aleksandr Herzen published them in London in their original French. Ekaterina Dashkova's (1743–1810) memoirs, first published in English in 1840, were also written in French, as were those of Varvara Golovina (1766–1821), finished in 1817 and published posthumously first in French and only in 1899 in Russian. Anna Labzina (1758–1828) wrote her memoirs about her provincial childhood and unhappy first marriage in 1810. They were first published in 1903 and provide insights into both her private and public life, blurring the boundaries, not unlike the way Dolgorukaia's memoirs put a private spin on events at court. Labzina's Russian language and spiritual discourse resemble Dolgorukaia's expressions of piety, and she, too, highlights her misfortunes against a childhood where patriarchy gives way to a decisive maternal influence.[10] Somewhat later, in the 1830s, Nadezhda Durova (1783–1866) wrote and published her memoirs in Russian under her male pseudonym, A. Aleksandrov. An introductory account of her childhood is followed by an unusual military memoir based on her participation in the Napoleonic wars as a cross-dressing cavalry officer. Her spirited rebellion against gendered social structures makes her memoirs quite different from Dolgorukaia's account of her mild rebellion against family advice. Durova's summary abandonment of her husband and son for military pursuits stand in stark contrast to Dolgorukaia's sacrifices in the name of traditional fidelity and marriage.[11] Sof'ia Skalon (1796/97–1861) wrote her memoirs in 1859, based on earlier journals, and they were first published in 1891. They describe her carefree Ukrainian childhood and contain particularly interesting information about many Decembrists.[12]

Dolgorukaia differs from her fellow women memoirists in that she was not a writer, nor did she participate actively in any cultural associations. Catherine as empress and Dashkova as the head of two academies obviously helped set the tone for eighteenth-century Russian culture and both wrote many literary works in addition to their memoirs. Golovina came from a family close to the court. She was a maid of honor at Catherine's court, participated in the court circles of Catherine's successors, and was an accomplished painter, composer, and salon hostess. Her memoirs focus on her friendship with the wife of Alexander I. Labzina participated in literary salons and Masonic cultural enterprises, including journalism, to a degree unprecedented for a woman, while Durova, after publishing her memoirs, authored numerous other literary prose works. Through her father, the writer Vasilii Kapnist, and famous relative, Gavrila Derzhavin, Skalon associated with top intellectuals and she personally knew the great nineteenth-century Russian writer, Nikolai Gogol, as well as prominent Decembrist activists. Dolgorukaia can claim no similar cultural activities and her writing is limited to her memoirs. It seems safe to assume that aspiration to literary style played a relatively small role in their composition. All of these memoirs give women's perspectives on life, but unlike most of them, Dolgorukaia's text concentrates on a very brief period, only a few years, briefer even than Labzina's fragmentary text. While Catherine, Dashkova, Golovina, Durova, and Skalon include broad pictures of court and cultural life, Labzina and Dolgorukaia pay greater attention to their personal and family lives.

Dolgorukaia's memoirs anticipate the travails of the Decembrist wives who also voluntarily followed their husbands into Siberian exile, and, for that matter, twentieth-century female witnesses of life in labor camps, such as Evgeniia Ginzburg (see Natasha Kolchevska's essay in this volume). However, neither Dolgorukaia's significance as one of the earliest Russian memoirists, as a witness to Russian history, as a linguistic phenomenon, or even as a woman exile, can explain why her text was read, quoted, imitated, amplified, and turned into poetry and drama probably more than any other Russian eighteenth-century text, or why it has been adapted for all classes and ages, and still continues to be published and discussed. To be sure, several generations of male Dolgorukiis used her text to enhance their proximity to subsequent courts, and to rehabilitate their name by showing both their hardships and the cruel punishments meted out by Anna's infamous "German party." Relatives have also used her text to highlight an upright female ancestor as compensation for missteps by male ancestors. Writers unrelated to Dolgorukaia have utilized her text for many other personal and political agendas.

One reason for the broad appeal of Dolgorukaia's memoirs is the very amorphousness of the genre itself, as described in the introduction to this volume: its "slippage" between unofficial history, artistic literature, subjective record, gossip, anecdote, and social or political document. Dolgorukaia's memoirs bear traces of all of these genres and lend themselves particularly well to a variety of readings. But perhaps the main reason for their lasting popularity is the specific image of humble, self-sacrificing, yet courageous and patriotic femininity that Dolgorukaia depicts—an image that has been surprisingly tenacious through major social, political, and cultural upheavals.[13]

I will examine the appropriation of Dolgorukaia's image of femininity, as well as devices subsequent writers have used to extol her above and beyond her self-image: their omissions and expansions, their emphases and distortions. My main concern is with the reception of the memoirs, with the *reading* of her text, in keeping with one of the goals of this volume.[14] I hope to show how Dolgorukaia's self-image entered Russian culture and lingered as a female role model for over two centuries. I will investigate how this woman's voice was recycled to reflect her readers' social perceptions of gender, their specific views of Russian history, their own political agendas, as well as different generic and stylistic approaches to her themes (courtship and marriage, life of the Russian aristocracy, political favoritism, court upheavals, exile, and so on).

Dolgorukaia's text penetrated virtually all spheres of literary culture directly and in a chorus with male relatives' reminiscences, oral legend, eyewitness reports, and historical documents.[15] Written in 1767, the memoirs were first published in 1810 in the journal *Drug iunoshestva* (*The Friend of Youth*) by her grandson who subsequently described how "all in Moscow were reading them with tears in their eyes" (cited in Pavel Dolgorukii, 207). The memoirs, perhaps unwittingly, fit the prevailing Sentimentalist demand that a text move its readers. From the very outset the instructional, pious, and patriotic potentials of Dolgorukaia's text were emphasized: *Drug iuno-* • *shestva* was directed at youth of both sexes with a broad content that would "awaken in the readers love of God, Tsar', Fatherland, and fellow humans."[16] Dolgorukaia's memoirs were meant to address the heart and to illustrate the inconstancy of human fates, spiritual fortitude, and a good old-fashioned understanding of marital fidelity (8–9). There is evidence that the memoirs circulated in some form even earlier.[17] The 1810 edition, together with subsequent editions by other male descendants and scholars, was heavily edited and "improved" both for style and content.[18] The memoirs came to be framed by gradually growing introductions and commentary, which tend to canonize Dolgorukaia and also increasingly to distract readers from her original text. Not until 1913 was her text published in accurate form.[19]

In high poetry, two major Romantic poems about Dolgorukaia stand out: a *duma* (historical ballad) published in 1823 by Kondratii Ryleev, most famed for his socially engaged poetry with Decembrist revolutionary fervor, and an 1828 narrative poem by Ivan Kozlov, a talented translator, journalist, salon host, and disciple of Byron, Zhukovskii, and Pushkin. She also makes a cameo appearance in her grandson's poem "I" (Ivan Dolgorukii, 5–6). Nikolai Nekrasov, Russia's leading Realist poet and champion of oppressed women (in poetry if not in life, as we see in the Gheith-Holmgren piece on Avdot'ia Panaeva), used her as a model for the Decembrist wives in his long narrative poem, "Russkie zhenshchiny" ("Russian Women"). She entered German literature via Sigismund Schreiber's 1828 translation of Kozlov's poem, where the translator honors her as a friend through a friend: "Er war mein Freund; was ihm Natalje war, / Ward sie auch mir."[20]

Dolgorukaia became a popular heroine in prose fiction as well. In 1857 her text joined the English epistolary tradition in a historical novel by James Arthur Heard, an English pedagogue who spent several years traveling in Russia founding Lancaster schools. Already in 1869 E. S., an unidentified contributor to *Semeinye vechera* (*Family Evenings*), boasted that she was famous "in all European literatures" (744). Popular novels, short stories, and dramas show traces of her text, as do Russian folk songs about the Sheremetevs and Dolgorukiis, anecdotes, and oral legends. Her memoirs have inspired entries in "pantheons" and encyclopedias, and numerous historical (or quasi historical) accounts feature her as a role model for girls.[21]

By 1886 D. Korsakov, who wrote several scholarly historical articles on the Dolgorukii family, refers to Dolgorukaia's story as "well-known to everybody" and he emphasizes the necessity to keep *reminding* readers of her (264). The moral effect of memory is invoked time and again. In 1889 the editor of *Deshevaia biblioteka* (*The Cheap Library*), a series intended for a broad audience, finds it "necessary to remind people of such a remarkable woman as often as possible" (*Zapiski kniagini:* iv). Sergei Glinka, the editor of the conservative, patriotic, not to say nationalistic, journal *Russkoi vestnik* (*Russian Herald*) apostrophizes Dolgorukaia with a prediction: "your name and deeds will live on until in human hearts all feelings of love grow cold, all veneration of greatness of soul and virtue [ceases]" (3–4). Nekrasov in "Kniaginia M. N. Volkonskaia" ("Princess M. N. Volkonskaia," 853–72)

traces a chain reaction of remembering: Dolgorukaia's sufferings, kept alive
by her descendents, were thus known to Volkonskaia, whose fate will in turn
be told by her great-grandchildren to their friends and future generations.
Collective human memory is stronger than man-made monuments and will
posthumously rehabilitate victims of male power plays, such as Dolgorukaia, while her tormentor is forgotten:

> Puskai dolgovechnee mramor mogil,
> Chem krest' dereviannyi v pustyne,
> No mir Dolgorukoi eshche ne zabyl,
> A Birona net i v pomine.
>
> May the marble of graves outlast
> A wooden cross in the desert,
> But the world has not yet forgotten Dolgorukaia,
> While there's not a trace left of Biron.
>   (II, 867–72)

By 1992 a historian E. Anisimov (*Svoeruchnye zapiski,* 103) resurrects
her memoirs after an eighty-year hiatus in their publication, in a nicely illustrated miniature edition with a background essay and notes (the pretty
format, no doubt, designed to appeal to girl readers). In 1996 Dolgorukaia's
fate sets the tone for Liudmila Tret'iakova's fourteen tragic romances, which
also seem designed for a popular female readership. Tonchu 1999 (where
Dolgorukaia merits more column space than Catherine II) commemorates
the ninetieth anniversary of the 1908 All-Russian Congress of Women. The
poetics of memory expressed in all these different genres and eras confer
special immortality on suffering women.

Authors of scholarly and popular texts in different genres justify their
appropriation of Dolgorukaia's memoirs in surprisingly similar *negative*
ways. As Holmgren points out in this volume's introduction, Russian biographies and collections of biographies of famous people started to flourish
in the heady days of post-Napoleonic nationalism. *Plutarkh dlia prekrasnogo pola (Plutarch for the Fair Sex),* first published in 1816, should be
seen in this context as promoting famous women, including Dolgorukaia—
a case where the memoir genre was quite literally transferred into a biographical context. The rhetoric accompanying such a *positive* promotion
abounds in almost apologetic negatives. Svetlana Kaidash in her collection
of women in Russian history, designed to expand *Plutarkh dlia prekrasnogo
pola,* points out that Dolgorukaia is "*not* famed for anything" and *lacks* the
historical significance of an Ol'ga or a Rogned (61, my italics).[22] T. Tolycheva in her immensely popular historical novel muses that Dolgorukaia
played *no* role in Russian history, had *no* claim to fame, intended her memoirs only for her son and *never* imagined that they would be published a
hundred years after her death (5, emphasis added).[23]

In the literary journal *Otechestvennye zapiski* (*Notes of the Father-land*), E-n introduces Dolgorukaia as an exception to the larger-than-life personalities and events of her era, suitable for "the novel, tragedy or drama," and accordingly bills his piece as "*not* a history, *not* a novel, and *not* a short story" but merely a "cursory sketch" in which Dolgorukaia is admired for *not* complaining about divine judgment or human injustices and *not* revealing others' vices (276, 300, 279, my italics). Kaidash (79) echoes this principle, pointing to Dolgorukaia's life as "a modest private life, reminiscent of *Domostroi* times," which seemed insignificant to her contemporaries used to "scandalous liaisons, brilliant favorites and notorious love affairs."[24] Tret'iakova (7) opines that the historical neglect of women stems from their ability to offer only love, rather than accomplishments, talents, or power, and Dolgorukaia's history is neither surprising nor striking. Dolgorukaia is consistently singled out for what she is *not* and her text, too, is frequently described negatively. A typical comment is that her memoirs lack historical veracity and add nothing to our factual knowledge of her era.

Losses and lacks inhere in Dolgorukaia's original plot, but her borrowers subsequently expanded this negative semantic field. All these secondary texts are regularly punctuated by deaths, and loss of material things accompanies loss of family, social status, liberty, and justice. Like the original, most texts emphasize Dolgorukaia's lack of maturity, good judgment, or physical strength. Some of her most important actions are also negational in nature—from her refusal to take her family's advice, to her initial refusal to accept exile for the Dolgorukiis or to succumb to depression, to her refusal to live with her wealthy brother or at court after exile (mentioned in several secondary texts). Several later accounts embellish on the original hint of other possible suitors by emphasizing Dolgorukaia's refusal to accept Empress Anna's offer of a worthy suitor, or the brilliant fiancé that Empress Elizabeth later presumably proffered (possibly a confusion with her sister-in-law whose postexile marriage was indeed arranged by Elizabeth). Her acts of refusal are made weightier by the royal rank of her advisors in others' accounts.[25]

Perhaps the most provocative mark of negativity shows in her successors' impulse to tell what Dolgorukaia herself does *not* and to "correct" her unhappy ending. Ryleev and Kozlov focus on events not described in the memoirs, and their folk songs detail the execution of the Dolgorukiis, which was not included in her memoirs. Dolgorukaia unwittingly creates suspense by ending her story so abruptly. Regretting that she ended "where her exile began," Ivan Dolgorukii had the urge to "write the history of this Heroine of our time" (cited in Pavel Dolgorukii, 207–8). Heard is titillated by the brevity that "serves to excite in the reader an earnest wish to know all the particulars of her life." He takes her "short sketch" as the foundation for his novel (iv–v) but is tempted to change the ending: "Had this work been

a romance or a novel . . . the author . . . would, most certainly, not have fore-
gone the pleasure of restoring his heroine to the arms of her husband, and
to happiness more than sufficient to have compensated her for all her past
sufferings" (258–59). Within Heard's novel Dolgorukaia's governess imagines how

> the youthful pair would flee away from these harassing scenes and continual
> intrigue and ambition, and allow me to guide them to the blissful valleys of
> peaceful Switzerland, where they would be surrounded by an honest and
> simple-hearted people, and might pass their days in peace and quietness,
> amidst some of the grandest and loveliest scenes with which nature has
> adorned this world of ours. (107)

Although the element of romance becomes more accented in novels, narrative poems, dramas, and popular "galleries" of Russian women for women
readers, the emphasis on suffering remains paramount.

The tendency to characterize a woman and her text in the negative
terms described above is latent misogyny, typical of Western definitions of
women.[26] Of course, multiple negatives may not intend a negative verdict;
quite the contrary, Dolgorukaia seems particularly good because she lacks
the pride of her sister-in-law, or the inconstancy and materialism of contemporary society belles.[27] As we have seen, she is placed above her contemporaries precisely by these negatively worded traditional feminine ideals. In
less patriarchal contexts the same qualities might equally well be described
positively as humility, constancy, altruism, and more positive aspects of her
life might have been stressed, but virtually all the secondary Dolgorukaia
texts convey positive femininity through negating formulations.

By the same kind of twisted and potentially misogynistic logic, readers are presumed *eager* to devour women's suffering, and female martyrdom is thought *pleasurable*. The "quiet, mild grumble of a sorrowful soul,
long since broken by sorrow and suffering" is for E-n (278) permeated with
"wondrous charm," and for Heard, Dolgorukaia's fate "will furnish amusement and instruction" (iii). Kozlov finds Ryleev's theme (Dolgorukaia's unfortunate fate) *"infiniment touchant."*[28] Many accounts, from popular
history (E. S.) to high literature (Ryleev and Kozlov) use the hagiographic
term "martyr" (*stradalitsa*) to characterize her.[29]

Texts by others, regardless of when and where they were written, tend
to make Dolgorukaia much more appealing than she is in her memoirs. Dolgorukaia herself reveals both envy and anger in her descriptions of her relatives' better fortunes, selfish behavior, materialistic orientation, hunger for
power, and constant squabbling. To greater or lesser extent, self-promotion
is inherent in the memoir genre, and Dolgorukaia is no exception: she tends
to look down on lower-class people, and some of her descriptions of her
own ability to withstand tribulations when others succumb sound boastful

even when she states that she does not wish to boast and attributes her fortitude to God's design. Such (justified or unjustified) belittling of others or boasting about herself, even when disguised, reflect poorly on Dolgorukaia herself, as does her insistent attention to material goods combined with her even more insistent disclaimers of material interests. Yet, these glimpses of her very human weaknesses make her own text more palatable than many subsequent hagiographies. Plays, prose fiction, and biographies written by others use a number of devices to dramatize negative behavior in others and deflect blame away from Dolgorukaia herself. Dolgorukaia's goodness is frequently heightened by her contrast to bad personages, and interjected parallels to other suffering women enhance her sufferings.

Ekaterina Dolgorukaia, her sister-in-law, the "sovereign-bride" engaged to be married to Peter II when he suddenly died, is the most frequently contrasted "bad" personage.[30] This contrast derives from the memoirs where Dolgorukaia juxtaposes her own naive failure to pack valuables for the journey against her female relatives' pockets stuffed with valuables. Most subsequent accounts also contrast the two women in terms of possessions. Whereas Natal'ia had "not much at all," Ekaterina brought along "a huge quantity of dresses . . . various valuables: a collar with eleven diamonds . . ." (Korsakov 1879, 42). According to family legend, Ekaterina's final deed was to order all her dresses burned so that nobody else could wear them,[31] while Natal'ia is poor and voluntarily even throws away her wedding ring.[32] Korsakov (1879, 42) contrasts Ekaterina's fancy Western-style apparel to Natal'ia's homespun Russian dresses, creating a sartorial barometer of patriotism.

Averkiev's 1876 play *Razrushennaia nevesta* (*The Ruined Bride*) revolves around Ekaterina's four (real and fictitious) aborted love affairs (with the Austrian Count Melissimo, the Russian nobleman Nesterov, Peter II, and the Siberian functionary Osip Tishin) together with various unseemly schemes threatening both her own and her family's position.[33] The sad moral of the play is expressed after Ekaterina rejected Tishin: her beauty first brought her the throne, then exile, and finally the ruin of her brothers (271–72). Natal'ia's fidelity and love are contrasted to Ekaterina's inconstancy and their relatives' hunger for power and glory. Her fidelity and innocence echo her memoirs but are here presented without the slightest self-promotion. Even in Averkiev's play, however, both women are ultimately the victims of male political power plays.

Ol'ga Golokhvastova's drama "Dve nevesti" ("Two Brides"), which appeared in 1877, polarizes the two women further. Ekaterina is made even more evil, actually *eager* to trade her "true" love for Melissimo for the power she will get as the tsar's wife. Indeed, she is portrayed as more evil than the men: it is she who insists on marrying the dying tsar, who orchestrates Peter's false testament, and who plots to marry Natal'ia's future husband, Ivan, to Elizaveta (Peter II's aunt and the future empress). Other women are shown to cuckold their husbands openly, and female inconstancy is the rule to which Natal'ia is the exception.[34] The sisters-in-law are jealous and unfairly critical of Natal'ia and the male characters are as opportunistic in love as in politics. The unnamed alternative suitor merely hinted at by Dolgorukaia herself (41) is here personified and dramatized as the philandering Count Löwenwolde.[35] Tolycheva in her novel also develops the contrast between Natal'ia and Ekaterina, and Mordovtsev in his pantheon perpetuates the comparison by placing his entry for Natal'ia (244–63) right after the Ekaterina entry (228–43), as does Tonchu (89, 89–92).

In the memoirs Natal'ia's brothers are not particularly evil although there are hints that their wealth troubles her (33) and her childhood stay with her older brother is described as utter misery. Her siblings try to dissuade her from keeping her vows to Ivan when the Dolgorukii fortunes turn, and they fail to attend Natal'ia's wedding, presumably due to illness. Yet they are shown to be generous and weep when she leaves for the wedding. Dolgorukaia's later correspondence shows her older brother Petr to be a miser who did not give her or her sons their fair share of the Sheremetev wealth.[36] On the other hand, she was quite fond of her younger brother Sergei (*Pamiatnye zapiski* 1867, 22). Fictional accounts tend to accentuate Dolgorukaia's disapproval of her older brother, as does Golokhvastova's play where he is even scheming with Löwenwolde to expose Ivan for treason. In the play Natal'ia is an even more virtuous and timorous bride than in her memoirs (which totally ignore Ivan's notorious libertinism) and she *chooses* to ignore Ivan's "crimes" even after she is made aware of them both by others' accusations and Ivan's own confession to premarital sex, womanizing, and falsifying Peter's testament to gain Elizaveta's (the future empress's) hand. She is tolerant beyond all credibility.[37]

Petr Furmann's 1856 novella for young girls is a broad popularization of the memoirs and other accounts (especially Kozlov's poem), designed both to instruct and entertain. He uses ominous parallels and female co-suffering to make Dolgorukaia's innocence and sufferings more palpable than in the memoirs. He emphasizes Ekaterina's true love for Melissimo and her agony over Peter's proposal (7–12; 27–32). Dolgorukaia's negative comments about members of her own family are entirely omitted, while her expressions of dislike or envy are often, as in the plays, "acted out" by the disliked characters themselves to enhance the saintly picture of Natal'ia.

In Heard's novel there is not a trace of nasty behavior by any Dolgorukii, other than the father, the generally acknowledged villain. As in Furmann, even Ekaterina presents a positive parallel to Natal'ia in her suffering. She is introduced (contrary to fact) as Natal'ia's childhood playmate in the idyllic Sheremetev garden (24, 87–88). The friendship motivates Ekaterina's later letter to Natal'ia (63–73), where she pours out her sorrow over sacrificing her true love (Melissimo) to parental ambition, thus anticipating

Natal'ia's later dilemma and her opposite decision to follow her own heart. The novel contains a number of such female parallels. The fate of Mariia Menshikova (who, ironically, preceded Ekaterina as the tsar's bride and who followed her father into a Siberian exile orchestrated by the Dolgorukiis) intertwines with that of the Dolgorukiis in a Sentimentalist Siberian fiction, ending with reconciliation, forgiveness, and repentance, that bears no resemblance to real events.[38] The sad stories of other female victims of historical events, Natal'ia Naryshkina (27), Evdokiia Lopukhina (xxi, 36), Ekaterina Skavronskaia (31–35), and even the Biron family (232–34) are woven in. Through this obsessive parallelism not only Natal'ia's life but the entire post-Petrine era is characterized by "vicissitudes," and Heard manages to achieve historical continuity and to generalize the mistreatment of Russian women into a virtually national characteristic. Mordovtsev similarly introduces her as one of the many women who during the troubled post-Petrine era were crushed by the juggernaut's wheel.

Several accounts, most recently Kaidash (129–30), extend the bad times to include the reign of Elizaveta, showing how exile was in turn meted out to those who had exiled the Dolgorukiis: Biron, Ostermann, Münnich, Golovkin, and others. Ekaterina Golovkina, for instance, voluntarily accompanied her husband, the vice-chancellor, into exile. Dolgorukaia's sentiments and words are easily recognized in her response to her empress in Korsakov's historical account: "What are honors and riches to me when I cannot share them with my beloved . . . I loved my husband in happy times, I love him in unhappy times too, and the only favor I ask is not to be separated from him" (Korsakov 1886, 280, cf. Townsend 40–41). Nekrasov extended the time frame to the post-1825 exiles. In all these texts Natal'ia's status as innocent victim is enhanced by female contiguity and in many texts Russia has reverted to "oriental barbarism," failing to keep up with European progress. Dolgorukaia becomes the vehicle for the authors' political criticism of autocratic injustices.

Several other good women figure silently in the original memoirs: Natal'ia's governess, her servant girl, and the two distant female relatives who represented the Sheremetev family at her wedding, when politics (or illness) prevented her immediate family from associating openly with the Dolgorukiis. These personages undergo amazing metamorphoses in subsequent accounts. As fellow sufferers they make Dolgorukaia's self-sacrifice a more generally feminine virtue, and as eyewitnesses to her sufferings they can testify to her greatness "objectively" and without tainting her image with undue pride. Averkiev combines all these faithful women into one composite personage named Anna Rodionovna, a distant relative whose name cannot but evoke Pushkin's famous nanny, Arina Rodionovna, one of the most tenacious positive images of simple Russian womanhood in all of Russian culture. Many of Dolgorukaia's exact memoir phrases are mouthed by this sainted relative (see, for example, Townsend, 46–47; Averkiev, 204). Like Dolgorukaia in the memoirs, Rodionovna, too, insists on Ivan's innocence and honorable deeds. A playful conversation between Natal'ia and Rodionovna culminates in a famous anecdote about Ivan's goodness, which goes well beyond the memoir account.[39] In the description of Natal'ia's wedding, the mute widows from the memoirs are replaced by the vocal Rodionovna whose refrain "not proper, not proper" gives us the same sense that the patriarchal Sheremetev absence makes this wedding woefully inadequate. Rodionovna also repeats Dolgorukaia's own medical excuses for her brothers' inability to attend her wedding and their tearful send-off.[40] Her words "It seemed that the very walls in my father's house helped me weep" (54) are here repeated almost verbatim by Rodionovna (Averkiev, 242).

In Golokhvastova's play we find similar character inventions and reassigned phrases, such as the new figures of Anis'ia, and her daughters who serve Natal'ia *in loco parentis*. Furmann resolves the problem of Dolgorukaia's piety by having Natal'ia gradually gain religious awareness from her governess and her husband (e.g., 91), as does Heard. One effect of these kinds of speaker substitutions and reassignments of worldly wisdom is that Dolgorukaia seems even more innocent and much less concerned about her own social position than she does in her memoirs.

The governess, identified as the Swiss Maria Stauden, is most creatively developed by Heard, who presumably even located part of the Dolgorukaia-Stauden correspondence.[41] Heard's novel combines these "authentic" letters with several invented ones by fictional and real personages, sections of narrator's narration, a verse epigraph, preface, introduction, and conclusion. The epistolary mode is a particularly felicitous choice for portioning out Dolgorukaia's monological account among several other speakers and points of view. Some events are given extra emphasis or more varied interpretations in multiple tellings by (or to) different persons, and especially the governess misses no opportunity to voice her admiration for Natal'ia. The death of the tsar, for instance, serves Madame D. (Heard's fictionalized governess) (100) mainly as a pretext to praise Natal'ia: "A passion so pure and disinterested seems to ennoble our nature, and to elevate it almost to a level with the nature of beings of a superior order" (102).[42] Heard's governess frequently explains or excuses Natal'ia's less than ideal behavior in the memoirs version: "Even poor Nathalia, whose gentle disposition was a stranger to all angry passions, could not help feeling deep indignation. The vexation, however, occasioned by this harsh proceeding was but of short duration" (126).[43] Natal'ia is depicted as "a kind of superior being" who already as a child sacrificed money given her "for jewels and dress" to rebuild a burned-down village—a case of typical Sentimentalist philanthropy and a foreshadowing of her adult disregard for possessions. In her memoirs, Dolgorukaia emphasizes the role of her own mother, but she omits practically all references to herself as a mother; her addressee-son would presumably have known firsthand. In Heard's novel the mother, even after her death, consistently guides both Natal'ia's and the governess's behavior and thoughts.[44] Featuring the governess as a surrogate mother allows Heard to double the emphasis on motherhood, and then to triple it as Natal'ia herself tells her governess about the births of her two sons (192, 194) and expresses concern for their upbringing, all of which does her credit. Heard's Dolgorukaia grows into a nurturing mother by learning from real and substitute mothers, and the monastically justified retrospective piety in the memoirs is in the novel turned into a more compassionate femininity channeled into idealized maternity.

In Furmann's novel Dolgorukaia is featured as a role model for the "the dear [female] readers." Generically his work is a bildungsroman showing her gradual maturation as a series of self-sacrifices to males: first to her father, then her husband, then her sons, and finally her Lord God. Ideal femininity as submission to men may be Furmann's main message to young girls. Dolgorukaia's personal maturation is, however, also significant. Her attitude to work, for instance, slowly improves as she matures from a spoiled girl into a good housewife. Some of this transformation into enforced adulthood can be gleaned in the memoirs as well,[45] but Furmann substitutes Dolgorukaia's eighteenth-century sensibilities with his own nineteenth-century views of women as housewives. In her memoirs Dolgorukaia is distressed over her failure to bring adequate supplies for the journey. Furmann (77) dramatizes the topic into a concrete incident where Ivan and Natal'ia go for a walk, miss dinner, and are told to fend for themselves. Natal'ia exclaims: "All the better! Ivan, I will be your housekeeper; I will cook for you only your favorite dishes." Similarly, the memoirs merely hint at manual labor. Dolgorukaia notes disparagingly that her sisters-in-law replaced her personal maid with a mere "laundress' helper who couldn't do anything but wash clothes" (71). Washing is for Natal'ia herself never more than a diversion. While on board ship she amuses herself by washing handkerchiefs between fits of weeping (75). Furmann presents her as a hardworking young housewife, cleaning, mending, and washing. He even addresses a paean to hard work and puts it in the perspective of Dolgorukaia's own times: "Would ever the valiant Count Boris Petrovich Sheremetev, the friend of the Great Emperor, recipient of the highest possible honors, would he ever have thought, amidst his might and untold riches, that his daughter, child of his own blood, would wash her own linen!" (124–25).[46] Furmann both expands the female network by enhancing and inventing female fellow victims and eyewitnesses, and injects his own era's more bourgeois view of women, together with the focus on quotidian *byt* that Realist recorders of women's lives tend to risk (as we shall see in the discussion of Panaeva)— all of which he uses to suggest that both the fragile feminine woman-child and the idealized subservient housewife are appropriate role models for young girls.

Dolgorukaia's memoirs emphasize a patriarchal male presence in subtle ways. Her *raison d'écrire* is mainly her son. Early on she mentions the joy of her *"father's* friends" at the birth of "a great *nobleman's* daughter" who "will attract all the prominent eligible young *men*" (added emphasis). Although her mother and sisters are important, Dolgorukaia thinks of her lineage patriarchally. Her father died when she was very young and initially gets little attention, but he is intermittently referred to as "the first field marshal" who was "much loved by the people" (39). Natal'ia's betrothal to "the foremost young [male] person in the state" (38) would "restore her family and raise her *brothers* to their *father's* estate" according to the common people (39).[47] And she constantly praises her husband Ivan, contrary to his known behavior. Iurii Lotman (299) even goes so far as to state that, in addition to her humility about her own life, she "writes a saint's life about him, turning her sinful and carefree husband into a martyr," in contrast to Labzina who does the reverse in her memoirs. Male deaths serve as milestones in her memoirs: those of her father and her tsar. Most subsequent accounts add those of her father-in-law, her husband, her younger brother, and her younger son.

The most obvious (mis)appropriations of Dolgorukaia's memoirs into a patriarchal context are her male relatives' "corrected" versions, which I have already mentioned. Her grandson's verse autobiography "I" (I. M. Dolgorukii, 5–6) shows her sharing everything with her husband, who was dearer to her than her own self. In him she lost everything. Her status as self-sacrificing wife was her most salient feature to her descendants. Popular accounts similarly represent her as an example of female virtue seen patriarchally: "the self-abnegation of mothers, the fidelity of wives, and the tenderness of daughters" (E. S., 731).

Furmann significantly develops the male context, and the information he garners from Dolgorukaia's text is supported by numerous (more authoritative) male sources, starting with Karamzin's *History*. He uses Kozlov's poem for a chapter epigraph and for several romantic interludes, together with unnamed historical sources, newspaper accounts (*Sanktpeterburgskie vedomosti*), P. Nebol'sin's travelogue, Pashkov's letters, the memoirs of Count de Liria (the Spanish minister), official government manifestoes, geography books on Siberia, local legends, and so on. Furmann sees Dolgorukaia as her father's devoted daughter. He expands her role as a mother, too, but her main quality is her devotion to a husband who is not nearly as positively described in Furmann's text as he is by Dolgorukaia herself. Much is made of the Sheremetev family's glory and the Dolgorukii family's power and the life of luxury she might have enjoyed. The role of her father is particularly embellished by the awe expressed by the "common folk." His fame extends internationally in her nanny's artless stories about his deeds among Germans and Swedes. Natal'ia internalizes her nanny's picture of her father and remembers him at key points in her life so that her actions, in a way, become doubly derivative. Even the description of Dolgorukaia's courageous rebellion when she marries Ivan against her family's advice emphasizes her as "a worthy daughter of her [by then deceased] father" (48), following his example, whereupon (with a little help from Kozlov) she kneels down before the paternal portrait "as if asking for his blessing" (65).[48] Later her father is cause for remembering better days (125) and she is singled out for an officer's compassion because of her father's great deeds (112–13). Furmann turns her into a product of male greatness.[49]

Poems about Dolgorukaia also emphasize male domination and male appropriation of Dolgorukaia's speech and acts. Ryleev's *duma*, while extracting some facts from her memoirs, is structured around the wedding ring legend.[50] Dolgorukaia is presented as a martyr during her final contemplation of her "dear friend," given her for a momentary taste of happiness. Her thoughts are centered on her past sacrifices for Ivan, and her only consolation is her memory of him. It is this memory that she now has to sacrifice by throwing her wedding ring into the Dniepr, as she tearfully prepares to renounce life itself and enter the monastic schema as if buried alive and fated to "dream only of the grave until the grave" (lines 50–56). Ryleev thus highlights her last act of self-sacrifice and reduces her very life to her relationship to her husband.[51]

Kozlov's poem was indebted to Ryleev (Maslov, 236), dedicated to a male poet, V. A. Zhukovskii, and framed by epigraphs from Dante ("There is no worse suffering than remembering days of happiness in times of misery") and Byron ("The lost on earth revived in heaven"). Both epigraphs lend male support to sentiments of sacrifice, lost happiness, and heavenly rewards, culled from the memoirs. An old man then utters specific words and ideas recognizable as Dolgorukaia's own from the memoirs, while a male infant and a male corpse guide her actions. Kozlov, following Dante, places Dolgorukaia's happy childhood in the perspective of her miserable return to Moscow, on foot, alone with a baby, and still ignorant of her husband's fate. At her childhood home, an ancient priest shows her true Russian hospitality and consoles her with Christian exhortations, stories about the former glory of Sheremetev, and the tragedy that struck his daughter, whom the priest does not recognize as the woman before him. Natal'ia is multiply present: as a child (through the priest's story, her own fleeting memories, and the surroundings) and as an adult (both as a postexile generic wanderer-mother and as the "real" but unrecognized Natal'ia). The adult Natal'ia is regaled with a male story about the young Natal'ia. These fictitious Natal'ias, but especially the young Natal'ia, are clearly recognizable from the memoirs, but the patriarchal old Russian layer is enhanced by a male survivor. Field marshal Sheremetev's larger-than-life image literally hovers above her as she kneels before his portrait as if asking him to bless her infant son. Her fervent wish to be united with her husband is the focal point and propels her to the Kremlin.[52] She arrives on a moonlit night and her beloved appears to her in a vision of a bloody hanged corpse.[53]

In Kozlov's poem the hazy atmosphere evokes Zhukovskii's verse as an intertextual background landscape. The Gothic tonalities of Russian pre-Romantic poetry are recreated in Dolgorukaia's fate which "has chained her / between a corpse and an orphan" (part 2, stanza 11). This dilemma sets the stage for the rest of the poem: her son grows up, she is free to enter a monastery, but even there she belongs to Ivan until she rids herself of the final symbol of earthly ties: her wedding ring. Kozlov concludes with the ring legend. N. A. Polevoi (549–50) tells us that the poem made Kozlov the favorite poet of female readers who could identify with women's suffering in a patriarchal world. In Dolgorukaia's memoirs the legend is twice prefigured: the ring is described as an example of the opulence of her betrothal (39) and she tells us how a pearl from her bracelet fell into the river (not the Dniepr, of course) while she bid farewell to her governess in Siberia (75). Whatever the origin of the ring legend, its persistent popularity in post-memoir texts foregrounds the two most prevalent images of old-fashioned patriarchal femininity presented to Russian readers over the centuries: faithfulness together with subordination to a husband, and piety together with the requisite suppression of earthly erotic love.[54] Kozlov encloses the *Domostroi* within a saint's life, enveloped in pre-Romantic wrappings.

As we have seen, Dolgorukaia's autobiographical statements are often reassigned to other characters in subsequent dramatic and epistolary texts. In prose versions an omniscient narrator frequently serves a similar role of enhancing, explaining, and mitigating original statements in narratorial digressions and interpretations. Glinka's narrator, for one, pauses between quoting and paraphrasing the memoirs to emote on or support what she has said or done, or to generalize her personal virtues into human ideals. The narrator even recasts her words into inclusive first-person plural form: "We, too, envy greatness! we, too, are tortured by the mediocrity of our lot! we seek, strive for those qualities that are the reason why those who have experienced greatness wish they hadn't been born" (Glinka, 37). Mordovtsev's equally sympathetic agreement with (261) or apologies for (251) memoir statements take the shape of phrases like "truly," "in actual fact," "indeed" (260) and he adds information that makes her suffering even more acute: "To this it must be added that Natal'ia Borisovna made this distant and difficult trip while pregnant" (261). This is the only direct reference to her pregnancy—a condition that Dolgorukaia herself might well have used to her advantage, had such biological data been proper themes for a nun.[55]

Many recycled versions of Dolgorukaia's memoirs have tried to "improve" the memoirs *stylistically*, by invoking canonical male authors. Kozlov, with his foregrounding of Ryleev, Zhukovskii, Dante, and Byron, also followed his male models stylistically by recasting the prose memoirs into verse. Furmann, from the very first chapter, uses learned male sources (Kozlov, Karamzin), not only to gain scholarly credence, but also to achieve "literariness." The most common Sentimentalist images and punctuation would be easily recognized even without his direct reference to Karamzin. Sentimentalism, which was by then (in 1856) decidedly hackneyed in high literature, seems to have persisted in popular literature, particularly texts which, like Furmann's, were written for young girls. On the level of plot, too, one can discern his Sentimentalist bent, reminiscent of Heard's and Kozlov's texts (e.g., part 1, stanza 9). Natal'ia's childhood philanthropy (she helps needy villagers and wipes the tears of those who suffer [6])[56] in combination with descriptions of a young girl's awakening and silent conversation with nature distinctly echo both Karamzin's "Frol Silin" and his eponymous boyar's daughter (2–4). Karamzinian rhythmical *periody* (passages with anaphoric repetition in syntactically parallel clauses, rhetorical questions and exclamations, emotive orthography) abound, and Dolgorukaia's simple conversational style gives way to Sentimentalist excesses.[57] But although Furmann seems to think that the outdated "feminine" Sentimentalist style was still appropriate for young girls, he is no pure Sentimentalist.[58] He also employs Realist techniques, such as speech differentiation, absent from Dolgorukaia's text. Furmann introduces lower class personages who speak in character, and he invents crowd scenes or dramatizes those embryonically present in the memoirs (16–19, 93–96, 118–19), for example, the dramatization of a boor engaged in a lofty literary discussion (Townsend, 44–45; Furmann, 136–40). Often folk wisdom is set against aristocratic pretense and Natal'ia matures as she comes to recognize the difference. Furmann also adds the kind of "inessential details" that so irked Konstantin Leont'ev in Tolstoy, for example, the piece of food that fell back onto the plate (8) or the fly that kept hitting the glass (80–81) or the dirty popular print in the peasant hut (79). The frequent food imagery connected to Ivan's unpleasant father (88, *passim*) is also a stock device of Realist prose. Although male critics accused women memoirists of using excessively quotidian details, some men were all too eager to follow the women's lead.

Heard, too, takes great stylistic liberties with Dolgorukaia's text, mainly by paraphrasing or introducing more sophisticated vocabulary, tropes and figures—presumably, like Furmann, to make his novel more literary. It seems that they thereby (unintentionally perhaps) deny Dolgorukaia status as a talented writer. Heard does not cater to a specific limited readership, but in his preface he addresses a general English educated public which knows little about Russia, and, as a good pedagogue, he begins with a lengthy historical survey of the state of the Russian empire from pre-Petrine to post-Petrine times.

While Furmann's attempts to adapt his prose for young girls tend to get lost in his stylistic eclecticism, and Heard's sophisticated prose seems all too purple today, Ostrogorskii's history in a children's journal consistently made the memoirs child-friendly both in content and style.[59] Words like *zolovka* (sister-in-law) and *dever'* (brother-in-law) or the foreign *kavaler* (cavalier) are glossed; others are replaced by more contemporary words or explained by appeal to contemporary phenomena; diminutives and child-language are ubiquitous, and selection of details (wedding gifts, adventures, toys and amusements, anecdotes) is meant to excite his young audience. Place names and dates are added for historical and geographical edification and Natal'ia's education is elaborated beyond the memoirs, no doubt to inspire emulation. Some harsher truths are avoided or toned down—for example, the horrible punishment of Ivan. The memoirs are clearly recognizable and occasionally quoted directly.

From Shcherbatov's plaints to the popular historical essay by E. S., Dolgorukaia's memoirs have been used both to glorify and vilify old Russian customs, and even to make them exotic. Dolgorukaia herself hints at her preference for "the good old days" (36). For Glinka she exemplifies old Russian virtues—superior to "the illness of imagination," the dangerous inclinations to dreaminess, the dissipation, the vainglory, and the luxury that characterize nineteenth-century Russia (11–12, 30–31). Dolgorukaia's memoirs are drafted into serving Glinka's own conservative russophilia and xenophobia (especially bironophobia). Dolgorukaia embodies the ideals of female abstinence, self-abnegation, and suffering, together with moderation and monogamy that are favored as particularly Russian by Glinka and expressed in old Russian texts such as the *Domostroi*.

Vladimir Mikhnevich, a professional nineteenth-century historian and author of fiction who was particularly prolific in chronicling women in Russian history, puts a different spin on Dolgorukaia's Russianness. In his "historical studies" published in 1896 he, too, waxes lyrical over Dolgorukaia's purely Russian character: "Such a delicate, generous and self-denyingly loving heart grew and blossomed in our native atmosphere under the warm breath of old family principles and traditions conveyed, perhaps, by an old nanny, a simple Russian woman" (23–24). He Russianizes even her foreign governess and idealizes her mother as "a woman of the old Moscow order," brought up in the *terem* and hardly influenced by Peter's innovations (40–41).[60] He contrasts Dolgorukaia's account of her birth as a happy occasion with the generally negative attitude to the birth of *daughters* in Russia (35–40) and, while criticizing the custom of hiring foreign tutors, he points to Dolgorukaia's governess as exceptional in devotion and self-sacrifice (93).

His chapter on love and courtship opens with an approving quote from the memoirs, contrasting Dolgorukaia's old-fashioned fidelity with current fashions, and he cites her to counter the opinion that in old Russia love was something "coarse, exclusively animal" (145–48). While glorifying old Russia, he uses Dolgorukaia's memoirs partly to criticize current courtship and marriage customs (158–59) and he transcends national boundaries when he likens her (by yet another appeal to male literary authority) to Shakespeare's Juliet as an ideal of femininity (164–67). Mikhnevich promotes Dolgorukaia to a type, in whom the best of old Russian customs and European ideals were felicitously combined (199–200).

Furmann retains the chronology and geography of Dolgorukaia's memoirs, but extends the time frame for educational reasons, and he introduces numerous additional historical, geographical, and ethnographical sources. The hardships of the Siberian journey are made both more credible and more exotic. While Siberia is exoticized as the outer reaches of empire, a whole new level of patriotism is reached by references to P. Nebol'sin's 1845 travels. Siberian beauty compares favorably to the Swiss alps, the Russian peasants are superior to their German counterparts, and the natural wilderness of the Ural region is extolled (128–31). Such comparisons make Russia superior to Europe in natural assets and also its equal as an empire engaged in colonizing the "oriental" Siberia.[61]

Since Heard addresses the *English* reader (vi), his frequent and lengthy excursions into Russian history, ethnography, and culture are justified. He aims for edification and names Manstein's memoirs among his numerous sources (225). One of Madame D's letters clearly draws on the real letters of Heard's compatriots, Lady Rondeau and her English addressee (81–90).[62] As Schmücker (*N. B. Dolgorukaja*, 33) points out, Heard is a Russian patriot, contrasting Peter the Great's accomplishments both to the preceding "hydra of ignorance and superstition" (Heard, xxii) and to the "vicissitudes" of the Menshikov, Dolgorukii, and Biron families. He does not blame Petrine Westernization, as do many Russian texts, but Peter's "ignorant" and "ill-disposed" successors (xxiii–xxiv), and Dolgorukaia's personality shines all the brighter against Russia's "Eastern barbarism" which persists *despite* Peter's great accomplishments. Heard's sympathies would qualify him as a Westernizer and he clearly welcomes Russia's "prominent station among the powers of Europe" (xxiv). The foreign governess in Heard's novel "orientalizes" Russia as "a fairyland, in which the magic wand of some capricious wizard is continually at work elevating the lowly to places of the greatest distinction, and with the same ease and celebrity stripping them of their splendour, and driving them forth from the gilded halls of the palace to the dark and dismal precincts of a smoky log-hut" (97–98). Heard's Natal'ia, representing European Russia, likens herself to a southern, "exotic plant" moved to "the very verge of human existence" where it is destined to wither and die (179). She contrasts Siberian nature to the flowering Sheremetev garden, and she vividly conveys her sense of otherness, not to say "civilized" superiority, in her "orientalist" discourse on the Ostiaks and Samoyeds, two native Siberian tribes: "The distance between a Newton or Leibniz, and one of these uncultivated children of ignorance and superstition, is so immense that it is difficult to reconcile oneself to the idea that they really belong to the same species" (180–81). Perhaps the most amusing example of exoticism is Ivan's description of "the bones of a gigantic animal," drawing on the sensational discoveries of frozen mammoths. Heard's novel is a channel for sharing, not to say showing off, what he himself has learned about Russia.

While this kind of cultural information makes accounts of Dolgorukaia more educational, it detracts attention from Dolgorukaia herself, making her now a representative of conservative slavophile patriotism and xenophobic cultural views, now a Eurocentric philosopher, now a pretext for authors to show off. On the other hand, when all attention is focused on Dolgorukaia, she tends to be sanitized and canonized into a paragon of virtue. Such are the formulaic images of Dolgorukaia in pantheons, encyclopedias, and historical essays. Already seven years before the first publication of Dolgorukaia's memoirs, a letter to the editor (Karamzin) of *Vestnik Evropy* in 1803 suggested that Dolgorukaia be included in a "Gallery of Great Russian Women." The letter summarizes her life with information that suggests that the writer has either seen the memoirs or heard family legends.[63]

Plutarkh dlia prekrasnago pola, ili gallereia znamenitykh rossiianok (1819) was, as mentioned before, one of the earliest women's "galleries." Dolgorukaia appears somehow out of place among four empresses, several other royal women, and Ekaterina Dashkova, the most prominent eighteenth-century woman intellectual. The Dolgorukaia entry is extracted and paraphrased from her memoirs (100–26), with a few pages added for editorial introduction and conclusion. The editor follows Glinka in introducing her as a "rare example of marital love and fidelity" demonstrating that "a woman's heart has as much strength as the heart of a man." The Sentimentalist editorial framework enhances her best qualities and smoothes out the rough edges of the memoir image.

In Mordovtsev's gallery (244–45) Dolgorukaia appears among nineteen notable eighteenth-century Russian women, continuing a long line of unfortunates. Like all these galleries, it is a compilation of the findings of other scholars, lacks a scholarly apparatus, and is restricted by its format to brevity. It is intended to highlight the role of Russian women in history either as direct agents of historical events or as "sensitive barometers" (xi) of their eras. Dolgorukaia is placed in the second category. Mordovtsev addresses his work to "educated Russian women of all ages," since he is not engaged in a scholarly investigation, implying that scholarly works are inappropriate for women. Most galleries seem to make this assumption implicitly or explicitly. The 1983 compilation *Sil'nee bedstviia zemnogo* is also presumably addressed to women since Kaidash presents it as a continuation of *Plutarkh dlia prekrasnogo pola,* and Tonchu's encyclopedia targets women by commemorating a women's congress. The latter two works attest that Dolgorukaia's presence in these sorts of galleries persists even today.[64] All these galleries summarize her life according to the memoirs that are frequently quoted and paraphrased by the authors who take her positive statements at face value and complement them with admiring male accounts (Kozlov, Glinka, and Heard in particular). Although Dolgorukaia's memoirs tend to be altered in these galleries, it is gratifying that she herself has the most say in presenting her life among and to persons of her own gender. The author of the popular account in *Semeinye vechera* even regrets that Kozlov's "melodious verse" is "unfortunately filled with fabrications" and prefers Dolgorukaia's memoirs to high literature (E. S., 745).

The contradictions in Dolgorukaia's personality are often made to represent femininity as physical weakness combined with spiritual strength. This kind of gender essentializing is nowhere more evident than in Furmann's chapter on the nature of woman (96–98). Although Natal'ia is here allowed to develop both intellectually and spiritually, certain traits remain constant. Physical weakness is present in her own memoirs in expressions of fear and complaints about ailments. Most subsequent accounts retain and amplify weakness as a positive characteristic of women and the most logical medical explanation for swoons, faints, and weak spells, namely her pregnancy, is notably absent in all but one account. Dolgorukaia, and women in general, are everywhere presented as excessively childlike, innocent, gullible, and inordinately fond of games. Furmann makes Dolgorukaia even more naive. His amplification of one specific memoir scene is telling. The memoirs describe how she would string up a sturgeon and have him swim along the ship on the Siberian river as they traveled north. Furmann turns this innocent amusement into a lesson on female obedience and ecology when Natal'ia liberates the fish, harkening to the advice of Ivan (the confirmed hunter!) against the torture of innocent animals (125–26). She is constantly in need of male protection and edification, yet mysteriously, a pillar of strength. Dolgorukaia's contradictory nature defines miraculous femininity for the ecstatic Furmann:

Who can explain the contradictions in a woman's nature?
    Natal'ia Borisovna with rare strength and fortitude endured the most difficult spiritual sufferings, constantly battling them and when she could not overcome them, at that minute she appeared in all her tender, feminine weakness . . .
    It sometimes turned darker than a southern autumn night before her eyes when she glanced into her future, but Natal'ia, not fearing this darkness, put her faith in the grace of the Almighty . . .

113

Moral sufferings pierced Natal'ia's heart sharper than any knife, but she endured this pain with angelic patience . . .

The stroke of fate hit her more strongly than a thunderclap, but Natal'ia did not waver . . . she knew how to transcend her fate.

Such boundless spiritual strength often appears in certain select women, who on the other hand, materially, physically speaking, preserve all their feminine weakness, given them by nature herself. (Furmann, 98, ellipses original)

Furmann enthuses for several more lines and concludes: "But such is the miraculous nature of woman!" Yet, *weakness* seems to be disproportionally stressed. Furmann's Natal'ia herself admits: "Of course I am a weak woman, but my spirit is firm!" (154). To her father-in-law she is "quite evidently a woman" and consequently a "weak creature," "a baby." After such accusations she begins to blame herself for being nothing but "a characterless, weak child" (100–1). Ultimately Furmann reduces a woman's strength to something charming and cute but all too fragile. Selfless love and sacrifice are the prime spiritual qualities for emulation in Dolgorukaia. They too are gendered: "Oh, in a woman's heart is an inexhaustible treasure! This treasure is that pure, chaste love, recommended by the Savior and bringing joy to people. This love consists of constant self-sacrifice" (114). The male Savior recommends purity and chastity and the main beneficiary of this female kenoticism is man. Golokhvastova exposes this implication most vividly, showing Dolgorukaia as her husband's guardian angel, *her* goodness transforming *his* evil ways, as does Korsakov (1879, 32; emphasis here and below added) when he points out that Natal'ia's sympathetic personality can reconcile even the strictest moralist with *Ivan's* frivolous ways. Her self-effacing love for him is "the best measuring stick of *his* true moral qualities, indisputable proof that prince Ivan by nature was worthy of a better lot in life than the one he got." Similarly, in some texts (E. S., 732) Dolgorukaia's sufferings atone for *her father's* failure to observe his monastic vows when he remarries.

We have seen how recycled versions of Dolgorukaia's memoirs almost without fail have a hagiographic tonality: Dolgorukaia gains in saintliness either by contrast to greedy or philandering male and female personages, or by a proliferation of parallel sympathetic women figures—be they victims of court machinations, fellow mothers, sisters, or tutors in feminine graces. Her martyrdom gains when memoir statements are revocalized by other personages or when the authoritative patriarchal genealogy or male literati context expands. She is further extolled by references to historical events, and her image is flexible enough to accommodate politically conservative or radical agendas or the new bourgeois ideals of authors far removed from Dolgorukaia's situation.

Dolgorukaia is set up as a role model for Russian girls and women, but the kind of virtue in distress Dolgorukaia represents is seen as rare, especially among women. Heard (iv), for instance, deems Dolgorukaia's "heroic display of virtue" even more alluring because it is found in a "young and beautiful lady, nurtured in the lap of luxury"—presumably an unlikely place for heroism or virtue. The ultimate irony is thus that while she is a role model, the ideal she represents is unattainable for normal young girls—she is not a woman but a saint, a martyr, an angel, a goddess, or a being from a higher realm. Glinka sees in her "all heavenly virtues," and he apostrophizes her ecstatically: "Born into greatness, born among all earthly blessings, you gave up everything, in life you died for the world and lived for Heaven! . . . your spirit ascended above all human greatness: you were *an Angel on earth*" (3–4, Glinka's emphasis). Tret'iakova includes her among the Russian goddesses of her title, and Polevoi (537–39) sees her memoirs not as an ordinary life description but a novel—making her not a woman, but a fiction.[65]

Notes

A 1990–91 grant from IREX, sabbatical funding from Macalester College and the Wallace Foundation, and the University of Illinois Summer Workshop for Slavic and East European Studies in 1995 supported research for this article—support I gratefully acknowledge. I am also grateful for feedback at the 1995 summer workshop of the Eighteenth-Century Russian Studies Association at the University of Illinois and at the 1996 AAASS convention.

1. See Townsend 3–7 for a concise calendar of Dolgorukaia's life, a map, and the Dolgorukii family tree. Korovin provides the most accurate historical context and his notes to Dolgorukov (1997, 352–54) contain an excellent discussion of the variant forms of the name Dolgorukii/Dolgorukov. Despite his preference for Dolgorukov and its derivatives I will use the form Dolgorukii and its derivatives following past practice in English for Dolgorukaia (except in source references where I follow the original).

2. I refer to Dolgorukaia's memoirs according to Townsend where the English translation faces the authoritative 1913 Russian edition.

3. I will refer to Dolgorukaia's text as "memoirs," although most Russian editions are labeled "notes" (*zapiski,* or *svoeruchnye zapiski,* or *pamiatnye zapiski*).

4. For appeals to God's mercy see 35, 41, 43, 47, 53, 55, 61, 65, 83. For references to other biblical precedents see 41.

5. Dolgorukaia's conversational style is analyzed in Townsend, "Pamiatnye zapiski" 1867; Bicilli 382, 400; and Nakhimovsky.

6. See for example, 53, 55, 67, 69, 71.

7. The fifteen-hundred-word supplement of "fitful rewritings and declamations" (Townsend, 3) might also show Dolgorukaia's intentions to reedit her work for a wider readership. See *Svoeruchnyia zapiski* 1913, 45.

8. Dolgorukaia sees Ernst-Johann Biron (or Biren, the empress's favorite from Courland) as the biggest villain and her class prejudice is heard in her scornful and erroneous description of him (cf. Korsakov 1886, 272). Other eyewitness descriptions of Anna and Biron are also negative and Biron's social strivings are well known. Even the usually charitable Lady Rondeau, who lived in Russia from 1728–34 as the wife of a minister at Anna's court and was an eyewitness to many of the relevant events, admits "an awfulness in her [Anna's] countenance" (Vigor, 71). Biron, the male foreign villain, is often pitted against Dolgorukaia, the "truly holy [Russian] woman," as in the popular historical essay in *Ezhemesiachnyi kalendar'* (482). See Bain 177–300 and Manstein 13–45 on Anna and her "German party."

9. *Pamiatnye zapiski* 1867 refers to Dolgorukaia's notebook (*zapisnaia knizhka*), which complements her memoirs as firsthand information about her life. Her notebook rubric echoes the memoirs: "Extract of my Troubled Life."

10. See Marker 2000. An annotated English translation was published in 2001 (Marker and May).

11. Two English translations of Durova's memoirs were recently published. For an excellent contextualization, see Mary Zirin's introduction to Durova 1989.

12. Tartakovskii is the most comprehensive reference work on Russian memoirs of the period, and Shchepkina's 1914 article in *Istoricheskii vestnik* provides a good survey of women's memoirs. See also Clyman and Vowles on the genre, and Costlow, Sandler, and Vowles on gender and sex. The recent attention to Russian women memoirists is seen in, for example, *Svoeruchnye zapiski* 1992, Tret'iakova, or the numerous new Russian editions of Catherine's and Dashkova's memoirs. The English Fitzlyon edition of Dashkova's memoirs is reissued with a new introduction and afterword (Dashkova 1995). Dashkova 2000 is the most exact annotated edition of Dashkova's memoirs in the original French. Dolgorukaia's memoirs appeared together with those of Dashkova, Sof'ia Skalon, and N. N. Mordvinova in Moiseeva 1990, but neither in Podol'skaia 1998 (which contains the memoirs of Elizaveta L'vova and Skalon among seven eighteenth-century male memoirists) nor in Bokova 1997, which contains the memoirs of E. A. Sabaneeva, Golovina, and Labzina.

13. On women in eighteenth-century Russia, see Shchepkina 1914 and 1890. Likhacheva 1890 and 1893 on women's education also contain valuable general information on women.

14. For competent analyses of Dolgorukaia's memoirs, see, for example, Townsend, Lotman, and Ahlbeck.

15. Korsakov (1886, 263–64) notes that Dolgorukaia's memoirs were "virtually the only source" for several biographical essays.

16. Foreword to *Drug iunoshestva* 1 (1807): xi. The journal was to cover all possible fields from politics to household matters, health, and "rules of education, like those of Ladies Edgeworth and Hamilton" (xiii).

17. See, for instance, "O dobrodetel'noi Kniagine."

18. M. Nevzorov, the editor of *Drug iunoshestva*, assures his readers that Dolgorukaia's grandson had submitted "the most faithful copy of the original in his keeping" (10)—a statement later contradicted by others. See Pekarskii 67.

19. On the idea that "framing" by (male) texts diverts readers from the fate of a woman, see Sandler 165–83. Townsend 8–13 outlines the main (but not all) editions up to 1913, changes to her manuscript by successive editors, and the fate of the manuscript.

20. In *N. B. Dolgorukaja*, xxx, Schmücker notes that little is known of the translator beyond his friendship with Kozlov.

21. *N. B. Dolgorukaja*, xxii–xxxviii discusses many poems, folk songs, and translations as instances of *Wirkungsgeschichte*. Korsakov 1886, 263–64 lists some of the earliest popular accounts.

22. *Plutarkh dlia prekrasnogo pola* was initially a translation from French. Following Karamzin's suggestion for a "gallery of Russian women, famous in history or worthy of this honor," several female students of history used Karamzin and other sources to compose a Russian sequel, volumes 5 and 6: *Plutarkh dlia prekrasnogo pola, ili gallereia znamenitykh rossianok*, published in 1819. See volume 1, editorial foreword, i–iv.

23. Tolycheva is a pseudonym for Ekaterina Novosil'tseva. The first edition appeared in 1874. The 1912 edition cited here is the fifth edition. Tolycheva (5, 16) notes astutely that Dolgorukaia's memoirs do not contain a single name, not even that of her husband.

24. *Domostroi* is a sixteenth-century authoritarian conduct manual, which was a staple in Russian gentry households well into the eighteenth century. It regulated religious practice, family life, and domestic economy. In the ideal family, the husband rules by violence and fear, and the primary feminine virtues are submissiveness, silence, decorum, and chastity.

25. References to the empresses' advice appear in numerous texts, for example, "O dobrodetel'noi Kniagine," (1803); Glinka (1815, 16, 42); and "Kniaginia" (1819, 99). Some texts elaborate her hints of alternative suitors into melodramatic tales of jilted lovers.

26. See Lloyd on gender bias in Western philosophy.

27. See, for example, the memoir account (Townsend, 28–29) of the few things she packed compared to her sisters-in-law—an account repeated approvingly in virtually all versions. Dolgorukaia's comparative poverty during the journey and the monetary gift of her governess she described in her memoirs are borne out by the official inventories taken in exile and accounts of gifts to locals (Korsakov 1879, 31–52).

28. Maslov (1912, 236).

29. Mikhnevich (199–200) uses Dolgorukaia as the prototype for "a whole series of women-martyrs for their husbands' sins." In "Kniaginiia Natal'ia Dolgorukaia," *Ezhemesiachnyi kalendar'zhurnal* (484), Kniaginiia Natal'ia Dolgorukaia summarizes her life as suffering "for forty years as a wife, mother and sister."

30. Most accounts of Ekaterina are unflattering, for example, Semevskii (1878, 739), Tolycheva (50), Ignat'ev (38–46), and Sulotskii (14–15). Korovin (295–99) tries to balance earlier accounts, but even so, negative traits dominate. Vigor (18, 22–26) gives an unusually sympathetic account.

31. See, for example, Dolgoroukow (371); Bantysh-Kamenskii, part 2 (245); Ignat'ev (45); Sulotskii (19).

32. Dolgorukaia's wedding ring became legendary. The ring legend was first published in *Drug iunoshestva* 1 (1810): 69, where I. Lpkhn [Ivan Lopukhin] tells how he saw Dolgorukaia (his mother's friend) in Kiev and heard about her struggle over Christian ideals and passions of the heart. She severed her ties with earthly love by throwing her wedding ring into the Dniepr before entering the schema. See also *Pamiatnye zapiski* (1867, 62–63); Glinka (46); "Kniaginia" (1819, 125); Dolgoroukow (1867, 370); Polevoi (541); Furmann (158–64); Sulotskii (14). The ring incident is even included in her genealogy in Dolgorouky (1859, 21).

33. Melissimo was related to the Austrian ambassador and was in Petersburg as embassy secretary. I have normalized the spellings of his and other names throughout. Ekaterina's affair with Melissimo is documented in Dolgoroukow (1867, 295); Vigor (18–19); Mordovtsev (230–33). I have seen no other references to Nesterov, but the Tishin incident is documented in most accounts of the exile, implicating the officer Ovtsyn, rather than Tishin himself (Mordovtsev, 239–40). Shubinskii (193–213) features several romances in Berezov, and shows that the spurned Tishin got his revenge by informing against the Dolgorukiis.

34. The Dolgorukiis (Ivan's father mainly, but according to many, Ivan himself, as well) created a false testament for Peter so that his fiancée, Ekaterina Dolgorukaia, would succeed him on the throne—an unsuccessful ruse that was among the causes for their exile. Many, most notably Shcherbatov, grumbled over post-Petrine moral corruption. Cuckolding was often satirized (see Pokrovskii).

35. Tret'iakova (19, 25) perpetuates the Löwenwolde plot. The rivalry between Count Löwenwolde and Ivan Dolgorukii may have originated in the fact that Ivan replaced Löwenwolde as court chamberlain (*kamerger*) to Peter and Löwenwolde was demoted to court marshall (*gofmarshal*) to Peter's sister, Natal'ia (see Korovin, 294).

36. See *Pamiatnye zapiski* (1867, 61–62) where Bartenev shows that Petr's miserliness was exaggerated and that most of his wealth came from

his wife. Dolgorukaia's letter to her son (54) sarcastically covets the crumbs from the rich table of "wretched Lazarus." Many subsequent accounts use the brothers to enhance Dolgorukaia's suffering. Korovin (318–19) points out that her sense of unfair treatment was felt for generations.

37. Anecdotes about Ivan's premarital womanizing are incorporated in the play. Shcherbatov (39–40) uses Ivan as proof of his century's dissipation: "he fell in love with or rather, appropriated, among others, the wife of Prince N. Iu. T., née Golovkina [Trubetskaia] for fornication and lived with her, openly." Ivan would harass the Trubetskoi household and rape women in his own quarters. Bartenev (*Pamiatnye zapiski* 1867, 9–10) points to youthful carousing. Korsakov (1879) tries to balance eyewitness accounts with historical and anecdotal sources. E. S. (733–34) and Korsakov (1879, 32) blame Ivan's bad behavior on foreign models, paternal influence, and post-Petrine mores. Ivan also presumably courted Elizaveta, Countess Iaguzhinskaia, and Count Ernst Münnich's oldest sister (see Korsakov 1879, 35–36; Münnich 20). Korovin (292–93) points out (312) that Ivan was a poor husband even in exile.

38. See 35, 38–48, 53, 88–90, 152–67. N. Kostomarov's novella "Samoderzhavnyi otrok" ("The Autocratic Child," 1878) contrasts Mariia Menshikova with Ekaterina and introduces Natal'ia positively, if more marginally.

39. Ivan presumably once bit the young tsar's ear to indicate the pain of a beheading and thus forestalled Peter's order for a beheading (Korsakov 1879, 33).

40. According to many accounts there were no valid medical reasons (see, for example, Dolgoroukow 1867, 346).

41. Korsakov (1879, 42) identifies her by financial letters the Dolgorukii family wrote. Three letters from the Dolgorukaia-Stauden correspondence are mentioned in *Russkii biograficheskii slovar'* without any further information (vol. 5, 22–25; see also Townsend 17, 137 and *N. B. Dolgorukaja. Das Journal*, xxxii). One wonders whether the authors might not confuse Heard's fiction with reality. "Found letters" are a traditional device of fiction and, without further proof, there is no reason to regard Heard's letters as historical documents. Townsend (137) points to the governess's valuable eyewitness descriptions of Russia, descriptions that Heard could equally well have made up himself during his extensive travels in Russia.

42. This and other multiple tellings of, for example, Ivan's death (205–6, 250) indicate Heard's familiarity with legends about the Dolgorukii family. See Dolgorukov, P. V., 100–1; Korsakov 1879, 50–51; Dolgorukii, Petr, 124–25.

43. Some of the memoir statements most damaging to the image of Dolgorukaia were also omitted in early editions of the memoirs. Heard may thus have been exposed to a nicer gentler Dolgorukaia than she was in her full text.

44. See 27, 63, 76, 137, 139, 141, 177, 186, 255.

45. Zirin (266) notes the theme of enforced adulthood in Labzina's memoirs as well.

46. In pre-Petrine Russia, women were in charge of household duties, but even the *Domostroi* did not mandate that an upper-class woman perform these duties herself.

47. Golokhvastova (39), in contrast, has Anis'ia practice political correctness *avant la lettre:* her Natal'ia will raise the station of her brothers *and sisters.*

48. In Kozlov's poem (part 1, stanza 12) the portrait figures *after* Dolgorukaia's return from exile. She thinks her father might have saved her from misery had he been alive. Many popular accounts (for example, E. S., 738) place the incident before the wedding.

49. In Averkiev's play Dolgorukaia's veneration of her father appears as directly quoted paternal guidance (201). From the epigraph on, Heard, too, sees Natal'ia mainly as wife, a view he lets Natal'ia herself present: "the only ties that now bind me to life are my children—his children" (244, italics original). Paternity subtly impinges on maternity.

50. Maslov (233) points to the 1816 and 1819 editions of the memoirs and "many manuscripts" as Ryleev's sources and connects the ring episode in the poem to the lost pearl in the memoirs (235). He holds that Kozlov appropriated the episode from Ryleev (237).

51. In her notebooks (Korsakov 1886, 276) Dolgorukaia herself makes that equation: "They took away my life, my unparalleled, gracious father and husband."

52. Dolgorukaia did not actually return on foot and she arrived with two children in Moscow in 1740 (Korsakov 1879, 51). She did not know the fate of her husband until her appeal at the end of 1739 to the empress to either join her husband if he was alive or to take monastic vows (*Pamiatnye zapiski* 1867, 52; Korsakov 1886, 278). She finally took monastic vows in 1758. See Semevskii 1867, 1168.

53. Kozlov's vision has been influential on other accounts. Golokhvastova's play, for instance, ends when Natal'ia enters adult life and the image of her future husband is mirrored to her as a bloody omen of future horrors.

54. Dolgorukaia's memoirs inspired many variations on the jewelry theme. Maksimov (138) uses Ivan's ring for a riches-to-rags plot and in *Ezhemesiachnyi kalendar'* (483–84) the ring turns into diamonds that Natal'ia used to erect a memorial church. Ignat'ev (44) describes how Ekaterina (now Countess Bruce) donates a diamond for an iconostasis. Sulotskii (14) details a ring legend preserved by inhabitants of Tomsk where Ekaterina entered a monastery but refused to give up her ring. Folk songs use a wedding ring as a gift to the executioner to ease Ivan's suffering. Bezsonov

(9, 11, 12, 13) even uses the ring image to identify the personages in the songs. In Tret'iakova (26), after the removal of the ring "the person who was called Natal'ia Dolgorukaia is no more." The ring, symbolizing her marriage to Ivan, comprises her very identity.

55. Dolgorukaia's failure to embellish her pregnancies may reflect pre-Petrine customs: the *Domostroi*, for instance, has virtually nothing to say about childbirth or physical motherhood. By contrast, Varvara Golovina, in her memoirs describes a particularly difficult pregnancy (Bokova, 97).

56. Philanthropy is also used to show Natal'ia's development. Later when she herself is poor, she nostalgically recalls being a "guardian angel" to the poor.

57. See, for example, Furmann (63) for a typical Karamzinian *period*.

58. Sentimentalism implied "feminization" of literature. Its style was modeled on conversational "feminine" language and catered especially to women readers. See Vinogradov 216; Uspenskii 41–67; and Vowles.

59. His history is most likely based on *Pamiatnye zapiski* 1867.

60. Her mother, Anna Petrovna (née Saltykova), was Sheremetev's second wife, thirty-five years his junior, widow of Peter the Great's uncle, Lev Kirillovich Naryshkin, and quite close to court circles, which surely exposed her to Petrine Westernization.

61. See Layton on empire building, "orientalism," and Russian literature.

62. Vigor 22–35.

63. Compare, for example, "O dobrodetel'noi Kniagine" (93) and the memoirs (42).

64. Dolgorukaia sets the tone for Kaidash's entire collection since its title quotes Kozlov's Dolgorukaia poem.

65. Polevoi's review shows how the memoirs penetrated that genre as well. Almost half of it is a summary of her life with many direct quotes from the memoirs.

Works Cited

EDITIONS OF NATAL'IA BORISOVNA DOLGORUKAIA'S MEMOIRS

"Zapiski ostavshiesia po smerti Kniagini Natal'i Borisovny Dolgorukovoi, docheri slavnogo Fel'dmarshala Grafa Borisa Petrovicha Sheremeteva, suprugi Kniazia Ivana Alekseevicha Dolgorukogo, blizhaishego liubimtsa Imperatora PETRA Vtorogo." *Drug Iunoshestva* 1 (January 1810): 8–69.

"Kniaginia Natal'ia Borisovna Dolgorukova." *Plutarkh dlia prekrasnago pola, ili gallereia znamenitykh rossianok* 6 (1819): 95–128.

"Pamiatnye zapiski kniagini Natal'i Borisovny Dolgorukovoi." Edited by P. Bartenev. *Russkii Arkhiv* 1 (1867): 1–64.

Zapiski kniagini Natal'i Borisovny Dolgorukoi s portretami i risunkami. Deshevaia biblioteka, 85. St. Petersburg: tip. A. S. Suvorina, 1889.

Svoeruchnyia zapiski kniagini Natal'i Borisovny Dolgorukovoi, docheri g. fel'dmarshala grafa Borisa Petrovicha Sheremeteva. St. Petersburg: Obshchestvo liubitelei drevnei pis'mennosti, tip. Sirius, 1913.

N. B. Dolgorukaja. Das Journal. Translated and edited by Alois Schmücker. Munich: Wilhelm Fink Verlag, 1972.

Townsend, Charles. *The Memoirs of Princess Natal'ja Borisovna Dolgorukaja.* Columbus, Ohio: Slavica Publishers, 1977.

"Svoeruchnye zapiski kniagini Natal'i Borisovny Dolgorukovoi." In *Zapiski vospominaniia russkikh zhenshchin XVIII—pervoi poloviny XIX veka,* edited by G. N. Moiseeva. Moscow: Sovremennik, 1990, 41–66.

Svoeruchnye zapiski kniagini Natal'i Borisovny Dolgorukoi, docheri g. feldmarshala grafa Borisa Petrovicha Sheremeteva. Edited by E. Anisimov, St. Petersburg: Khudozhestvennaia literatura, 1992.

OTHER SOURCES

Ahlbeck, Malin. "Resistance through Martyrdom? A Study of Russian Women's Early Autobiographical Writing." Master's Thesis, Department of History, Åbo Akademi, Finland, 1999.

Anisimov, Evgenii. "'Zapiski' Ekateriny II: sillogizmy i real'nost'." *Zapiski Imperatritsy Ekateriny II.* 1859. Reprint, Moscow: Kniga, 1990, 3–24.

Averkiev, D. V. "Razrushennaia nevesta. Drama v chetyrekh deistviiakh s epilogom." *Russkii vestnik* 121 (January 1876): 175–276.

Bain, Nesbitt. *The Pupils of Peter the Great. A History of the Russian Court and Empire from 1697 to 1740.* New York: New Amsterdam Book Company, 1899.

Bantysh-Kamenskii, D. "Dolgorukaia, Kniagin'a Natal'ia Borisovna." In part 2, *Slovar' dostopamiatnykh liudei russkoi zemli."* Moscow: V tip. S. Selivanovskago, 1836, 228–40.

———. "Dolgorukaia, Kniazhnia Ekaterina Alekseevna." In part 2, *Slovar' dostopamiatnykh liudei russkoi zemli."* Moscow: V tip. S. Selivanovskago, 1836, 240–45.

Bezsonov, P. A., ed. *Pesni sobrannye P. V. Kireevskim izdany Obshchestvom liubitelei rossiiskoi slovesnosti.* In part 3, issue 9, *Vos'mnadtsatyi vek v russkikh istoricheskikh pesniakh.* Moscow: V tip. Bekhmeteva, 1872, 1–14.

Bicilli, P. "Die 'Haus'-Literatur und der Ursprung der klassischen Literatur in Russland." *Jahrbücher für Kultur und Geschichte der Slaven* 10, 1/2 (1934): 382–420.

Bokova, V. M., ed. *Istoriia zhizni blagorodnoi zhenshchiny*. Moscow: Novoe literaturnoe obozrenie, 1996.

Clyman, Toby W., and Judith Vowles, eds. *Russia Through Women's Eyes. Autobiographies from Tsarist Russia*. New Haven, Conn.: Yale University Press, 1996.

Costlow, Jane T., Stephanie Sandler, and Judith Vowles, eds. *Sexuality and the Body in Russian Culture*. Stanford: Stanford University Press, 1993.

Dachkova, Ekaterina. *Mon histoire. Mémoires d'une femme de lettres russe à l'époque des lumières*. Edited by Alexandre Woronzoff-Dashkoff, Catherine Le Gouis, and Catherine Woronzoff-Dashkoff. Paris: L'Harmattan, 2000.

Dashkova, Ekaterina. *The Memoirs of Princess Dashkova*. Translated and edited by Kyril Fitzlyon, with an introduction by Jehanne M. Gheith. Durham: Duke University Press, 1995.

Dolgorukii, Ivan Mikhailovich. "Ia." In vol. 2, *Bytie serdtsa moego ili stikhotvoreniia*. Moscow: V universitetskoi tipografii, 1817, 5–13.

Dolgorukii, Pavel Ivanovich, ed. "Materialy dlia russkoi istorii. Avtobiografiia ottsa moego kniazia Ivana Mikhailovicha Dolgorukova." *Moskvitianin* 6, 11 (1844): 197–213.

Dolgorukii, Petr. *Skazaniia o rode kniazei Dolgorukovykh*. St. Petersburg: V tip. Eduarda Pratsa, 1840.

Dolgoroukow, Pierre. *Memoires du Prince Pierre Dolgoroukow*. Vol 1. Geneva: Cherbuliez H. George, 1867.

Dolgorouky, Pierre. *Notice sur les Principales familles de la Russie*. Berlin: Ferdinand Schneider, 1859.

Dolgorukov, I. M. *Kapishche moego serdtsa ili slovar' vsekh tekh lits, s koimi ia byl v raznykh otnosheniiakh v techenie moei zhizni*. Edited by V. I. Korovin. Moscow: Nauka, 1997.

Dolgorukov, P. V. *Iz zapisok kniazia P. V. Dolgorukova. Vremia Imperatora Petra II i impreatritsy Anny Ioannovny*. Translated from French by S. M. Moscow: Obrazovanie, 1909.

The Domostroi. Rules for Russian Households in the Time of Ivan the Terrible. Edited and translated by Carolyn Johnston Pouncy. Ithaca: Cornell University Press, 1994.

Durova, Nadezhda. *The Cavalry Maid: Memoirs of a Woman Soldier of 1812*. Translated and edited by John Mersereau and David Lapeza. Ann Arbor, Mich.: Ardis, 1988.

Durova, Nadezhda. *The Cavalry Maiden: Journals of a Russian Officer in the Napoleonic Wars*. Edited and translated by Mary Fleming Zirin. Bloomington: Indiana University Press, 1989.

E. S. "Natal'ia Borisovna Dolgorukaia." *Semeinye vechera* 12 (1869): 730–45.

E-n, Ia. G. "Kniaginia Natal'ia Borisovna Dolgorukaia." *Otechestvennye zapiski, ucheno-literaturnyi zhurnal* 116, 1 (1858): 275–300.

Furmann, Petr. *Natal'ia Borisovna Dolgorukova. Povest' dlia devits.* St. Petersburg: V tip. Eduarda Pratsa, 1856.

Glinka, Sergei. "Obrazets liubvi i vernosti supruzheskoi, ili bedstviia Natal'i Borisovny Dolgorukoi, docheri Fel'dmarshala Borisa Petrovicha Sheremeteva, suprugi Kniazia Ivana Alekseevicha Dolgorukogo." *Russkoi Vestnik* 1 (1815): 3–47.

Golokhvastova, O'lga A. *Dve nevesty. Istoricheskaia drama v piati deistviiakh.* Moscow: V universitetskoi tip. (M. Katkov), 1877.

Heard, James Arthur. *The Life and Times of Nathalia Borissovna, Princess Dolgorookov.* London: Bosworth and Harrison, 1857.

Ignat'ev, R. "Iz zhizni Gosudaryni-nevesty kniazhny E. A. Dolgorukovoi." *Russkii arkhiv* 1 (1866): 38–46.

Kaidash, Svetlana. "'Sil'nee bedstviia zemnogo' sud'ba Natal'i Dolgorukoi." In *Sil'nee bedstviia zemnogo.Ocherki o zhenshchinakh v russkoi istorii.* Moscow: Molodaia gvardiia, 1983, 61–79.

"Kniaginia Natal'ia Dolgorukaia." *Ezhemesiachnyi kalendar'-zhurnal* 6 (1869): 479–84.

Korovin, V. I. "Kniaz' Ivan Dolgorukov i 'Kapishche moego serdtsa.'" In Dolgorukov, I. M., *Kapishche moego serdtsa ili slovar' vsekh tekh lits, s koimi ia byl v raznykh otnosheniiakh v techenie moei zhizni.* Moscow: Nauka, 1997, 283–350.

Korsakov, D. "Khniaz' Ivan Alekseevich Dolgorukoi (favorit i oberkamerger imperatora Petra Vtorago) (1708–1739)." *Drevniaia i novaia Rossiia* 1 (1879): 31–52.

———. "Kniaginia Natal'ia Borisovna Dolgorukaia." *Istoricheskii vestnik* 23 (February 1886): 263–82.

Kostomarov, N. "Samoderzhavnyi otrok." *Drevniaia i novaia Rossiia. Ezhemesiachnyi istoricheskii illiustrirovannyi sborniik* 1 (1878): 5–58.

Kozlov, I. I. "Kniaginia Natal'ia Borisovna Dolgorukaia." In *Polnoe sobranie stikhotvorenii.* (Biblioteka poeta. Bol'shaia seriia). Edited by I. D. Glikman. 2nd edition. Leningrad: Sovetskii pisatel', 1960, 377–408.

Layton, Susan. *Russian Literature and Empire: The Conquest of the Caucasus from Pushkin to Tolstoy.* Cambridge: Cambridge University Press, 1994.

Likhacheva, E. *Materialy dlia istorii zhenskogo obrazovaniia v Rossii (1086–1796).* St. Petersburg: Tip. M. M. Stasiulevicha, 1890.

———. *Materialy dlia istorii zhenskogo obrazovaniia v Rossii (1796–1828).* St. Petersburg: Tip. M. M. Stasiulevicha, 1893.

Lloyd, Genevieve. *The Man of Reason: "Male" and "Female" in Western Philosophy.* Minneapolis: University of Minnesota Press, 1984.

Lotman, Iurii. "Dve zhenshchiny." In *Besedy o russkoi kul'ture. Byt i traditsii russkogo dvorianstva (XVIII–nachalo XIX veka).* St. Petersburg: Iskusstvo—SPB, 1994, 287–313.

Maksimov, S. *Sibir' i katorga. Politicheskie i gosudarstvennye prestupniki.* Vol 3. St. Petersburg: Tip. A. Transhelia, 1871.

Manstein, C. H. von. *Contemporary Memoirs of Russia from the Year 1727 to 1744.* London: Frank Cass and Co., 1968.

Marker, Gary. "The Enlightenment of Anna Labzina: Gender, Faith, and Public Life in Catherinian and Alexandrian Russia." *Slavic Review* 59, 2 (2000): 369–90.

Marker, Gary, and Rachel May, eds. *Days of a Russian Noblewoman: The Memories of Anna Labzina.* Translated and edited by Gary Marker and Rachel May. Dekalb: Northern Illinois University Press, 2001.

Maslov, V. I. *Literaturnaia deiatel'nost' K. F. Ryleeva.* Kiev: n.p., 1912.

Mikhnevich, Vl. *Russkaia zhenshchina XVIII stoletiia. Istoricheskie etiudy.* Kiev: Iuzhno-Russkoe Knigoizdatel'stvo F. A. Iogansona, 1896.

Moiseeva, G. N., ed. *Zapiski i vospominaniia russkikh zhenshchin XVIII— pervoi poloviny XIX vekov.* Moscow: Sovremennik, 1990.

Mordovtsev, D. "Natal'ia Dolgorukova. (Kniaginia Natal'ia Borisovna Dolgorukova, urozhdennaia grafinia Sheremeteva)." In *Russkie zhenshchiny novogo vremeni. Biograficheskie ocherki iz russkoi istorii. Zhenshchiny pervoi poloviny XVIII veka.* St. Petersburg: A. Cherkesov, 1874, 244–63.

Münnich, Ernst. *Rossiia i russkii dvor v pervoi polovine XVIII veka. Zapiski i zamechaniia gr. Ernsta Minikha.* St. Petersburg: Tip. V. S. Balasheva, 1891.

Nakhimovsky, A. "A Syntactic, Lexicological and Stylistic Commentary on the Memoirs of Princess Natalja Borisovna Dolgorukaja." *Folia Slavica* 8, 2–3 (1987): 272–301.

Nekrasov, N. A. "O dobrodetel'noi Kniagine Natal'e Borisovne Dolgorukoi. (Pis'mo k Izdateliu)." *Vestnik Evropy* 12 (1803): 92–94.

———. "Russkie zhenshchiny. 1. Kniaginia Trubetskaia. 2. Kniaginia M. N. Volkonskaia. (Babushkiny zapiski)." In vol. 2, *Polnoe sobranie stikhotvorenii v trekh tomakh.* (Biblioteka poeta. Bol'shaia seriia). 2nd edition. Leningrad: Sovetskii pisatel', 1967, 309–74.

Nevzorov, M. "Predislovie." *Drug iunoshestva* 1 (January 1807): vii–xiv.

Pekarskii, P. "Russkie memuary XVIII veka." *Sovremennik* 4 (1885): 53–90.

Plutarkh dlia prekrasnogo pola, ili zhizneopisaniia velikikh i slavnykh zhen vsekh natsii, drevnikh i novykh vremen. Moscow: V universitetskoi tip., 1816–19.

Podol'skaia, I. I., ed. *Russkie memuary. Izbrannye stranitsy. XVIII vek.* Moscow: Izdatel'stvo Pravda, 1988.

Pokrovskii, V. "Rogonostsy v epigrammakh XVIII veka." *Chteniia v Imperatorskom obshchestve istorii i drevnostei rossiiskikh pri moskovskom unviversitete* 4, 215 (1905): 3–48.

Russkii biograficheskii slovar'. Edited by A. Polovtsov. Vol. 5. St. Petersburg: Tip. G. Lissnera i D. Sovko, 1916.

Ryleev, K. F. "Natal'ia Dolgorukaia." In *Polnoe sobranie stikhotvorenii.* (Biblioteka poeta, Bol'shaia seriia). 2nd edition. Leningrad: Sovetskii pisatel', 1971, 167–70.

Sandler, Stephanie. *Distant Pleasures: Alexander Pushkin and the Writing of Exile.* Stanford: Stanford University Press, 1989.

Semevskii, Mikhail. "Chelobitnaia kniagini N. B. Dolgorukovoi imperatritse Elizavete Petrovne 1757 g." *Russkii arkhiv* 7 (1867): 1167–68.

[Semevskii, Mikhail?]. "Kniazia Dolgorukovy v 1730–1740 gg. Zametka." *Russkaia starina* 23, nos. 10–12 (1878): 735–46.

Shchepkina, E. *Starinnye pomeshchiki na sluzhbe i doma. Iz semeinoi khroniki (1578–1762).* St. Petersburg: Tip. M. M. Stasiulevicha, 1890.

————. *Iz istorii zhenskoi lichnosti v Rossii. Lektsii i stat'i.* St. Petersburg: Tip. B. M. Vol'fa, 1914.

————. "Vospominaniia i dnevniki russkikh zhenshchin." *Istoricheskii vestnik* 8 (1914): 536–55.

Shcherbatov, M. *O povrezhdenii nravov v Rossii kniazia M. Shcherbatova i Puteshestvie A. Radishcheva.* London: Trübner, 1858. Reprint, Moscow: Nauka, 1983.

Shubinskii, S. N. "Berezovskie ssyl'nye." In *Istoricheskie ocherki i razskazy.* 6th edition. St. Petersburg: Tip. A. S. Suvorina, 1911, 193–213.

Sulotskii, A. "Kniazhna Ekaterina Alekseevna Dolgorukaia v ssylke v Berezove i v monashestve v Tomske." *Russkii vestnik* 148 (1880): 5–19.

Tartakovskii, A. G. *Russkaia memuaristika XVIII–pervoi poloviny XIX v.* Moscow: Nauka, 1991.

Tolycheva, T. [Novosil'tseva, E. V.]. *Natal'ia Borisovna Dolgorukaia i berezovskie ssyl'nye.* 5th edition. Moscow: Tip. T-va I. D. Sytina, 1912.

Tonchu, Elena. *Rossiia–zhenskaia sud'ba.* St. Petersburg: Obshchestvo Znanie, 1998.

Tret'iakova, Liudmila. *Rossiiskie bogini. Novelly o zhenskikh sud'bakh.* Moscow: Izdatel'stvo Izograf, 1996.

Uspenskii, B. A. *Iz istorii russkogo literaturnogo iazyka XVIII–nachala XIX veka. Iazykovaia programma Karamzina i ee istoricheskie korni.* Moscow: Izdatel'stvo moskovskogo universiteta, 1985.

Vigor, Mrs. William. *Letters from a Lady who Resided some Years in Russia to Her Friend in England.* 2nd edition. London: Dodsley, 1777. Reprinted as *Letters from Russia,* New York: Arno Press, 1970.

Vinogradov, V. V. "Russko-frantsuzskii iazyk dvorianskogo salona i bor'ba Pushkina s literaturnymi normami 'iazyka svetskoi damy.'" In *Iazyk Pushkina. Pushkin v istorii russkogo literaturnogo iazyka.* Moscow-Leningrad: Academia, 1935, 195–236.

Vowles, Judith. "The 'Feminization' of Russian Literature: Women, Language, and Literature in Eighteenth-Century Russia." In Toby W. Clyman and Diana Greene, eds. *Women Writers in Russian Literature.* Westport, Conn.: Greenwood Press, 1994, 35–60.

Zirin, Mary. "Butterflies with Broken Wings?—Early Autobiographical Depictions of Girlhood in Russia." In *Gender Restructuring in Russian Studies,* edited by M. Liljeström, E. Mäntysaari, and A. Rosenholm. Tampere, Finland: University of Tampere, 1993, 255–66.

Jehanne Gheith and Beth Holmgren

Art and Prostokvasha: Avdot'ia Panaeva's Work

IN THE AGE OF Russian realism, writers and critics together welcomed the real-world material—the nationally or regionally specific characters, settings, speech, and artifacts—that memoirs inventoried for literary use. Realist fiction aspired to the memoir's authenticity and particularity, and to that end often imported its thematic foci and representative strategies. Yet the same critics who cheered this seemingly democratic impulse in literature also arbitrated what and whose realia signified for inventory and import, and how such goods and practices should be displayed. The realist era marked Russian writers' first collective attempt to inscribe the ambiguous phenomenon of *byt*, a concept that neutrally designates the daily round and human relations, yet also can connote a soul-deadening materialism, a philistine immersion in the quotidian. A century later, novelist Iurii Trifonov, accused of "bytovizm," would lament its lingering toxicity for Russian readers and critics (Trifonov 1987, 541–42). In both nineteenth and twentieth centuries, socially approved representation of *byt* in whatever literary form required expert, gloves-on handling, a projection of at once intimate knowledge and critical distance.

As Russian women writers were to be told, they could not manage the job without contamination. Although women had published fiction regularly since the 1830s, they reportedly struggled against nature to achieve critical approval and transcendent value. The scope of their lives was deemed confining, their experience leveled by domestic concerns, and their creative faculties blinkered by biology. The king-maker critic Vissarion Belinskii made plain these perceived limitations in his 1840 review of Mariia Zhukova's works:

> Men are, by nature, more all-embracing than women; men are gifted with the capacity to go beyond their individual personalities and enter all kinds of situations that they have not only never experienced, but cannot experience, while a woman is locked into herself, into her female and feminine spheres, and if she goes beyond these, then she becomes an abnormal creature. That is why a woman cannot be a great poet. (Belinskii 1978, 369)[1]

Acclaimed Russian realist masters such as the novelist Ivan Turgenev and the dramatist Aleksandr Ostrovskii volunteered corollary observations of women's uncontrolled, emotionally driven creation, works that appear "unliterary, rushing straight from the heart, not thought through" (Turgenev 1956, 123).[2] To paraphrase Ostrovskii's more detailed taxonomy, women "naturally" write outraged feelings and unreconstructed *byt*:

> The works of female authors . . . differ from works of the male pen in that, while often inferior in artistry, they excel in their wealth of petty details, elusive psychological nuances, a particular kind of energy and fullness of feeling, very often high indignation. Women are wanting in quiet creation, cold humor, defined, finished images; on the other hand, they evince more of the touching, the denunciatory, the dramatic. It cannot be otherwise, for women are connected to the world more emotionally than men. (Ostrovskii 1952, 141)

What these various male authorities in nineteenth-century Russia judged to be intellectually limited and emotionally overwrought we today revalue as alternative, equal, and sometimes subversive in value and approach. Instead of instilling critical distance, nineteenth-century women writers often reveled in emotional immediacy and intensity, investing their characters with many elements of their own identity and experience. Instead of staging politically allegorical battles between male generations (fathers and sons) or different social classes, these authors often spotlighted their "confined," socially assigned areas of expertise: individual psychology and the "female" worlds of domestic activities and social exchange. By focusing on family, on the mechanics of daily life, and on female characters as key players in literature and society, their writings—both fictional and nonfictional—evoked the art and argued the value of individual relationships and daily tasks.

Let's consider, then, the illustrative case of Avdot'ia Iakovlevna Panaeva (born Brianskaia, pseud. N. Stanitskii [1819/20–93]), a woman writer whose oeuvre spanned the entire realist period and articulated, first in fiction and finally in memoir, her provocative engagement with *byt*. The daughter of well-known actors, Panaeva spent her life and made her literary and social reputation in St. Petersburg, an urban center that enabled her contact with famous cultural figures and distinguished her experience from that of many women writers residing in and writing about the provinces (Zirin 1994, 74). At the age of eighteen, she fled her parents' abusive home through marriage-misalliance with the writer and aristocrat, Ivan Panaev, and thereby was drawn into the publication and social scene surrounding *The Contemporary* (*Sovremennik*), a radical, highly influential thick journal her husband cofounded and coedited with the poet Nikolai Nekrasov. Soon unhappy with the gambling, philandering Panaev, she entered into a sixteen-year professional and romantic relationship with Nekrasov, serving as hostess, editor, feature/fiction writer, and mentor to young talent. Her writing career developed in her collaboration with Nekrasov and largely for *The Contemporary*, launched with *The Tal'nikov Family* (*Semeistvo Tal'nikovykh*, 1848), her fictionalization of her brutal childhood; highlighted by such influential works as the novels *Lady of the Steppes* (*Stepnaia baryshnia*, 1855) and *A Woman's Lot* (*Zhenskaia dolia*, 1862) as well as two novels coauthored with Nekrasov, *Three Countries of the World* (*Tri strany sveta*, 1848) and *The Dead Lake* (*Mertvoe ozero*, 1851); and summarized, to a certain extent, in her 1889 *Memoirs*. The texts that bracket this career—*The Tal'nikov Family* and the *Memoirs*—comprise her most original work and elaborate her distinctive assessment of and involvement with *byt*, a relationship that frankly informs her style, values, self-image, and self-worth. Read in sequence, *The Tal'nikov Family* and her *Memoirs* suggest a fiction-memoir symbiosis that privileges the domestic backstage and the unsung workers and dependents in the Russian home.

The most autobiographical of all her fictions, *The Tal'nikov Family* first starkly limns Panaeva's difference in the emerging movement of Russian realism. An account of girlhood, the novel predates, but in no way anticipates, the boyhood-focused works of Sergei Aksakov and Lev Tolstoy. In fact, *The Tal'nikov Family* did not register on the contemporary scene because the tsarist censor forbade its publication, damning (and revealing) it as "cynical," "immoral," and "undermining of parental power" (Kurova 1952, 41). Panaeva's novel sooner connects with Dostoevsky's fictions than male-authored gentry memoirs in its cast of impoverished, unhappy city dwellers and its captive fascination with pathological behaviors. Its almost relentless chronicle of abuse resembles, but eclipses, even Maxim Gorky's shocking early twentieth-century account of his childhood. Unlike Gorky's autobiography, Panaeva's fiction resurrects no adult heroes.

Furthermore, although this novella intimates an analogy between the Tal'nikov family and the larger political oppressions of tsarist Russia, its chief target for exposure and reform is the narrator's abusive kin. A fictitious "editor's" endnote justifies publishing this "sharp account of all possible coarseness and immorality in the home" with the hope that similarly abusive parents might recognize themselves in it and repent (Panaeva 1952, 357). Its first-person narrator, the "escaped" daughter Natasha, fearlessly and sometimes cynically exposes characters and deeds then inadmissible in contemporary Russian fiction. Like Gorky's *Childhood*, *The Tal'nikov Family* unveils its harsh focus with an initial display of the dead, but here the body of Natasha's six-month-old sister, potentially the most stunning icon of human loss, elicits no sorrow but the wet nurse's laments about her curtailed income. Natasha's testimony necessarily blends childish perception with adult knowledge—a common first-person strategy in memoirs of childhood also reflective of her early initiation into adult pathology. This prematurely cynical survivor-child inks portraits of a narcissistic, card-addicted mother who ghettoizes and neglects her many children; a father subject to murderous rages and devoted solely to household pets and hunting expeditions; a sadistic uncle who relishes beating Natasha's brother, a child off-loaded by the improvident Tal'nikov parents; a well-meaning grandmother who drinks herself to a comforting incapacity; and a cowardly, crazy, breast-beating grandfather. According to Natasha's unflinching purview, the claustrophobic Tal'nikov household also crowds together dependent unmarried aunts, a hateful governess, eight or more children (a number varying by birth, death, and even adoption!), dogs, birds, and the flies and roaches that infest the nursery and afford the children dismal entertainment.

Panaeva trains her novella on this bad family *byt* to strong aesthetic and psychological effect. Her narrator does not analyze or prescribe general stages in her development, and elaborates no socially contextualized family history. Rather, she details the dramatic, grotesque incidents of adult abuse and the often ignoble exigencies of the children's survival. From her vantage point as victim, the daily round of meals, schooling, play, socializing, and frequent illness threatens incessant danger and demands her vigilant testimony. In the overcrowded nursery, a drunken laundress literally frightens a sickly baby brother to death, and a feverish Natasha nearly dies as she symbolically dreams that she and her siblings lie burning in a room intentionally locked by her father (Panaeva 1952, 275, 294). What the narrator *can* generalize about is her siblings' burial:

> Funerals usually proceeded this way: a carriage was hired, and Mother and Father were asked if they wished to view the body. Mother bore such difficult moments with remarkable calm, attesting to her great strength, and she'd conclude the scene very quickly. She'd walk up to the casket, make the sign of the cross over the child, and carelessly kiss its forehead, saying: "God be with him! There's nothing to cry about, there are enough of them left . . ." Besides, she needn't have uttered these comforting words, since the faces of those present displayed all the courage necessary to cope with such a loss. Father, who didn't like to stay home, sometimes didn't show up for the removal of the body. (Panaeva 1952, 275–76)

As the above passage indicates, Natasha often conveys *byt* as a kind of chamber theatre, a continuous performance mainly orchestrated by her hypocritical actress mother and rendered through vividly sketched action, extensive dialogue, and Natasha's wry "reviews." Given her actor parents' regard for public show and distaste for the demands of family life, this sort of performance description best serves Natasha as a means of self-preservation and an effective, emotionally *understated* narrative strategy: her experience verges on the melodramatic, but her style does not. Both her mother and father impose a divide between the finer public space of their quarters and the cramped ghetto of the nursery, which they typically close off to guests and infrequently visit. But even the "backstage" nursery lends itself to the internal spectacles of sickness, death, and punishment. Courtship, on the other hand, transforms the entire household into a more public stage, with the children cast as props or stagehands. When a highly eligible suitor courts the aunts in their room adjoining the nursery, the exceptional appearance of Natasha's mother forces the children into mute poses, sent to bed or frozen "like statues in a family crypt" (Panaeva 1952, 282). A ball mounted for the same suitor's pleasure temporarily frees Natasha to plumb the dressing room secrets of her hated governess's toilet (thick make-up, false braid, too-tight corset); to spy with the other children on the dancing itself from the wings; and to script the governess's humiliation after she has punished their spying. Ultimately, Natasha's own surprise courtship ushers her onstage and out, allowing her a brief starring role as she bids farewell to an assembled line of family and servants at the novella's end.

In her self-representation, Natasha suffers and escapes, but does not transcend, the petty, sordid life of the Tal'nikov household. Despite her ironic "reviews" of adult abuse, she chronicles *byt* in which she is both trapped and complicit. Her characterizations do not denounce her victimizers, but painstakingly register their deeds and speech; her narrative charts the disturbing ambiguity of their behavior. That admission extends to her own actions, as she details how she and her siblings squabble over scarce resources or conspire to exact ugly vengeance. Her "I" often elides into the children's "we," which sometimes swells to absorb dependent aunts, the outcast grandfather, the drunken grandmother, and assorted servants—anyone, that is, who suffers the father's indifference and the mother's grand airs. What kindnesses Natasha commemorates are invariably those shown one underdog to another—the solicitude of the lone aunt she will genuinely miss when she marries, or the parental protection her poor little brother Vania (the uncle's whipping boy) affords a child whom their mother adopts and then forgets. The self Natasha intimates in *The Tal'nikov Family* is fused with an abused, resourceful collective and keenly attuned to power relations and survival skills, not individual ambition and model development. Her story significantly concludes with her escape and incipient individuation.[3]

Panaeva's *Memoirs*, heavily censored and issued in the *Historical Herald* (*Istoricheskii vestnik*) in 1889, would seem to make good on that escape to mark her extraordinary achievements since her novel debut. In *The Tal'nikov Family* a young woman vents a terrible childhood in fiction; the *Memoirs*, penned by a mature woman, bear assured witness to the most important, compelling period (1840s–1860s) of the *Contemporary* circle, in which Panaeva figured as the anomalous female insider. With her memoirs Panaeva liberates her life story from her coercive family circle and charts her circulation in an elite world, abandoning the shelter of fiction to assume the public prowess (and accountability) of memoir writing. Both moves attest to her greater self-confidence as a writer and a public person. In her *Memoirs* she flourishes her credentials as witness and chronicler with a leisurely description of her childhood, summoning up her impressions of such historical events as the 1824 Petersburg flood and the Decembrist uprising and showcasing her encounters with such cultural celebrities as the poet Aleksandr Pushkin and the ballerina Istomina. Whereas her narrator persona in *The Tal'nikov Family* was bound to the roles of victim and conspirator, her memoir persona surely wields control over recollecting and interpreting history.

Yet there persist certain important parallels of narratorial attitude and backstage focus. Both Natasha and Panaeva's memoiristic "I" insists on narration uncensored by decorum or sentiment, and their self-representation valorizes their own unconventional behaviors. They fix their attention, respectively, on the matter-of-fact melodrama of family abuse or the unprepossessing physical, material, and psychological aspects of celebrity interaction. In both memoir and autobiographical fiction, Panaeva's narrators persistently violate moral and social taboos in what they dare to disclose or repeat; the memoirist regularly declares that "I'm just passing on what I heard" (*peredaiu to, chto slyshala*). To varying degrees, both do sound the "denunciatory and dramatic" tone Ostrovskii ascribed to women writers, but that tone in Panaeva's work purposefully targets the sacrosanct institutions of family, intelligentsia, and even the grand enterprise of nineteenth-century Russian literature.

Panaeva's *Memoirs* also emerged from a different kind of desperate situation. She wrote this final work for money in her impoverished old age, abandoned by Nekrasov (who pursued a French actress rather than marry her after Panaev's death), widowed by her second husband, Apollon Golovachev, and left the sole support of her surviving children, including her daughter, the future writer Evdokiia Nagrodskaia.[4] Panaeva sketches the direst of straits in an 1889 letter to the critic Nikolai Chernyshevsky: "I haven't a red cent these days, and I've got to write, but how can you write when all you think of is feeding your family?"[5] Driven by need, Panaeva shrewdly opted to trade on her most valued cultural commodity—her associations with famous men. Her effort paid off chiefly for posterity, when Kornei Chukovskii, ever the scrupulous editor, restored and annotated her complete, uncensored manuscript in 1928, according the same high premium to her contacts with such "frequent guests" as Belinskii, Aleksandr Herzen, Chernyshevsky, Nikolai Dobroliubov, Mikhail Saltykov-Shchedrin, Tolstoy, Turgenev, Ivan Goncharov, Aleksei Pisemskii, Ostrovskii, Dostoevsky, Dmitrii Grigorovich, and Mikhail Sleptsov (Chukovskii 1986, 5). A new Soviet publishing industry welcomed her glowing tales of its radical prehistory.

Nevertheless, Chukovskii, a specialist on Nekrasov and a deferential, scholarly portraitist of Russia's literary greats, admits objections to this woman's writing that interestingly echo the charges of nineteenth-century male critics. "Unfortunately," the critic admits, "Panaeva sometimes pays too much attention in her memoirs to local, insignificant details and remembers too well every possible intrigue and squabble" (Chukovskii 1986, 6). In Chukovskii's judgment, Panaeva misses the forest of ideas and principles for the trees of *byt*—details about dress, appearance, bad behavior, and troubled relations. Panaeva otherwise commits the somewhat more pardonable sin of partisanship (given her radical democratic tendencies), for she excoriates the liberal gentry ascendant in the 1840s and champions the *raznochintsy* and seminarians who ushered in the radical 1860s. But Chukovskii cannot quite forgive Panaeva's recurring critique of Turgenev, because she desecrates the words and image of a "classic."

Once again, a woman writer stands faulted for excessive detail and emotion, yet, in a gratifying qualification, Chukovskii also concedes her excesses some artistic power:

> This surfeit of everyday detail (*bytovye melochi*) in large part facilitates her account's fictionalization, which, of course, gives it extraordinary value. Each person she describes in her book lives once more before her: she sees his face, and she loves or hates him as if he were still alive. Historical personages long passed from the scene come alive in her book's pages. Remembering their old talks and debates, Panaeva reproduces these verbatim, as if she were hearing them at this very moment. (Chukovskii 1986, 7)

Chukovskii's argument hinges on fascinating paradoxes—that an abundance of detail and vehement partisanship render Panaeva's memoir fictional, yet thereby improve on history through their animating force. The critic generally acknowledges that Panaeva has effected a potent mix of real-world reference and dramatic fiction, thus resurrecting, rather than merely recording, the past.

Chukovskii's salutary observation furnishes an excellent point of departure for our perusal of Panaeva's "enlivening" techniques. Underpinning this *non*fiction is her cautiously selective focus. In title and reference Panaeva's work contracts with the reader to present the truth, and Chukovskii conscientiously corrects her text for factual mistakes and probable embroideries. Yet some important facts necessarily lie beyond his editorial reach. Panaeva's memoir persona, unlike her fictional alter ego Natasha, actually suppresses her traumatic childhood, qualifying herself instead as a stable witness to well-known events and personalities. For example, she represents her father by brief eccentric portrait rather than villainous role; neutrally worded generalizations about his laziness and distance minimize the disgraceful performance she elaborated in her novella. Even more sobering, perhaps, is Panaeva's censorship of her married life. The *Memoirs* carry forward a narrator who eschews personal intimacy: Panaeva features both

Panaev and Nekrasov and implies her charge over their joint household, but she divulges nothing about her turbulent romances, the children she bore and then lost in infancy, and the humiliations she suffered in her irregular relationship with Nekrasov.[6] Nor does Panaeva venture beyond the limelight of her famed associations to chronicle her second marriage, surviving children, and the sixteen years "she lingered on inconspicuously" following Golovachev's demise (Ledkovsky 1974, 431). Her self-censorship protects her and her flawed family and friends from the memoir's capacity for public shaming, and allies her, unsurprisingly, with her female contemporaries, for most Russian women writers of her day skirted the potentially self-indicting topics of women's bodily experience (Kelly 1994, 70; Holmgren 1994). Yet Panaeva's selective purview also shrewdly foregrounds proven celebrities and fashions a comradely self-image that promises readers her equanimity, reliability, and muted sexuality. As Catriona Kelly discerns, the memoirist's "reticence" here signals "probity" as well as virtue (Kelly 1994, 71).

Indeed, Panaeva hugs an advantageous low ground in her *Memoirs*. She gleans arresting images and, often, damning details from viewing the famous obliquely or from a subordinate, if somewhat irreverent, position. Panaeva remembers Pushkin as the curly haired man who ogled her pretty young aunts through their apartment windows (Panaeva 1986, 35). Her memories of the great ballet master Didelot (whom she likens to a snipe) characteristically report the beatings he administered to his pupils and the bruises her aunts would exhibit on returning from his classes (Panaeva 1986, 29). Panaeva's perspective, not unlike Natasha's, generally transcribes the experience of the unprivileged insider—the abused pupil, the personal servant, the poor relation, the wife. She collects and transmits all the curious or damaging facts, anecdotes, and gossip that constitute the insider's chief entertainment and mode of aggression. Here is a memoirist who readily carries tales about Turgenev's improvidence with other people's money; Nekrasov's self-destructive addiction to cards; Natal'ia Goncharova's highhanded bargaining with Pushkin's publisher to pay for a new ball dress; and the rumors about Ostrovskii's private life—"that he drank nonstop and a fat village woman ran his affairs" (Panaeva 1986, 227). The stuff of everyday life still yields this observant critic extraordinary melodramatic and comic material.

With little analytical shaping, Panaeva's memoirs adhere to the basic chronology of her meetings and involvements during her satellite existence with Panaev and Nekrasov—her tour of Western Europe, Moscow visits, summers at rented dachas, and daily business with *The Contemporary* in St. Petersburg. Her chapters, titled with a subject index for the delectating reader, typically compile sketches of a subject's looks, mannerisms, and attitudes; what Panaeva implies to be key facts about her subject's family and financial situation; entertaining anecdotes and rumors; and much quoted dialogue. In vivid contrast to Aleksandr Herzen's *My Past and Thoughts*, the masterfully analytical memoirs of the nineteenth-century intelligentsia, Panaeva regales her audience with these self-styled character readings that hallow the poor underdog and rage against the hypocrite, tantalizing us with her empathetic or sardonic view of a public person's private life.

Panaeva's impressions of Elizaveta Granovskaia, the painfully shy wife of the eminent Moscow University professor and salon figure, Timofei Granovskii, assemble a characteristically positive portrait of the underdog. These pit social prejudice against Panaeva's superior judgment, commencing with rumors Panaeva has heard favoring Herzen's magnificent wife over the clumsy, dim German *hausfrau* Granovskii reportedly has wed. Panaeva's subsequent meeting with Granovskaia rebuts this slander with a sympathetic sketch accentuating the woman's loving acts and hidden talents:

> Granovskii's wife was not noted for her beauty. She was remarkably shy, but her every word expressed sincere simplicity. We got on famously from the start, as if we'd known each other a long time. We held a great many views in common. I had a delightful time with her and promised to return the next day.
>
> The Shchepkin family was at their dacha and the Aksakovs had gone to their estate, so none of my acquaintances remained in Moscow, and the Granovskiis pressed me to dine with them whenever Panaev was invited elsewhere. Spending almost entire days at the Granovskiis, I can speak of their home life. It was nice to see harmony between husband and wife; they both sincerely loved each other without demonstrative affection. Granovskii's wife did not speak of her love for her husband, but it was manifest in her efforts to preserve his peace, to keep him from any household disturbances. Granovskii absolutely loved a clean house and a good table, and his wife assiduously saw to both. Granovskii's income was limited to his professor's salary, and so his wife necessarily had to care for the household. It turned out that she possessed an excellent knowledge of German literature, read a great deal, and was a good musician, so that her education and accomplishments distinguished her among other women, but, due to her modesty, it never occurred to her to advertise this in the circle she now frequented as Granovskii's wife. (Panaeva 1986, 135)

Passing quickly and kindly over Granovskaia's unexceptional looks, Panaeva opts for a more intimate endorsement through shared conversation and long observation. Virtually adopted by the Granovskiis while her husband presumably goes about more important business, Panaeva is positioned to probe and empathize where other circle members have not bothered to go. She discloses the private life hidden from the circle's semipublic gaze, the pitiful economy and housewifely skills that enable Granovskii's intellectual work, the love and harmony quietly manifest between the "dimwitted" wife and her eminent husband. Panaeva thus articulates and approves the emotional relationships and domestic tasks that dominate any wife's existence, and she delves further to discover ("It turned out . . .") the *wife's* intellectual distinction. In Panaeva's memoirs, the mute, dull wife is re-viewed and redeemed.

Granovskaia's posthumous rehabilitation constellates a number of Panaeva's core values. The German woman's domestic industry and public self-effacement, especially in Granovskii's intimidating circle, recommend her to Panaeva over Herzen's wife, the intelligentsia's "darling," whom Panaeva trounces as blandly beautiful and undeservedly self-important. Panaeva explicitly casts her lot with Granovskaia, confessing her reluctance, as a "prosaic woman," to meet with a reportedly "exalted" example of her sex, and then critiquing Herzena's conversation-cum-examination administered in "flowing tones" (Panaeva 1986, 137). The discrepancy between the "artificial" Herzena and the "prosaic" memoirist recalls the morally freighted inequity between actress mother and dependent child in *The Tal'nikov Family*, between the empowered hypocrite and the shrewd underling.

Moreover, Panaeva is repeatedly enlisted in Granovskaia's defense— to ease her great shyness in visiting the Herzen household, to manipulate Granovskaia's martinet father when he visits, and to distract her from her anxiety over her husband's welfare in later years. Her recorded intercessions simultaneously honor the historically obscured Granovskaia's sensitivity and vulnerability and exhibit Panaeva's own considerable capacities as family counselor and champion of the oppressed. In a kind of compensatory application, Panaeva represents herself deftly managing the awkward or abusive situations that necessarily victimized her fictionalized alter ego.

Perhaps most important, Panaeva awards herself oblique recognition in commending Granovskaia's "clean house and good table." Her *Memoirs* infrequently allude to her overwhelming obligations as hostess, which Marina Ledkovsky characterizes as keeping "a perpetual 'open house' for the greatest of the Russian intelligentsia":

> For approximately the following thirty years, first in Moscow for a short period, then mainly in St. Petersburg, Panaeva received her literary friends every day and invariably treated them to breakfast, tea or dinner, depending on the time when they "dropped in." Belinskii, Herzen, Bakunin, Odoevsky, Turgenev, Goncharov, Granovskii, Tolstoy, even Alexandre Dumas during his stay in Russia, and a host of other no less prominent writers and critics were entertained by Panaeva. (Ledkovsky 1974, 424)

Nineteenth-century American and British women writers, empowered by their societies' cult of domesticity, elaborated in their fiction what one critic has termed "home plots" that focus on housekeeping, detailing and decoding domestic "processes, order, and rituals" (Romines 1992, 293). Panaeva's circle of radical intelligentsia, however, neither identified nor embraced a domestic ideal. The labor of the hostess or the household manager was presumed, but not honored as a significant cultural activity by intellectuals publicly invested in the "woman question" and swayed by the nihilists' self-abnegating lifestyle.[7] Such attitudes likely encouraged Panaeva's reticence about domestic routine, the more so because she, like other Russian women writers of her day, so evidently espoused them, readily empathizing with abused household servants and shunning the company of conventional society women.[8] Yet Panaeva did value her domestic work for its pragmatic benefit and emotional balm, an interpretation she conveys by highlighting selective domestic interventions. As in the *Tal'nikov Family*, so here Panaeva generally intimates the domestic circle as a revelatory forum that she is superbly qualified to critique: "Everyone's character is best discerned in their home environment" (Panaeva 1986, 279). In her *Memoirs*, however, Panaeva can muster examples of her own and others' *good* housekeeping.

Indeed, hospitality and good household management constitute defining virtues in Panaeva's text and inform her judgments and sympathies. Her opprobrium falls heavily on the stingy and the parasitic. Pavel Annenkov is blackmarked several times for his miserliness. In a lengthy sketch, Panaeva pillories Turgenev for his false hospitality, when he grandly invites his Petersburg friends to sample the excellent cooking at his summer place and then neglects to alert his chef. The spendthrift Turgenev is likewise faulted for imposing on Nekrasov's generosity, exploiting his editor friend as a liaison with moneylenders or relying on an open line of credit with *The Contemporary* despite his claims not to write for money. Panaeva invariably discloses the financial details that burdened or compromised her subjects, and almost as regularly presents herself articulating others' financial woes. It is significant that she breaks her customary silence in intellectual circles to mention the unmentionable—that is, the desperate financial straits of a Belinskii or a Bakunin. Her intercession distinguishes her as an egalitarian among self-absorbed liberals, as well as a pragmatist among self-denying radicals.

Panaeva fully admits her readers into her own domestic backstage in a comic episode, thus highlighting her talents and exercising her anger at a safe remove. The setting is a small rented dacha near Oranienbaum, and the uninvited guest the renowned French writer, Alexandre Dumas père, who, as it turns out, seeks a full-service home away from home:

> Grigorovich informed us that Dumas desired absolutely to meet the editors of *The Contemporary* and their co-workers, and he argued heatedly that we should entertain Dumas in European style. I merely insisted that we host him in our city apartment because our dacha was small, and I already had my hands full feeding unexpected guests since we had to send for provisions to Peterhof, four versts away. It was decided, therefore, that we'd treat Dumas to a gala breakfast in town to which we'd invite all *The Contemporary* contributors spending the summer in Petersburg. (Panaeva 1986, 234)

For the first time, Panaeva initiates us into the calculations and hazards of playing hostess. As the inconsiderate Dumas nonetheless descends on their country place every few days like a hungry French locust, we learn more about her culinary ingenuity and wry diplomatic skills. Dumas's first breakfast, hastily assembled, includes a full plate of *prostokvasha* (curds and whey), a homely peasant dish that nonetheless delights the iron-stomached Frenchman. With more warning, Panaeva strategizes a "Russian dinner" heavy enough to ground him: "Once I purposely prepared such a dinner for Dumas that I was fully convinced I'd be spared his visits for at least a week. I fed him cabbage soup, a fish and kasha dumpling, roast pig with horseradish, ducks, fresh pickles, fried mushrooms, and sweet pastry with jam. Dumas cheered me up when he spoke of his extreme thirst after dinner and he drank a great deal of seltzer water with cognac" (Panaeva 1986, 239). Yet Dumas's digestive capacity prevails and the Frenchman returns repeatedly for "chère dame Panaieff's" hospitality, to the counterpoint of her vociferous objections behind the scenes and her devising to escape his conversation.[9] Many years after this imposition, her *Memoirs* at last disclose her deft sabotage and once more convey her critique of a great male author's everyday insensitivity.

In other episodes, Panaeva puts her homemaking skills to virtuous use, ministering to the poor and sick in her famous set. Still a young bride, she slips into an informal, plain speaking friendship with the critic Belinskii, and provides him the practical and emotional support his male companions would not think to offer. It is Panaeva who urges the group to find easier and steadier literary work for Belinskii; who divines in him a needy family man and convinces him to marry; who alone knows the particulars of his courtship and wedding and outfits his new household for him at his request. Her account of her domesticating good deeds exonerates her as the lone woman—the manager of *byt*—among intellectual men, and the attractive young hostess who retains her virtue in the company of avowed womanizers. The rumors linking her and Belinskii, she declares in a rare admission of her sexuality, were patently untrue (Panaeva 1986, 105). Belinskii, moreover, doubly valorizes Panaeva's work with his praise for her *writing*. A seriously ill Belinskii reportedly drags himself from his deathbed to congratulate her on *The Tal'nikov Family*, a powerful important work he never would have guessed she'd authored because she seemed to him to be "eternally preoccupied with housekeeping" (Panaeva 1986, 179–80). Once again, Panaeva arranges for oblique recognition, citing the opinion of a renowned critic to remind readers of the "hidden" talent a "preoccupied housekeeper" may possess.

Panaeva of course played real wife to both Panaev and Nekrasov, although her *Memoirs* convey their various interactions as more comradely than intimate. In fact, a separate text Panaeva devoted to Nekrasov's "domestic life" largely features anecdotes about his servants (Panaeva 1986, 380–406). Panaeva's short-lived children are also disturbingly absent in her *Memoirs*. Her most loving maternal relationship is enacted instead with Dobroliubov, the ascetic radical who, in Panaeva's painstaking and elaborate portrait, desperately mourned his mother, attempted to parent his younger siblings, and died tragically young.

Panaeva's text has primed her readers for the heroic entrance of the seminarians, the lower-class, unpretentious, hardworking intellectuals she implies as her soul mates. Here her quoted voice unusually resonates, as she defends their characters against the liberals' attack: "'As you see, Belinskii made his mark; intellectual development nevertheless *has* penetrated into society's other classes'" (Panaeva 1986, 263). Dobroliubov, whom Nekrasov has settled against her wishes in rooms adjoining their apartment, soon ingratiates himself as a shy, serious, and sensitive young man in great need of her attentions. The caretaking routine she prescribes for him reads like a nurse's clinical log, in sharp contrast to her ironic "menus" for Dumas:

> At first I'd send morning tea and breakfast to Dobroliubov's room, because Nekrasov and Panaev woke up late and at different times, but he soon asked permission to have tea with me (I rose early), explaining that his rooms could then be cleaned and he could begin work immediately afterwards.
> At morning tea I made Dobroliubov eat some kind of meat because he sometimes came to the table with no sleep, having worked the night through. Since I also insisted that Dobroliubov rest a half hour after eating, Chernyshevsky began to show up for tea in order to chat with Dobroliubov during his free time. (Panaeva 1986, 268)

Unlike Belinskii, the sickly Dobroliubov never marries, and Panaeva oversees his and his family's domestic arrangements almost until the day he dies. On more than one occasion, her famous charge expresses his great appreciation for her "hygienic concerns" (272) and sensible advice, and she reproduces "verbatim" his appeals for help (at one point he summons her home from a European cure) and their bedside conversations as his illness worsens. Dobroliubov intuits Panaeva's maternal gestures, and Panaeva, in turn, links him with her heretofore favorite beneficiary:

> Dobroliubov began to speak feelingly about how smart, enlightened, and good a woman his mother had been, and that her loss had been so terrible to him that he first thought of committing suicide.
> To distract Dobroliubov from such gloomy memories, I told him stories about Belinskii, about whom he'd already asked a great deal. (Panaeva 1986, 303)

Although Dobroliubov moves out of the Panaev-Nekrasov household a few days before his death to spare his hostess extra work, Panaeva attends him faithfully, earning the touching benediction: "'You've done for me what my mother alone could do'" (Panaeva 1986, 313). An otherwise unsentimental narrator risks transcribing a fellow radical's paean to her *mothering;* once again, Panaeva validates a traditional female role through temperamental affinity and comradely relations rather than suggesting her adherence to any bourgeois domestic ideal.

Panaeva thus revalues the venerated world she surveys in her *Memoirs* through her manifest bias; her defiantly humble vantage point as wife, mistress, hostess, caretaker, and worker for *The Contemporary;* her motley cast of celebrities and their overshadowed associates, families, and servants; and her primary attention to domestic details and embarrassing gossip rarely reported in other intelligentsia memoirs. To bear credible witness to others' lives in the terms of her intelligentsia contemporaries, she divests her persona of an abusive childhood, sexual relationships, and maternal losses, thereby fashioning herself into an untouchable female observer, an anomalous female comrade who distances herself from the contaminating company of both society ladies and self-absorbed literati. But, unlike her radical sisters, Panaeva frankly owns her modest origins and caretaking skills. Her *Memoirs* occupy those intersections of fame and family, art and domesticity, that prescribed her roles as writing "wife" and intelligentsia hostess. Panaeva views her famous subjects from the perspective of one who serves and speaks to the point, not to philosophize or pontificate.

As this sharp-eyed hostess sketches and judges assorted famous characters, she curiously recreates a cultural scene in which the arts form topics of *other* people's extensively quoted monologues, yet human relations, habits, and maintenance demand her immediate engagement and description. In lieu of worshiping at the feet of the masters, her *Memoirs* incarnate them as messy, needy human beings, and hallow instead the key values of decency, generosity, solicitude, hard work, and material care. This means that in Panaeva's world the *byt* well managed by the housewife, hostess, secretary, or servant merits periodic inscription and steady appreciation, for it proves vital to the life of the mind. Critics of nineteenth-century Western domestic fiction have argued this literature obfuscates class conflicts and radical politics and exclusively invests in middle-class values.[10] But Panaeva's helpmate perspective and tales of domestic ministry operate subversively in her social context, disproving any detachment of politics from personalities or intellectual life from the daily round. The values she insinuates are not those of a middle-class hostess, but of a woman who binds powerful radical sympathies with traditional gestures of benevolence and mercy. In her case, domestic deeds are sanctioned by the proper politics and sanctified by an unconventional "good woman." Just as a clean home, good table, and parental love—a *family* reform, as it were—would have redeemed

Natasha's nightmarish childhood in *The Tal'nikov Family,* so Panaeva in her memoirs suggests a new brand of heroinism through her hands-on care, in word and deed, for the abused, maligned, and overlooked in Russian culture. In her autobiographical novella Panaeva's alter ego is shown to be tempered in the crucible of *byt,* schooled in the survival skills of critical observation and solidarity with the oppressed. In her *Memoirs* Panaeva then "authenticates" her triumphant maturation into an enlightened, willing manager of domestic tasks and human relations, ministering to and daring to measure Russia's elite by her passionate, pragmatic example.

Notes

1. See also Catriona Kelly's discussion of "the special role which Belinsky, and other critics like him, assigned to women writers, who were assumed to be only concerned with depicting discrimination against women in society and in the family" (Kelly 1994, 25).

2. Turgenev's portrait of the woman writer does sketch a creature of great appetite and no formal control: "For a woman, even a writing woman, the obstacles that would stop a man at the very outset do not exist. She is not afraid to fill up dozens of pages either with pointless stories or simply chatter, she is not afraid of making mistakes. She writes greedily, rapidly, with a kind of involuntary respect for writing in general, without literary manners or embellishment" (123).

3. Kelly categorizes *The Tal'nikov Family* as an example of the "escape plot" in which the heroine is ultimately liberated (by marriage or professional opportunity) from her oppressive family (62–63).

4. For particulars on Panaeva's post-Nekrasov life, see Sobel 1994, 1999.

5. Quoted in Chukovskii 1986, 10.

6. For more information about the Panaeva-Nekrasov relationship, see Richard Gregg's article, which charts the discrepancy between Nekrasov's real-life mistreatment of the women he loved and their substantially reworked images in his poetry.

7. The Russian radical intelligentsia's disdain for any domestic ideal did not mean, however, that no domestic ideology was promoted in educated Russian society. See Greene 1998 for one discussion of this ideology's contents and dissemination.

8. Focusing on Russian women's prose in the 1840 to 1880 period, Kelly remarks that "the oppression of domesticity . . . is almost invariably encapsulated by showing the heroine at her hated embroidery frame" (70).

9. During one of Dumas's visits, Panaeva begs her visiting nieces to pretend their ignorance of French so that she will have a pretext not to speak

with the Frenchman (Panaeva 1986, 240). It bears noting that Chukovskii finds much that is "inexact and invented" in this segment of the *Memoirs* and cites Panaev's and Grigorovich's reminiscences as correctives! (Panaeva 1986, 458).

10. See Cohen 1998, 8, as well as the monographs of the two critics she cites, Nancy Armstrong and Mary Poovey, for an elaboration of how "domestic ideology represented by cultural products like novels can be seen as middle-class political interest masquerading as psychology."

Works Cited

Armstrong, Nancy. *Desire and Domestic Fiction: A Political History of the Novel*. New York: Oxford University Press, 1987.

Belinskii, V. G. "Povesti Mar'i Zhukovoi." Vol. 3. *Sobranie sochinenii*. Moscow: Khudozhestvennaia literatura, 1978, 364–72.

Chukovskii, Kornei. "Panaeva i ee vospominaniia." In Panaeva's *Vospominaniia* (Moscow: Pravda, 1986), 5–14.

Cohen, Monica F. *Professional Domesticity in the Victorian Novel: Women, Work and Home*. Cambridge: Cambridge University Press, 1998.

Greene, Diana. "Mid-Nineteenth-Century Domestic Ideology in Russia." In *Women and Russian Culture: Projections and Self-Perceptions*, edited by Rosalind Marsh. New York, Oxford: Berghahn Books, 1998, 78–97.

Gregg, Richard. "A Brackish Hippocrene: Nekrasov, Panaeva, and the 'Prose in Love.'" *Slavic Review* 34, no. 4 (December 1975): 731–51.

Holmgren, Beth. "For the Good of the Cause: Russian Women's Autobiography in the Twentieth Century." In *Women Writers in Russian Literature*, edited by Toby W. Clyman and Diana Green. Westport, Conn.: Greenwood Press, 1994, 127–48.

Kelly, Catriona. *A History of Russian Women's Writing 1820–1992*. Oxford: Clarendon Press, 1994.

Kurova, K. S. "Tvorchestvo A. Ia Panaevoi v 60-e gody." *Uchenye zapiski Kazakhskogo gosudarstvennogo universiteta im. S. M. Kirova*, v. 14, vyp. 1, Alma Ata, 1952.

Ledkovsky, Marina. "Avdotya Panaeva: Her Salon and Her Life." *Russian Literature Triquarterly* 9 (1974): 424–32.

Ostrovskii, Aleksandr. "Oshibka." Vol. 13. *Polnoe sobranie sochinenii*. Moscow: Gosizdat khudozhestvennoi literatury, 1952, 139–49.

Panaeva, A. Ia. *Semeistvo Tal'nikovykh*. In vol. 2, *Russkie povesti XIX veka: 40–50-kh godov*. Moscow: Khudozhestvennaia literatura, 1952.

———— (Golovacheva). *Vospominaniia*. Moscow: Pravda, 1986.

Poovey, Mary. *Uneven Developments: The Ideological Work of Gender in Mid-Victorian England*. Chicago: University of Chicago Press, 1988.

Romines, Ann. *The Home Plot: Women, Writing and Domestic Ritual.* Amherst: University of Massachusetts Press, 1992.

Sobel, Ruth. "Panaeva, Avdot'ia Iakovlevna." In *A Dictionary of Russian Women Writers,* edited by Marina Ledkovsky, Charlotte Rosenthal, and Mary Zirin. Westport, Conn.: Greenwood Press, 1994.

———. "Avdot'ia Panaeva." In vol. 1, *Russian Women Writers,* edited by Christine D. Tomei. New York and London: Garland Publishing, 1999.

Trifonov, Iu. V. "Net, ne o byte—o zhizni!" Vol. 4. *Sobranie sochinenii.* Moscow: Khudozhestvennaia literatura, 1987, 541–45.

Turgenev, I. S. Review of *Plemiannitsa* by Evgeniia Tur, in vol. 11, *Sobranie sochinenii.* Moscow: Khudozhestvennaia literatura, 1956, 118–36.

Zirin, Mary Fleming. "Women's Prose Fiction in the Age of Realism." In *Women Writers in Russian Literature.* Westport, Conn.: Greenwood Press, 1994, 77–94.

Natasha Kolchevska

The Art of Memory: Cultural Reverence as Political Critique in Evgeniia Ginzburg's Writing of the Gulag

AS SOVIET SOCIETY AWOKE in fits and starts from the Stalinist nightmare, one of the more significant developments in mobilizing collective memory was the emergence of a body of testimonial writing that addressed the high crimes committed by the Soviet state against its citizens in the decades following the October Revolution. While many Gulag survivors (and their families) wrote primarily to record the destruction inflicted by totalitarian terror on lives and limbs, others made it their mission not only to chronicle personal tragedy but also to testify to the devastation of traditional Russian culture and cultural values. In the post-Stalin period, Gulag survivors such as Aleksandr Solzhenitsyn or Evgeniia Ginzburg (or, as was the case with Nadezhda Mandelstam, widows of the nonsurvivors) took upon themselves the tattered mantle from their spiritual forebears among Russia's intelligentsia to do this work of documentation, commemoration and/or mourning the passage of a lost culture. Continuing the nineteenth-century intelligentsia's self-imposed "civilizing mission," as Catriona Kelly has characterized it (1998a, 238), in the post-Thaw decades these writers assumed the moral high ground to scrutinize the implications of the new order for a range of social, political, and cultural questions generated by recent Soviet history.

However, as Sheila Fitzpatrick and others have pointed out, in Soviet Russia, culture has often been the site of contested terrain in the struggle for power among various classes and groups: "it was generally accepted that the Russian intelligentsia was the guardian of culture and 'cultural values'; (*kul'turnye tsennosti*). . . . 'Power' was sometimes a synecdoche for the Bolshevik Party, 'culture' for the intelligentsia," she writes. "'Culture' was also one of the primary spheres of revolutionary contestation, like politics and economics. It was a locus of struggle, an area in which power (hegemony) could be won or lost" (1–2).[1] Fitzpatrick has in mind here the 1920s and the years leading to the "Cultural Revolution" at the end of that decade, yet the same situation held in the years after Stalin's death. Memoirists such as Evgeniia Ginzburg (born 1904), and later, Aleksandr Solzhenitsyn (born 1918), were both the benefactors and the victims of this power struggle between Russia's political and intellectual leaders. These writers returned from the Gulag and exile in the 1950s, often with little in the way of family, status, or economic or social support, armed only with a pen and a collective, subconscious remnant of an idea that they must resume the intelligentsia's traditional mission to enlighten the people and serve as the conscience of the state.

Evgeniia Ginzburg's *Krutoi marshrut* (published in English in two volumes, *Journey into the Whirlwind* and *Within the Whirlwind*) has been among the most widely read and praised by readers and fellow writers in the Soviet Union and abroad.[2] As we learn episodically in the course of her memoir, Ginzburg's life traced a trajectory that was virtually paradigmatic for the first generation of postrevolutionary Soviet "priviligentsia," to borrow Leona Toker's term (53): born in Moscow into a middle-class, assimilated Jewish family, she joined the Communist Party and matriculated in history at the University of Kazan' in the early 1920s. Ginzburg married Pavel Aksyonov, chairman of the city Soviet in Kazan' and bore him two sons before her arrest in 1937. Over the next eighteen years, she served two sentences in labor camps in the Soviet Far East, then lived in exile in Magadan until her return to Moscow in 1955, where she worked as a contributor to and editor for several pedagogical journals. Like many Gulag survivors, after Khrushchev's secret speech at the Twenty-second Party Congress in 1956, she began writing her memoir as a testament (initially for her son, then for an as yet unborn grandson). As hopes for publishing her memoir in the Soviet Union waxed and waned, it began to circulate in *samizdat*, was "miraculously" published abroad, with the first volume appearing in English in 1967, and the second posthumously, in 1979.[3] Ginzburg died in Moscow in 1977.

Aside from the excellent, often novelistic quality of its writing, one of the reasons for the reception of *Whirlwind* as one of the most significant works of its genre and period has been the way that both the experiences narrated and the positions taken in the text, as well as that text's own history, embody so much of the Soviet experience. Although (thanks to her husband's rank) Ginzburg moved in relatively privileged Party circles, she was not of the stature that would unequivocally make her the focus of readers' attention (as was, for example, the case with three other memoirs avidly read by very different audiences—those of Nadezhda Mandelstam, widow of the poet Osip Mandelstam; Svetlana Alilueva, Stalin's daughter; or Anna Larina, widow of the prominent Bolshevik, Nikolai Bukharin). Nonetheless, Ginzburg life's journey was played out against and intertwined with major

146

historical events of the early Soviet period: the promotion by the new Soviet government of egalitarian (in terms of class, gender, and ethnicity) policies in the areas of education and professionalism in the 1920s, the reappearance of consumerism in the mid-1930s, the purges and arrests of the latter part of the 1930s, the impact of World War II even on the far reaches of the Gulag in the 1940s, and the fluctuating cultural policies of the post-Stalin years. The publication history of *Whirlwind* followed a similarly paradigmatic course: rejected by *Novyi mir*, the leading Soviet journal of literary and social commentary, it was published in various *tam-* and *samizdat* forms in the 1960s and 1970s, tracing a map taken by many nonconformist Soviet writings.[4] In the second half of the following decade, during a period of intense historical and cultural scrutiny of the Stalin legacy initiated by Gorbachev's glasnost policies, *Whirlwind* found a broader audience, first with an adaptation of the memoir staged in 1988 at the *Sovremennik*, one of Moscow's premier theaters, followed by serial publication in a Latvian journal, *Daugava*, in 1989, and finally, in 1990 (after Solzhenitsyn's *Gulag* had been fully serialized in *Novyi mir*), in a separate edition of 100,000 copies.

Ginzburg's memoir has traditionally been read as one woman's true story of survival and spiritual growth as she made her way through the Gulag system and subsequent exile in the Soviet Far East. When *Whirlwind* was finally published in the Soviet Union, the writer Vasil' Bykov chose to focus on its truth value in his introduction to the 1990 volume: "This is not a novel or any of the other accepted literary genres. This is an echo filled with the pain of our recent past, [an echo] which nevertheless cannot help but resonate in the human soul with half-forgotten fear and trembling" (3). Similarly, Toker focuses in her analysis of Ginzburg's memoir on the shifts in this once ardent Marxist's ideology prompted by her camp experience (52–54), even as she later acknowledges its self-conscious construction, its many ironic reversals and mythic patterns, and the difficulty of "distinguish[ing] the gifts of spontaneous memory from those of imagination" (130). I do not argue against such readings of Ginzburg's memoir: they function to fill an important national need to actively reclaim and transmit an unofficial past out of the rubble of totalizing, official, historical narratives, to validate the importance of individual experience within a national historical tragedy, to provide an opportunity for both writers and readers to reestablish control over the discursive realm, and to write a counterhistory (or histories) that is more "trustworthy."[5] Paradoxically, the very subjectivity of its author's position made *Whirlwind* more credible to its audience than the synthesizing, "objective" narratives written by professional historians who, in the Soviet context, worked for the state and wrote their studies accordingly.

Postmodernist critics have argued that "all claims to truth are merely stories" (Jameson, 3). Without necessarily fully agreeing with that totalizing position, I would like to use it as a springboard for examining the transformation from fact to art in *Whirlwind,* the interweaving of the multiple narrative strategies that cohere in the course of Ginzburg's autobiographical "journey." I have discussed her adoption of such generic models as the adventure tale and the bildungsroman elsewhere.[6] Here I want to focus on Ginzburg's autobiographical narrative as an intersection of the literary and the historical, of individual and social memory, and on the contribution of these modes to a narrative that simultaneously incorporates and resists her culture's sustaining myths. For, as much as it is a "chronicle" that moves its heroine forward through time, *Whirlwind* is also an exploration backward, an examination of origins and causes. Parallel to her physical journey through the Stalinist Gulag lie other journeys, other storylines, through which Ginzburg traces her growth as an individual, from naïveté to consciousness, and from a false social role to a more meaningful one. As a result, even as she writes her individual life story, Ginzburg also attempts to scrutinize a national cultural self-identity in her exploration of one woman's trajectory from *kul'turnost'*, a false, consumerist sense of culture, to *kul'tura,* in which protection of traditional cultural values becomes the goal.[7] Coming as she did from a bourgeois (and therefore suspect) family, Ginzburg was not one of the *vydvizhentsy*—that cohort of "yesterday's workers and peasants" (Fitzpatrick, 11) who had been educated during the crash program established by the First Five-Year Plan, yet she was of their generation and, in many respects, shared their tastes and values in her prearrest life. Like her cohort, she was "politically loyal rather than politicized" and more important for my purposes here, she had "no specific cultural agenda" (Fitzpatrick, 13). Rather, as Stalin (partially) reintroduced traditional cultural values in the 1930s, the consumption (rather than the production) of culture became another goal or benefit of political loyalty, education, and privilege, so that for the pre-Gulag Evgeniia, cultural products had the same value as did her gold watch or the Ford that she was entitled to as a party functionary's wife. Ironically, only with the loss and suffering of the Gulag does she produce a significant cultural artifact. Through the "steep trajectory" alluded to in the memoir's title, Ginzburg inscribes a circle that goes back to Russia's first and arguably only culturally hegemonic class—the nineteenth-century intelligentsia—thereby repeating the familiar Marxist-Leninist model of explaining the present as a culmination of a series of moments in the past.

However, in *Whirlwind* she turns that model on its head (or goes over the head of that model) by inscribing a cultural genealogy that includes a much broader range of contributors to a national consciousness. Finding herself on the opposite side of an ethical divide from a world that she had once embraced—and that had embraced her—she uses her memoir to testify, enlighten, and promote a cultural and moral vision to a community she perceives has lost its cultural and moral anchors. This critique explicitly refers to the situation of the text's production and to the author herself. Writing in a culture in which historical discourses have been repeatedly discredited when the state has appropriated them, Ginzburg turns to the autobiographical mode, with its requisite focus on the individual consciousness, as a compromise position from which to speak. She can do so because that consciousness, while it is singular, simultaneously participates in its culture, lending it a double-voicedness that will mediate between individual memory and official history.[8] Ginzburg thus enters into an "autobiographical pact" with her readers, by which they accept her version of a specific context rather than academic or state-sanctioned accounts.

Evgeniia Ginzburg's life and attitudes, conscious and unconscious, as revealed in her narrative, reflect, and reflect on, many of the sociocultural constructs and preoccupations of her generation. Benefitting from women's rights legislation and policies passed in the 1920s that significantly changed, at least on paper, women's independence and access to professional possibilities, Ginzburg immediately introduces herself in the multiple roles— wife, mother, Communist Party member, university lecturer—expected of an educated Soviet woman. However, in these opening chapters, the bewildered heroine focuses more on protecting her privileged life than she does on comprehending the events unfolding around her. As a result, in an unacknowledged twist on Hegel, Ginzburg implies that despite her education, profession, and status—"external" factors as it were—she is not truly an *intelligentka* because she lacks awareness, and that the "steep trajectory" of her memoir's title will be a matter not just of experience but also of consciousness. Through her narrative, as she suggests from the beginning, she will move from being an *intelligentka* "in form"—as a result of her education and her academic position—to being one "in substance," to paraphrase Katerina Clark (1993, 303).

Many of Ginzburg's paradigms of self-representation, as well as her account of *Whirlwind's* epically complicated journey from secret journal to publication, are derived from classical Russian and European concepts of heroism: even the difficult journey of the text itself, with its peril-filled passages complete with death and resurrection (the author burns her first draft) evokes the famous examples of Gogol and Bulgakov. It is also worth noting that some of the tropes in *Whirlwind*—the heroine's drive to overcome physical and natural obstacles, episodes of near death and subsequent resurrection, her delight in labor well done, and the aura of grandeur in all of her life in spite of its many adversities, to mention the most obvious examples—are also familiar to readers of socialist realist narratives. However, Ginzburg's purposes in using these paradigms diverge dramatically from those in state-sanctioned Soviet literature, for in her memoir she assails the state for destroying not only its citizens but also its own culture, and the processes of reeducation and coming to consciousness are now used to track the development of an oppositional Soviet heroine. Critical to Ginzburg's definition of a role for herself is her identification with the prerevolutionary intelligentsia, which had exemplified and promoted Russia's strongest national myth—that of its peculiar destiny and spirituality, as manifested in its literature and culture. She insinuates through her narrative that by destroying the bearers of Russian culture, Stalinist policies also eradicated, possibly forever, Russia's traditional claim to superiority, or even parity, with other nations. Ginzburg's representation, in the chapters of *Whirlwind* leading to the heroine's arrest, of "an inauthentic life," full of tense professional and domestic privilege but devoid of spiritual value, is intended to remind us of possible literary ancestors. In her reading of the nineteenth-century Russian classics, Virginia Woolf has suggested that "[their] stories are always showing us some affectation, pose, insincerity—the soul is ill; the soul is cured; the soul is not cured. Those are the emphatic points of the story" (182). Woolf's detection of a sense of falsity, and its reversal, as well as her observation that the heroes of Russian tales "appear as if they 'have lost their clothes in some terrible catastrophe,'" which enables them to speak for the whole of humanity," as Boym adumbrates (84), go to the heart of Ginzburg's opening strategies in *Whirlwind*. Until her arrest, both material and human relationships, with the sole exception of the mother/child bond, the most inviolable in Russian culture, are strained, politicized, and "inauthentic." But arrest removes both privileges and constraints as she literally "loses her clothes" (except for a tattered box that accompanies her throughout her long travels), and years after that loss, takes up the pen to sew a new, more authentic, literary outfit.

Trained as an historian, employed as university lecturer in her prearrest life, when she turns to the writing of her memoirs, Ginzburg incorporates these two biographical facts into the writing of what is as much a staged, "performed," and aestheticized work of literature as it is a "remembrance." While her narrative may read as a chronologically, spatially, and experientially predetermined account of the eighteen years that its author spent in the Gulag and in exile, its distinguishing features owe more to novelistic strategies than they do to traditional, synthesizing historical discourse, thus allowing its author to reinterpret and reaccent those experiences in the light of a perspective acquired, and understood, only much later. Ginzburg addresses this directly in the epilogue to the second volume when, after listing the numerous writers, historians, and ordinary readers who acknowledged her role in revealing the consequences of Stalin's policies from the viewpoint of one of his victims, she ends on a personal rather than historic note. Wondering about the fate of her memoir (this at a time when the first volume had appeared only abroad), she concludes,

Whatever happens, I consider it my duty to finish the book. Not so much because I want to record the facts about my later years in camp and exile as to reveal to the reader the heroine's spiritual evolution, the gradual transformation of a naive young Communist idealist into someone who had tasted unforgettably the fruits of the tree of knowledge of good and evil, a human being who amid all her setbacks and sufferings also had moments (however brief) of fresh insight in her search for truth. It is this cruel journey of the soul and not just the chronology of my sufferings that I want to bring home to the reader. (2: 423 [597])

In this paragraph, which comes at the very end of her memoir, Ginzburg recapitulates the tension between historical and novelistic imperatives (experience recorded as it happened versus experience re-created and ordered, so as to find or attribute meaning), cognitive versus intuitive ways of knowing and learning, and the negotiation of the chronicler's social task from the standpoint of the truth seeker's more individualized one.

It should come as no surprise that in this historian's memoir, confessional and conversion narratives intersect with firsthand "reporting," and displace the confident historian's voice that had characterized her earlier academic work. In *Whirlwind*, the former Communist Ginzburg's text increasingly opens to practices, such as religion, which Marx had characterized as "the opiate of the people," while her attentiveness to bodily, biological, and other forms of "intuitive" knowledge lead her to try experiences unavailable to the prearrest heroine. In one early passage, sitting with other newly anointed "enemies of the people" in a Kazan' prison built before the revolution, she admits that

> . . . it was no use trying to think of things "on a world scale." Tonight I cared nothing for the world, only for my children orphaned twice over.
>
> I sat up and looked around. Everyone was asleep except Lydia, who had left her bunk and stood beside me, her obsessed eyes for once looking at me with simple human kindness. She stroked my head and repeated several times, in German, the words of Job: "For the one thing which I greatly feared is upon me, and that which I was afraid of is come unto me."
>
> This broke the spell. All night I had wanted to cry and couldn't. My eyes and heart were burning in arid sorrow. Now I fell sobbing into the arms of this strange woman from a world unknown unto me. She stroked my hair and said again and again in German: "God protects the fatherless. God is on their side." (1: 119 [78])

Here, in a move typical of Ginzburg's multilayered reconstruction of her "memory," Ginzburg assembles a scene rich in symbolic gesture and cultural allusion. Lydia Mentsinger, a "fanatical" Seventh-Day Adventist, as we have learned earlier (I: 106–7 [70]) is, or rather was, culturally, ideologically, linguistically, a stranger, an enemy even, to someone like Ginzburg. Ironically, it is Lydia's quoting of an "enemy" text, that is, the Old Testament, in the language of both Luther and Marx, and her physical gesture that undercut the thrall of the heroine's first religion, Communism, and direct her, like Saint Paul or Saint Augustine, toward conversion to a higher truth.[9]

Why did Ginzburg not return to teaching history once she was free and permitted to live in the Far Eastern city of Magadan? This can be explained as a biographical fact—she was offered a job teaching Russian language and literature to Gulag administrative personnel—and as an authorial strategy—writing a personal memoir was easier (more possible) and less risky than writing any history of the Stalin era. If we are to believe her, Ginzburg, like many Russian memoirists before her, initially took up the pen strictly for personal and familial reasons, for "it did not occur to me that there could be any question of publication" (2: 418 [593]). Nonetheless, she burns that first "family" memoir to attempt, again according to her epilogue, something more public, composed, and intentional, and in so doing she reaches for a "truth" that her experience has proven to be beyond the historian's grasp. Her first version, she apologizes, was "not a book but only the raw material for one . . . haphazard, and too loosely put together" (2: 419 [593]). Significantly, it is when she is finally given her own apartment, that is, when the *"unheimlich"* spaces of her years as a rejected Soviet citizen come to an end and she is literally reinstalled in her community, that the work of self-construction in its full sense, as woman, mother, professional, and *intelligentka,* can begin.[10] It is at this intersection of training and experience, of historic fact and poetic "truth," and of individual and collective memories that Ginzburg's published memoir assumes its rightful place. Ginzburg makes the paradoxical statement that this second version is remarkable for its "truthfulness" rather than its literary merit, and yet is marred by self-censorship (2: 420 [594]). She thus conveniently ignores what readers of her memoir have often observed: that *Whirlwind* reads like a novel, has a polished narrative exposition, a strong authorial voice alternating with dialogue that is staged and characters who perform, a grasp of the difference between "real" and narrative time, and a wealth of literary and cultural references.

In a word, *Whirlwind* is a highly *kul'turnyi* work of real art in the Tolstoyan sense, one that intends to fulfill important ethical, didactic, and aesthetic functions simultaneously. Moreover, unlike an "oral history," whose merits also lie in its proximity to an individual truth that lies outside the context of ruling elites, Ginzburg's "remembering" resembles the memoiristic practices of those elites. As Paul Connerton has written,

> These writers of memoirs see their life as worth remembering because they are, in their own eyes, someone who has taken decisions which exerted, or can be represented as having exerted, a more or less wide influence and which have changed part of their social world. The 'personal' history of the

memoir writer has confronted an 'objective' history embodied in institutions . . . They have been inserted into the structure of dominant institutions and have been able to turn that structure to their own ends. It is this perceived capacity of making a personal intervention that makes it possible for the writers of memoirs to conceive their life retrospectively. (19)

Connerton further distinguishes between the life histories of elite and subaltern groups by arguing that what is lacking in the latter "is precisely those terms of reference that conduce to and reinforce [the] sense of linear trajectory, a sequential narrative shape: above all, in relation to the past, the notion of legitimating origins" (19). It is this search for legitimacy, and her redefinition of legitimacy in cultural rather than political terms, that I suggest argue for reading Ginzburg's Gulag memoirs as a work of cultural recovery as well as a model of prison camp literature. Cast out of her socialist paradise, Ginzburg the heroine and Ginzburg the author simultaneously embark on a journey in search of a meaningful community. For the memoir's heroine, this means breaking out of her privileged but constrained world into one in which family, friendship, selfhood, and destiny are redefined and restructured. For its author, reordering her experience into a document about a fallen culture, namely, Russian culture, enables Ginzburg to inscribe herself into the one community—the intelligentsia—that can give meaning to the chaos created by the Stalinist state.

Faced with the collapse of a meaningful world, Ginzburg is forced to search for what Benedict Anderson has termed "another style of continuity [where] what . . . was required was a secular transformation of fatality into continuity, contingency into meaning" (11). This explains the polarity that Ginzburg establishes between the unpredictability and illogic of the world of arrests, Gulags, and denunciations, and the continuity and meaning that she finds in Russian, and to a lesser extent, Western European culture. While the Soviet state had positioned itself as a model of logic and organization, Ginzburg discovers that the opposite is true. All state action is beyond comprehension (even to its own henchmen): "for the first time, I came up against that reversal of logic and common sense which never ceased to amaze me in the more than twenty years that followed" (1: 10 [10]). This is the first of many observations scattered throughout *Whirlwind* on the illogic of this universe. Cognitive facility and practical impulse count for naught in the design of the Gulag: "With all my teacher's training, I could not explain to this child of another world what exactly I was being accused of" (1: 56 [38]); "the main preoccupation was the floors. Camp bosses everywhere had a mania for clean floors. The whiteness of the floor was the one criterion of hygiene" (2: 5 [273]);[11] "It doesn't really make sense. First they educate me, give me university degrees . . . then they send me off to fell trees or, as an exceptional favor, to work in the chicken house" (2: 67 [320]). "I had long since made up my own mind that in our world the nor-

mal chain of cause and effect had been broken. At that time I had read neither Kafka nor Orwell" (2: 161 [392]).

Ginzburg, like many similarly educated Soviet citizens of her generation, had been brought up on the "magnificent illusion," to quote Andrei
Sinyavsky, that they live in a world that is "explained, harmonious, comprehensible . . . a scientifically constructed and scientifically organized utopia"
(30). When the purges and arrests bring that utopian dream to an end, and
the state begins to devour its best and brightest, Ginzburg turns to Russian
culture to fill the space so recently filled by a fervent faith in leader and system. In a textual move that parallels the way that various "communities"—
prison, chicken farm, orphanage, surrogate family, school, ex-prisoners—
impart meaning to the social spaces of her "life," pre-Soviet Russian culture
anchors the heroine of *Whirlwind* in a self-legitimizing originary narrative.
Abandoning the youthful superiority of the prearrest heroine in respect to
unsanctioned people and texts, Ginzburg now appeals to pre-Revolutionary
Russian culture to provide the arrangements that will bring meaning and
order to her life. Tellingly, her imagery echoes that of Sinyavsky:

> We were creatures of our time, the epoch of magnificent illusions. We were
> not making our way to Communism via "the low road of the mines, the sick-
> les, and the pitchforks." No, we were "flinging ourselves into Communism
> from the poetic heights." In effect, for all our youthful devotion to the cold
> formulas of dialectical materialism, we were out and out idealists. Under the
> blows of the inhuman machine that descended upon us, many of the "truths"
> we had been parroting all those years lost their sparkle. But no blizzards
> could extinguish that candle flickering in the wind, the spirituality of the Rus-
> sian intelligentsia, which my generation accepted as a secret gift from the
> thinkers and poets of the beginning of the century who had themselves been
> the targets of our critical shafts.
>
> It had seemed to us that we had toppled them from their pedestals in the
> cause of a newly acquired truth. But in the years of trial we realized that we
> were flesh of their flesh. Because even the selflessness with which we sought
> to establish the new path came from them, from their disdain for the satis-
> factions of the flesh, and from their unquenchable spiritual fervor.
>
> . . . we were far from being wise. On the contrary, it was with the great-
> est difficulty that our reason, weighed down with ready-made concepts,
> groped toward the light of reality. Nevertheless, we did manage to carry our
> "lighted candles" into solitary confinement, into the huts and punishment
> cells, and through the blizzard-lashed marches in Calami. Those lamps of
> ours alone were what enabled us to emerge from the pitch-darkness. (2:
> 100–1 [345–46])

The above passage makes it clear that Ginzburg's debt to literary models
(and their authors) goes beyond mere citation. In these lines, as succinct and
evocative as any written by Aleksandr Blok, one of the pivotal figures in the
Russian cultural landscape, Ginzburg appropriates key imagery and con-

cepts from the prerevolutionary intelligentsia and redefines it on her own, experience-based terms, often to ironic effect. Neither her generation, with its smug belief in itself as the embodiment of history's course, nor the preceding ones, going back to the nineteenth-century intelligentsia's paradoxical mode of "unity through alienation" (Billington, 388), escape her critical eye. Never one to minimize her role, be it in the camps or in post-Stalinist dissidence, Ginzburg traces a romantic, heroic culture. Ginzburg's text muddles monolithic, Stalinist cultural categories as she assumes responsibility and takes action for the actions of her foremothers and fathers among the Russian intelligentsia. Here, she acknowledges both the flaws in her spiritual origins and their durability: no Communist rhetoric ("cold formulas") or officially sanctioned teachings ("newly acquired truth[s]," "ready-made concepts") could substitute for the "secret gift" inherited from her spiritual predecessors.

Thus, it is possible to read *Whirlwind* as a search for a legitimate genealogy, for the proper forebearers worthy of a survivor of the camps who is a remarkable woman, not least in her own eyes. In this respect, however, Ginzburg would be surprised to find herself in the company of Soviet state-sanctioned cultural products. As Katerina Clark has argued in her seminal studies of Stalinist culture, one of the critical points in high Stalinist culture "has been a marked proclivity for writers . . . to articulate their model of the present in terms of a particular historical figure. . . . The society is legitimized in a myth of origins and a line of succession . . . stretching from that line of origin to the present."[12] For Ginzburg, that "line of succession" is actually made up of many lines that crisscross temporal and spatial barriers and social and linguistic terrains, but they are all rooted in a unified notion of humanistic, Russian/European culture. In a kind of a cultural omnium-gatherum, Ginzburg's lineage embraces a fellow elderly prisoner's bundle of tattered belongings as much as Dante's *Inferno;* Giordano Bruno and his iron mask explain the present, as do "Nekrasov's most hackneyed lines" (I, 228 [145]); public health posters remembered from childhood hang in her imaginary library next to shelves of Shakespeare, Alexandre Dumas, and Aleksandr Pushkin. The canonical points that justify her own claim to literary (and social) authority, however, reside in classical, prerevolutionary Russian poetry, in Pushkin and in Blok, and in the paragons of post-Stalinist dissident culture: Pasternak, Mandelstam, Akhmatova. They become her models, she is "flesh of their flesh," and it is their work that she must continue, even as she ostensibly writes a prison camp memoir.[13] As she prepares to spend her first New Year's in prison, Ginzburg reflects

> once again on the power which literature exerts on us in that state of spiritual composure which prison life induces, and which makes us strive, devoutly and humbly, to drink in an author's words to the full. I have never loved human beings so devotedly as in those months and years when, cast away in the inhuman land and imprisoned behind stone walls, I absorbed

every line of print as though it were a message radioed from Earth, my distant mother and homeland, where I had lived with my human brothers and sisters, and where they lived still. (I, 228 [145])

And so, on this New Year's Eve, significant both as a traditional holiday and as the first in her life spent in prison, she chooses to be consoled in her text (or does "truth" so dictate?) by Nikolai Nekrasov, a prerevolutionary poet canonized in the Soviet era because of his progressive views and civic poetry. On this occasion, she sees him in a new light:

Even Nekrasov's most hackneyed lines were now as moving as a letter, charged with emotion, from a distant friend. I used to read to Julia "Knight for an Hour" and "The Russian Women." Strange to say, the passages which struck one most forcibly were those which one had hardly noticed. For example, "Sleep is for others, not for me"—the poet's exclamation on a moon-lit, frosty night. . . . I had learned those lines at school and they had merged with dozens of other lines . . . without making any deep impression on me, but now . . . ! Outside our cell window was that very same frosty night, and however cold it might be we never closed the chink through which a trickle of fresh air come in to us, and with it our beggar's dole from the table of life. I also brought with it Nekrasov's tingling frosty night, and I felt as if no one before us could have fully appreciated the words: "Sleep is for others, not for me." (1: 228 [145–46])

Culture, and her memoir, thus become a bridge, a "solution for continuity" that imparts meaning and order to a world that has lost both. To return to Clark's argument, Ginzburg incorporates a paradigm widely used by official culture, but reaccentuates that originary topos with her own meaning.

Ginzburg's memoir is full of digressions such as the one above that perhaps belong more in an essay than in fictional narrative. Throughout *Whirlwind*, she also adopts numerous novelistic strategies to better "remember"—that is, impart meaning—to the biographical facts. Thus, chronological time alternates with narrative time: "The year 1937 began, to all intents and purposes, at the end of 1934—to be exact, on the first of December," she writes in her opening sentence. Here, the narrative perspective is not that of the straightforward chronicler or recorder, but rather that of the narrator laying out the *Vorgeschichte* or background of her narrative. As the telephone rings, forebodingly, at four o'clock on that morning to summon Ginzburg to a party meeting, she introduces the fused public/private paradigms that defined Soviet social life in the 1930s:

My husband, Pavel Vasilyevich Aksyonov, a leading member of the Tartar Province Committee of the Party, was away on business. I could hear my children in the next room breathing evenly in their sleep.

"You're wanted at the regional committee office, Room 37 (38 in the Russian text-NK), at six A.M."

This order was given to me as a member of the Party. (1: 3 [6])

Ginzburg's identification of her husband and herself as Party members (although with a difference in status—he is "a leading member," and introduced by his name and patronymic, while she is merely "a member of the Party"), the narrator's isolation (her husband is away), her children's innocent breathing, the ominous timing of the phone call—her "remembering" of these multiple, suggestive details alert careful readers to their entry into a consciously constructed narrative space.

In the following paragraphs, Ginzburg leaves for the meeting, symbolically abandoning for what will be the first of many times the home, family, and material security that her marriage, education, and party status had given her, and introduces the first-person confessional voice that will enable her to inscribe her physical and spiritual journey from naive, innocent "child" to a mature woman of considerable self-insight and resilience:

> Without waking anyone, I ran out of the house long before there was any traffic in the street. I can still remember the still snowfall and the strange lightness of my walk.
>
> I don't want to sound pretentious, but I must say in all honesty that, had I been ordered to die for the Party—not once but three times—that very night, in that snowy winter dawn, I would have obeyed without the slightest hesitation. I had not the shadow of a doubt of the rightness of the Party line. Only Stalin—I suppose instinctively—I could not bring myself to idolize, as it was already becoming the fashion to do. But if I felt this vague disquiet about him, I carefully concealed it even from myself. (1: 3 [6])

Far from being a static preface to the journey to come, these paragraphs introduce the dramatis personae performing symbolically, almost archetypically, laden roles: absent husband, blameless children asleep (one of whom will die in the siege of Leningrad), heroine taking the initial steps of her danger-filled, life-altering journey. Through a careful arrangement of these first, seemingly quotidian details, Ginzburg invokes paradigms that are articulated not only through her life story, but also through the major discourses of Russian-Soviet social and cultural life that have engaged Russian writers from Pushkin and Tolstoy through Platonov and Tolstaya: home and homelessness, domesticity and public life, individual responsibility and collective morality.

Nevertheless, for all of its literary gestures, in its author's mind, *Whirlwind* is an autobiographical memoir that derives its power, as Ginzburg asserts in her Epilogue, from its "truth" value. Having established herself as the recipient of that "secret gift" from the prerevolutionary intelligentsia, Ginzburg insists on the validity of her memory and its role in authenticating the author's position between truth and official history's falsifications. Through her memoir, that gift is now revealed to a select group of readers, those who have entered into a "pact" with the author to accept her writing of the truth as she knew it. Writing as an ex-historian in a post-Stalin soci-

ety in which the state had played a decisive role in disfiguring history, Ginzburg turns to the autobiographical (or memoiristic) mode as a compromise
position, for it is closer to memory than the historical mode, at least as understood in modern thought. Memory, and its literary manifestation in poetry, she argues, are essential for human and cultural survival. As she relates
in the epilogue, soon after her arrest, physical survival becomes inextrica-
ble from textual survival:

> Readers often ask me: "How could you keep such a mass of names, facts,
> place names, and poems in your memory?"
>
> Very simply: because just remembering it all to record it later had been the
> main object of my life throughout those eighteen years. The collection of
> material for this book began from the moment when I first crossed the thresh-
> old of the NKVD's Inner Prison in Kazan'. All those years I had no opportu-
> nity to write anything down, to prepare any preliminary sketches for a future
> book. All that I have set down has been written from memory. When I began
> to work on the book, the only landmarks in the labyrinth of the past were my
> own poems, also composed without benefit of pencil or paper, but thanks to
> the efficiency of my memory where poetry is concerned, clearly imprinted on
> my brain. I am fully aware of the homemade, amateur quality of my prison
> verses. But to a certain extent, they did duty for the notebooks I did not pos-
> sess. And that is their justification. (2: 417–18 [592–93])

In this revealing passage, Ginzburg addresses the vital yet paradoxical
interaction between poetry and memory, through which poetry distorts
"facts" and "truth" to arrive at a higher or deeper "truth." This interaction
is central to understanding Ginzburg's distinctive negotiation of the camp
memoir form, and the sense of authority and urgency that she conveys. By
putting poetry at the core of her memory, she reflects her generation of
Soviet dissident intelligentsia, for whom, as Liudmila Alekseeva writes, "a
passion for poetry became a sign of the times" (Gessen, 11). In addition, by
writing a memoir that pays tribute to a destroyed Russian culture (and the
Western European heritage that Russia shared) as much as it does to
Stalin's victims, Ginzburg reveals her indebtedness to a classical tradition,
to Homer, about whom it has been said that "to versify was to remember,"
and to Simonides of Ceos, who established the centrality of images, and of
their organization (Le Goff, 64, 66). Like the Homeric epic, Ginzburg's
memoir, in addition to its discourses of witnessing and self-fashioning,
mourns various types of loss, all intertwined through culture and personal
experience: of children and family, of youth, and perhaps most important
for our purposes here, of Russian culture. For Ginzburg as for Homer,
poetic mourning of this scope heroicizes the mourner, and both write in response to a perceived national need, the victim's corrective, as it were, to a
national tragedy. Like Simonides, she "visualizes the places occupied by the
victims of a disaster of which he [was] the only survivor,"[14] reproducing

them in narrative that relies for its momentum on the "efficiency" of her poetic memory.

Ginzburg's insistence on the orality of her poetry is similarly evocative of the oral roots of Western culture, of the beginnings of history in myth and story. It is telling that for the early Greeks, Mnemosyne was both the goddess of memory and the mother of history, and "she [both] reminds men of the memory of heroes and their high deeds, and . . . presides over lyric poetry," as Le Goff observes (64). Moreover, he continues, "The poet is thus possessed by memory, [he] is a diviner of the past . . . when poetry is identified with memory, this makes the latter a kind of knowledge, and even of wisdom, of *sophia.*" It is this wisdom, with its connection to what Ginzburg accepts as the core of human experience, that explains the position of authority that she gradually grows into, through her life experience and her reflection on that experience, first through her memorized poetry, then through its written reflection.

As the author returns to Moscow and takes up her pen years later to write what will become her published memoir, she writes as Mnemosyne's priestess (remember the "secret gift"), for through her "cruel journey of the soul," she has traced a dual journey, forward in biographical time, but backward to a past that the Stalinist interregnum has made inaccessible to subsequent generations. At the end of her memoir, after she has finally received her rehabilitation certificate from the Soviet state, she is stunned by the thought that her long journey is finally over, that at last "I was just like everyone else," as she says with a hint of irony. She sits down to catch her breath:

> Suddenly, two country cousins (*provincialy*) came over to me—a man and a woman with heavy suitcases in their hands and rucksacks over their shoulders.
>
> "Would you please tell us, young lady, how we get to the Kazan' station?"
>
> This apparently trivial happening immediately put me in a good mood again. For one thing, they had called me "young lady." So, even in my late fifties I didn't look like an old woman. And for another, they had asked me how to get to the Kazan' station. Not to Mylga, not to Elgen, not to Vaskov's House and not to Lefortovo, but simply to the Kazan' station. And I did my very best to explain to them in detail where to change trains and where to cross the street. (2: 415 [590])

In this, the last "public" gesture of her memoir, Ginzburg again blends personal experience with obvious cultural symbolism. Invoking through these "country cousins" the nineteenth-century myth of the Russian people or *"narod"* turning to an urban *intelligentka* for direction, she uses this minor incident to textually guide the reader back in time and place from the Soviet present to Kazan' station, one of Russia's ancient cities on the Volga River, mother of all Russian rivers. In the Russian mind, the road from

159

Moscow to Kazan' resonates with multiple cultural and historical associations: Kazan' was the home of the famous icon of the Kazan' Virgin, the site of Ivan the Terrible's historic battle with the Mongols, a hotbed for sympathizers with the Decembrists, and the site of a famous university, Ginzburg's alma mater. In the author's consciousness, that question erases the names (the auditory ugliness of which she had noted more than once in her memoir) of the Gulag camps (Mylga, Elgen), the administrative offices where she had to report weekly even after her release from the prison camp (Vaskov's house), and Lefortovo prison, Moscow's infamous site of interrogation for many of the victims of the great purges. Like the "road that leads to the church," (a church no longer standing) that literally frames the narrative in Tengiz Abuladze's perestroika-era film, *Repentance,* the seemingly innocent image of Kazan' station here makes something happen that can happen only in a culturally created text.

Edward S. Casey has noted that Mnemosyne for archaic Greek culture embodied "a way of getting (and staying) in touch with a past that would otherwise be consigned to oblivion: it was a fateful fending off of forgetfulness" (Casey, 13). By the fifth century, however, with the emergence of Platonic philosophy and the shift of the historical paradigm away from remembering and toward analysis, "the highly personified figure of Mnemosyne disappears" (13)—the female figure of Mnemosyne, with its implications of direct access to the past through myth and image is replaced by the male historian's distancing synthesizing discourses, and knowledge is privileged over wisdom. A comparable appropriation was made by the future-oriented, analytic, and abstracting modes of Marxism-Leninism. There is no indication that Ginzburg had any profound knowledge of classical scholarship, much less of such a shift in classical thought: in the only passage in the memoir in which she speaks of her father, she admits that, as a child "when he took me out for walks, he used to teach me strange Greek words . . . Born in the nineteenth century, he had learned both Latin and Greek in high school" (1: 246 [158]). Nonetheless, I suggest that she writes her memoir to access and preserve from extinction Russia's cultural past, particularly in its literary and poetic forms, many of which are indebted to traditional folk forms (*skazki,* traditional rituals, folk sayings, prisoners' songs and poetry, and so on).

In the prison and camp context, which has often been used as a metonymic trope for Soviet society as a whole, a society in which production of and access to the printed word were highly restricted, Ginzburg substitutes the oral composition and "remembering" of her own poetry for the absent notebooks. In the tradition of prison poetry, those organized images that she carries around in her brain represent the last border that cannot be transgressed by a system that has violated her life and her body in every other way. Ginzburg counterposes "the efficiency of my memory where poetry is concerned," which has produced this text, to the massive inefficiency, described by her in detail, of the Gulag. Ginzburg suggests a different kind of history or record, one based on poetry ("images"). However, she also counterpoises that memory, intact and efficient within her body as long as she is alive, to the fragility of the text that she launches into a dangerous world. Unlike individual (or collective) memory, texts can be appropriated ("kidnapped" to use her image) by institutions or subsequent generations of readers.

Ginzburg's recognition of the dilemma she faces when she commits to inscribing her "efficient," irreproachable, but ultimately mortal, memory in a text that she knows will be the defining narrative of her life explains the contradictory positions that she takes toward writing and the fate of her memoir in the epilogue to *Whirlwind*. If her memory for "truth" is infallible, its recording and publication make it highly vulnerable for reasons that Russian readers and students of Soviet history would quickly recognize. Once the text moves from the private, familial arena to the public stage, Ginzburg points out the detours and distortions that threaten its very integrity. In a gesture that Billington has described (speaking of Soviet writers in general) as "anticipatory self-censorship" (535), these begin with the author's own urge to edit her text, to make it more palatable to the editors who will decide its fate:

> together with my hopes of publication the missing inner editor came into being. He carped at every paragraph: "You won't get that past the censor." I started looking for more streamlined formulations, and I not infrequently spoiled passages that had come out well, comforting myself with the thought that, after all, a sentence or so was not much sacrifice for the sake of publication, of reaching people at last. (2: 419 [594])

Launched into a contingent world, the text of *Whirlwind* follows its own trajectory through editorial offices and *samizdat* readers. Pleased, on the one hand, that letters "from Leningrad and Krasnoyarsk, from Saratov and Odessa," marked her narrative's journey beyond the confines of the Moscow dissident community, Ginzburg expresses both dismay and pride that ". . . I had completely lost control over the astonishing life of my unpublished book" (2: 420 [594]) And, if these letters from her secret readers, and from prominent intellectuals of the Brezhnev era, were "reassuring," she is alternatively chagrined and angered by other responses to the same text. Aleksandr Tvardovskii, the chief editor of *Novyi mir*, the leading journal of Russian intellectual life in the postwar period, responds negatively.[15] After submitting her manuscript to *Iunost'*, a widely circulated though less revered journal, she learns that her manuscript would not be published there either, but rather would be "forwarded . . . for safekeeping to the Marx-Engels-Lenin Institute where, as the cover note put it, 'It might serve as material on the history of the Party'" (II, 422 [595]).

Consequently, Ginzburg worries that in a literate, historicized culture, memory must be mediated through a text for it to become public, but once made public, at least in the Soviet context, it becomes subject not only to distortion, but to destruction, or to convenient forgetting in dusty Party archives. Cultural memory, Ginzburg's memoir reminds us, is based on experience and individual and collective will. Textual production and reproduction are only one of several, and by no means the most reliable, modes for its preservation. She learns many lessons from her eighteen years in the Gulag, not the least of which is that literature—oral or written—and other forms of cultural production driven by myth and story (remembering, dreaming, daydreaming) derive power from their ability to arrange experience into meaningful—sense-making and symbol-using—patterns. Those patterns are generationally predetermined as much as they are transcendent and eternal, and Ginzburg's memoir should be read in the context of her generation of Brezhnev-era dissidents, during which "a new stock figure emerged in films and literature, the martyred intellectual as tragic bearer of cultural memory." (Clark 1993, 298) Not dismissing the memoir's capability to act as cultural policeman as well as cultural preserver, I would nonetheless argue that the presence of the autobiographical "I" here mediates between those conflicting positions: Ginzburg's memoir speaks to present and future readers because of the seductiveness of a narrative written from the position of the unmediated "I," an I that is historical, mortal, contingent—and "cultural." There is something paradoxical, after all, between her desire to write herself into the nineteenth-century intelligentsia, and at the same time her distrust of the printed word—in its own and subsequent generations' eyes, the intelligentsia's highest achievement. What saves *Whirlwind* from becoming consumed by a vision of past cultural glory is Ginzburg's understanding of culture not as a product, a result, or a given, frozen in time and canon, but rather a constant negotiation of the perpetually renewing paradoxes that it presents for the individual, the writer, and the reader. It is here, I would argue, that the cultural work of this memoir takes place.

Notes

1. Indeed, that is the central idea of Fitzpatrick's book. For a more recent treatment of the same topic, see Louise McReynolds's and Cathy Popkin's "The Objective Eye and the Common Good," in Kelly and Shepherd, 57–98. Steve Smith's and Catriona Kelly's observation in their essay in the same volume, "Commercial Culture and Consumerism," is also relevant: "Possession of education and 'culture' was at least as important as the possession of wealth in determining social status, and marked out the narrow band of its possessors from the dark 'masses'" (154).

2. Among the most informative discussions in English of Ginzburg's memoir are the following: Adele Barker's entry in *Dictionary of Russian Women Writers*, ed. Marina Ledkovsky, et al. (Westport, Conn.: Greenwood Press, 1994), 205–6; Edward J. Brown, *Russian Literature Since the Revolution* (Cambridge: Harvard University Press, 1982), 287–91; Olga Cooke, "Evgeniia Ginzburg," in *Reference Guide to Russian Writers*, ed. Neil Cornwall (London: Fitzroy Dearborn, 1998), 320–22; Barbara Heldt, *Terrible Perfection: Women and Russian Literature* (Bloomington: Indiana University Press, 1987), 153–56; Beth Holmgren, "For the Good of the Cause: Russian Women's Autobiography in the Twentieth Century," in *Women Writers in Russian Literature*, ed. Toby Clyman et al. (Westport, Conn.: Greenwood Press, 1994), 131–34; Catriona Kelly, *A History of Russian Women's Writing, 1820–1992* (Oxford: Clarendon Press, 1994), 367–68; Natasha Kolchevska, "A Difficult Journey: Evgeniia Ginzburg and Women's Writing of Camp Memoirs," in *Women and Russian Culture: Projections and Self-Perceptions*, ed. Rosalind Marsh (New York: Berghahn Books, 1998), 148–62; Nadya Peterson, "Dirty Women: Cultural Connotations of Cleanliness in Soviet Russia," in *Russia°Women°Culture*, ed. Helena Goscilo and Beth Holmgren (Bloomington: Indiana University Press, 1996), 180–97, *passim;* Marschal Schatz, "Soviet Society and the Purges of the Thirties in the Mirror of Memoir Literature," *Canadian-American Slavic Studies* 2, no. 2 (1973): 250–61; Leona Toker, *Return from the Archipelago: Narratives of Gulag Survivors* (Bloomington: Indiana University Press, 2000), 52–55, and *passim.*

3. *Krutoi marshrut* was first published in Russian by émigré presses in 1967 and 1979. (See Works Cited.) All citations are from the English editions, followed by the page numbers in the 1990 Russian text. For brevity's sake, I use *Whirlwind* for all references in the text to Ginzburg's work.

4. After the appearance of her memoir in the West, Ginzburg continued to insist that the manuscript translated and published in Italy and Germany had been taken out of the Soviet Union and printed against her wishes. *Journey into the Whirlwind* was first published in Italian translation in Milan in 1967, and shortly thereafter a Russian edition appeared in Frankfurt-am-Main. Soon afterward, Ginzburg was expelled from the Soviet Union of Writers.

5. Beth Holmgren addresses the multiple roles the memoir can play in this volume's introduction.

6. See my "A Difficult Journey," endnote 2.

7. Catriona Kelly's general summary of the development of the Soviet intelligentsia into cultural consumers could have been written about the pre-Gulag Ginzburg: "the Stalinist regime did succeed in imposing a broad consensus regulating life and mentality in Russian cities and large towns . . . this consensus took for granted the importance of 'culture.' In the 1920s

and 1930s, this signified above all technological and scientific progress, but in the late 1940s, it came primarily to signify nineteenth-century Russian art, with Pushkin, Gogol, Tolstoi, Gor'kii, the painters Repin, Shishkin, and Levitan, the composers Glinka, Tchaikovsky, and Rimskii-Korsakov, elevated to the new national pantheon. The key significance of the intelligentsia, above all writers, in expressing cultural values through moral pronouncements was also accepted" (Kelly 1998b, 315).

8. The challenge that factographic and fictionalized first-person narratives present to official history has been a topic of considerable scrutiny. For a range of views on the question, see Donald Fanger, "Conflicting Imperatives in the Model of the Russian Writer: The Case of Tertz/Sinyavsky," in Gary Saul Morson, ed., *Literature and History: Theoretical Problems and Russian Case Studies* (Stanford: Stanford University Press, 1986), 111–24; Jane Gary Harris, "Diversity of Discourse: Autobiographical Statements in Theory and Practice," in *Autobiographical Statements in Twentieth-Century Russian Literature,* ed. Jane Gary Harris (Princeton: Princeton University Press, 1990), 3–35, *passim;* and Andrew Baruch Wachtel, *An Obsession with History: Russian Writers Confront the Past* (Stanford: Stanford University Press, 1994).

9. Toker traces a very direct development from Marxism to religious faith in Ginzburg's work: "In the mid-forties, Ginzburg's break with Marxism took a religious form . . . in spite of the residue of Soviet patterns of conduct and thought, she turned to Christianity" (54). Ginzburg's marriage to her second husband, Anton Walter—a German-Russian, Catholic, homeopath and "jolly saint"—replays this pattern on a more multidimensional level.

10. In "Narrating Space," her illuminating essay on the relationship between space and the construction of social and cultural identity, Patricia Yaeger uses but also cites several critiques of this distinction between the concepts of "place" and "space": "place is associated with the *heimlich* work of self-construction versus the *unheimlich* anonymity of space" (4, n. 5).

11. For a perceptive reading of the relationship between gender, cleanliness, and resistance in the camps, see Nadya L. Peterson's "Dirty Women: Cultural Connotations of Cleanliness in Soviet Russia," *Russia*❋*Women*❋*Culture,* ed. Goscilo and Holmgren, 177–205.

12. Clark 1993, 289. See also her *The Soviet Novel: History as Ritual* for a wide-ranging discussion of mythic paradigms in Soviet literature.

13. Ginzburg's turn to icons of European culture in her memoir is also reminiscent of the fondness of Bulat Okudzhava, the 1960s semiunderground Soviet bard, for the *poet maudit* figure of Francois Villon.

14. See Natalie Zemon Davis's introduction to a special issue of *Representations* 26 (spring 1989): 3, devoted to history and memory.

15. Vasily Aksyonov, Ginzburg's son and a prominent writer and commentator on Soviet and post-Soviet literary politics, explains Tvardovsky's rejection of Ginzburg's memoir for publication as part of the editor's prejudice against intellectuals, whom he perceived as privileged, writing about the sufferings of the Russian people. Talk given at the American Association for the Advancement of Slavic Studies national convention, Washington, D.C., October 1995.

Works Cited

Aksyonov, Vasilii. Remarks made at a "Roundtable on Evgeniia Ginzburg." AAASS, Washington, D.C., October 1995.

Anderson, Benedict. *Imagined Communities*. 2nd ed. London: Verso, 1991.

Billington, James H. *The Icon and the Axe: An Interpretive History of Russian Culture*. New York: Vintage Books, 1970.

Boym, Svetlana. *Common Places: Mythologies of Everyday Life in Russia*. Cambridge: Harvard University Press, 1994.

Casey, Edward S. *Remembering: A Phenomenological Study*. Bloomington: Indiana University Press, 1987.

Clark, Katerina. *The Soviet Novel: History as Ritual*. Chicago: University of Chicago Press, 1981.

———. "Changing Historical Paradigms in Soviet Culture" in *Late Soviet Culture From Perestroika to Novostroika*, edited by Thomas Lahusen with Gene Kuperman. Durham, N.C.: Duke University Press, 1993, 289–306.

Connerton, Paul. *How Societies Remember*. Cambridge: Cambridge University Press, 1989.

Davis, Natalie Zemon. "Introduction," *Representations* 26 (spring 1989): 1–6.

Fitzpatrick, Sheila. *The Cultural Front: Power and Culture in Revolutionary Russia*. Ithaca: Cornell University Press, 1992.

———. *Everyday Stalinism: Ordinary Life in Extraordinary Times. Soviet Russia in the 1930s*. New York: Oxford University Press, 1999.

Gessen, Masha. *Dead Again: The Russian Intelligentsia after Communism*. London: Verso, 1997.

Ginzburg, Eugenia. *Journey into the Whirlwind*. Translated by Paul Stevenson and Max Hayward. San Diego: Harcourt Brace Jovanovich, 1967.

———. *Within the Whirlwind*. Translated by Ian Boland. San Diego: Harcourt Brace Jovanovich, 1979.

Ginzburg, Evgeniia. *Krutoi marshrut: Khronika vremen kul'ta lichnost*. Vol. 1. New York: Possev-Verlag, 1967. Vol. 2. Milan: Arnoldo Mondadori, 1979. Volumes I and II were reprinted together in *Krutoi marshrut: Khronika vremen kul'ta lichnosti*. 1990. Moscow: Sovetskii pisatel'.

Jameson, Frederic. Foreword to J. F. Lyotard, *The Postmodern Condition: A Report on Knowledge.* Translated by G. Bennington and B. Massumi. Minneapolis: University of Minnesota Press, 1984.

Kelly, Catriona. "New Boundaries for the Common Good: Science, Philanthropy, and Objectivity in Soviet Russia." In *Constructing Russian Culture in the Age of Revolution: 1881–1940,* edited by Catriona Kelly and David Shepherd. Oxford: Oxford University Press, 1998, 238–55.

———. "From 'Russian Empire' to 'Soviet Union.'" In *Constructing Russian Culture,* 1998, 314–17.

Kolchevska, Natasha. "A Difficult Journey: Evgeniia Ginzburg and Women's Writing of Camp Memoirs." In *Women and Russian Culture: Projections and Self-Perceptions,* edited by Rosalind Marsh. New York: Berghahn Books, 1998, 148–62.

Le Goff, Jacques. *History and Memory.* Translated by Steven Rendall and Elizabeth Claman, New York: Columbia University Press, 1992.

McReynolds, Louise, and Cathy Popkin. "The Objective Eye and the Common Good." In *Constructing Russian Culture,* 1998, 57–105.

Peterson, Nadya. "Dirty Women: Cultural Connotations of Cleanliness in Soviet Russia." In *Russia*Women*Culture,* ed. Beth Holmgren and Helena Goscilo. Bloomington: Indiana University Press, 1996, 177–205.

Sinyavsky , Andrei. *Soviet Civilization: A Cultural History.* Translated by J. Turnbull with the assistance of Nikolai Formozov. New York: Little, Brown and Co., 1990.

Smith, Steve, and Catriona Kelly. "Commercial Culture and Consumerism." In *Constructing Russian Culture,* 1998, 106–64.

Toker, Leona. *Return from the Archipelago: Narratives of Gulag Survivors.* Bloomington: Indiana University Press, 2000.

Woolf, Virginia. *The Common Reader.* New York: Harcourt Brace Jovanovich, 1953.

Yaeger, Patricia. "Narrating Space." In *The Geography of Identity,* edited by Patricia Yaeger. Ann Arbor: University of Michigan Press, 1996.

Galya Diment

English as Sanctuary: Nabokov's and Brodsky's Autobiographical Writings

This is the use of memory:
For liberation—not less of love but expanding
Of love beyond desire, and so liberation
From the future as well as the past.

—T. S. Eliot

"A WRITER'S BIOGRAPHY is in his twists of language," Joseph Brodsky wrote in "Less than One," the first essay in the volume by the same title (Brodsky 1986, 3). By that he meant, most likely, that there is no real need for a writer's biography since it already exists in that writer's very language which, twisting along the same paths as the artist's life, reflects and records the most vital developments of his or her being. Ironically, as Brodsky was writing that essay in 1976, his own biography was beginning to be paralleled in the "twists" of not one language but two: Joseph Brodsky was rapidly becoming a bilingual writer.

Literary bilingualism is one of the most fascinating developments of literature in exile, and it has been drawing increasing critical attention in recent years. While Samuel Beckett still remains the most critically well charted territory in this respect, there are now a number of works discussing not only other bilingual writers but also whole cultural traditions of literary bilingualism.[1] Regardless of how we define it, "literary bilingualism" is, of course, not a totally modern phenomenon. Quite a few Western European writers of previous centuries, including Thomas More and John Milton, chose to write certain works in Latin rather than their native tongues. Likewise, in Russian literature of the eighteenth and nineteenth centuries, one now and then comes across literary works (like Petr Chaadaev's famous *Philosophical Letters* [1829]) written in French. Brodsky himself alluded to this fact in a 1990 interview in which he stated that "Sposobnost' operirovat' dvumia iazykami nichego iz riada von vykhodiashchego soboi ne predstavliaet: vspomnim khotia by XIX vek" ("An ability to operate with two languages is nothing extraordinary—let's remember, for example, the nineteenth century" [Vail', 27]).[2] But bilingualism obviously became a much more frequent phenomenon in the literature of the twentieth century. Cataclysmic wars and revolutions as well as a greater degree of mobility all contributed to numerous instances of twentieth-century writers going into exile, whether a self-imposed one, as in the case of Samuel Beckett, or a forced one, as in the case of Joseph Brodsky.

We are told we owe it to Auden that Brodsky first attempted to write in English. He simply wanted, he said, "to find myself in closer proximity to the man whom I considered the greatest mind of the twentieth century: Wystan Hugh Auden" (Brodsky 1986, 357).[3] I believe he really thought that Auden was the sole reason behind his desire to write in English—yet one of his first English essays also happened to be autobiographical. It was not the "closer proximity" to Auden that he sought there but the closer proximity to his own past and to his late parents. His choice of English to record his Russian memories may appear surprising. However, more than twenty-five years before him, Vladimir Nabokov, another prominent Russian bilingual exile, made the very same, seemingly illogical choice.

Nabokov and Brodsky took different paths to becoming bilingual writers. Nabokov simply stopped writing in Russian after he came to the United States, save for some poetry and a Russian version of his 1950 autobiography. Brodsky, on the other hand, most actively and successfully used both Russian and English after his emigration in 1972. The two also became bilingual, most likely, for largely different reasons. "When a writer resorts to a language other than his mother tongue," wrote Brodsky in his tribute to Auden,

> he does so either out of necessity, like Conrad, or because of burning ambition, like Nabokov, or for the sake of greater estrangement, like Beckett. . . . [I]n the summer of 1977 I . . . set out to write (essays, translations, occasionally a poem) in English for a reason that had very little to do with the above. . . . My desire to write in English had nothing to do with any sense of confidence, contentment, or comfort; it was simply a desire to please a shadow. (Brodsky 1986, 357, 358)

Aware of a tempting parallel between himself and Nabokov, and pinpointing Nabokov's "burning ambition" as a driving force behind his transformation into an American writer, Brodsky liked to emphasize his own lack of any ambition. "If I have become, to a certain extent, an English writer," he told an interviewer, "this has happened against my ambition, it has been a side effect rather than a conscious goal" (Bethea 1989, 38).[4]

One can easily perceive that Brodsky hated being always compared to Nabokov—just as Nabokov himself detested being always compared to Conrad. That Brodsky and Nabokov are, in fact, more different than they are alike should be plainly evident. Suffice it to say that Nabokov actively disliked most of the authors whom Brodsky respected. In Nabokov's estimate, Dostoevsky was a "third-rate writer" (Nabokov 1980, 172), T. S. Eliot "a big fake" (Nabokov 1989, 90), Auden easily mistakable for Aiken (Nabokov 1980, 163),[5] and Blok a better poet than Mandelstam (Nabokov 1981, 97). He also did not care much for Brodsky's own poetry when he first read it in 1969—it "is flawed by incorrectly accented words," he wrote, "lack of verbal discipline and an overabundance of words in general" (Nabokov 1989, 461).

In his turn, Brodsky never made a secret of *his* lack of respect for *Nabokov's* poetic output. In his conversations with Solomon Volkov, Brodsky remembered with much distaste how the editors of *The Kenyon Review* had asked him in 1979 to translate a Russian poem by Nabokov ("Otkuda priletel? Kakim ty dyshish' gorem," 1924) into English: "Oshchushcheniia byli samye raznoobraznye. Vo-pervykh, polnoe otvrashchenie k tomu, chto ia delaiu. Potomu chto stikhotvorenie Nabokova ochen' nizkogo kachestva. On voobshche, po-moemu, nesostoiavshiisia poet . . . Ia byl protiv etoi idei, no oni nastaivali." ("I had very mixed feelings about it. First of all, complete disgust for what I was doing because Nabokov's poem is of very low quality. He, in general, in my opinion, never materialized as a poet . . . I was against that idea but they kept insisting" [Volkov, 169].)[6]

Brodsky did, however, admire Nabokov's prose (as he had informed Carl Proffer back in the late 1960s, when still in the Soviet Union), and, as David Bethea showed in his 1990 paper on the similar symbolism of the butterfly as an image for art in Nabokov and Brodsky, there does exist an occasional—and quite essential—similarity between the two which makes one want to look at them side by side.[7] Their possible reasons for recording their early memories in English definitely provide such an occasion.

Elizabeth Klosty Beaujour makes a curious statement regarding bilingual writers and their linguistic choices. "There are," she writes, "even fairly frequent instances when a bilingual writer will choose the language in which he writes a work *against the logic of subject matter and context*. Take, for example, the decision of several bilingual Russians to write their childhood memoirs first in a language other than their mother tongue even at periods when they were actively using Russian for other literary purposes" (Beaujour, 45, emphasis modified). Elementary logic would, indeed, suggest that there is nothing more natural than describing your childhood experience in the language of this childhood, and one is likely to pity the author who is seemingly forced by his or her financial situation in a new country to write an autobiography in a different language. Especially when this author directly asks for pity—as Nabokov did in his introduction to *Drugie berega* (the Russian version of his autobiography), where he complained that his original English autobiography, *Conclusive Evidence,* "took the longest time to write (1946–50) and writing it was particularly excruciating since the memory was attuned to one key—which was musical, sketchy, and Russian—but was forced to use another key—a detailed English one ("pisalas' dolgo" [1946–50] s osobenno muchitel'nym trudom, ibo pamiat' byla nastroena na odin lad—muzykal'no nedogovorennyi, russkii—a naviazyvalsia ei drugoi lad, angliiskii i obstoiatel'nyi," Nabokov 1978, 8). But before we actively pity Nabokov for his hardships let us forget for a moment this statement, which was made postfactum and to the Russian audience who Nabokov knew would be hurt and suspicious if he did not strongly profess his loyalty to the mother tongue, let us consider his sentiments at the time of actually writing *Conclusive Evidence*.

First, it is important to establish that while Nabokov obviously did intend to make his book a financial success, his reasons for writing the autobiography were more personal, therapeutic, and artistic than they were commercial. He did say that he was "determined to make some money with the book" (Nabokov 1989, 90) and in 1946 the time *was* right for a book about Russia since Russia was on everybody's mind at the end of the war it helped to win—but all that was secondary to an overwhelming desire to revisit his past. "When I'm done with the novel [*Bend Sinister*]," he wrote to his sister in May of 1946, "I'll get going on a detailed autobiography, something I have long wanted to write" (Nabokov 1989, 68). He obviously intended from the very beginning to write the book in English even though only a year earlier he had complained to Wilson that his "urge to write is something terrific but as I cannot do it in Russian I do not do it at all" (Nabokov 1980, 156).

Back then Nabokov was just recovering from a rather painful attempt to render a vastly Russian experience into English in the form of a 1944 literary biography of Nikolai Gogol. "This little book has cost me more trouble than any other I have composed," he wrote to his editor, James Laughlin, in 1943:

> The reason is clear: I had first to create Gogol (translate him) and then discuss him (translate my Russian ideas about him). The recurrent jerk of switching from one rhythm of work to the other has quite exhausted me. I never would have accepted your suggestion to do it had I known how many gallons of brain-blood it would absorb. . . . I would like to see the Englishman who could write a book on Shakespeare in Russian. (Nabokov 1989, 45)

He also complained that "switching from one [language] to another by means of spasmodic jumps causes a kind of mental asthma" (Nabokov 1989, 42).[8]

Logic would suggest that a similar attempt to render his own Russian experience into English would lead to the same "kind of mental asthma." And yet, contrary to his statement in *Drugie berega*, there is much "conclusive evidence" in his letters of the period that the work was enjoyable and went smoothly. "My new book is developing nicely," he wrote to Wilson in 1947 (Nabokov 1980, 193) and he informs his sister in 1948 that he has already written a series of *"avtobiograficheskikh shtuchek"* (little auto-biographical items) and sent them to *The New Yorker* (Nabokov 1985, 52). The Russian word *shtuchki* here, with the built-in "cuteness" of its diminutive suffix, has a certain degree of lightness and playfulness which would be difficult to associate with the kind of hard labor referred to in the Russian version of his autobiography. And even though his sister would be a logical person to appreciate his dilemma of having to write his memoirs in English rather than Russian, Nabokov, interestingly enough, does not even mention it. Instead, when, in 1947, some Russian friends ask him why he is not writing in Russian, he responds: "As for Russian prose, I seem to have completely lost the knack, but I can still manage verse" (Nabokov 1989, 74).

Furthermore, in 1953, while working on *Lolita,* which did prove to be a product of "monstrous misgivings and diabolical labors," Nabokov actually claims that *Conclusive Evidence* together with *Pnin* had turned out to be "brief sunny escapes from [*Lolita's*] intolerable spell" (Nabokov 1989, 140). As a matter of fact, it was his Russian *Drugie berega,* and not *Conclusive Evidence* that, according to his letter to Wilson in 1954, was excruciatingly difficult to write and "has left me quite limp and hysterical" (Nabokov 1980, 285).

His apparent difficulty with the Russian text, and a relative lack of such with the English one, poses an interesting question. Elizabeth Beaujour quite legitimately attributes some of Nabokov's difficulties with *Drugie berega* to the inevitable pains of self-translation, which he once likened to "sorting through one's own innards" (Beaujour, 90). Beaujour also suggests that this agony of self-translation is quite common among bilingual writers. But Nabokov's professed distaste for self-translation only explains, it seems to me, why he chose to *forego* a close self-translation into Russian, departing freely from the original text and creating, instead, what many believe to be a largely independent work (see, for example, Grayson, 141–54). Thus one should most likely look for the reasons for the relative ease with which he appears to have written the English text, as opposed to the Russian version, elsewhere. They may actually lie in the simple fact that at the time Nabokov started working on his autobiography, English stopped being just the language of financial necessity for him and became largely the language of his *choice.* It afforded him distance to create art, therapy to soothe the pain of his losses, and freshness to escape trivializing that which he wanted least to trivialize.

We cannot of course claim that by 1946 Nabokov was more comfortable with English than with Russian: the opposite was true. Nabokov's mastery of his native Russian was superb and he knew he could never hope to attain a similar mastery in another language. From the very start of his career as an American writer, Nabokov's confidence in the quality of his English tended to be rather shaky. (In public he frequently asserted that he had been a truly bilingual child and that English was, in fact, his *first* language since it was in that language that his aristocratic and Anglophilic parents preferred to speak to their children.) In his biography on Nabokov, Brian Boyd relates an amusing anecdote concerning Nabokov's English during his first years in America. In 1942 Nabokov wrote one of his first (and best known) poems in English—"On Discovering a Butterfly"[9]—and sent it to *The New Yorker:* "[T]he fair copy of the poem . . . showed all too painfully the occasional thinness of his English. The ninth line now reads 'My needles have teased out its sculptured sex.' In the fair copy he sent off to *The New Yorker,* the line ended: 'its horny sex.' When *The New Yorker* editors explained why the phrase was impossible, he thanked them 'for saving that line from an ignorance-is-bliss disaster. And that nightmare pun. . . . This has somewhat subdued me—I was getting rather pleased with my English'" (Boyd 1991, 54). To Wilson, Nabokov called his language "imitation English" and "pidgin English" (Nabokov 1980, 36, 39), and throughout his life referred to it as "this second instrument . . . a stiffish, artificial thing . . . which cannot conceal poverty of syntax and paucity of domestic diction" (Nabokov 1981, 106).[10]

It appears, however, that it was precisely this artificiality that greatly facilitated Nabokov's experience with writing his memoirs. Nabokov, as we know, never believed in autobiography as means of self-exposure. "I hate tampering with the precious lives of great writers," he was to write later, "and I hate Tompeeping over the fence of those lives—I hate the vulgarity of 'human interest,' I hate the rustle of skirts and giggles in the corridors of time—and no biographer will ever catch a glimpse of my private life" (Nabokov 1981, Lectures, 138). And, understandably, no reader either. He seems to have been particularly sensitive about not trivializing the lives of his late parents. Like Fyodor in *Dar*, Nabokov painfully sought the best medium in which to cast the portrait of his father, finally admitting in 1950 that he "may drop altogether the idea of writing a special piece about my father since various material concerning his activities finds adequate niches here and there in my book" (Nabokov 1989, 96). It was his father's brutal death (V. D. Nabokov was assassinated in 1922 in Berlin by Russian monarchists) that proved to be the most difficult subject for reflection. "Again and again throughout [his autobiography]," writes Brian Boyd, "Nabokov returns obliquely to his father's death as if it were a wound he cannot leave alone but can hardly bear to touch. For Nabokov the love of those closest to the heart—a parent, a spouse, a child—distends the soul to dwarf all other feeling" (Boyd 1990, 8).

The orphaned son craved therapy, impersonality, and distance to ease his pain: he even chose to call the book *Conclusive Evidence* because he believed it was "the most impersonal title imaginable" (Nabokov 1980, 259). In his early years in the United States he often mused about the detached quality of his literary English: in 1942, for example, having just completed his first novel in English, he confessed to a Russian friend that it was "as though I created the person who composed *The Real Life of Sebastian Knight* and the poems in *The New Yorker* and all the rest, but it's not I who am creating—my relation to it is in the category of the pleasure one experiences in sport" (Field, 249). The same detached and artificial flavor of the new language was of immense help when it came to his desire to assume control over his personal and often painful memories and distance himself from them.

Nabokov's need for therapeutic detachment and his fear of trivializing his feelings for his family make his autobiography what it is—the book where, as Elizabeth Bruss once noted, "the most private moments of [Nabokov's] life, the assassination of his father, the courtship of his wife, are merely hinted at, anticipated, or mentioned only when they have already taken place offstage" (Bruss, 136). When dealing with his father's death, Nabokov not only limits himself to "hints"; he also, as Boyd points out, "organizes these hints in terms of . . . chess and fate as a tribute to the love for chess problems and the fascination with fate that . . . he and his father shared in life" (Boyd 1990, 100). Aloof, impersonal art seems to have been the only way in which Nabokov was willing to relive and even redeem the losses of his parents and to record "the beating of [his] loving heart" and "the torture an intense tenderness is subjected to" (Nabokov 1974, viii).

He obviously wanted to use his artistry to erect a lasting temple where he could immortalize and freely worship loved ones while at the same time keeping them away from curious stares of unworthy outsiders. In an earlier article on *Speak, Memory,* I have already discussed some striking instances in which Nabokov actually elevates his parents—as well as his wife and son—to the status of immortals by physically removing them from the ground. In one scene, his father is tossed up in the air by happy peasants. In another his parents appear to the disturbed boy, who is fearful for his father's life, on a landing *above* him, "where a Greek statue presided over a malachite bowl for visiting cards" (Nabokov 1950, 136; in the later version of his autobiography, the statue of Venus was actually transformed into merely "an armless Greek woman of marble" [Nabokov 1966, 193]—the two people standing next to her were, most likely, much truer gods in the eyes of their son). I call this technique "otstranenie," that is, "a removal," and suggest that together with "ostranenie" it constitutes the quintessence of Nabokov's authorial control over his personal materials.[11] It was, I believe, precisely Nabokov's use of *English* that became for him the perfect mechanism for such defamiliarization. Not only an "alien tongue" but also a tongue of "alienation," it provided a natural medium for "ostranenie," which made his elevation of the loved ones, or "otstranenie," all the more possible.

"Whenever I start thinking of my love for a person," he was to write in *Speak, Memory,* describing his desire to elevate those he loved above mortality,

> I am in the habit of immediately drawing radii from my love—from my heart, from the tender nucleus of a personal matter—to monstrously remote points of the universe. Something impels me to measure the consciousness of my love against such unimaginable and incalculable things as the behavior of nebulae (whose very remoteness seems a form of insanity), the dreadful pitfalls of eternity, the unknowledgeable beyond the unknown, the helplessness, the cold, the sickening involutions and interpretations of space and time. . . . When that slow-motion, silent explosion of love takes place in me, unfolding its melting fringes and overwhelming me with the sense of something much vaster, much more enduring and powerful than the accumulation of matter or energy in any imaginable cosmos, then my mind cannot but pinch itself to see if it is really awake. . . . I have to have all space and all time participate in my emotion, in my mortal love, so that the edge of its mortality is taken off, thus helping me to fight the utter degradation, ridicule, and horror of having developed an infinity of sensation and thought within a finite existence. (Nabokov 1966, 296–97)

That "something" that impelled him to project his love into the remote unreachable realm *and* to render it in a "defamiliarized" new language was a combination of the "infinity" of his feeling[12] and his fear that this feeling could lose its "immortal" edge through association with numerous other declarations of love which often reduce the notion of love to the level of *"poshlost'"* (banality) or "poshlust," as Nabokov liked to spell it. "'Poshlust' . . . is especially vigorous and vicious," he wrote in *Nikolai Gogol,* "when the sham is *not* obvious and when the values it mimics are considered, rightly or wrongly, to belong to the very highest level of art, thought or emotion" (Nabokov 1961, 68, his emphasis). The kind of trivialization that Nabokov was trying to escape was, of course, quite universal. It was the same trivialization of love that Joyce mocked in *Ulysses:* "Love loves to love love. Nurse loves the new chemist. Constable 14A loves Mary Kelly . . . His Majesty the King loves her Majesty the Queen" (Joyce 1961, 333). Nabokov chose to use English to avoid trivializing his book not because he thought that the speakers of this language were *intrinsically* any less prone to render "the very highest level of art, thought or emotion" banal but because to *his* Russian ears, as yet less sensitized to "poshlust" in English than in Russian, commonly used and abused words sounded better in a nonnative language.

By the time we get to Brodsky, however, the autobiographer's choice of English as an appropriate language to write about his parents is already dictated by a fear of a much more deadly—and specifically Soviet rather than universal—trivialization: that of not only people's feelings but of their whole lives.

Brodsky's situation in regards to English and Russian was even more drastic than Nabokov's. Like Nabokov's, Brodsky's association with English went back to his years in Russia. Yet he was a product of a different time and a different milieu, and his middle-class Jewish family did *not* routinely converse in English and could not supply him with imported English tutors. Whereas for Nabokov English was the language of his aristocratic Arcadian childhood, for Brodsky his largely self-taught English became one of the most precious acquisitions of his mature life, sustaining him during the long months of his non-Arcadian exile in a cold Northern region of the Soviet Union. It was there that he came to know Yeats, Eliot, and Auden in the language in which their poetry was written. He once called his transition into an English-writing author "an organic one" since English-language culture "has never been alien to me" (Ezerskaia, 109). But having produced some of the most original and daring poetry ever written in Russian, Brodsky could have even less hope than Nabokov that he would be able to reach equally lofty linguistic summits in English.[13]

"[I]t is . . . interesting that [Brodsky] chose to write about his most intimate memories—childhood, home, and family—in English rather than in Russian," notes Beaujour (159). It is especially interesting because in his first autobiographical essay Brodsky actually lamented that "[t]he little I remember becomes even more diminished by being recollected in English" (Brodsky 1986, 4). He also complained that "any experience coming from the Russian realm, even when depicted with photographic precision, simply bounces off the English language, leaving no visible imprint on its surface" (Brodsky 1986, 30).

The truth is, however, that while he did not consider it possible that English would ever become the permanent language of his poetry,[14] prose essays were a different matter, and, all limitations aside, he liked having an option of writing them in a nonnative tongue. "Belonging to two cultures, or, simply put, bilingualism to which one is doomed [in exile] . . . is a very interesting situation, psychologically," he told his interviewer once: "Potomu chto ty sidish' kak by na vershine gory i vidish' oba ee sklona . . . Proizoidi chudo, i vernis' ia v Rossiiu na postoiannoe zhitel'stvo, ia by chrezvychaino nervnichal, ne imeia vozmozhnosti pol'zovat'sia esche odnim iazykom." ("Because it is as if you sit on the top of a mountain and see both of its sides. . . . If a miracle were to happen, and I were to return to Russia for good, I would be very anxious about not being able to use a second language" [Volkov, 200].)

In "In a Room and a Half," he leaves us with no doubt as to why he made his linguistic choice. "May English . . . house my dead," he proclaimed, referring to his late parents in this 1985 essay. "In Russian I am prepared to read, write verses or letters. For Maria Volpert and Alexander Brodsky, though, English offers a better semblance of afterlife, maybe the only one there is, save my very self. And as far as the latter is concerned, writing this in this language is . . . therapeutic" (Brodsky 1986, 461). Thus by 1985, Brodsky already knew that his impulse to write about his past in English stemmed from much more than just his admiration for Auden. Similarly to Nabokov, Brodsky wanted to use his English in order to build a sanctuary for his parents, protecting them from the inhumanity of trivialization and allowing himself to take at least some edge off his pain. Through English Brodsky also hoped to attain that very degree of "greater estrangement" that he craved no less than did Beckett or Nabokov. "The ability to distance oneself is a unique thing," he wrote in 1974, "it . . . indicates the scale on which [one's] consciousness is working" (Brodsky 1977, 8).

"I want Maria Volpert and Alexander Brodsky to acquire reality under 'a foreign code of conscience,'" he writes in "In a Room and a Half," "I want English verbs of motion to describe their movements. This won't resurrect them, but English grammar may at least prove to be a better escape route from the chimneys of the state crematorium than the Russian" (Brodsky 1986, 460). Even more than Nabokov, Brodsky obviously gave much thought to his use of English and what it allowed him to do. "The English language is not only the language of a culture but it also evokes a specific vision of the world," he once told an interviewer. "The English language is permeated with a spirit of responsibility, it can look things straight in the eye. While hearing a Russian, French, German or Italian sentence we first think: does it 'sound well'? When hearing an English sentence, we immediately think of reality; we think: Is it true?" (Bethea 1989, 38–39). This is, of course, a very subjective evaluation of the language and the kind of evaluation that many native speakers of English will not necessarily agree with. What is interesting in that assessment, however, is that Brodsky is willing to lump his native Russian together with "French, German or Italian" while his non-native English stands markedly alone, distinguished from the rest through such admirable qualities as "truth" and "responsibility." Later on in the same interview he also noted the beneficial changes that his second language had brought into the first one: "English has certainly influenced my Russian. It's difficult to determine how, but I've noticed, for example, that unwittingly I try to apply to Russian the precise analytical mechanism characteristic of English. I used to write without deliberation; now I ponder every line" (Bethea 1992, 243). "The precise analytical mechanism" may not be necessarily characteristic of everyone's English but it was definitely characteristic of Brodsky's nonnative English (he simply had to think more when using it). In a strange twist of his artistic biography—and, of course, in strange "twists of [his] language(s)"—Brodsky's English, with its built-in nonnative detachment, even aided in renewing and defamiliarizing his native Russian.[15]

Brodsky's strongly positive sentiments about his second language may seem at variance with our stereotypical image of a "bitter exile" where a writer cherishes his native language as one of the rare valuable possessions that he was allowed to bring from the country of his birth. It is, ironically, the same image that Brodsky himself evoked in 1988 when he stated that "the condition we call exile is, first of all, a linguistic event: an exiled writer is thrust, or retreats, into his mother tongue. From being his, so to speak, sword, it turns into his shield. . . . What started as a private, intimate affair with the language, in exile becomes fate—even before it becomes an obsession or a duty" (Brodsky 1988, 18). The key words here are, however, "obsession" and "duty": "obsession" negates a possibility of detachment, "duty" is incompatible with enjoyment and "play." In the condition of forced exile, as in the cases of Brodsky and Nabokov, one's native language often stops being a "private" and "intimate" means of artistic expression and becomes an instrument of one's political fate.[16] It is probably for that reason that Brodsky associates English not only with "responsibility" and "truth" but also with "freedom." "I write this in English," he wrote in "In a Room and a Half," "because I want to grant [my parents] a margin of freedom: the margin whose width depends on the number of those who may be willing to read this" (Brodsky 1986, 460).[17] He also wanted, of course, to grant the same "margin of freedom" to himself.

Unlike Nabokov, Brodsky refused even to contemplate writing his memoirs in Russian—"To write about them in Russian would be only to further their captivity, their reduction to insignificance, resulting in mechanical annihilation" (Brodsky 1986, 460). What separates Brodsky and Nabokov in this instance are, of course, seventy years in which most intimate Russian words, like "love" or "mother" and "father" had been further compromised not only by the onslaught of trivial usage but also by all the dehumanizing and hypocritical connotations added to them by the rhetoric of the Soviet state. "I know that one shouldn't equate the state with language," writes Brodsky, "but . . ." (Brodsky 1986, 460). But to write about his parents in Russian would have been for him like placing them once again in their dreadful communal apartment, which together with "strip[ping] off any illusions about human nature" (Brodsky 1986, 454–55) stripped off one's human dignity as well.

It is not, after all, that surprising that Nabokov and Brodsky chose to write about their mothers and fathers in a language other than their mothers' and fathers' tongue. Neither should it come as a surprise that the two are far from the only writers in exile who, given that choice, prefer—for reasons more personal and artistic than commercial—to write their intimate recollections or reflections in the language of the country of their exile rather than their native language. Thus one of Brodsky's favorite poets, Marina Tsvetaeva, chose to record some of her reminiscences in French rather than Russian. Curiously enough, her choice may have been at least partially dictated by the same desire to find the most appropriate linguistic medium for writing about her parents. As Elizabeth Beaujour points out, "[a]lthough economic motives explain Tsvetaeva's decision to try writing in French, . . . they do not explain why these *particular* sketches were chosen. . . . The answer may be that, while Tsvetaeva wrote about her relations with her mother only in Russian, these [French] texts are about the period after her mother's death and concern Tsvetaeva's relations with her father" (131, Beaujour's emphasis).

Beaujour goes on to suggest that "[t]he impetus to write in French *precisely these sketches,* about her father . . . may have been furnished by the plaster bust of an Amazon which plays a major role in 'Charlottenburg' [the title of one of the autobiographical sketches written in French], thus providing a thematic link with Tsvetaeva's previous work in French, the 'Lettre à l'Amazone'" (131, Beaujour's emphasis). But Tsvetaeva's reasoning may have been more intricate than mere association. Brodsky is right to call Tsvetaeva's autobiographical prose "a breather" that is "lyrical and temporary." It is, he writes, "not the 'when-nothing-is-known-yet' childhood of a certified memoirist. It is the 'when-everything-is-already-known' but 'nothing-has-begun-yet' childhood of the mature poet caught up in the middle of her life by a brutal era . . . [its] role is purely therapeutic" (Brodsky 1986, 183, 184). Tsvetaeva may have sought to heighten the "therapeutic" effect of some of her sketches even further by using a nonnative language—as Brodsky and Nabokov did.

One rarely thinks of James Joyce as a "bilingual" writer, for although Italian was often the language he and his wife spoke to their children, he rarely used it for writing. When he did—as in a series of nine articles he wrote for a paper in Trieste (*Il Piccolo della Sera*)—he did so mostly for money and for whatever little fame those articles could bring him.[18] Yet one article, written in 1912, stands somewhat apart from the rest. It is devoted to Charles Stewart Parnell (1846–91), a famous Irish statesman who was an idol and, in some ways, a "father" figure of Joyce's youth. In 1912 Parnell was still a tragic hero for Joyce and his feelings for the man were both very personal and very complex. The subject for the article was Joyce's own choice—and a somewhat surprising one, given the newspaper's preference for more current and general topics. In "L'Ombra di Parnell" ("The Shade of Parnell") Joyce bestows the blame for Parnell's fall (after it became known that he was engaged in an extramarital affair with a married woman) and subsequent death on both the English and the Irish: "In his final desperate appeal to his countrymen, he begged them not to throw him as a sop to the English wolves howling around them. It redounds to their honour that they did not fail this appeal. They did not throw him to the English wolves; they tore him to pieces themselves" (Joyce 1964, 228). Writing about Parnell in Italian rather than in English, the language spoken by those on both sides of the Irish Sea whom Joyce held responsible for betraying and humiliating the Irish leader, must have granted Joyce and his hero the same "margin of freedom" which Brodsky sought when he refused to write about his parents in the language of those who abused and humiliated them.

The list of examples could go on—but it is hardly necessary to make our point. When one uses memories to create memorials—as Brodsky and Nabokov do—the availability of an excellently functional but less "familiar" language can be an immense asset: it can help to bring about that very "liberation—not less of love but expanding / Of love beyond desire, and so liberation / From the future as well as the past,"[19] which many writers actively seek when they sit down to write their memoirs. The artifact of a new language can also facilitate the crucial artistic need for authorial detachment in autobiographical writings where the convenient mediation of traditional artifacts of fiction or poetry is usually not available. Distance, in its turn, could bring therapeutic comfort—often the primary reason for writing autobiographies in the first place—inasmuch as it affords one a certain control over one's life. Taking all that into consideration, Brodsky's and Nabokov's decision to use a nonnative language to describe their "native" experiences is not at all illogical. It may be, on the contrary, the most logical choice they could have made.

Notes

This article is an updated and slightly revised version of the article that appeared in *Slavic and East European Journal* 3 (fall 1988): 353–72. I would like to thank *SEEJ* for allowing me to reprint it in this volume.

1. See, for example, Leonard W. Forster, *The Poet's Tongues: Multilingualism in Literature* (1970), Brian T. Fitch, *Beckett and Babel: An Investigation into the Status of the Bilingual Work* (1988), Elizabeth Klosty Beaujour, *Alien Tongues: Bilingual Russian Writers of the 'First' Emigration* (1989), Yael S. Feldman, *Modernism and Cultural Transfer: Gabriel Preil and the Tradition of Jewish Literary Bilingualism* (1986), James Phillips, *Yvan Goll and Bilingual Poetry* (1984). Those works raise interesting linguistic and psychological questions; some of them, like Elizabeth Klosty Beaujour's book, even bravely venture into such spheres as mental geology and neurolinguistics. But defining literary bilingualism can sometimes lead to shaky ground. James Phillips, for example, defines a bilingual writer as "the author who is at ease in two languages and whose works have enjoyed a certain celebrity as well as retained critical attention in the different languages and countries concerned" (Phillips, 1). But is not a bilingual writer simply a writer who writes in two languages, regardless of his or her literary reputation or lack of such? And even if we were to accept

Phillips's dubious premise that only "noteworthy" authors should be considered "bilingual writers" we would still find his definition highly unsatisfactory. For one thing, being "at ease in two languages" sounds much too casual for the kind of ability it takes to establish lasting literary reputations. Phillips's other sine qua non for literary bilingualism—the evidence of a writer's works enjoying "a certain celebrity as well as . . . critical attention in the different languages and countries concerned"—is even more problematic. Only a few years ago such a condition would have excluded from the ranks of "truly" bilingual most of the émigré Eastern European writers whose works were mercilessly suppressed in their native countries and who therefore were deprived of any "celebrity" or "critical attention" in at least one of the "countries concerned." This obviously applies to both Nabokov and Brodsky. Never published in the Soviet Union while he was alive, Nabokov is only now attaining (and retaining) the wide celebrity and attention which is his due as a Russian writer. Likewise, for many years, Joseph Brodsky was much better known and acclaimed in the West than he was in the former Soviet Union. Needless to say, there are still many bilingual authors around the world whose works have yet to receive official attention in their native countries.

2. For more on early nineteenth-century bilingualism (mostly French-Russian), see William Mills Todd III, *The Familiar Letter as a Literary Genre in the Age of Pushkin*, 140–55. Unless specified otherwise, all translations from Russian are mine.

3. Brodsky could be, on occasion, decidedly more cynical about his reasons for writing his essays in English: "Chto zhe do esse, kotorye ia pishu glavnym obrazom po-angliiski, to ia sochiniaiu ikh skoree po neobkhodimosti—finansovoi ili intellektual'no-prikladnoi chtoby, naprimer, razveiat' u angloiazychnogo chitatelia te ili inye illiuzii." ("As far as the essays that I write mostly in English are concerned, I write them largely out of necessity, either financial or applied intellectual in order, for example, to debunk this or that illusion that an English-speaking reader may have" [Vail', 26–27].) It is also interesting to note here that when pressed to find a parallel for Auden among Russian poets, Brodsky, shocking his interviewer, named Nikolai Zabolotsky who, in his opinion, was a largely "underestimated figure" and "a poet of genius," especially in his later works (Volkov, 152). For more on Zabolotsky, see Sarah Pratt's article in this volume.

4. In his Nobel Lecture, Brodsky designated "fate" as the driving force behind his literary bilingualism—"the two cultures to which fate has willed me to belong" (Brodsky 1988, 27). The original (Russian) text of the lecture is available in a supplement to *Kontinent* 55 (1988).

5. Nabokov also criticized Auden as a translator of Russian poetry: "I . . . know a few of his translations—and deplore the blunders he so lightheartedly permits himself" (Nabokov 1981, 151).

6. The translation ("Demon") can be found in *The Kenyon Review* 1 (winter 1979): 120. Nabokov's original poem is in Vladimir Nabokov, *Stikhi* (Ann Arbor, Mich.: Ardis, 1979), 145. For Brodsky's overall negative assessment of Nabokov as a poet, see also "A Poet and Prose": "Some, like Nabokov, for example, have tried to the very end to convince themselves and those around them that even if they were not primarily poets, they were poets all the same" (Brodsky 1986, 177).

7. See Proffer's notes for "A Stop in the Madhouse: Brodsky's *Gorbunov and Gorchakov*," 351. The Nabokovs were apparently so pleased to hear from Carl Proffer that Brodsky was a great fan of the writer that in 1969 they "arranged for jeans to be sent in their name to poet Joseph Brodsky" (Boyd 1991, 570). Likewise, in his interview with Volkov, having criticized Nabokov's poetry Brodsky then praises his prose: "On zamechatel'nyi prozaik" ("He is a remarkable prose writer" [Volkov, 169].) David Bethea's paper, entitled "Nabokov and Brodsky: Two Butterfly Poems," was presented at a Nabokov conference in Moscow, USSR (May 1990). Some of it found its way into Bethea's *Joseph Brodsky and the Creation of Exile*, 218.

8. Brodsky mentioned a similar "mental asthma" of switching languages when he talked about "the typical schizophrenic nuances" (*tipichnye shizofrenicheskie niuansy*) when using two languages: "inogda snabzhaesh' angliiskoe sushchestvitel'noe russkim suffiksom, ili v kachestve rifmy k russkomu slovu vyskakivaet slovo angliiskoe." ("Sometimes you add a Russian suffix to an English noun or an English word jumps out as a rhyme to a Russian word.") He went on to say that he is perfectly resigned to this situation: "No ia privyk k elementu breda v svoem sushchestvovanii i ne rassmatrivaiu podobnye situatsii kak nechto nenormal'noe, skoree naoborot" ("But I have gotten used to the element of delirium in my existence and do not view such situations as something abnormal. The opposite is more like it" [Vail', 27]).

9. Usually entitled "A Discovery" (sometimes "The Discovery") in subsequent publications.

10. Nabokov's feelings about his languages are best revealed in a 1942 letter to Wilson where he claims "to know Russian better than any living person—in America at least—and more English than any Russian in America" (Nabokov 1980, 66). Needless to say, to know English better than "any Russian in America" would not, in Nabokov's eyes, be as remarkable an achievement as knowing *Russian* better than any Russian in America—or anywhere else, for that matter.

11. For more on that, see my article "'Nabokov' Doesn't Rhyme with 'Love'? On Love and Control in *Speak, Memory*."

12. Brian Boyd rightfully thinks that this passage "states the problem Nabokov addresses throughout his art: what can we make of the breach between the limitless capacity of consciousness and its absurd limitation? To answer this, he has searched relentlessly for some consciousness beyond

the boundaries of the human" (Boyd 1990, 10). Boyd is referring here to to the theme of "potustoronnost'" (the otherworldly) in Nabokov which has been explored by Vladimir Alexandrov in *Nabokov's Otherworld.*

13. In a 1991 documentary, *Joseph Brodsky: A Maddening Space,* Brodsky observed how important it was for him from the very beginning of his exile to achieve a firm command of literary English: "I could not permit a situation to emerge where a poem in English [would] be . . . less supple, less tactile than . . . in Russian" (Brodsky 1991, 20). For a brief but helpful discussion of Brodsky's bilingualism, see also chapter 7 ("The Consequences of Nomadism: Late Bilingualism and Posthumous Biographies") of David MacFadyen's *Joseph Brodsky and the Baroque.*

14. For more on that, see his exchange with Solomon Volkov in *Razgovory s Iosifom Brodskim,* 165–200.

15. Unless Brodsky was deceiving himself, and the process of "ponder[ing] every line" was merely an inevitable outcome of the diminishing immediacy and spontaneity of his Russian. For his fear of forgetting Russian, see his interview with Ezerskaia ("Pust' oni chitaiut Prusta"; "Let Them Read Proust") in *Evreiskii zhurnal (Jewish Magazine):* "'Vy zhivete vne Rossii uzhe mnogo let. Kak vy perenosite otorvannost' ot rodnogo iazyka?'—'Teper' mne uzhe ne tak trevozhno, kak pervye nedeli v Vene. Kak-to ia ne mog naiti rifmu i sprosil sebia—neuzheli takoi russkoi rifmy net voobshche? Mozhet ia nachinaiu zabyvat' rodnoi iazyk?'" ("'You have lived outside of Russia for many years. How do you tolerate your isolation from your native language?'—'Now it's not as alarming to me as it was during my first weeks in Vienna. I could not find a rhyme and asked myself—is it possible that such a rhyme does not even exist in Russian? Am I beginning to forget my native language?'" 58).

16. Brodsky openly questioned this traditional image of "bitter exile" in *Joseph Brodsky: A Maddening Space.* While responding to the questions posed by another bilingual poet—and exile—Derek Walcott, Brodsky vigorously mocks the stereotype and then proceeds to formulate the single most important artistic benefit of living in a culture which is not your own—a chance of remaining a detached observer. Here is some of their discussion:

BRODSKY: I've made a conscious decision to pretend . . . that nothing happened, that it's a normal transition, it's a normal continuum. . . . After all, any country, every country is a continuation of the space. . . .[G]radually, that sort of mask became a real face, in a sense. That's what you're looking at, basically. [. . .]

WALCOTT: . . . you have never really been displaced then.

BRODSKY: Of course not. Of course not. Of course never. No. It's . . . all in the eye of a bunch of silly beholders.

WALCOTT: . . . but . . . [what] about "Brodsky the exile . . ."?

BRODSKY: Well, that's . . . exactly the eye of a silly beholder. [. . .]

WALCOTT: But that's painfully true of Ovid as well, though . . .

BRODSKY: Well, you know, [in] his time it was more true, because he was kicked into one hundred percent uncongenial area . . . I got kicked out from the . . . backward [country] into the advanced trail. . . . In a sense, the opposite happened . . . I am more or less in a more congenial condition here. Derek, you know that full well, better than anybody else that . . . to be on the outside is the core of the whole thing. Because apart from anything else, you are . . . on the outside . . . from the outset, because you observe. . . . [W]hen you find yourself in a country which is not your own . . . you are in a sense, well, in the most ideal, technically speaking, for an artist, condition. (Brodsky 1991, 18, 44–46)

Brodsky dwelled on the same notion of a "beneficial" exile also in his earlier interview with Ezerskaia: "Genrikh Bell' kak-to zapisal v dnevnike, chto chem dal'she pis'mennyi stol khudoznika budet stoiat' ot otechestva, tem luchshe dlia khudozhnika." ("Heinrich Boll once wrote in his diary that the further the writer's desk is located from his native land, the better it is for the artist" [Ezerskaia, 106].) At the very least, Brodsky maintains, there is no palpable difference between writing "at home" and "in exile": "[P]oskol'ku ia zanimaius' tem zhe samym, i v usloviiakh, kak mne kazhetsia, napominaiushchikh te, v kotorykh ia zanimalsia etim doma to . . . [n]ikakogo razryva net. Absoliutno nikakogo . . . Vsiakaia novaia strana, v konechnom schete, lish' prodolzhenie prostranstva." ["Since I am doing the same thing and under conditions which, I think, are reminiscent of those I had back at home, there is no break. Absolutely none. Every new country is, in the long run, just a continuation of space" (Ezerskaia 108).] See also his other interview in *Evreiskii zhurnal:* "'Kak povliiala zhizn' v Amerike na vashe poeticeskoe tvorchestvo?'"—'Nikak.'" ["'How has life in the United States influenced your poetry?'—'Not at all'" ("Pust' oni chitaiut Prusta," 60).]

    17. Svetlana Boym's insightful commentary on this passage is worth quoting: "Some things could only be written in a foreign language; they are not lost in translation, but conceived by it. Foreign verbs of motion could be the only ways of transporting the ashes of familial memory. After all, a foreign language is like art—an alternative reality, a potential world" (Boym, 260). Interestingly, in *Joseph Brodsky: A Maddening Space,* Brodsky offered an additional—and strangely "adolescent"—explanation for why he had chosen to write "In a Room and a Half" in English: "[M]y parents died about a year before, and I was in considerable trouble. There was a girl whom I liked very much. And I knew that no matter what I'm going to do, [nothing] is going to please her. So I decided to write that piece. I would somehow introduce that realm to her, whether she cares or not. I thought that . . . [would] make . . . me more palatable to her" (Brodsky 1991, 50).

18. As Mason and Ellmann point out in their introduction to Joyce's essays for *Il Piccolo della Sera,* Joyce "also liked to display his graceful and idiomatic Italian" (Joyce 1964, 187).

19. Those lines, which also serve as the epigraph to this article, are taken from Eliot's *Four Quartets* ("Little Gidding," III, lines 8–11).

Works Cited

Alexandrov, Vladimir E. *Nabokov's Otherworld.* Princeton: Princeton University Press, 1991.

Beaujour, Elizabeth Klosty. *Alien Tongues: Bilingual Russian Writers of the 'First' Imigration.* Ithaca: Cornell University Press, 1989.

Bethea, David. "Exile, Elegy, and Auden in Brodsky's 'Verses on the Death of T. S. Eliot'." *PMLA* 107 (March 1992): 232–45.

———. *Joseph Brodsky and the Creation of Exile.* Princeton: Princeton University Press, 1994.

———. "A Valediction Forbidding Mourning: Exile, Elegy, and 'Audenticity' in Brodsky's 'Verses on the Death of T. S. Eliot.'" Given as a paper at AAASS conference (November 1989). Published in revised versions as an article in *PMLA* (see above) and a chapter in *Joseph Brodsky and the Creation of Exile,* 120–39.

Boyd, Brian. *Vladimir Nabokov: The American Years.* Princeton: Princeton University Press, 1991.

———. *Vladimir Nabokov: Russian Years.* Princeton: Princeton University Press, 1990.

Boym, Svetlana. "Estrangement as a Lifestyle: Shklovsky and Brodsky." In *Exile and Creativity: Signposts, Travelers, Outsiders, Backward Glances,* edited by Susan Rubin Suleiman. Durham: Duke University Press, 1998.

Brodsky, Joseph. "The Condition We Call Exile." *The New York Review of Books* (January 21, 1988): 16–20.

———. *Joseph Brodsky: A Maddening Space. A Transcript.* Media Transcripts, New York Center for Visual History, 1991.

———. *Less than One: Selected Essays.* New York: Farrar Straus Giroux, 1986.

———. Preface to *Modern Russian Poets on Poetry.* Ann Arbor, Mich.: Ardis, 1977.

———. "Pust' oni chitaiut Prusta: Interv'iu s Iosifom Brodskim." In *Evreiskii zhurnal* 1 (1991): 58–60.

———. "Uncommon Visage. The Nobel Lecture." Translated by Barry Rubin. *The New Republic.* (January 4 and 11, 1988): 27–32.

Bruss, Elizabeth W. *Autobiographical Acts: The Changing Situation of a Literary Genre.* Baltimore: John Hopkins University Press, 1976.

Diment, Galya. "'Nabokov' Doesn't Rhyme with 'Love'? On Love and Control in *Speak, Memory.*" *Journal of Evolutionary Psychology* 3, no. 4 (August 1989): 275–82.

Ezerskaia, Bella. "Esli khochesh' poniat' poeta . . ." In *Mastera.* Ann Arbor, Mich.: Hermitage, 1982, 103–12.

Feldman, Yael S. *Modernism and Cultural Transfer: Gabriel Preil and the Tradition of Jewish Literary Bilingualism.* Cincinnati: Hebrew Union College Press, 1986.

Field, Andrew. *Nabokov: His Life in Part.* London: Hamish Hamilton, 1977.

Fitch, Brian T. *Beckett and Babel: An Investigation into the Status of the Bilingual Work.* Toronto: University of Toronto Press, 1988.

Forster, Leonard Wilson. *The Poet's Tongues: Multilingualism in Literature.* Cambridge: Cambridge University Press, 1970.

Grayson, Jane. *Nabokov Translated.* Oxford: Oxford University Press, 1977.

Joyce, James. *Ulysses.* New York: Random House, 1961.

———. *The Critical Writings.* Edited by Ellsworth Mason and Richard Ellmann. New York: Viking, 1964.

MacFadyen, David. *Joseph Brodsky and the Baroque.* Montreal: McGill-Queen's University Press, 1998.

Nabokov, Vladimir. *Conclusive Evidence.* New York: Harper, 1950.

———. *Nikolai Gogol.* New York: New Directions, 1961.

———. *Speak, Memory.* New York: Putnam, 1966.

———. *Bend Sinister.* New York: McGraw-Hill, 1974.

———. *Drugie berega.* Ann Arbor, Mich.: Ardis, 1978.

———. *Lectures on Russian Literature.* Edited by F. Bowers. New York: Harcourt, 1981.

Nabokov, Vladimir, and Elena Sikorskaia. *Perepiska s sestroi.* Ann Arbor, Mich.: Ardis, 1985.

———. *Selected Letters: 1940–1977.* Edited by Dmitri Nabokov and Matthew J. Bruccoli. New York: Harcourt, 1989.

Nabokov, Vladimir, and Edmund Wilson. *The Nabokov-Wilson Letters: 1940–1971.* Edited by Simon Karlinsky. New York: Harper, 1980.

———. *Strong Opinions.* New York: McGraw-Hill, 1981.

Phillips, James. *Yvan Goll and Bilingual Poetry.* Stuttgart: Hans Dieter Heinz, 1984.

Proffer, Carl. "A Stop in the Madhouse: Brodsky's *Gorbunov and Gorchakov.*" *Russian Literature Triquarterly* 1 (1971): 342–51.

Todd, William Mills III. *The Familiar Letter as a Literary Genre in the Age of Pushkin.* Princeton: Princeton University Press, 1976.

Vail', Petr, and Aleksandr Genis. "V okrestnostiakh Brodskogo." *Literaturnoe obozrenie* 8 (1990): 23–29.

Volkov, Solomon. *Razgovory s Iosifom Brodskim.* New York: Slovo, 1997.

Marina Balina

The Tale of Bygone Years: Reconstructing
the Past in the Contemporary Russian Memoir

"IN THE LAST FEW YEARS memoir has become one of the most popular literary genres," state the editors of the journal *Voprosy Literatury* (*Literary Issues*) in their January 1999 roundtable discussion titled *Memoirs on the Cusp of the Epoch.*[1] Acknowledging the fact that more and more literary figures take the opportunity to "write directly of themselves and their times," the editors posed the following question to contemporary memoirists: "Why did you decide to write memoirs?" The result of this survey of eighteen was quite unexpected: most of the writers do not consider themselves memoirists and vehemently resist classification of their work as such.

This roundtable discussion temporarily united a very diverse group comprised by such well-known fiction writers as Grigorii Baklanov and Andrei Bitov; poets and prose writers Konstantin Vanshenkin, Anatolii Naiman, Semen Lipkin, Naum Korzhavin, Elena Rzhevskaia, and Sergei Gandlevskii; literary critics Pavel Basinskii, Leonid Zorin, and Emma Gershtein; publicist and well-known economist Nikolai Shmelev; poetry translator Andrei Sergeev; surgeon and documentary writer Iulii Krelin; Orthodox priest Mikhail Ardov; and actor and poet Vladimir Rezepter. In keeping with this trend of resisting the memoir classification of his writing, Anatolii Naiman states, "I have not yet written a memoir and don't know if I ever will" (30). It seems that he leaves it to his reader to decide the genre of his work, *The Honorable End of a Dishonorable Generation.* Andrei Sergeev remarks, somewhat less negatively, that although he does not believe his *Stamp Catalog* "is a work of pure memoir genre," he also realizes that discussion of such "purity" is extremely difficult and proposes to "abandon the division of prose into separate genres" (32). Genre division could be superseded, in his opinion, by a division into greater and lesser prose (*bol'shaia i malaia proza*) where the definition would simply be based on length rather than the features of a too loosely defined literary canon. Nikolai Shmelev maintains, "No, no, I don't write memoirs," instead characterizing his work as painting "pictures," which he believes demand "less responsibility than memoirs" (34). Vladimir Rezepter defines memoir not as a self-sufficient genre, but as "a search for a genre" (31). Iulii Krelin proposes a new genre, diary-memoir, which is most closely tailored to his goal: "to leave a noticeable presence of existence and, in some cases, of direct action" (24). Pavel Basin-skii and Sergei Gandlevskii both reject outright the notion that they are writing memoirs. Basinskii protests that, "I am too young and not mature enough for that [memoir writing]." While Gandlevskii admits that his work, *Trepanation of the Cranium,* has "a memoir-like undercurrent," for him it is not "a memoir in its pure form" (13). Memoirists of the older generation, such as Konstantin Vanshenkin, Emma Gershtein, and Daniil Danin, admit to the memoir status of their creations, but actively try to separate them-selves, if not from the memoir genre, then from its past socialist realist tra-dition of subverting facts to ideological demands. "Faith in the credibility of literary recollections is indeed hard to maintain," writes Danin (20). Bor-shagovskii states that the chief driving force behind contemporary memoir is Deception ("precisely Deception with a capital 'D'" [11]). The desire to overturn this Deception "paradoxically supports the existence and relative increase in the production of memoir literature" (12).

This unanimous reluctance to be considered a memoirist is in no way prompted by a lack of respect for the genre in general. Basinskii pro-nounces the genre high, complex, and noble, "where one cannot hide" (6). Gershtein also recognizes the high demands that the genre places upon the author. Many of the roundtable participants refer to Aleksandr Herzen's *My Past and Thoughts* as a quintessential example of the memoir genre. Yet in all of the commentaries one feels that the authors are heeding an over-whelming urge to step over or reject the closest time stratum, that of the memoir of the Soviet period, in order to escape the implications and suspi-cions of contributing to a genre well known for its political compromise.

Nevertheless, contemporary post-Soviet memoir is a Soviet phenom-enon to a much greater degree than a continuation of the "interrupted" classical tradition (Tartakovskii, 40). Formalized under the aesthetic domi-nance of socialist realism, the Soviet memoir over the years developed a stern and all-controlling etiquette[2] that has deeply entrenched itself in the genre memory,[3] requiring current memoirists to confront precisely this model in their work.

Early Soviet memoir discourse, as well as auto/biographical discourse, was rooted in obituary. Katerina Clark writes that Nikolai Bukharin's obitu-ary of Yakov Sverdlov "realized the biographical metaphors for the life and death of the true revolutionary" (Clark, 72). The condensed form of an obit-uary allowed its author to concentrate on service to the revolution and the qualities essential to performing this task. Brooks states that "Bolshevik leaders and journalists used the obituaries not only to mark the end of a significant life, but to promote their agendas" (Brooks, 31). Obituary, in its very essence, doesn't leave room for the private and subjective; it presents to the reader "a public person," a person who, according to Bakhtin, "has nothing for himself, nothing that could not be accountable to public and state" (Bakhtin, 169). In his discussion of the chronotope which lies at the core of the rhetorical auto/biography of antiquity, Bakhtin identifies encomion, the funeral speech at a citizen's burial, as the main source for the formation of the genre of auto/biography. Encomion was not a work of "literary character," but was "a civic verbal act of a political nature, aimed at public glorification or a public account of real individuals" (Bakhtin, 168). This approach to life, one's own or another's, demands a laconic brevity of discourse which is subjugated to the main goal, one's civil service.

Precisely this discourse was adopted by Lenin in his obituary for Ivan Vasilievich Babushkin, first published in 1910 in the pages of *Workers' Gazette*. This piece relates to us in a condensed way the ground rules of a memoir etiquette that for decades would dominate the memoir of socialist realism. Babushkin, executed by a firing squad without a proper trial for the illegal transport of a great number of firearms to support an organized uprising in Siberia, is presented in this obituary as a true martyr who lived and died for the people.

One can see here the sharply outlined key points of the narrative: joining the revolutionary struggle, an action equated with rebirth, and death "for the right cause—the future victory of proletariat" (Lenin, 79), making the depiction of his death a purely didactic example. In fact, Lenin doesn't even try to hide his intentions to transform such reminiscences into a propaganda weapon: "We appeal to our comrade workers to collect such reminiscences of the revolutionary struggle and any additional facts from the life of comrade Babushkin. We intend to publish a brochure with the life stories of such workers. . . . Such a brochure would be the best reading material for young workers, who would learn from it how an active worker needs to live and fight" (Lenin, 82–83). Thus, the facts of Babushkin's life became valuable not as uniquely subjective experiences that the memoirist would like to share or as objective historical material, but rather as didactic propaganda elements which later would become an essential part of socialist realist memoir discourse. A binary evaluative scale was implemented to judge the events of human life, dividing them into "positive" (that is, affirmative of the authoritative position) and "negative," which differed from the former to a very minute degree. Jeffrey Brooks points out that " the obituary was the only description of individual life in the 1920s that appeared regularly during the whole period" (Brooks, 30).

The 1930s saw the completion of the formation of a memoir etiquette in Soviet literature. Under the heading of "Memoir Literature" in volume seven of *The Literary Encyclopedia*, published in 1934, "the propagandistic role of the memoir genre" (148) was particularly highlighted. This same text lists the obituary as one of the forms belonging to this literary genre. Thus, the memoir was transformed into a textbook example category, the main task of which was to support and illustrate the postulates implemented by political leadership.

However, the 1930s added a new dimension to the art of recollection by making reminiscences gauges of political loyalty on the fast changing scene of the Stalinist purges. "A memoirist," stated Anatolii Vasil'evich Lunacharskii, a literary critic, journalist, revolutionary, and politician who was from 1917 to 1929 the People's Commissar of Education and Culture, "should be trusted no more than any other chronicler. While dealing with this raw material, a true Marxist should subject it to a rather careful critique . . . I can say that the result of this analysis can produce the picture of an objective reality that a Marxist can comment on, on the other hand it can reflect upon the personality of a Marxist himself, stating his class interests" (Lunacharskii, 18). The Soviet state's ability "to police individual expression" (as Beth Holmgren states in this volume's introduction) was realized in response to the demand to become first and foremost "a Marxist," therefore rendering individual interests (in our case—recollecting the past) directly dependent on class interests. Thus, the process of remembrance was completely subordinated to official history, which controlled not only the selection of the facts but put its stamp of approval on the memoirist as well. The important quality of the memoir to depict events in retrospect was completely paralyzed: the memoirist could pay with his or her own life for what he or she chose to remember. The delicate balance between subjective and objective time in the memoir was directly sabotaged: the singularity of human life appeared to be crushed by the weight of official history. The very concrete and real fear of referring to forbidden subject matters and the self-censorship that resulted violated any personal relationship with events. The world of what was once experienced was replaced by the world of what one was allowed to remember. Individual stories at first became controlled and, by the end of the 1930s, finally were absorbed by official history.[4]

This period in memoir writing is perhaps best illustrated by one official memoir, *The History of the Communist Party*, and its author, Joseph Stalin (Dobrenko, 639), who presented his own version of the facts of revolutionary history, thus correlating the past with his own involvement in it. The direct result of these policies was that, as stated by Kardin, "at the end of the 1930s, publication of memoir literature began to dwindle and gradually virtually disappeared" (10).

The rebirth of memoir literature started in the second half of the 1950s. The Thaw period slowly removed former taboos and liberated human memory from the burdens of official history. But the socialist realist memoir discourse shaped by Stalinist culture was so indelibly rooted in genre memory that the memoirs of the 1950s as well as the 1960s and 1970s still reflected a model dominated by official history. The process of de-Stalinization that Khrushchev started in February of 1956 focused on rearticulating objective facts. The liberalization processes of the post-Stalin period allowed for the inclusion of previously censored names and a rewriting of the events previously excised from official history. A new process of *rewriting* history began, and the "human document" (memoir, autobiography, diary) was called on to fill the gaps in the collective memory of the society.

However, the newly rewritten history of the Thaw period continued to stringently control individual recollection of the past. Two important features of the memoir—its subjective vision and the right to an individual reading of history and objective depiction of events—were subordinated to the rewritten version of official history.[5] The memoir continued to maintain its propagandistic and didactic functions. In fact, writes Kardin, "the revolutionary hero becomes the hero of a memoir, thus influencing its narrative character. His life and deeds are dedicated to the people and his story is aimed at the masses" (Kardin, 56).[6]

The influence of socialist realist memoir etiquette was so prevalent that it penetrated dissident memoirs, rendering their structures strikingly similar to officially legitimized memoirs. The dissident memoirists charged themselves with the same task of writing or rewriting history as did their socialist realist counterparts. Both focused on their version of history and confronted the officially accepted Soviet model of objective reality. In their declaration of war against the model of official history, the dissident writers tried to replace it with their own equivalent. They often referred to the same factual materials used in official literature, providing their own ways to prove the "correct" readings of the facts. Thus, Lev Kopelev starts his memoir with the most critical period in Russian history, the "summer of 1917" (15). The linear mode of narration is dominant in *Hope Against Hope* by Nadezhda Mandelstam and *Within the Whirlwind* by Evgeniia Ginzburg.[7] Both official and dissident memoirists concentrate on the image of a protagonist as a figure martyred for the "right cause." The "right" cause is determined by the particular version of history reconstructed to meet the author's needs.

For both groups the private subjective elements of their reminiscences became secondary to proving the accuracy of the objective reality they tried to recreate. While official memoirs presented their protagonists as creators of the established political system, their dissident counterparts focused on various manifestations of the struggle against this system, be it in the reality of the camps (Evgeniia Ginzburg) or inner exile (Nadezhda Mandelstam). During the 1960s and 1970s both groups contributed to the creation of the dominant memoir model, which was "constructing a life so it fits into and illustrates some prior conception or didactic point the narrator wishes to press" (Winslow, 65).

Simultaneous with the processes described above another genre appeared on the periphery of the literary world. While it never tried to inscribe itself into the Soviet literary canon, it baffled critics, who were at a loss as to its categorization. It was given titles as diverse as "autodocument" (Urban), "lyrical prose" (Bal'burov), "documentary prose" (Yavchunovskii), "memoir-autobiographical prose" (Shaitanov), or "free prose" (Bank). Yet one thing was certain, this new genre was different from the conventions of memoir of the time. Konstantin Paustovsky introduced this genre with his trilogy *Story of a Life.* Its first book, *Distant Years,* appeared in 1955 and paved the way for a new type of memoir. As Edward Crankshaw has stated, "Paustovsky in his soft and gentle voice declared that it's time for Soviet literature to open a new page, and the sooner it gets over the horrors of the past, the better" (12).

Paustovsky titled his reminiscences a novel, from the very outset sabotaging any possible connection with the stereotypical memoir. By defining his work as a novel, the author reserved for himself the right to freely interpret the events of objective reality without being concerned about their truthfulness or legitimacy. Personal life experience, rather than well-known historical fact, triggers the narrative. For instance, in his memoirs the Russo-Japanese War has only contextual meaning, serving to justify the appearance of mysterious uncle Iuzia. The horror of the pogroms in Kiev is expressed through the figure of the neighboring Jewish tailor whose family is given refuge by the author's parents. There is no single episode in which Paustovsky tries to offer the judgment or generalization that had become standard in the Soviet memoir. Before the reader's very eyes, the seemingly indestructible structure of the memoir of socialist realism started to disintegrate. First to go was the linear narrative: flashbacks were mixed with flash-forwards within the boundaries of a single episode. The utter disconnectedness of the narrative created a long-forgotten feeling of freedom to move about in time that before had been precluded by Soviet memoir etiquette.

The new memoir questioned the established linear retrospective nature of the genre by pointing out that this approach is destructive to the very nature of the process of remembering. Iurii Olesha stated that this process is truly "remarkable. We remember a thing for a reason unknown to us. Ask yourself to recall something from your childhood. Close your eyes and ask yourself to do it, and you will recall something absolutely unexpected. No will power is involved" (26).

Nataliia Iashina suggested that reminiscences "run against each other as snatches. What is it? The most vivid impression? Why is this insignificant event remembered when another essential event is completely missing from memory" (77)? Vera Ketlinskaia constructed her memoir based not on "how the events happened, but how they would be recalled in memory" (16). She came up with the definition of her reminiscences as "spills" (*ras-sypushki*). Viktor Shklovskii addresses the "flocked" (*klochkovaia*) nature of the memoir and observes that "it never unfolds straightforwardly" (18). An attempt to construct the memoir according to the nature of memory removes the distance between the memoirist and the object of his or her reminiscences, including the author and the protagonist of his or her narrative into one tidily connected life cycle. Thus, one of the last "bulwarks" of the conventional memoir of socialist realism, its hierarchical nature, was destroyed. *The Holy Well* and *The Grass of Oblivion* by Valentin Kataev serve as the best examples of such new memoirs.[8]

In this new memoir official history ceases dominating subjective narrative and historical facts serve as stage backdrop or decor. The subjective memoir "highlights" moments from officially accepted history randomly when those events and facts are relevant to the depiction of an individual experience.[9] This mode of memoir writing is represented by the works of Ol'ga Berggolts (*Daylight Stars*), Victor Shklovsky (*Once Upon a Time*), Veniamin Kaverin (*Lighted Windows*), Vera Ketlinskaia (*Evening. Windows. People*), and Il'ia Brazhnin (*The Magician's Bag*). The turn to historical fact by those memoirists is not only spontaneous and achronological, but also constitutes an appeal for a different history. Revolutionary events and socialist conquests are displaced in these new memoirs by a cultural history that revisits the most crucial turning points of contemporary culture.

Writing reminiscences as subjective stories frees the memoirist from the necessity of organizing individual memory in accordance with the demands of official history, but the genre memory very unexpectedly recalls its socialist realist model with its constant request for the legitimization of the narrative's truthfulness. This paradox is reflected in the memoir's inclusion of different kinds of documents: evidence from private archives (Kaverin's *Interlocutor*), excerpts from notebooks (Kron's *The Eternal Problem*), and private letters (Ravich's *Portraits of Contemporaries*). Objective time, supported by documents, takes over the function of official history, pushing the latter outside the temporal model of the memoir. The "intrusion" of documents destroys the traditional closed nature of the socialist realist memoir and connects the text with such related genres as autobiography (Soloukhin's *Drop of Dew*), literary portrait (Paustovsky's *Alone With the Autumn*), and the travelogue (Konetskii's *Dreams of the Sea*).

A decade later, literary critics explained this phenomenon as a "lack of impenetrable partitions between the genres" (Shaitanov, 11), and addressed it as "a desire to create simultaneously the artistic unity of two different realities [subjective and objective]" (Balburov, 41), as an attempt to present "a synthetic portrait of the epoch" (Bank, 228). All these observations are correct, but all of them avoid remarking on the emergence of a new un-conventional genre within the outer boundaries of Soviet literature, the genre known in the West as life writing. Marlene Kadar explains that life writing is "the most flexible and open term available for autobiographical fragments and other kinds of autobiographical-seeming texts. It includes the conventional genres of autobiography, journals, memoirs, letters and other texts that neither objectify nor subjectify the nature of a particular cultural truth" (10).[10] During the last two decades of its existence, life writing has developed its own genre characteristics that allow us to unite such seemingly different narratives as those listed above and to address them as works that belong to one genre. These characteristics include spontaneity and fragmentation in presenting factual material in order to reflect the ir-regularity of human memory. By focusing on the events of a particular life disconnected from the narrative of official history, the writer stresses that life's uniqueness and upsets the dominance of official history over personal story. In the Soviet environment life writing became an alternative to the political dictates of official history. An appeal to the cultural experience of the generation appears in the memoir. A high level of subjectivity influ-ences the structure of the narrative and helps to create the memoir's own objective reality, one which has begun to exist as a direct opposite to the of-ficially accepted version of the same reality. Life writing presented Soviet literature with a new model of memoir that would portray "characters and events that are given in depth and often with opposite characteristics" (Winslow, 65).

Memoir writing in the 1970s and 1980s became the real battlefield for establishing the new genre of life writing. The struggle commenced after the speech given by Egor Ligachev at the "Meeting of Directors and The-ater Workers" published in the April 20, 1986, issue of *Pravda*. It signaled the official beginning of the rewriting of recent Soviet history. Citing in the 1980s a "blossoming of the memoir genre" (Vorob'ev, 3), the critics of this period of "late Soviet culture" once again exhorted memoirists to "fill in the blank spots of history" (Vorob'ev, 3). Like the memoirs of the Thaw period, the narratives of the 1980s were called on to fulfill the duty of returning to the reader "many of those names, events, and works of literature that would contribute to the full restoration of real history" (Vorob'ev, 3). Once again, triggered by the changing political atmosphere, memoirs had to submit to the pressure of a changed version of absolute time, and factual material was again placed at the core of the narrative. The reminiscences of this period attracted the reader with sensational facts that were grouped together to uncover "false" history. In this way the memoirs of glasnost merged within the genre the discourse practices of both the dissident memoir and the memoir of the Thaw, fostering an approach to history akin to a "draft" full of blots, a "draft that needs to be corrected again and again" (Katanian,

227). This approach once again restored the facts that had formed the background in the literature of life writing to primary importance.[11] If the previous memoir model emphasizing official history was strictly binary, placing the memoirist in a position to either support the official history or destroy it in the dissident memoir, the reminiscences of the 1980s "throw" the entire body of historical facts together so that the confused reader cannot discern where official history is being validated or objective reality is being reconstructed. The abundance of memoirs that focused on the same factual material undermined the very authenticity of the objectivity of both facts and official history. This authenticity had eroded completely, and so the disoriented reader simply stopped believing in any kind of facts. The only history that remained reliable under such circumstances in the eyes of the reader was the writer's personal story.

Two memoirs of the 1980s primarily influenced the development of life writing in the 1990s: Lev Ginzburg's *Only My Heart is Broken* and *House Upside Down* by Iurii Trifonov, a memoir written in the form of the travelogue. Both Ginzburg and Trifonov use the subjective time of their life experience as the focus of their narrative and demonstrate an extremely close affinity with autobiography: both texts concentrate on reexamining the author as public persona and as private person. However, the autobiographical mode with its focus on a single life experience is constantly violated. The openness of their life writing is characterized not only by shifts from one narrative mode to another, but also by a constant "intrusion" of wholly different texts. This innovation differs from the 1970s device of life experience legitimization through quotations from documents. Through the organic inclusion of another text into one's life experience, the author represents not only his or her own life, but also the life experience of a generation. Excerpts from encyclopedias, literary translations, telegrams, and quotes from philosophical essays refer to a shared objective experience between the memoirist and his or her audience. Such a text does not lose its authenticity in a constant compromise with official history, but instead preserves a mutual cultural code of the author's generation, expressed variously through literary history (Ginzburg and Trifonov), film (Trifonov), music (Ginzburg), sport (Trifonov).

These narratives create a world of objective reality that is at the same time concrete and transcendental, since the very well defined borders of "a culture of one's own" in no way coincides with the world of officially accepted culture. This focus on unique cultural experience is utilized to counter and protect against a dominant official history. Thus, Ginzburg chooses moments from world cultural history to comment on his personal dilemmas. Citing the example of Carl Off, the composer of *Carmina Burana*, to illustrate creative life under the totalitarian regime of Nazi Germany, Ginzburg refers to the composer's nonparticipation and withdrawal into his own world of music as a possible "resistance by weakness: the inability, the impossibility of participating in violence" (189). The essence of this resistance is an attempt to survive "when one is supposed to die," an attempt "to know when ignorance is obligatory" (189). Knowledge of culture, one's own as well as the world's, becomes a necessary tool of survival. Ginzburg's reminiscences on cultural memory, along with his recollection of facts, displace events of objective reality. He forms a reality of his own that is densely populated by Hartmann Von Aue, the medieval author of *Poor Heinrich*, Heinrich Heine, Bishop Galen, and Dostoevsky. Knowledge of culture serves as the unifying element for the realities of the fragmented and disconnected world in which he, his parents, his deceased wife, his new love, and his dissatisfied children exist along with the characters of his translations. Ginzburg is telling his story, which appears as a cultural paradigm of a generation that attempts through its knowledge of the world's culture to reestablish the connection with world history that had been severed in the Soviet period.

Trifonov inscribes himself in history by substituting his personal story for "historical" periods and events. This subjectivization of life experience is *extreme* in Trifonov's narrative. The form of the travelogue is not chosen by accident. A travelogue permits the narrative to unfold in both directions: forward and backward. Both movements support the composition of the text and are linked with a change of geographical location as well as the ability to recall the past.[12] Utilizing this particular feature, Trifonov's narrative travels back to the self at the core of which the reminiscence is rooted, but again it is reminiscence about the self the writer used to be. The narrative incorporates the same device of an unfinalized and incomplete depiction of life experience with fragmentary descriptions of objective reality, but differs from Ginzburg's reminiscences in its coherence. While the link between the scattered recollections of the past in Ginzburg's narrative is a cultural memory, the personal "I" in Trifonov's reminiscences fulfills this role by liberating itself from the influx of different memories. This is the story about the "I" that the writer used to be and which he lost through constant compromise with official history. The writer intends to recover ownership over his personal experiences and not to make his past or the past of those whom he remembers a didactic example. His goal is of a different nature: it is motivated by self-discovery, or rather rediscovery. To accomplish this goal the writer "recalls" the very conventional socialist realist genre pattern and begins to rewrite the past, thus effectively replacing it with the history of his personal experience. In this way conventional rewriting of history is replaced in life writing with the rewriting of personal story.

The programmatic story that opens Trifonov's travelogue, *House Upside Down*, is called "Cats or Rabbits." This story recollects the author's visits to a small Italian city where on his first visit eighteen years ago he ate roasted rabbits. He returns to this town eighteen years later and wants to repeat the same experience, but learns that he apparently had been deceived, having been served not rabbits, but cats. The fact of the deception is not proven; there are only rumors, but nevertheless a feeling of deep disappointment does not leave the author, who is unable to forgive himself for being so trusting. In his recollection he recognized that he was driven by the desire to try something new and exotic, that he wanted to be deceived. These reminiscences presented to the reader as a travelogue allow the story to develop regressively rather than progressively. Still, the narrative does not develop vertically into the past, but rather makes constant references to the present. Thus, Trifonov states: "I came to the city eighteen years ago after I had been here the first time. Then . . . I ran, jumped, smoked with a passion, could work nights, . . . now . . . I don't run, I don't jump, I don't smoke, and I can't work nights. Then everything fascinated me, I wanted to remember everything, I was driven by the urge to write, . . . now nothing fascinates me and I don't particularly feel like writing" (Trifonov, 193). These flashbacks interwoven with flash-forwards depict the life cycle of an individual who is constantly tortured by his memory. It offers a different form of cycle that is completed by reliving the human life experience. The time between his present and his past is so comprised that it does not leave any space for exotic details or entertaining facts about objective reality. Objective time, in fact, does not matter at all. Restricting the narrative to subjective time only, the story depicts the disappointment of a representative of the generation that grew up nourished on "cats"—images of the time of official history.

The highly subjectified model of Trifonov's memoir and Lev Ginzburg's reminiscences, with their appeals to cultural memory, serve as cornerstones for the memoirists of the 1990s. The focus on subjective time in such memoirs as Anatolii Rybakov's *Novel of Remembrance,* Nina Gorlanova's *Time as a Parody of Eternity,* Pavel Basinskii's *Prisoner of Moscow,* and Sergei Gandlevskii's *Trepanation of the Cranium* conveys to the reader a multidimensional portrait of a generation. Relying on subjective reality as the only true one available to them for their inspiration, this new generation of writers recollected rather than wrote against their Soviet past.[13]

These new memoirs signify another step toward ejecting official history from their highly subjective narratives. However, it should be said that it was much easier to dismiss official history from the texts of the 1990s since this history had become highly fragile and disconnected from real human life in the former USSR. Constant attempts to tell the truth about the past of the country or an individual have produced so many versions of this past that society in general felt deprived of its own history. The subjective experience of an individual became the only tangible and real experience in which one could trust and with which one could identify.

These four memoirists focus their narratives on recreating their subjective world, thus employing different approaches to depict objective reality. Rybakov and Basinskii present their lives as stories of a constant struggle with the world outside. As a representative of the older generation, Rybakov's memoir becomes a revelation of his *nonbelonging* to the official mainstream of the Soviet literary establishment. Basinskii's narrative constitutes his struggle *to belong* to the Moscow intellectual elite. Gorlanova and Gandlevskii manage to successfully push objective reality out of their lives by simply omitting it from their narratives. As a working mother of four, Gorlanova has very little time to pay attention to the ongoing changes around her. The only *real* and trustworthy experience in her life is her family with its everyday demands and worries. Thus, the story of a cat's illness carries much more weight in her narrative than the story of Russia's rediscovery of its grim past. Gandlevskii uses his drinking as an excuse not to remember or to remember selectively. His "amnesia" is triggered by a device similar to Gorlanova's: the subjective world takes over and subordinates the events and facts from outside of his life. The memoirs of the 1990s finally free the genre from its Soviet past by returning to the eyewitness the right to select and comment on the events that surround one's life.

Rybakov states at the beginning of his memoir that "reminiscences cannot be subordinated to the actual chronology of time. I have written three stories about childhood and three novels about youth in which I have mixed reality and fiction, now it is difficult for me to separate one from another" (5). Here his memory unfolds before the reader in a linear narrative, progressing from a depiction of the prehistory of his family, the time before his birth, to his parents' very painful relationship, one that radically affected him as a child, to his adult successes in literature.

This memoir possesses all the structural qualities of the new genre of life writing. It includes quotations from diaries, and it incorporates documents from his personal archive on his rehabilitation as a victim of Stalinist "purges" as well as newspaper clippings, personal letters, official statements to Brezhnev, and evaluations of his works from the editors of journals in which he published. This overwhelming quantity of factual material creates a dual effect. On the one hand, Rybakov's memoir reminds us in its structure of the memoir by Lev Ginzburg, wherein the writer used an abundance of factual material to separate himself from official history. Rybakov, however, brings this history back into his narrative but prefers to choose particular events that would illustrate *his struggle* against the dominance of this history in his life and writing (for instance, stories connected with the publication of his novel *Heavy Sand*).

Rybakov's reminiscences are composed of forty separate chapters, but every chapter that presents a new fragment of his memory is self-sufficient. Each ends with a short and brief summary of Rybakov's life experiences over the time depicted, and lessons he has to learn from them in order to move forward. Thus, describing his expulsion from the institute and the alienating behavior of his former school friend, then secretary of the local Komsomol organization committee Grisha Eidinov, Rybakov notes that, "He [Grisha] embodied for me the degeneration of the idea I grew up with and believed in. At that period of my life I did not possess any knowledge as to whether this idea would again be reborn or if the starting process of degeneration would finally destroy it" (42). This constant commentary on the meaning of each episode of his life in the future, not only his own but his country's as well, presents the reader with a constant mixture of two realities, subjective and objective, where subjective life experience eclipses the importance of objective facts. At first glance it seems as though the author is adapting the Trifonov memoir model with its high level of subjectivity and its depiction of human life as a circle of diverse experience, but Trifonov doesn't pretend to draw any conclusions and his narrative *bears no didactic message.* He poses the rather rhetorical question of the meaning of life that he does not pretend to know how to answer.

By completing every episode of his private life, every encounter and recollection of real life events with a general didactic conclusion, Rybakov transforms his subjective experience into the common life pattern of the Soviet "lost" generation, "children of World War II" who made many mistakes in their life, but still "grow up as moral people" (218). They are the ones who suffer for their "support and participation in Gorbachev's reforms" since they are left with no salaries and minimal pensions, but this generation is "incapable of participating in any criminal activity" (Rybakov, 222). The memoirist recreates the past of this generation of "martyrs." "The time of Brezhnev's reign is called a 'calm time' but it was a calmness of the doomed" (257). "Nonparticipation" becomes the moral quest for righteousness in this generation, so Rybakov's real actions, private or public, are judged according to the very concept of nonaction. Thus, he declares: "I have never, orally or in writing, participated in any official action of condemning or approving of political or cultural events. No such letters have ever borne my signature" (261). Nonparticipation as a form of resistance is known to us from Lev Ginzburg's memoir, but Ginzburg offers knowledge of cultural history as a form of resistance, whereas Rybakov suggests a compromise with official history, a balancing act, at the core of which is an ability to reach an equilibrium within the flow of official history in order to not permit it to destroy one's subjective existence. His memoir presents several examples of such successful balancing acts—Valentin Kataev's *The Grass of Oblivion* (1967), Veniamin Kaverin's *Lighted Windows* (1983). Rybakov's reminiscences became a cultural model for a generation fully exposed to the most crucial moments of Soviet history: from the "purges" of the 1930s to the dissolution of the Soviet Union. This model strongly influenced the memoirs of Semen Lipkin (*Sketches and Thoughts*), Evgenii Fedorov (*Fried Rooster*), Grigorii Pomeranets (*Notes of an Ugly Duckling*), and Alexander Volodin (*An Attempt to Repent*).

Pavel Basinskii "remembers" the very concept of struggle (the class struggle in the conventional memoir of socialist realism) in his narrative and places it at the core of his reminiscences. Basinskii, the provincial boy who decided to conquer the capital city of Moscow and its literary establishment, reminisces over the story of his battle with the city. In a very strange way Basinskii's memoir resembles those of the early revolutionaries. The depiction of his life starts with his arrival in Moscow. Everything that happened before—birth, family, study at the provincial university—did not matter: "My first serious encounter with Moscow started in August of 1980" (100). His Moscow life and the people he meets and reflects on in his life are in one way or another important for the fulfillment of his two most important deeds—becoming part of the literary and artistic establishment of Moscow and succeeding in professional life. His goal is to conquer the capital, to squeeze out of himself, drop by drop, his "stupid provincial soul" (Basinskii, 132). The memoir is full of references to the literary atmosphere of the 1980s: the political difficulties of self-expression for young critics, the significant change of scene in the beginning of the 1990s. His memoir is full of short narrative vignettes depicting the Moscow literary establishment of Evgenii Vinokurov, Igor' Zolotusskii, Lev Anninskii, Andrei Nemzer, and Viacheslav Kurizyn.

Basinskii mixes names and events, but all facts that contribute to the accurate depiction of objective reality undergo highly controlled selection. In no way is his memory "unfolding freely"; rather, his choice of factual material carefully fulfills his "ideological" task to present himself as a conqueror and not a loser. Basinskii assays a definitive memoir of his generation more bluntly than any other contemporary memoirist. Like Rybakov, he constantly makes general summarizing statements, "All students of the Gorky Literary Institute could be divided into three categories" (108), or "In every provincial person one can find a trace of captain Kopeikin" (112).[14] Unlike Rybakov, however, he does not use his generalizations as conclusions but rather inserts them freely throughout the narrative. The effect of this device is twofold: it supports the illusion of the freedom essential to the new life writing style while revealing another structure within the narrative that supports a highly self-centered story of a single success. This narrative is deprived of open and free interaction with other forms of subjective self-expression (autobiography, diary). The history of success, the story of "Napoleon" (Basinskii, 109), is the actual driving force behind the creation of this memoir. Thus, an attempt to create a generational picture is undermined, but this peculiar doubled narrative reveals the old cultural stereotype of Balzac's Rastignac, and the provincial conqueror of the world capital is revealed. The knowledge of world culture on which Lev Ginzburg so desperately relied influences not the narrative mode of Basinskii's text but the very structure of his memoir and *decodes* its hidden message.

Nina Gorlanova's memoir *Time as A Parody of Eternity* undermines the whole aspect of time as the organizing component of the narrative. In fact, this writer never *has* time: she is a mother of four burdened with the constant struggle to find money to feed her family, meet their everyday needs, and simply remain focused in the turbulent world of her own household. Her life is a constant compromise. However, it is not official history she is compromising. This history, with its terrifying and destructive nature, is constantly downplayed and destroyed on the pages of her reminiscences, reminiscences that depict a very short distance in time between what has happened and what is described. In her world, politics, art, and nursing a child are joined together. "Well, it was the Andropov period . . . I had the luck to be a nursing mother. But even during the time of Andropov the nursing mother and Fellini are two noncomparable things . . . how is one to fit in the time for a movie with the baby's nursing schedule and have it so that the older children would already have come back from school?" (Gorlanova, 356). The Andropov period, however, also means that one could have been arrested at the movie theater. In his struggle to increase discipline in the workplace, Andropov, the former KGB chief, instituted patrols that combed the cinemas and stores during working hours looking for people absent from the workplace. Taken to the local police stations, people would spend hours trying to provide a reason for their absence from work. Gorlanova fears getting caught between Soviet politics in everyday existence and the needs of her everyday life. The solution is quickly found: if caught, she decides she will attack the KGB patroller by splashing him with her breast milk! (357). This is not to say that Gorlanova pretends that she is not afraid. Elsewhere in the text she confesses that, "there is nothing entertaining in being followed by the KGB" (348). But she doesn't have any choice. Her life goes on, and must go on, and, in order to preserve it, she learns to dismiss the objective reality of Soviet life. The dominance of official history over human life is destroyed by its being ridiculed. Linear narrative is abandoned and the memoir presents an open circle of human life centered on subjective experience. "Time stands still" (349), writes Gorlanova in reference to the time *outside* of her life.

Gorlanova's time, however, is very chaotic: she establishes separate, seemingly closed circles in the "still time" that reflect on her subjective existence. These are the circles of her university friends in Perm'; poets Vitalii Kalpidi, Lev Shukhman; writers Anatolii Korolev, Leonid Iusefovich; her family circle with her husband, children, and relatives; the circle of her co-workers at the publishing house; her friends from the young writers' studio; and the neighbors of her communal apartment. But clear definition of those circles does not prohibit Gorlanova from constantly moving them around, mingling their participants, and creating an image of an active and productive cultural life for the 1970s, which was marked officially as "the time of stagnation." Her narrative conveys a fragmented, seemingly disconnected reality (*klochkovataia real'nost'*) that seeks no legitimizing correlation with official history. Student folklore of the 1970s, period jokes, and postcards from friends written on many family occasions are interwoven with events in the present: fights with kids, small chats with friends, arguments with neighbors. Thus, the image of an unfinalized state of human life is created, with the greatest value assigned its most subjective manifestation—the family.

Gandlevskii tells the reader about his fight against a tumor and calls his recollections "History of an Illness." In Russian "*istoriia bolezni*" (in its English translation "medical chart") literally means "the history of someone's medical problems." The memoirist stresses the double meaning that he implied in his subtitle. It is not only the history of his deteriorating health, but also the story of the battle of his generation of *sorokaletnie* (literally, forty-year-olds) with life. "It [his head] was constantly hurting, from the very beginning of the day. So starts the story" (Gandlevskii, 111). Referring to his illness as the starting point of his narrative, Sergei Gandlevskii establishes the temporal dimensions of his objective reality—before the operation and after. What happens after nobody knows, although the writer has a certain wish list: to be able to make a living with his literary career, to learn foreign languages, and so forth. The depiction of his illness is not even the depiction of struggle, of which he, a true representative of his generation, is incapable. The stagnation of the period he lived in made him a nonbeliever in any type of resistance. It taught him that the only tool of defense was ignorance. His constant drinking helped him to ignore the objective world and strengthened within him his image as an outcast. His illness makes Gandlevskii revisit his past and relearn the value of human life. The wish list that he puts together symbolizes that this ignorance is disappearing and that the narrator *wants* to live.

Gandlevskii is definitely following the memoir model of Trifonov by presenting his life experience in a highly subjective manner. His life's journey appears to be complete. From the pre- to postoperational times Gandlevskii comes closer than any other memoirist of the 1990s to realizing this new form of life writing. His narrative is open in time, interrupted with memory flashes of dialogues with friends and relatives, with letters, and with his and his fellow poets' poetry. It creates an image of the chaos of life, the preferred topic of postmodern literature. This chaotic world is about to destroy the memoirist. His ignorance as a mode of nonaction could make him submit to the chaos of reality, but it does not happen. Gandlevskii is stimulated by fighting his physical pain to revisit his personal history and start his "dialogue with chaos" (Lipovetsky, 33).

This memoir thus gains transcendental meaning: afraid to lose his memory as a result of trepanation, the author reserves it as a last resort, and discovers that there is hope there. Trying to bring order to his chaotic life as he prepares for the worst, Gandlevskii is not ignorant any longer. Fighting death becomes synonymous with fighting ignorance, and life completes the full cycle: a wasted life in an objective world that could not stimulate or even recognize his gift, a near death experience, and a return back to life, unique and unrepeatable, where the greatest value is placed on simply *being alive*. Gandlevskii's memoir represents complete liberation from such socialist realist components as life for the cause, in which living is constantly evaluated by measuring achievements and successes. The generation of *"sorokaletnie"* was sentenced to become a generation of nonachievers in the doomed world of Soviet reality. Their voices were hardly heard, their works seldom published. In order to regain the lost years, they need not look back, but forward to life "after pain."

What is the future of the memoir in contemporary Russian literature? The present picture is very diverse. As a result of the complicated process of reclaiming ownership of their own life experiences, these writers have to confront the many features of the genre that have accumulated throughout the years of its existence in Soviet literature. As literary critic Marina Abasheva remarks, "It seems that no works of postmodernism would affect our burning curiosity for the real facts of life" (6). Sergei Gandlevskii, referring to the high popularity of memoirs in post-Soviet literature explains that this phenomenon is due to two reasons: one historical and the other literary.[15] The memoir with its focus on the past is, in his opinion, "the only vehicle that can connect the new post-Soviet generation with the generation of their parents. Soviet memory vanishes so fast. Posed to our children today, the once indisputable question 'What does the abbreviation USSR mean?' garners in our present environment this almost standard reply: 'A tattoo on Uncle Vania's arm'" (*Voprosy literatury*, 14). "Whether we want it or not," continues Gandlevskii, "we all became historical figures" (*Voprosy literatury*, 15). This statement illustrates the different dynamics today between official history and the story of everyday real existence that was suppressed in the Soviet memoir for almost seven decades. The value of the depiction of real life experience has dramatically increased in a country that lived for such a long time in a world of utopian dreams and deceptions. The memoir of the 1990s fulfills the honorable task of resurrecting this once suppressed reality for generations to come.

Notes

I would like to thank Beth Holmgren, Mark Leiderman (Lipovetsky), and Valerie Orlando for their helpful comments and editorial suggestions. Research for this article was supported by a grant from the Kennan Institute for Advanced Russian Studies of the Woodrow Wilson Center. All translations are my own, except where noted.

1. A similar attempt was undertaken in 1974 by the same literary journal, *Voprosy Literatury*. The round-table discussion titled "Responsibilities of the Witness, Rights of the Artist" that included predominantly prominent literary critics rather than writers (Korallov, Kardin, Makashin, Bragin) stressed the importance of the memoir to reflect on the "great victories of the Soviet people on all fronts of socialist labor" (45). The biggest achievement of memoir literature, according to this forum, was its ability to "reveal the most typical trends of the epoch" (58).

2. I have employed here the definition of literary etiquette developed by Dmitrii Likhachev in his study of Old Russian Literature. By literary etiquette, Likhachev meant special landmarks that existed to guide the writers in their search for an appropriate literary form. Likhachev stated that those landmarks reflected the demands of the outside world and were rooted in the politics of feudal society. According to the scholar's observation, those landmarks formed a well-defined etiquette—a set of rules and regulations that would have been applied to literary genres and affect both form and content. Likhachev specifically stressed the compulsory (*prinuditel'nyi*) nature of such etiquette. Elsewhere I have argued that the literature of socialist realism demonstrated the same kind of subordination to the landmarks imposed on it by the official party line. (See my article on "Literatura puteshestii i socialisticheskii realism" in *Sotsrealisticheskii kanon*, edited by E. Dobrenko and H. Guenther [St. Petersburg: Akademicheskii proekt, 2000].)

3. First expressed in Bakhtin's *Problems of Dostoevsky's Poetics* (1963), the idea of genre memory was based on Bakhtin's thought that a genre "possesses its own objective memory that preserves its peculiar features" (121). According to Bakhtin, "a genre lives in the present but always *remembers* its past, its beginning. Genre is a representative of creative memory in the process of literary development" (106). I would like to suggest that the memoir in Soviet literature recalls the main features of the obituary with its given finalized images, retrospective but linear narrative, obsession with facts, and purposely dry nonemotional discourse. As I hope to demonstrate, the memoir, at different periods in Soviet and post-Soviet literature, would resist this genre memory and try to merge with other closely related genres, such as autobiography, travelogue, and diary.

4. The formation of the Commission for the Study of Party History and the History of the October Revolution in 1920 could be identified as the first attempt to simultaneously organize and control the very process of memoir writing. This Commission initiated the creation of local affiliates in order to collect materials in the provinces and established centers for the

collection of reminiscences deemed relevant to local revolutionary history. Revolutionary memoirs appeared as separate publications (Lepeshinskii's *On the Turn*, Ol'minskii's *From the Past*, Bobrovskaia's *From the Notes of an Ordinary Revolutionary*) and also in special sections of the periodicals of the day, such as *Press and Revolution* (*Pechat' I Revolutsiia*) and *Messenger of Life* (*Vestnik Zhisni*). At the same time, literary and historical magazines such as *The Past* (*Byloe*, 1900–26) and *Voice of the Past* (*Golos Minuvshego*, 1913–23) continued to publish memoirs. New publications, *Penal Servitude and Exile* (*Katorga i Ssylka*, 1921–35), and *Red Archive* (*Krasnyi Archiv:* 1921–41), focused on past revolutionary history. At Gorky's initiative, the Memoir Cabinet (a library collection dedicated to memoirs) was opened. The creation of this institution was motivated by his belief that "memoir literature, by introducing the young generation to the unknown, plays an integral cultural as well as educational role" (Gorky, 32). Concurrently a special book series, Memoir Library (Biblioteka memuarov), began its publication.

5. In 1960 a volume of memoirs entitled "Commanders of the Civil War" reinstated repressed generals Tukhachevskii, Bliukher, Kovtiukh, Egorov, and Putna into the canon of Soviet history. Yet, in the same year, Tvardovskii refused to publish the sixth chapter of Il'ia Erenburg's *People, Years, Life* in *Novyi Mir*, since it described the not yet reinstated figure of Bukharin as a leader of a Bol'shevik school organization (Frezinskii, 328).

6. The late 1960s and the 1970s finalized the literary production of such memoirs. In 1966 a special session of the Executive Committee of the Russian Federation Writers' Union was called. The decision was made to organize memoirists into a special unit as well as to start production of "ideologically charged memoirs in honor of the fiftieth anniversary of the October Revolution." In 1972 Anastas Mikoian, member of Politburo CPSU from 1926 to1966, joined the ranks of Soviet memoirists by publishing his reminiscences *On the Road to Struggle* in *Novyi Mir*. In 1978 he was joined by General Secretary Leonid Brezhnev. He awarded himself the Lenin State Prize in Literature for his trilogy *Little Land, Rebirth* and *Virgin Land*. Thus, the memoir became an official "court genre" of Soviet leadership.

7. In my remarks on the similarities between the structures of the official memoir and the dissident memoir I do not question the literary value and the complexity of Nadezhda Mandelstam's *Hope Against Hope* or Evgeniia Ginzburg's *Within the Whirlwind*. Natasha Kolchevska in her article on Evgeniia Ginzburg in this volume and Beth Holmgren in her monograph *Women's Works in Stalin's Time: On Lidiia Chukovskaia and Nadezhda Mandelstam* (Indiana University Press, 1993) have successfully delineated these texts' extraordinary literary features. My assertion of a dominant

socialist realist etiquette present in these narratives concerns their outer structure, not the intricacies of their plots.

8. For an extensive discussion on Kataev's memoirs, see chapter 5 in Richard C. Borden's *The Art of Writing Badly*, 110–37.

9. In her introduction to this volume, Beth Holmgren refers to this process as the "deliberate aestheticization of the Russian memoir" (32).

10. Donald Winslow stresses the more inclusive nature of life writing. However, he restricts this term to the union of biography and autobiography. In this way Kadar's definition is much broader and is more appropriate for the description of the works discussed in this article. In her attempt to describe the features of life writing, Kadar, stresses that "in all the life writing genres, life and writing identify to their mutual benefit" (159). The scholar does not provide a more detailed definition of this genre except to refer to "some features of narrativity." For my future discussion of the memoirs in Soviet/post-Soviet literature, I adopt the term *life writing* based on Kadar's general description of its all-inclusive nature and make my own attempt to provide the characteristics of this new genre.

11. Publications in such *thick journals* ("tolstye zhurnaly") as *Novyi Mir* illustrate this new obsession with factual material. Thus, Diana Tevekelian reconstructs the history of the 1978 publication of Brezhnev's reminiscences in *Novyi Mir* (Tevekelian, 201–9), Savva Golovanivskii reflects on the destruction of writers' groups and literary unions at the beginning of the 1930s (Golovanivskii, 52–60), and Daniil Granin describes his meetings and negotiations with Kosygin while he was working on his *Blockade Book*. The attention of the memoirists is focused on concrete events of objective reality, but these still pertain to the time of official history and not the real-life events of the personal story. Featured are, for example, the events that surrounded the preparation of the special issue of *Literaturnaia Gazeta* dedicated to the Victory Parade of 1945 (Berser, 211–20), the doctors' plot of 1953 (Rapoport, 14), and the illness and death of the father of socialist realism, Maxim Gorky (Kruchkov, 5).

12. On the discussion of the travelogue structure in socialist realist literature see my articles: "A Prescribed Journey: Russian Travel Literature from the 1960s to the 1980s" (*Slavic and East European Journal* 38: 2 (1994); "Literatura puteshestvii" in *Sotsrealisticheskii kanon*, ed. Hans Guenther and Evgeny Dobrenko (St. Petersburg: Akademicheskii Proekt, 2000: 896–910), as well as Evgeny Dobrenko's article "Iskusstvo sotsial'noi navigatsii: ocherki kul'turnoi topografii stalinskoi epokhi" (*Wiener Slavistischer Almanach* 45 [2000]: 93–134).

13. Only two memoirists identify their prose as memoir in the title, although they still use the device (familiar to readers of the 1970s) of qualifying their memoir with extra description. Gorlanova uses the adjective

"not serious" in front of the definition "memoir." Rybakov inserts the word "novel" into his title immediately before the word "reminiscences" (*roman-vospominanie*), from the very beginning asserting the author's right to freely interpret history.

14. Captain Kopeikin is a character of "The Tale of Captain Kopeikin," the story inserted into chapter 10, part 1 of Nikolai Gogol's famous novel *Dead Souls.* Kopeikin, a one-legged and one-armed war invalid, comes to St. Petersburg to get his military pension for his service in the war of 1812 against Napoleon. I believe that Basinskii's statement refers to the desire "to have it all and now" that Captain Kopeikin experiences when he first approaches the capital and is blinded by its richness.

15. In his essay in this volume, Alexander Prokhorov attributes the great popularity of memoirs to their entertainment value in post-Soviet Russia. I would agree with this statement but only partially. Today Russian readers can satisfy their interest in the private lives of foreign and domestic movie stars, or be introduced to the details of the Kremlin wives' and children's existence. I suggest, however, that *skandal'nye* (scandalous) memoirs play only a limited part in this process of resurrecting reality. As Prokhorov observes later in his essay, it is the attempt "to construct a unified, harmonious self" (1) that moves the memoirist to perform the task of writing. I believe that the same desire to "reconstruct" selves and lives and to liberate those lives from the burden of reality foisted on them from above promotes reader interest in this genre.

Works Cited

Abasheva, M. "Parki bab'e lepetan'e . . ." Introduction to Nina Gorlanova. *Vsia Perm'*, 1996, 5–13.

Ardov, M. *Legendarnaia Ordynka: sbornik vospominanii.* St. Petersburg: INAPRESS, 1995.

Bakhtin, M. M. *Voprosy literatury i estetiki.* Moscow: Khudozhestvennaia literatura, 1975.

Bal'burov, E. A. *Poetika liricheskoi prozy: 1960–1970-e gody.* Novosibirsk: izd. "Nauka," 1985.

Bank, N. *Nit' vremeni. Dnevniki i zapisnye knizhki sovetskikh pisatelei.* Leningrad: Sovetskii pisatel', 1978.

Basinskii, P. "Moskovskii plennik. Ispoved' provintsiala." *Oktiabr'* 9 (1997): 100–33.

Berggolts, Ol'ga. *Dnevnye zvezdy.* Leningrad: Sovetskii pisatel', 1971.

Borchshagovskii, A. *Zapiski balovnia sud'by.* Moscow: Sovetskii pisatel', 1991.

Brazhnin, I. *Sumka volshebnika.* Leningrad: Lenizdat, 1978.

Brooks, Jeffrey. "Revolutionary Lives: Public Identities in Pravda during the 1920s." In *New Directions in Soviet History,* edited by Stephen White. Cambridge: Cambridge University Press, 1991, 27–41.

Clark, Katerina. *The Soviet Novel: History as Ritual.* University of Chicago Press, 1981.

Crankshaw, Edward. "Back to the Real Russia," quoted in P. Genri. "Povest' o zhizni" K. Paustovskogo v vospriiatii anglichan." *Literaturnoe obozrenie* 11 (1992): 45–50.

Danin, D. *Bremia styda.* Moscow: Moskovskii rabochii, 1996.

Dobrenko, E. "Mezhdu istoriei i proshlym: pisatel' Stalin i literatyrnye istoki sovetskogo istoricheskogo diskursa." *Sotsrealisticheskii kanon:* 639–673.

Fedorov, E. *Zharenyi petukh.* Moscow: MP "Itlar" "Carte Blanch," 1992.

Gandlevskii, Sergeii. "Trepanatsiia cherepa." *Znamia* 1 (1994): 99–151.

Ginzburg, Evgeniia. *Krutoi marshrut.* Frankfurt/Main: Possev-Verlag, 1967.

Ginzburg, L. *Razbilos' lish' serdtse moe.* Moscow: Sovetskii pisatel', 1983.

Gor'kii, A.M. *Gor'kii i sozdanie istorii fabrik i zarodov. Sbornik dokumentov i materialov.* Moscow, 1959.

Gorlanova, Nina. "Vremia kak parodiia na vechnost' (neserieznye memuary)." In *Vsia Perm'.* Perm': Iuriatin, 1996.

Ianskaia, I; Kardin, V. *Predely dostovernosti: ocherki documental'noi literatury.* Moscow: Sovetskii pisatel', 1986.

Iashina, N. *Vospominaniia ob ottse.* Arkhangel'sk: Severo-zapadnoe izd., 1977.

Iavchunovskii, Ia. *Dokumental'nye zhanry.* Saratov: Saratovskii gos. universitet, 1974.

Istoriia sovetskogo obshchestva v vospominaniiakh sovremennikov: 1917–1927. Annotirovannyi ukazatel' memuarnoi literatury. Zhurnal'nye publikatsii. Moscow: Gos. Biblioteka im. Lenina, 1961

Istoriia sovetskogo obshchestva v vospominaniiakh sovremennikov: 1917–1957. Annotirovannyi ukazatel' memuarnoi literatury. Moscow: Moskovskii universitet, 1958.

Istoriia sovetskogo obshestva v vospominaniiah sovremennikov. 1928–57. Annotirovannyi ukazatel' memuarnoi literatury. Zhurnal'nye publikazii. Moscow: Kniga, 1967.

Kadar, Marlene. "Coming to Terms: Life Writing—from Genre to Critical Practice." In *Essays on Life Writing: from Genre to Critical Practice,* edited by Marlene Kadar. Toronto: University of Toronto Press, 1992, 3–12.

Kardin, V. *Segodnia o vcherashnem: memuary i sovremennost'.* Moscow: Voennoe izd., 1961.

Kataev, V. *Sviatoi kolodez. Trava zabveniia.* Moscow: Sovetskii pisatel', 1969.

Kaverin, V. *Osveshchennye okna.* Moscow: Sovetskii pisatel', 1983.

———. *Sobesednik: Vospominaniia i portrety.* Moscow: Sovetskii pisatel', 1973.

Ketlinskaia, V. *Vecher. Okna. Liudi.* Moscow: Molodaia gvardiia, 1974.

Konetskii, V. *Morskie sny.* Moscow: Sovetskii pisatel', 1975.

Kopelev, L. *I sotvoril sebe kumira.* Ann Arbor, Mich.: Ardis, 1978.

Kron, A. *Sobranie sochinenii.* T.3. Moscow: Sovetskii pisatel', 1990.

"Kruglyi stol: Memuarnaia literatura i ee problemy." *Voprosy literatury* 4 (1974): 45–130.

Lenin, V. I. *Sobranie sochinenii* 20 (*Collected Works*): 79–83.

Likhachev, D. *Poetika drevnerusskoi literatury.* Leningrad: Khudozhestvennaia literatura, 1971.

Lipkin, S. "Zarisovki i soobrazheniia." *Novyi Mir* 8 (1994): 36–52.

Literaturnaia Entsiklopediia. T.7. Moscow: Sovetskaia entsiklopedia, OGIZ RSFSR, 1934, 131–49.

Lunacharskii, A. V. *Revolutsionnye siluety.* Izd.2. Gosudarstvennoe Izdatel'svo Ukrainy, 1924.

Mandel'shtam, Nadezhda. *Vospominaniia.* New York, 1970.

"Memuary na slome epochi." *Voprosy literatury* (January–February 1999): 3–56.

Naiman, A. *Slavnyi konets besslavnykh pokolenii.* Moscow: Vagrius, 1998.

Olesha, Iu. *Ni dnia bez strochki. Iz zapisnykh knizhek.* Moscow: Sov. Rossiia, 1965.

"O memuarnoi literature. Po materialam plenuma Komissii po khudozhestvenno-istoricheskoi literature Pravleniia Soiuza pisatelei RSFSR." *Voprosy istorii KPSS* 2 (1966): 150–53.

Paustovskii, K. *Naedine s osen'iu: Portrety, vospominaniia, ocherki.* Moscow: Khudozhestvennaia literatura, 1967.

Paustovskii, K. *Povest' o zhizni: Dalekie gody.* Moscow: Sovetskii pisatel', 1955.

Pomeranets, Grigorii. *Zapiski gadkogo utenka.* Moscow: Moskovskii rabochii, 1998.

Rappoport, Ia. *Na rubezhe dvukh epokh. Delo vrachei 1953.* Moscow: Kniga, 1988.

Ravich, L. *Molodost' veka.* Leningrad: Sovetskii pisatel', 1957.

Rybakov, A. *Roman-vospominanie.* Moscow: Vagrius, 1997.

Sergeev, Andrei. *Omnibus: Al'bom dlia marok.Portrety. O Brodskom. Rasskaziki.* Moscow: Novoe literaturnoe obosrenie, 1997.

Shaitanov, I. O. *Kak bylo i kak vspomnilos': sovremennaia avtobiograficheskaia i memuarnaia proza.* Moscow: izd. Znanie, 1981.

Shklovskii, V. *Zhili-byli.* Moscow: Sovetskii pisatel', 1966.

Soloukhin, V. *Kaplia rosy.* Moscow: Molodaia gvardiia, 1960.

Tartakovskii, A. "Memuary kak fenomen kul'tury." *Voprosy literatury* 1 (1999): 35–56.

Trifonov, Iu. *Oprokinutyi dom. Sobranie sochinenii* (*Collected Works*). Moscow: Khudozhestvennaia literatura, 1987, 4.

Urban, Adol'f. "Avtodokumental'naia proza." *Zvezda* 10 (1970): 193–204.

———. "Khudozhestvennaia avtobiografiia i document." *Zvezda* 2 (1977): 192–209.

Volodin, Aleksandr. *Popytka pokaianiia.* St. Peterburg: Isd. Petropol', 1998.

Winslow, Donald J. *Life-Writing: A Glossary of terms in Biography, Autobiography, and Related Forms.* 2nd ed. Honolulu: University of Hawaii Press, 1995.

"Za pravdivoe osveshenie zhizni i deiatel'nosti V. I. Lenina." *Voprosy istorii KPSS* 5 (1958): 183–91.

Zorin, L. *Avanstsena: memuarnyi roman.* Moscow: Slovo, 1997.

Contributors

Marina Balina is a professor of Russian at Illinois Wesleyan University. Her publications include *Endquote: Sots-Art Literature and Soviet Grand Style* (with Nancy Condee and Evgeny Dobrenko), *Soviet Treasure: Culture, Literature, and Film* (with Evgeny Dobrenko and Jurii Murashov), and articles on contemporary Russian and Soviet life writing (autobiography, memoir, and travel literature). She served as a special editor of *a/b: Auto/Biography Studies Journal* and completed a special issue entitled *Rethinking Russian Autobiography*. She is working on an anthology of Russian/Soviet fairy tales (with Helena Goscilo and Mark Lipovetsky).

Galya Diment is a professor and the chair of the Department of Slavic Languages and Literatures at the University of Washington, Seattle. She is the author and editor of four books, including *Pniniad: Vladimir Nabokov and Marc Szeftel*, and is coediting volumes on Russian and Soviet film and approaches to Nabokov's *Lolita*, as well as working on a cultural biography of Samuel Koteliansky, a Russian translator for Bloomsbury's Hogarth Press.

Jehanne Gheith is an associate professor of Slavic and the director of Comparative Area Studies at Duke University. She has edited several volumes on Russian women and has authored the book *Finding the Middle Ground: Krestovskii, Tur, and the Power of Ambivalence in Nineteenth-Century Russian Women's Prose*. She is writing essays based on a series of interviews with survivors of the Gulag.

Helena Goscilo, UCIS Research Professor of Slavic at the University of Pittsburgh, writes on gender and culture in Russia. She has authored and edited more than a dozen volumes, including *Balancing Acts, Skirted Issues: The Discreteness and Indiscretions of Russian Women's Prose, Fruits of Her Plume, Dehexing Sex: Russian Womanhood during and after Glasnost, TNT: The Explosive World of T. Tolstaya's Fiction*, and *Russian Culture in the 1990s*. Her other projects include a cultural study of the New Russians (with Nadezhda Azhgikhina), an edited collection of folkloric and

211

literary fairy tales (with Marina Balina and Mark Lipovetsky), and the construction of a comprehensive digital library devoted to Stalin(iana) (with Susan Corbero and Petre Petrov).

Gitta Hammarberg is DeWitt Wallace Professor of Russian at Macalester College in St. Paul, Minnesota. Her specialty is Sentimentalism and eighteenth-century Russian literature. She is the author of *From the Idyll to the Novel: Karamzin's Sentimentalist Prose.* Her recent publications are devoted to such topics as women's albums, early Russian women's journals, bouts-rimés, dandyism, dogs/doggerel, and gender and genre.

Jane Gary Harris is a professor of Russian literature at the University of Pittsburgh. She is the editor and cotranslator of *Osip Mandel'stam: The Critical Prose and Letters;* the author of *Osip Mandel'stam;* and the editor of *Autobiographical Statements: Essays on the Autobiographical Mode in Twentieth-Century Russian Literature, American Contributions to the Tenth International Congress of Slavists,* and *Lidiia Ginzburg: In Memoriam.* She has published various articles on Petr Bitsilli, G. R. Derzhavin, Lidiia Ginzburg, Osip Mandel'stam, Aleksandr Solzhenitsyn, problems of autobiography and fiction, life writing, and the Russian women's periodical press. She is preparing an edition of Ginzburg's selected writings, working on a manuscript on the Russian women's periodical press of the early twentieth century, and editing a volume of essays entitled *Gender Critique and Gender Studies in Russia and East Europe* from the 2000 ICCEES Tampere Congress.

Beth Holmgren is a professor and the chair of the Department of Slavic Languages and Literatures at the University of North Carolina at Chapel Hill. Her books include *Women's Works in Stalin's Time: On Lidiia Chukovskaia and Nadezhda Mandelstam* and *Rewriting Capitalism: Literature and the Market in Late Tsarist Russia and the Kingdom of Poland.* Her recent publications focus on various aspects of Russian and Polish émigré culture in the United States, and she is at work on a cultural study of the life and legacy of the Polish American actress Helena Modjeska.

Natasha Kolchevska teaches in the Department of Foreign Languages and Literatures at the University of New Mexico. She is the author of numerous scholarly publications on late-nineteenth- and twentieth-century Russian women's autobiography, Russian modernism, prison camp literature, émigré writers, and post-Soviet literature. Her edition and translation of S. V. Kovalevskaya's *Nihilist Girl* was published by the Modern Language Association. She is completing a book on Russian women's memoirs and writing on violence in Russian culture.

212

Contributors

Sarah Pratt is a professor of Russian in the Slavic department at the University of Southern California and serves as the dean of academic programs in the College of Letters, Arts, and Sciences. She is the author of *Nikolai Zabolotsky: Enigma and Cultural Paradigm, Russian Metaphysical Romanticism,* and *The Semantics of Chaos in Tjutcev.* She has published numerous articles on Russian poetry, the Russian critic Lidiia Ginzburg, the American theorist Harold Bloom, and Russian women's autobiography.

Alexander Prokhorov is an assistant professor of Russian language and culture at the College of William and Mary. He is the editor of *Springtime for Soviet Cinema: Re/Viewing the 1960s* and has written articles on contemporary Russian film, literature, and cultural theory. He is writing a book on early post-Stalinist culture.

Index

Index

Brintlinger, Angela, xxvii
Briusov, Valerii, 20
Brodsky, Joseph, xi, xxx, 167–69, 174–85; choice of English for essays, 175, 180n. 3, 181n. 8; choice of English for memoirs, 168, 174–79; "In a Room and a Half," 175–76, 177
Brooks, Jeffrey, 187–88
Brooks, Peter, 55
Bruss, Elizabeth, 173
Bukharin, Nikolai, 146
Bulgakov, Mikhail, 149
Bykov, Vasil', 147
Byron, George Gordon, 109
Byt, 105–6, 128, 129, 130, 131, 132, 134, 139, 141, 142

Carnival Night (film, 1956), 71
Casey, Edward S., 160
Catherine II: conditions of her reign for memoir production, xvi, xvii; memoirs of, 94, 95
Cement (Gladkov), 60
Chaadaev, Petr, 167
Chernyshevsky, Nikolai, xxvi, 133, 140
Childhood (Tolstoy), xxvii
Children of the Famous (television memoirs), 72
Chudakova, Marietta, 12
Chukovskaia, Lidiia, xxiii, 64, 73
Chukovskii, Kornei, xxii, 133–34, 142–43n. 9
Clark, Katerina, 40, 155, 156, 187
Conclusive Evidence (Nabokov), 169, 170, 171, 172
Connerton, Paul, 152–53
Conrad, Joseph, 168
Contemporary, The (journal), 130, 132, 135, 138, 141
Conversation about Dante (O. Mandel'stam), 13
Couser, G. Thomas, xiii
Crankshaw, Edward, 191

Danin, Daniil, 187
Dante, 107, 109, 155
Dar [*The Gift*] (Nabokov), 172
Dashkova, Ekaterina, 94, 95, 112
Daylight Stars (Berggolts), xxix, 192
Dead Lake (Nekrasov-Panaeva), 130
Decembrists, memoirs of, xviii; wives of, 95

Declassified Lives (memoir series), 70
De Man, Paul, 54
Derzhavin, Gavrila, 95
Diment, Galya, xxx
Dobin, Efim, 16–17, 19
Dobroliubov, Nikolai, 133, 140–41
Dolgorukaia, Natal'ia, xi, xxvi, 93–127; biography, 93; features of her memoirs, 93–94; female foils, 101–2; as "feminine" ideal and role model for female readers, 96, 97, 98, 99, 100, 102, 103, 104, 105, 106, 109, 110, 111, 112–13, 114–15; good women doubles, 103–5; high stylization of, 109–10; realism and rewriting of her image, 105, 109; "Russianness" of, 110–12; Sentimentalism and rewriting of her image, 103, 109; valorized by male authorities, 106–8; vis-à-vis other female memoirists, 94–95
Domostroi, 108, 110, 117n. 24
Dostoevsky, Fyodor, 130, 133, 168–69
Drugie berega, 169, 170, 171
Drug iunoshestva (journal), 96
Dumas, Alexandre (*pere*), 138–39, 140, 155
Dunham, Vera, 72
Durova, Nadezhda, xviii, xx, 95

"Early Years, The" (Zabolotsky), xxiii–xiv, 35–36, 37, 39–46; relationship to Soviet "coming of age" myth, 39–40; Russian Orthodox experiences in and influences on, 37, 38–39, 42–46
Eikhenbaum, Boris, xxvii, 8, 9, 10, 12, 16
Eisenstein, Sergei, 76–77, 78, 82
Eliot, T. S., 168–69, 175
Engel, Barbara Alpern, xx
Engels, Friedrich, 37, 38
Erenburg, Il'ia, xxiii
Ermash, Filipp, 82
Erofeev, Venedikt, xxx
Esenin, Sergei, 80
Evening. Windows. People (Ketlinskaia), 192
Extraordinary Adventures of Italians in Russia, The (film 1974), 79

Family Chronicle (Aksakov), xix, xxvi, xxvii
Fathers and Sons, 18, 54
Fedin, Konstantin, xxvii
Fedorov, Evgenii, 198–99
Fedorov, Nikolai, 38

Index

Index

Index

Index